£7-50

Policy-m[aking]
in
Education
THE BREAKDOWN OF CONSENSUS

The Open University

This reader is one part of an Open University integrated teaching system and the selection is therefore related to other material available to students. It is designed to evoke the critical understanding of students. Opinions expressed in it are not necessarily those of the course team or of the University.

Policy-making in Education

THE BREAKDOWN OF CONSENSUS

A Reader edited by

IAN McNAY

and

JENNY OZGA

at the Open University

PERGAMON PRESS

OXFORD · NEW YORK · TORONTO · SYDNEY · FRANKFURT

in association with

THE OPEN UNIVERSITY

U.K.	Pergamon Press Ltd., Headington Hill Hall, Oxford OX3 0BW, England
U.S.A.	Pergamon Press Inc., Maxwell House, Fairview Park, Elmsford, New York 10523, U.S.A.
CANADA	Pergamon Press Canada Ltd., Suite 104, 150 Consumers Road, Willowdale, Ontario M2J 1P9, Canada
AUSTRALIA	Pergamon Press (Aust.) Pty. Ltd., P.O. Box 544, Potts Point, N.S.W. 2011, Australia
FEDERAL REPUBLIC OF GERMANY	Pergamon Press GmbH, Hammerweg 6, D-6242 Kronberg-Taunus, Federal Republic of Germany

Selection and editorial material copyright © 1985 The Open University

All Rights Reserved. No part of this publication may be reproduced, stored in a retrieval system or transmitted in any form or by any means: electronic, electrostatic, magnetic tape, mechanical, photocopying, recording or otherwise, without permission in writing from the copyright holders.

First edition 1985

Library of Congress Cataloging in Publication Data
Main entry under title:
Policy making in education.
1. Education and state—Great Britain—Addresses, essays, lectures. I. McNay, Ian. II. Ozga, Jennifer III. Open University.
LC93.G7P64   1985   379.41   85-9372

British Library Cataloguing in Publication Data
Policy making in education: the breakdown of consensus: a reader.
1. Education and state—Great Britain
I. McNay, Ian   II. Ozga, Jennifer   III. Open University
379.41   LC93.G7

ISBN 0-08-032671-4 (Hardcover)
ISBN 0-08-032670-6 (Flexicover)

Printed in Great Britain by A. Wheaton & Co, Ltd., Exeter

Preface

This reader consists of a collection of articles which form part of the Open University Course E333, Policy-making in Education. The course critically examines ways of analysing education policy, discusses the structure and process of educational policy-making in central and local government, and analyses educational policy in practice through case studies of particular policy issues.

The primary concerns of this reader are the exploration of ways of understanding educational policy-making and a reassessment of the 'partnership' between central government, local government and the teachers. Because the reader forms only one part of the course (much of which consists of written texts or broadcasts discussing issues raised in the reader articles) it cannot claim to offer a complete picture of educational policy-making. The selection of articles has been made with the overall course content in mind. It has been designed to highlight specific problems and to develop the students' critical understanding. Opinions expressed within articles are, therefore, not necessarily those of the course team nor of the university. However, the editors believe that the selection, though not comprehensive, focuses on major issues in educational policy-making, and will be useful to anyone with an interest in the area.

There are three other readers, also published by Pergamon Press, and related to case studies of educational policy which are discussed in course material. These readers are:

Curriculum and Assessment: some policy issues. Edited by P. Raggatt and G. Weiner.
Education, Training and Employment: towards a new vocationalism? Edited by R. Dale.
Race and Gender: equal opportunity policies in education. Edited by M. Arnot.

It is not necessary to become an undergraduate of the Open University in order to study the course of which this reader is part. Further information about the course associated with this book may be obtained by writing to: The Admissions Office, The Open University, PO Box 48, Walton Hall, Milton Keynes MK7 6AB.

Contents

Introduction: perspectives on policy
    Jenny Ozga and Ian McNay   1

Section 1   *Education Policy in Context*

1. Education Policy and Values   11
   Maurice Kogan

2. Education and the Economy: changing circumstances   25
   W. F. Dennison

Section 2   *Some Perspectives on Policy-making*

3. Educational Politics: a model for their analysis   39
   Margaret S. Archer

4. The Politics of Administrative Convenience: the case of middle schools   65
   Andy Hargreaves

5. Social Policy and the Theory of the State   85
   Claus Offe

Section 3   *The Collapse of Consensus?*

6. Changing Relations between Centre and Locality in Education   103
   Stewart Ranson

7. Distributing Resources   125
   W. F. Dennison

8. The DES   145
   Brian Salter and Ted Tapper

9. Competition...and Competence?: education, training and the roles of DES and MSC   159
   D. L. Parkes

10. The British University Grants Committee 1919–83: changing
    relationships with government and the universities   173
    Michael Shattock and Robert Berdahl

11. School Governing Bodies and the Political-Administrative System 195
    M. Kogan, D. Johnson, T. Packwood and T. Whitaker

Section 4   Teacher Unions and Teacher Numbers

12. Pushing for Equality: the influence of the teachers' unions—the
    NUT   217
    Paul Lodge and Tessa Blackstone

13. The National Union of Teachers   233
    Ken Jones

14. Teacher Numbers: the framework of government policy   251
    Kieron Walsh, Roland Dunne, Bryan Stoten and John D. Stewart

Section 5   A Policy Re-examined: equality of opportunity

15. Education and Social Policy   275
    John Lawson and Harold Silver

16. Poverty and Educational Priority   291
    Keith Banting

17. Class Inequality in Education: two justifications, one evaluation
    but no hard evidence   315
    James Murphy

Index   335

Introduction
Perspectives on policy

The academic study of educational policy-making has been dominated by two related and mutually supportive traditions, which may now be ripe for reassessment. This book is an attempt to sketch out the basis for such a reassessment: it presents major theoretical and empirical evidence towards that end. For further discussion of the interpretation of the evidence the reader is referred to the Open University Course E333, Policy-making in Education.

The two dominant perspectives on educational policy-making may be roughly distinguished from one another by characterizing one, pluralism, as the major theoretical perspective and the other, case study, as the principal methodological means of supporting and illuminating the theory. In practice the division has not been so tidy, and, indeed, it might be more accurate to suggest that the accumulation of case studies has encouraged the growth of a broadly pluralist protective theoretical cover. There are, of course, wide variations in the use of case study methodology. Some case studies are principally concerned with the accumulation of detail and exist as images of events rather than analysis of them, in others the weighting of analysis and description is more even-handed. Whatever the weighting, the tendency for case studies of educational policy-making has been to support or modify the pluralist framework rather than challenge it.

A pluralist would retort that this simply demonstrates the elegance and completeness of the theory. This may be the case, but we need to be convinced. Certainly, pluralism is an accommodating theory, a broad church which may contain a number of potentially damaging heresies and yet survive so long as its taken for granted assumptions are not too closely scrutinized. Again, pursuing the parallel with the church, the critic of pluralism can easily be branded a heretic, because the essential premises of pluralism are seen as fundamental to a democratic society. An attack on pluralism is an attack on it.

Central to these assumptions is the idea that policy outcomes are the result of negotiations, bargaining, competition and co-operation among various groups—principally, in the context of education, the Department of Education and Science (DES), the Local Education Authorities (LEAs), the teachers, but also various 'pressure' and 'interest' groups. Tied to this is the idea of the 'system' as untidy, unstructured, 'loose'—a federation of interests, sometimes competing, sometimes mutually supportive.

A relatively sophisticated version of this characterization of the system is Briault's[1]* 'triangle of tension', which consists of the DES, LEAs and teachers, welded together yet held apart by the stress in the system, a tension maintained by the different protagonists pulling in different directions, and by conflict over resources.

However, this triangular configuration is unusual, the dominant image is one of tripartite partnership, the triple alliance, the educational trinity. The unity of the partners is maintained by a broad agreement about the intrinsic worth of education: there may be divisions about priorities within that broad agreement, and there may be little that is specific in the creed that unites the partners, but there is a shared belief, a faith, in the value of the enterprise.

The existence of the broad consensus permits a division of labour: the DES promotes particular policies and establishes the general direction of policy, the LEAs make provision, and the teachers interpret the word within their own classrooms. Particularly thorny issues may disrupt the harmony from time to time, but this is to be expected in such an untidy and loosely controlled system.

A further assumption, following from these, is that the senior partner, the DES, is reluctant to encroach on the territory of the others and trespass on LEA and teacher autonomy. This view has been voiced as a criticism of the DES for its failure to specify educational aims, and its reliance on precedent and existing provision; in Fowler's words, this reduces policy-making to 'disjointed incrementalism'.[2]

Many case studies draw on this broad framework and simultaneously support it: studies of comprehensive reorganization which stress LEA autonomy, studies of resource allocation within LEAs which emphasize their differences and hence their autonomous status as policy-makers,[3] studies of teacher union effectiveness which emphasize the success of negotiation and the failure of militancy.[4] Many studies of schools have emphasized the autonomy of their policy-making, the divergence of practice among them and the differences between the intentions of policy-makers at central and local government levels and institutional practice. This has provided support for the theoretical analysis of the system which emphasizes its distributed nature and the claims to partnership status of the major protagonists.

Pluralism has, however, been affected by changes in educational policy-making in the 1970s and 1980s. The impact of falling rolls and declining resources has resulted in a modified version which places greater emphasis on conflict and attaches greater importance to the control of resources. The emphasis is on competing rather than co-operating interests—for example,

* Superscript numbers refer to Notes at the end of the article.

the DES and the Manpower Services Commission (MSC) are described in these terms, as are the erstwhile partners. The change in 'climate' is blamed for this sharpening of conflict and erosion of consensus.

The disintegration of the alliance, the breakdown of partnership, might lead us to question the explanatory value of pluralism, rather than to place the responsibility for change solely on the changing climate. It is, after all, not unknown for adversity to strengthen relationships; in the cold educational climate, could not the partners have huddled together for warmth? Re-examination of the relationship, apparently so fragile under stress, may lead us to wonder about the extent to which it was a partnership at all.

For example, if we consider the question of the broad consensus about educational aims, we must disinter the extent to which deep divisions about the interpretation of equality of opportunity became concealed in administrative debates, and subsumed within the human capital approach to education. These conflicts began to resurface with Callaghan's unsuccessful bid to steal the Conservatives' clothes in the 'Great Debate', and have been put into sharp focus by the current government's concern with standards and revival of selection.

The consensus, if it existed, was a fragile one. A more convincing image would permit the different participants to hold different views of what they were doing, yet all believed that it amounted to some broad extension of opportunity. The ideological function of consensus was to conceal the conflicts among participants and the enormous gap between policy rhetoric and practical reality.

Thus the concept of partnership could well be subjected to serious historical scrutiny, informed by scepticism about much of the evidence for consensus and local and teacher autonomy. A first step would be to explore the origins of 'partnership', which seem to be relatively recent, in the 1944 Act. This raises two questions. If, as Shipman argues,[5] the 1944 Act was the cumulation of a process of increased strengthening of central control of education, how has it come to be used as evidence of *lack* of control? Time and again we read section 1, followed by the comment that only a foreigner would think this *really* meant that education was under the control and direction of the Secretary of State. Why has a document which caused considerable political problems at its introduction because of its centralizing tendencies come to be seen as a cornerstone of devolution?

The second question concerns the placing of 'partnership' in its historical context. Why do we begin with 1944, with its emphasis on rebuilding, rejuvenation and reconstruction? Does this not cause us to lose sight of the origins of our 'system', and its earlier characteristics? If we take a long view, how convincing is the 'partnership' thesis then?

The historical view, of course, places firmly at the centre of the agenda a question which pluralist theorists about educational policy-making have tended to dodge, and that is the question about the function of education.

Historical evidence of policy-makers' perceptions of education as a tool of wealth creation, and the means of production of a skilled work force, as the 'gentler' of the masses, as the force to break down class barriers, is readily available: it is a missing dimension in contemporary studies of educational policy-making. The pluralist emphasis on consensus, or taken-for-granted assumptions about the purpose of education and its essential worth, has distracted us from these fundamental questions.

For attempts to examine educational policy and educational systems with those questions in mind we must be grateful for incursions into educational policy-making by sociologists. A number of recent publications raise questions with which protagonists of the partnership thesis and pluralists —modified or otherwise—are bound to take issue.[6] Nor is it sufficient—as some have attempted—to apply the heretic label (Marxist) to such analyses and condemn them to the figurative stake. The relatively unsophisticated characterization of education by some neo-Marxists as an ideological state apparatus producing classified and labelled workers for the fulfilment of capital's needs has been successfully ignored by many in the mainstream of educational policy analysis—as well as by teachers and students—because it fails to accord with their own interpretations of both the structure of the system and the content of their educational experience. However, this does not mean that analyses which concentrate on the role of the state in educational policy—whether Marxist or not—can be safely dismissed. Admittedly many such analyses are offered at a level of abstraction which renders them vulnerable to criticism from pluralists with extensive and detailed system and subsystem knowledge; the work of bringing together case study analysis and sociological perspectives on policy-making has barely begun. Such analysis would use the best of the pluralist-informed methodology—the detailed case study, observation and description of the various participants—to counter the tendency to over-generalized explanation, and the location of all change in the monolithic state. At the same time, concentration on the purposes of educational policy, recognition of the role of the state and debate about its coherence, the extent of contradictions within it, and the extent of autonomy of the local state, would give a sharper focus to education policy issues than the blurred, soft-focus imagery of pluralism. Taken together with historical studies and studies of the ideological functions of concepts like 'partnership' and 'professionalism', the area could produce both theory and case study which provided better accounts of educational policy-making in the 1980s than modified pluralism.

As we have indicated, most of that work needs to be done, though there has been some, particularly from educational sociologists who are moving into the area of policy studies. In this Reader we include a range of approaches: some of them fall within the pluralist framework, some are very sophisticated extensions of pluralism, incorporating historical and political dimensions.

This Reader, therefore, does not offer a prescription for future developments, but highlights some of the areas of difficulty we have outlined here. For example, we reassess the state of the 'partnership', consider the influence of (diminished) resources on policy-making, and examine the role of a major interest group. We also look again at the impact of policy for equality of opportunity through a historical overview of its interpretation from the beginnings of state provision to the EPA experiment. Because we have concentrated on specific problems—i.e. the 'partnership' concept, the role of resources, the changed climate, different explanatory models—we have not attempted an encyclopaedic approach to educational policy. Some of the items not included here may be covered in the other three course readers.

However, the collection does have a sharp focus on major changes in policy-making and on major developments in ways of understanding educational policy; for this reason we hope that it will prove a useful and lasting contribution to an important debate. The collapse of the educational consensus and the erosion of the partnership have raised doubts about the explanatory value of the dominant paradigm in educational policy studies; in the following pages you will find a reassessment of that paradigm, and evidence both for and against it.

The Reader treats issues at the broad level of 'system'. It deals with agencies outside the institution in the main. Policy-making *within* institutions is treated in two other Open University courses: E323 and E324.

Section 1 of the Reader places educational policy-making within the general context of change. Kogan discusses changes in attitudes to education and different interpretations of its purposes, Dennison surveys the changed economic and demographic circumstances of the 1980s.

Section 2 looks at ways of understanding the policy-making process from different theoretical perspectives: Archer describes a model for the analysis of educational politics, Hargreaves argues for detailed empirical work supported by theoretical development, Offe places analysis of the state and its role at the centre of the study of social policy.

Theorizing about policy-making in education has been dominated by the idea of partnership, at least in England and Wales. Section 3 reassesses the state of the partnership under the strain of scarce resources, competing demands and pressure for accountability. Ranson looks at shifts in the relationship between the central and local government of education since the 1944 Act, Dennison analyses the influence of central government over policy through its control of resources.

Salter and Tapper concentrate on the role of the DES, which in the early 1980s seemed to be taking second place in directing new initiatives in education to the Department of Employment through the Manpower Services Commission. This shift in initiatives within central government ministries carries with it implications for the nature of education. Parkes looks at the emergence of the Manpower Services Commission, particularly in provision for 16–19-year-olds.

Introduction

The MSC is one of a number of 'intermediate bodies' operating in education, particularly in curriculum areas from which, traditionally, central government has distanced itself. Increasingly, however, the determination of strategic developments is being located in the hands of bodies which combine both curriculum and resource responsibilities. The MSC is one of these; in higher education the National Advisory Body for public sector higher education in England, its equivalent in Wales, and a likely equivalent in Scotland originally had remits relating to resource rationalization with curriculum implications, but have increasingly achieved an equality of treatment between those two areas. The longest standing of such intermediate bodies is the University Grants Committee (UGC) and the article by Shattock and Berdahl examines its uneasy place as a buffer between the universities and central government. A similar intermediate status can be seen in school governing bodies, discussed by Kogan et al., which may identify and align themselves with either the head and teaching staff of the school, or the local authority and its education committee, while providing a forum also for representation of other 'community' interests, especially parents.

Teachers constitute a third 'partner' in education policy-making and Section 4 looks at the strategies for influencing policy open to teachers through an examination of a major teachers' union. Lodge and Blackstone take a conventional interest group approach to the analysis of union influence, Jones argues that changed circumstances have rendered the conventional strategies inappropriate, and identifies a number of problems facing organized teachers in terms of loss of morale, salary erosion and external pressures.

The final article in this section, by Walsh et al., examines the way in which the DES attempted to implement policy for the management of teacher numbers in the 1980s.

Section 5 re-examines the major principle in British education, that of equality of opportunity. The origins of the principle and its reflection in various patterns of provision are explored in an extract from Lawson and Silver's historical study. The impact of the principle on practice is assessed by Banting in his examination of Educational Priority Area (EPA) policy. Finally, Murphy looks at the contribution of educational sociology to shifts in the meaning of the concept of equality of opportunity.

REFERENCES

1. Briault, E.W.H., A distributed system of educational administration: an international viewpoint, *International Review of Education*, Vol. 22, No. 4, pp. 429–39, 1976.
2. Fowler, G., Morris, V. and Ozga, J., *Decision-making in British Education*, Heinemann/Open University Press, London, 1973.
3. See, for example, Byrne, E., *Planning and Educational Inequality: a study of the rationale of resource allocation*, NFER, Slough, 1974.

4. For example, Parry, N. and Parry, J., The teachers and professionalism: the failure of an occupational strategy, in Flude, M. and Ahier, J. (eds.), *Educability, Schools and Ideology*, Croom Helm, London, 1974.
5. Shipman, M., *Education as Public Service*, Harper & Row, London, 1984.
6. For example, Ahier, J. and Flude, M. (eds.), *Contemporary Education Policy*, Croom Helm, London, 1983.

SECTION 1

Education Policy in Context

Education Policy and Values

MAURICE KOGAN

Educational policy and values interact with the moods and circumstances of their periods. Education is a social artefact embodying aspirations about the good life for the individual and the best arrangements for the whole society. It is, therefore, particularly prone to change as social and economic circumstances change.

This article charts movements in educational values and policies from 1945, a period which amply exemplifies how the aims of education can change, at least at the level of the governing authorities, within the space of one generation. It then discusses ways in which values might be classified and how they evince themselves operationally.

Values are moral propensities or feelings about what ought to be. They underpin ideologies which are value preferences attached to some kind of programme for, or aspiration to, action. Changes in values must be set in their context of movements in social arrangements and assumptions, and in the state of the economy. Values themselves become a context in which other factors affecting policies are grounded. Values are implicit in the power and institutional relations which are both the contexts and the results of different value positions.

POLICY CONTEXTS FROM 1945

Following the Second World War, the education service was concerned first with implementing the 1944 Act and with repairing the neglect of the war years. Amidst steel and timber rationing, shortages of building labour, imbalance between the numbers of teachers and pupils, the first post-war Labour Government sought to implement the Act by providing secondary

Specially commissioned for this volume, © 1985 The Open University.

education for all up to the age of 15 (in 1948), by the 'roofs over heads' policy, by remanning schools through the emergency training scheme, and by the first build-up of further education.

When the Conservatives took office in 1951 they were not at first disposed to divert the products of economic growth into the public sector. The first post-war Conservative Minister of Education, Florence Horsborough, seemed particularly well suited to Treasury policies. A new era began when she was replaced in 1955 by Sir David Eccles, as a result of the unpopularity of a bill which increased teacher pension contributions.[1]

As Britain's position in the world declined, there was widespread optimism that nevertheless it might be a productive and benign society. During the Eden and Macmillan administrations a long consumer boom began, constrained though it was by recurrent economic crises. Social barriers between the different classes and age groups were thought to have become weaker. Poverty seemed on the way out, although, by the mid-1960s, the concept of relative deprivation embodied growing unease about new manifestations of poverty. Education benefited from these attitudinal and social changes as well as from the natural demography of the baby boom and the policy-induced demography of a raised school-leaving age.

Sir David Eccles represented a different style from that of his predecessor. His value positions were expansionist, ameliorist and consensual—those of the liberal postwar Conservative, of whom he, Boyle and, on a larger stage, Macmillan were the personifications. They believed in a good life for all, and that it was the responsibility of the state to ensure basic minima and open up opportunity. They were exponents of the 'soft' concept of equality. They did not shirk using public resources for the reinforcement of individual capacities to make good.

Eccles, as did Boyle later, set about increasing public support for public education. They talked to the constituencies about the need to level-up opportunities. Eccles provoked a warning from the Prime Minister to be more careful when he told a Conservative conference, 'all those women in hats', that they should send their children to maintained primary schools.

He sought to improve rather than to radically alter the system. He later reflected that expansion was favoured in general terms, but that no one was clear about how to use the money.[2] But the advances were remarkable. In the early 1960s building programmes were launched to improve the quality of schools, technical education and the training of teachers. In 1956 he had announced plans for the reorganization of rural schools, a relatively cheap reform (about £50m in capital building) which appealed to him as a county member. During the 1960s as many as two new schools were being opened each day.

Technical education was more important, although hardly, he thought, a vote catcher, except for the self-made man then entering Conservative politics, but he persuaded Churchill to let resources flow by telling him that the Russians had twenty times as many places as we had.[3] The circulars issued in 1960 display expansion all round, including mandatory awards for students and expansion of the youth service. Higher education expanded until further accelerated by the recommendations of the Robbins Report (1963).

To the liberal Conservatives, teaching and accommodation were more important than structure. When interviewed later, Eccles thought that selection at 11+ created anxieties mainly in towns, that farmers liked secondary modern schools and preferred them to the 'rat-holes' of old fashioned and small grammar schools.

Eccles gave witness to his assumptions of consensus in the course of the Crowther debate (1 March 1960):

> ... I expected (the Report) would tell us that the post-war revolution in employment and the spread of wealth should modify, perhaps radically, the pattern of educational advance which seemed right at the beginning of the war. But the Council did not take that view. The report endorses, with the utmost conviction, the principles of educational reform laid down by the 1944 Education Act.

Eccles gave a glowing account of progress. People were voting for education with their feet: 'HM Inspectors are repeatedly telling me of schools where staying on suddenly becomes a fashion. First, the able children and those from more responsible homes take the lead and set the example. It catches on.' So did a junior minister point to the self-reinforcing demand for education: 'We are now having to reinforce the success of the earlier education drive which began some years ago and which is now producing as its fruits an intensified demand for more and better education everywhere in the country.'[4]

In 1960 the large issues concerning secondary school selection had not yet become salient. Higher education was to be the next important area for change. Jo Grimond demanded a Royal Commission on the universities. Eirene White attacked the Government's failure to plan educational advance—'activity is no substitute for policy'—and the lack of coherence in policy as between universities and other forms of higher education. Eccles promised an enquiry. He referred to

> the race to get to university which is doing great harm... the conclusion is inescapable. Many more university places must be available... even if it means sacrifices in other directions, the money must be found for education... education is the response which a free society makes to the claims of each individual child to be cared for, not for what he produces, but for what he is. We must remain a strong nation.

This anti-instrumental view expressed by a Conservative minister of the 1960s was of a piece with his declaration that poverty would be abolished within a decade. In 1963, on the day of publication, the Home government accepted the recommendations of the Robbins Committee. 'Courses of higher education should be available for all of those who are qualified by ability and attainment to pursue them and who wish to do so', was the key concept.

Ultimately the proportion of each age group admitted quadrupled—from 3 per cent to over 12 per cent between 1945 and the early 1970s, when demand for higher education began to slow down.

The United Kingdom was thus set for progress towards mass, if not universal, higher education. New universities and thirty polytechnics were created. In their train came the Open University, although not part of the original Robbins mandate, and the Council for National Academic Awards. The scale and texture of the system were thus radically altered.

In the period before the return of the Labour Government in 1964 the zest for expansion continued unabated. In 1962 education expenditure reached £1000m for the first time. It took 3.2 per cent of the gross national product in the mid-1950s, 5 per cent in 1965, and 6 per cent in 1969.[5]

If unequivocal about the need to extend opportunity, the Conservatives were gradualist about much else. They assumed that the schools could meet changes in social needs, including those posed by the recent arrival of immigrants. Boyle was non-doctrinal about selection for secondary education. 'We no longer regard any pattern of organisation as "the norm" compared with which all others must be stigmatised.'[6]

The 1964 Labour Government inherited expansionism from its predecessors and the main area of dissensus was how far education should promote equality. Hitherto, opportunities for all had meant virtually no displacement of existing privileges. Incorporating the positive concept of equality must mean that there would be some losers. On all of the main issue areas—the speed with which selective secondary education should be abolished, the neutralization of the private schools, and implementing the Newsom (1963) and Plowden (1967) policies of positive discrimination—successive ministers proved hesitant. This has led some to assume that there was a 'social democratic' consensus between the main parties, a point to which we shall return later.

THE CASE OF HIGHER EDUCATION: FROM EXPANSION TO CONTRACTION

The changes in higher education raise questions about the values involved. In continuing expansion and in establishing the binary system, the Labour Government created an uneasy amalgam between public utility, this being the primary justification for the polytechnics, as stated by Crosland and their other protagonists,[7] and elitism, this remaining the justification for the expanded university sector.

Not all change derives from ideology, however. Large-scale expansion leads to changes in the relationships between the universities and the state. Responsibility for the University Grants Committee shifted from the Treasury to the Department of Education and Science (DES). Growth brought a greatly more costly system. In 1939 perhaps 30 per cent of university funding was met from the public purse. By the 1960s it reached 90 per cent. By the early 1970s universities no longer received quinquennial grants but were given what the government thought fit and on assumptions which increasingly responded to DES notions of utility rather than their own concepts of how to fulfill their functions of teaching, scholarship and research.

With expansion, higher education became more hospitable to a wider range of courses, catering to students whose purposes in attending were different from those of the pre-war 3 per cent. Larger institutions meant the assertion of more managerial and less collegial forms of organizational behaviour, and with them came stronger staff unionization and student politicization.

The Robbins principle of social demand was renounced in 1981 when the universities were suddenly deprived of 9 per cent of their funds, at a time when the 18-year-old cohort was at its peak, and the UGC decided to preserve 'the unit of resource' by cutting about 20,000 places. Their resources had already shrunk by about 10 per cent in the previous decade. When the government relented, it did so in pursuit of its own preferences. Some money was restored so that information technology, genetic engineering and business studies could be funded. The universities came under pressure to change the tenure rules which had always been regarded as central to the maintenance of academic freedom. At the same time, the public sector came under a rationalization exercise performed by the recently created National Advisory Body for Local Authority Higher Education.

THE PATTERN OF CHANGING VALUES

Several value issues were thus deployed in the case of British higher education. In the early 1960s there was bipartisan agreement about expansion. The underlying motives were those of widening opportunities for the able—the 'soft' concept of equality; of furnishing the economy with educated manpower; of maintaining at the same time provision for high-class scholarship and research, even in those areas with no obvious economic justification. The system did not entertain some of the broader objectives established elsewhere, of open access and comprehensive universities, and there was no attempt, as in Sweden, to increase the number of work experienced students returning to education later in life. At the end of the Labour administration, however, a DES Report, *Higher Education into the 1990s* (1978), canvassed ways in which the impending demographic downturn could be put to advantage by widening opportunities.

The radical Conservative Government of 1979 introduced a wholly different range of values. Whilst protesting belief in holding open opportunity, it favoured more exclusive access. It pursued particular instrumental objectives thought to be conducive to a productive economy.

Some recent interpretations[8] identify a 'social democratic' consensus between Labour and Conservative politicians during the period before the 1979 Conservative Government. This view assumes that the underlying motives were not general amelioration, but that education policies were used to maintain the existing social structure and the needs of 'capital'. Policy was directed to sustaining 'social cohesion', encouraging the working classes, and women, to accept their lot rather than to acquire the consciousness needed to achieve a more radically equal society through a thorough-going redistribution.

Labour and Conservative ministers did share a belief in expansion and that education was an undisputed good. Both shared a belief in its contribution to the economy, to growing distribution of wealth, and to individual happiness. Neither saw any reason to believe that in its existing evolutionary modes education would reinforce deprivation or inequality. Both made explicit statements to the contrary. Both believed that teachers would seek the best for clients from a combination of professional expertise and altruism. But ministers such as Crosland shared no consensus on the need for universal comprehensive education or the damage done to the majority by the perpetuation of public schools. His principal speeches and his 'The Conservative Enemy' do not lend themselves to such an interpretation.

Postwar conservatism moved a long way in allowing the drift to comprehensives, the endorsement of 'progressive' primary education and the expansion of higher education. Given the Conservatives' radically expansionist mood, it is not surprising that Labour's efforts seemed no different from those of their predecessors. If determined socialist policies were never fully promoted, the Labour governments did mark the beginning of an ideological divide. By the mid-1960s the weak concept of equality was proving insufficient for the Labour administration, which at first tried to complete comprehensivization by 'request', but, just as it was to lose office in 1969, prepared to legislate against those local education authorities which remained obdurate.

In 1970 Mrs Thatcher became Secretary of State, and although still, in her 1972 White Paper, committed to continued growth of higher education, and prepared to accept backbench persuasion that nursery education should be expanded, began the first instalments of confrontation politics. Free school milk and subsidies for school meals were abolished or reduced. Within three days of taking office she withdrew the circular requiring local authorities to make all of their secondary schools comprehensive.

Between 1973 and 1979 policy was marked by uncertainty. The economic blizzard of 1972 finally put paid to the optimism which had lasted for nearly thirty years. The Black Papers[9] attacked the liberal modes of education as selling children short on the skills they needed. A group of cognoscenti from the London Institute of Education[10] had earlier criticized the developmental assumptions of the Plowden Report (1967) which had sponsored the progressivism of primary schools. At the same time, the authority of knowledge was questioned by the sociology of knowledge which pointed to the artificial nature of its hierarchies and the extent to which its received authority depended upon its social provenance. The effects of these critiques on academic self-confidence and the standing of education in society can only be a matter for speculation.

Teacher status had never been secure, but the professionals had been allowed to develop their own systems and philosophies. In the 1970s these autonomies were challenged partly by the onset of corporate management but also by demands that the schools should be more responsive to the wishes of clients. The ideal of the school as a beneficent institution run by altruistically motivated professionals was challenged in Avon, where the chief education officer resigned rather than yield to non-professional control. The case of William Tyndale Junior School, and the Auld Report which followed it, laid out the rights of parents and the duties of local authorities in controlling the ways teachers were to provide for children. The Taylor Report (1977) proposed greater power for governing bodies and to distribute it more evenly between the local authority, teachers, parents and the community. The DES later attempted [11] a consumerist version of control; parents were to form the majority on governing bodies which would decide the educational policies of individual schools. This was thought to be going too far, even for ministers determined to weaken the control of both teachers and local authorities, and the Green Paper incorporating these suggestions seemed likely to be withdrawn at the time of writing. The 1981 Act had given parents the right to choose their children's schools, and had also provided assisted places in independent schools for able pupils who would otherwise not have been able to afford them. All of these moves added up to a considerable onslaught on professional power by heroic politicians.

The process of bringing the schools under greater political and central control had its timid beginnings in 1974, with the creation of an Assessment of Performance Unit (APU), in the warning given in 1976 in James Callaghan's speech at Ruskin College, Oxford, that parents were anxious about educational standards, and by a flow of DES circulars and HMI publications about the need to monitor performance and to establish the core essentials of the curriculum.

By 1985, however, the Secretary of State was threatening to enforce the competence testing of teachers, and had already made decisive moves towards the quality control of teacher education, and had forbidden the training of social science graduates for primary school teaching. The DES in 1984[12] used withheld local authority money (£35m) to promote curriculum development schemes of its own choice. It promoted inservice training schemes which again enabled it to assert its own instrumental preferences.

By early 1985 quite precise skills, deriving from the pursuit of technologies, but also from classic subjects, had won back territory from the new styles of learning, and particularly those areas where social problem-solving and experientially based learning had begun to make progress. The government diverted parts of local authority rate support grant to the Manpower Services Commission (MSC). The MSC put £150m into Technical and Vocational Educational Initiative schemes which were criticized by teachers and local authorities as being unrelated to the rest of the curriculum.

The rights of the DES over educational content have always been uncertain, for the control over the curriculum is delegated by law to local authorities, whilst the Secretary of State is required to promote the education of the people of England. In the past the central authorities possessed considerable authority. Until 1902 the Board of Education adjusted grants according to the results of tests administered to pupils by HMIs. Even after the abolition of payment by results, the work of the schools was subject to the Elementary Code, although an increasing amount of leeway was allowed the schools. In the period following the 1944 Act the schools became increasingly free of central instruction or persuasion. Such developments as Mode 3 of the Certificate of Secondary Education (CSE), which allowed for examinations to be internally set and examined but assessed externally, were evidence of ministers' wishes to allow the schools to be the prime agents in educational development. The novelty of the changes in the 1980s rested in the quite particular and instrumental preferences expressed by the DES and the non-consultative way in which it behaved.

CLASSIFYING VALUES AND POLICIES

On the basis of this account of educational policies from 1945 to the present day (1985), it is possible to pose two questions. How do values in education originate, and who has authority to implement them? Are there different kinds of values and do they operate in different ways?

The history demonstrates how value issues emerge unsystematically from the beliefs entertained by individuals or groups of individuals or interest groups or parties. They become policies when power is gained and the values become authoritative. Some policy movements derive less from *a priori* assumptions about what is morally right than from the observation and experience of practitioners. Practitioners identify the best ways in which pupils learn and what should be learned. These judgements involve assumptions about the kind of adult that education should produce and the world he or she should inhabit.

Practitioner-based value setting is conditioned by the larger system and the values which flow through it; resource allocations, external examinations, maintaining schools as efficient organizations, all tap different sources of values and ways in which they are made authoritative. Recent policy moves, to incorporate presumed employment needs and parental demands, add to the range of values which teachers have to take on board. Ultimately it is they who select from them, because it is through teachers that the principal discernible products of education emerge.

As we move from the curriculum to more social or economic objectives, so the sources of values and groups affecting their adoption become more diffuse. Some teachers sponsored the equality norm, but the issues were most cogently identified by social scientists and brought home to roost by politicians.

This modified pluralist account of value setting assumes negotiation between loosely coupled groups, none of them plainly constituting a certain and permanent elite, yet not immediately speaking directly from the viewpoint of most clients and schools. Even granted the recent incursions of the centre, the power to install values remains diffuse and multi-level. Over time, there are cyclical shifts in the balance of power between those controlling the political-administrative system and those who administer the curriculum and sustain the relationships with clients in the schools.[13]

GROUPING OF VALUES

We can now take up the questions of their origins and types by analysing educational policy-making through four crudely defined sets of values: educational, social, economic and institutional. They are not clearly boundaried from each other, and appear in different mixes in different policy packages. Different values can be held in tension in any one policy at any one time: the educational may conflict with the social or economic justifications.

What are some of the properties of these value groupings? When writing on these issues ten years ago,[14] the author assumed that some values operated continuously as if intrinsic to education. Others were thought to emerge in an innovative or discontinuous fashion. Two factors might affect the continuousness of values in education. They might be protected because most obviously within the zone of concern of the professionals who run education; the values enshrined in the curriculum are an obvious example. Issues of a predominantly social or economic kind are less likely to concern teachers with long-distance commitments to the professional task. Where teachers have engaged in them they have found it difficult to sustain consensus, as, for example, the teacher unions' reluctance to sponsor comprehensive education until quite late in the day.[15] Teachers' interests and values take on different perspectives according to whether they are operating in the classroom or in their professional association settings.

Continuity is enhanced by the delegation of authority which enables values to be maintained at different points in the system. If educational continuities are now being severely tested by ministers who take no traditional educational assumption for granted, it is not, however, against nature for teachers' concepts of child development to be challenged by 'outsiders'. Economic instrumentalism or radical egalitarian policies may conflict with the notion that children should develop largely at their own pace. Some teachers might object to the labelling implied by social engineering.

Educational values largely derive from views of the proper nature of the educated person and respond to such basic values in individuality and self-determination. Values derived from concepts of the educated individual are modified by assumptions about what society and employment expect of schools. This antinomy is expressed in the organization of schools which simultaneously allow for the mediation of social control and for the individual treatment of pupils' needs.

Some educational values such as individual satisfaction and autonomy derive from a long tradition of acceptance of the thinking of Froebel, Montessori, Dewey, Susan Isaacs and Piaget. These value positions are backed by a scientific view of how children best learn. Values are not easily separated from questions of what is the best technique to adopt.

SOCIAL VALUES

Educational and social values are adjacent to each other. Concepts of learning entail views about the relationships between individuals and society. The social issues of most concern have been socialization and equality. Socialization is the process by which each generation is inducted into the norms of society. It can therefore respond to a wide range of values, depending on the purposes for which children are to be socialized. The dominant norms are highly variable between societies and can range widely within any particular society. Indeed values pluralism is itself a dominant value in British society and one sponsored by education.

At the same time, the schools have never been detached from the promotion of particular value assumptions. Patriotism, the work ethic, individuality, multi-culturalism, have jostled with legal requirements to teach religious education and offer acts of worship. Socialization has, on the whole, favoured value eclecticism, but with tilts towards the assumptions of a liberal capitalist society. The dominant social issue has been that of equality.

Egalitarianism has shaped many of the key policies: comprehensives, the raising of the school-leaving age, for example. It remained an important if submerged issue in the 1970s as Labour administrations both central and local wrestled with problems of installing comprehensives. The equality value encountered several problems. First, there were the operational difficulties of putting it into effect: those of attitudes, of institutional structure and finance. Second, there were the conceptual problems of reconciling it with other and more heuristic educational practices and values. Third, it was necessary to determine which species of equality was being sought. The 'soft' or 'weak' concept argued for equality of opportunity to compete for educational chances. The 'hard' or 'strong' (these being Anthony Crosland's distinctions) concept argued for positive attempts to compensate for social disadvantage. A further stage is now concerned with securing maximum take-up and impact and brings education back to concern with individualized attention. These complexities, operational and conceptual, have presented virtually insuperable problems to social planning. Comprehensive education called for reconciliation between differentiated learning for individual and common provisions for all children. These were not new problems, but many had hoped that the schools would have a new mandate with which to tackle them. The evidence had convinced educationists that selection should go; the 1970s showed that securing an effective replacement was not easy.

ECONOMIC VALUES

Education has always been justified by its contribution to the economy. Even when non-instrumental views prevailed, it was claimed that education produces the flexibility of mind and creativity needed to sustain the economy and society. The issue has thus been not whether there will be a return on educational investment but whether the return will justify a particular level of investment.

The values underlying the economic arguments have been no less ambivalent than in more general social areas. Good economic performance can be argued both for its value to the individual and to society, as a way to sharpen acquisitiveness and as enabling society to afford welfare programmes. The basic values should not be taken for granted.

Economic arguments mainly favoured educational expansion for most of our period, but are now being turned against it. For example, both the original expansion and the current contraction of higher education have been justified on economic grounds. Expenditure on education is at the mercy of economic policy at large which has been both discontinuous and external to education. Current policies pull education towards zones of control well outside the policy networks of the education interest groups and the DES. The present yielding of ground by the DES and local authorities to the Department of Employment and the MSC implies that education as the developer of the whole person is less important than as the creator of specific employable skills for wealth creation.

INSTITUTIONAL VALUES

Institutional values do not relate directly to the outcomes of education, which are learning and teaching, but nonetheless elicit basic values. Such policies as the defence of local authority powers against the centre, the place of parents on governing bodies, the powers of teachers, the freedom of the universities, the representation of students, can be argued in terms of equity, freedom, or the advancement of a sense of community. Almost all views of how institutions should be governed start from a liberal democratic standpoint which notoriously leads to outcomes differing according to the viewpoint of different interested groups. For example, 'participation' may mean that parents should govern the school, or that they should have the right to criticize teachers who retain control over the school, or that teachers should be governors and thus modify the clients' ability to criticize. Or it can be construed traditionally as the right to elect and dismiss councillors who might not pay much heed to the views of parents or teachers.

Institutional values also justify the maintenance of systems which appoint teachers, build and maintain capital plant and are responsible for thousands of pupils. They have to be accountable and reliable. Such characteristics depend upon combinations of social and individualistic values for their justification: equitable treatment between individuals, or preserving communal assets, for example. If, however, institutions prize procedures above the basic values that procedures are meant to implement, organizational pathology has set in.

CONCLUSION

In this paper an attempt has been made to relate recent educational policy to underlying values. The historical themes have been used to consider how values operationalize themselves in terms of continuity and permeability to influences outside education itself. Throughout, the ambivalence and context-relatedness of values in education have been emphasized. A final point must be made. Not all policies derive from conscious motives. Many politicians enjoy power for the sake of it and act from pragmatism rather than principle. The values game is worth playing, but not to death, and not in the face of commonsense evidence about intentionality.

REFERENCES

1. Interviews with two Conservative and one Labour MP, reported in Kogan, M., *Educational Policy Making: a study of interest groups and Parliament*, Allen and Unwin, London, 1975, on which much of the material contained in this chapter is based.
2. Interview with Lord Eccles, March 1974.
3. Ibid.
4. Kenneth Thompson, MP, House of Commons, 30 November 1960.
5. Vaizey, J. and Sheehan, J., *Resources for Education*, Allen and Unwin, London, 1968.
6. Annual Conference, Association of Education Committees, 1963.
7. For example, Robinson, E., *The Polytechnics*, Cornmarket Press, London, 1968.
8. For example, Education Group, Centre for Contemporary Cultural Studies, *Unpopular*

Education, Schooling and Social Democracy in England Since 1944, Hutchinson, London, 1980.
9. Cox, C.B. and Dyson, A.E. (eds.), *Black Paper 1 (Fight for Education)*, and *Black Paper 2 (The Crisis in Education)*, Critical Quarterly Society, 1969, 1970.
10. Peters, R.S. (ed.), *Perspectives on Plowden*, Routledge & Kegan Paul, London, 1968.
11. DES, *Parental Influence at School. A New Framework for School Government in England and Wales*, Cmnd 9242, HMSO, London, 1984.
12. Kogan, M., Curriculum innovation: the impact of central government initiatives, *Secondary Education Journal*, Vol. 14, No. 3, October 1984.
13. Wirt, F., Reassessment needs in the study of the politics of education, *Teachers' College Record*, Vol. 78, No. 4, May 1977.
14. Kogan, M., *Educational Policy Making*, chapter 3.
15. Kogan, op. cit.

2

Education and the Economy
changing circumstances

W.F. DENNISON

Were education not publicly provided, there would still be need to consider numerous interactions with the economy. Teacher supply might be more subject to market forces, student participation rates could be more influenced by economic activity levels, but many components in the relationship would continue unaltered. The dominant question concerns the willingness and the ability of the economy to support an education service, and relatedly the effects on the intentions and functions of the service of economic factors. Clearly, the inverse question has also to be posed, about the economic contribution of education—the benefits sought and achieved by the provision of the service.

As regards each of these issues the three decades of the 1960s, 1970s and 1980s provide quite different perspectives. The 1960s were a period of unprecedented growth, following the expansions achieved since 1945. All sectors of education benefited, with substantial growth in real terms and relative to most other measures. In brief, the education service expanded more rapidly than the public economy as a whole, which itself took a rising proportion of GDP.[1] The educational components, if not the economic costs, of such a policy were accepted without equivocation. When concerns were expressed, on political grounds or whatever, it was the methodologies or the priorities within the policy which were questioned, not its main thrust. The intention of more education for a greater number of clients seemed wholly acceptable. As a result, schools and FE increased enrolments, more children stayed beyond minimum leaving-age, new colleges and polytechnics were established and provision for youth services and the handicapped was raised. Yet across this whole range of increased expenditure few overt

Source: Dennison, W.F., *Educational Finance and Resources*, Croom Helm, London, 1984.

attempts were made to differentiate consumption from investment components. Clearly, the introduction of a polytechnic was biased towards investment, because of the anticipated economic returns from college graduates, as compared to the development of a special school, but a discrete separation was neither intended nor sought. More practically, a major effect of expansion was an increased education work force: not only in relation to teacher and lecturer numbers, but also in the evolution of a large supportive infrastructure, from education psychologists to domestic and cleaning staff.

The 1970s started similarly, with continuous growth and an expectation of its continuance. The Education White Paper (1972) envisaged a 53 per cent rise in recurrent school expenditure over the next ten years (63 per cent for higher education).[2] Significantly, the main theme was consolidation and improvement, to supplement previous expansions, as well as concentrating on activities which had up to then received little attention. Recurrent expenditure on nursery education, for example, was projected to increase almost threefold but these plans remained unfulfilled, for by the end of the decade the general situation had altered totally. In terms of expansion, instead of education occupying a premier position within a public expenditure sector advantaged relative to GDP, spending on education was forecast to decline more rapidly than any other comparable major programme within a government spending programme itself projected to shrink.[3] The actual turn-round was swift, given the cumbersome nature of the decision-making machinery, taking no more than three years (1973-76): starting with capital expenditure, as this presents fewer problems, educational spending was rapidly transformed from expansion, through a short period of staticity to shallow decline. As for growth, no sector or activity was exempt. Naturally, this rapid transition, after such a lengthy period of sustained growth, provoked a view that the change was no more than a temporary abnormality, to be replaced at some stage by expansionism. Towards the end of the decade there were indications that these perceptions might prove correct, with some limited expansion in 1978 and 1979 (although without altering the relative position of education in public expenditure programmes)[4] but, in retrospect, these gains represented more a correction for previous underspendings and a pre-election boost than a prediction of what was to follow.

It is highly probable that by the end of the 1980s educational expenditure as conventionally defined—that is setting aside, for the time being, any measures associated with the MSC—will be several percentage points lower than the levels existing at the start of the decade: possibly (for reasons to be considered later) the decline may be much greater. The more detailed projections for the mid-1980s continue the pattern first established almost ten years previously of steady decline more or less evenly spread across the main sectors of education. Between 1983-84 and 1985-86 educational spending should rise by 6 per cent in cash terms but, with the accommodation of pay and price increases, the volume of educational activity seems certain to continue its decline. While education's share of public expenditure should decrease only marginally from 12.22 per cent to 12.15 per cent, this is within a total where restriction is a main objective of government economic policy.[5] The effects of these changing circumstances are less marked in relation to the actual conditions under which schools and colleges function, as compared to the changes in attitudes and practices that accompanied and followed the transition. Someone returning towards the mid-1980s, after an absence of 25 years, would not meet enormous classes with under-paid staff in outdated buildings: although they would discover shortages of equipment, books and specialist staff. Depending, of course, on individual situations it would be difficult to find schools and colleges which, in terms of real inputs per head, did not receive considerably more in 1983-84 than 1958-59.

However, this contrast, relative to attitudes, is much less important than the year by year situation. A rate of growth of 3 per cent, say, does not seem too much different to a 1 per cent contraction (after all 99 per cent of the original resources are still available) but the implications for attitudes and priorities are considerable, particularly if these respective rates are sustained: attitudes, because of the advantages perceived by staff of working in an environment where additional resources are continuously being generated: priorities, as difficult decisions about what activities are no longer viable need never be made during growth. For example, views about resource shortages may be related more to funding levels than might have been anticipated without contraction than to absolute assessments of deprivation. Additionally, expansion itself initiated arrangements and practices which made conversion more difficult, particularly by introducing inflexibilities if spending ever had to be reduced. The large numbers of staff, for instance, recruited as the service grew, joined on the assumption that they had a job until they chose otherwise, and that reasonable aspirational levels would be satisfied. Indeed, job security may have been a factor which attracted them to the work in the first place. Obviously, they react adversely to possible job losses, and to a related decline in promotional opportunities: even to the extent of resisting practices more appropriate to the new circumstances, particularly if they can convince themselves that these circumstances are only temporary. The whole situation is exacerbated by an age profile in which teachers recruited in their twenties, during the expansionist era of the 1960s and early 1970s, dominate.

Two factors directly related to the system go some way towards explaining this movement from growth to contraction. The first, more tangible and less contentious, results from pupil shortage in schools, following birth-rate decline. The rate was high from the late 1950s onwards, peaking in 1964, falling slowly to 1971 and then more substantially. As a result primary school rolls began to drop from the mid-1970s, with a small upturn anticipated in the mid- and late 1980s, because of a birth-rate rise, centred around 1980. For secondary education, numbers in compulsory schooling did not begin to fall until the early 1980s, but the trend will continue for at least ten years with only a limited expansion likely in the mid-1990s.[6] Therefore, it was much more than coincidence that the transition from growth to shrinkage occurred simultaneously with the first real appreciation of the likely effects of birth-rate decline. Since 1945 much of the expansion had been to cope with additional pupils: by the mid-1970s total numbers were soon to fall—eventually by almost 35 per cent. In other words, the most effective and persuasive lobby for extra resources was about to evaporate. Since then arguments that unless new schools are built, and additional staff employed, statutory obligations cannot be fulfilled, have largely ceased for most LEAs and are unlikely to be re-established, at least this century. Even the anticipated increases in numbers already mentioned will be relatively small, raising the respective primary and secondary school population to well below the peaks of the 1970s and early 1980s.

It is more difficult accumulating evidence to substantiate the second explanatory factor, as it involves assessments of the public standing of the education service. Most directly, there has been a reduction in confidence in relation both to the processes and outcomes, and a resultant decline in public esteem, reflected in the translation from top to bottom placing in public sector resource distribution. Of course, an empiricist is entitled to ask questions about this erosion of public confidence (its level and extent, the time scales involved, the previous standing of the service, the differential effect on sectors, etc.) and whether, in fact, it has occurred at all. Without a sophisticated approach based on market survey techniques and already established before the transition, answers to these questions cannot be elucidated. However, it does not follow that the main statement has no substance. There is sufficient qualitative evidence to confirm the point, not indisputably of course, but to the extent that the education service should be concerned. It would be inappropriate, and highly complacent, for educationists to dismiss the 'Great Debate' of 1977, for example, as an irrelevant exercise.[7] There were reactive elements sponsored by the DES. Criticisms particularly from employers, about the quality of school-leavers had to be considered, if not answered.[8] A forum offered that opportunity: more cynically, it diverted attention from more important issues, and the actual decision-making machinery. However, proactive factors also surfaced, in that the DES, by launching the initiative, announced its attention towards more interventionism in those school processes it had traditionally left to professional staff. Similarly, the establishment of the APU during the mid- and late 1970s, had both reactive and proactive components. Those, such as 'Black Paper' writers, who claimed that standards were falling, had to be assuaged by demonstrating that, at least, these standards were to be more systematically monitored than previously.[9] On the interventionist side, by being seen to be highly supportive of such an arrangement, the DES registered growing concern for processes and outcomes to LEAs and school staff. More recently, the emergence of the Youth Training Scheme (YTS) for school-leavers, in effect an additional year of education and training, but not school-based, can be viewed as an expression of government dissatisfaction with the outcomes when the leaving age was raised in 1972. On this occasion, by dominating resource determination and using high youth unemployment, it has sponsored alternative institutional arrangements.

The greater interventionism, illustrated by these examples, is best viewed as part of the evolution of a corporatist policy-making strategy, in which the DES (and government) organizes co-operation. In the case of YTS, by ensuring that its own organization (MSC) has sufficient resources, and control of their use, government offered colleges, staff, LEAs and firms no feasible alternative but to work with it.[10] Perhaps the most striking example of the ability to organize co-operation was the local authority response to the government, the Technical and Vocational Education Initiative (TVEI) (1983). The intention was to provide a four-year curriculum for low-achieving 14–18-year-olds (that is, a wider brief than the YTS arrangements) containing general, technical and vocational education including work experience, with the aim of developing a range of occupational skills and competencies.[11] Many LEAs were opposed, both politically and ideologically, to the idea of separate arrangements, and more particularly direction towards low-grade employment, for a minority of 14–18-year-olds, even as a pilot scheme, as it impinged directly on their responsibilities, yet over two-thirds were willing to participate. Such was the response that the initial scheme was soon extended to cover more projects.[12] With this process of corporatism the pluralist strategy employed previously, whereby a neutral government adjudicated, when necessary, between participants who themselves were generating much of the policy, becomes defunct. In this context, with pluralism, it was the professional staff (assisted by the LEA) and the examination boards which represented the main interests at institutional level: while nationally the local authority associations, the teacher unions and (to a limited extent) the DES were dominant.

Quite possibly this change of strategy would have occurred irrespective of other events. It was not restricted to education: major alterations in the government's relationships with other activities—manufacturing industry, local government services in general, nationalized industries, the health service—occurred almost simultaneously. Of course it can be argued that the DES sponsored the erosion in public confidence to justify the new approach. There is, perhaps, no better way to further lessen esteem for a service, than by publicizing a 'debate' in which reasons for reductions in this esteem receive scrutiny. However, to pursue this argument overlooks a crucial issue. As the accusations of lack of control of process, lower quality of outcomes, and reduced standards proliferated, they were not countered successfully, either because they could not be (that is, by implication, they were true) or because they were thought irrelevant and unimportant (because the system was too introspective). Whatever the reason, the DES could change strategy largely unimpeded and, more significantly, a positive lobby, to prevent or dilute the government-initiated change in the resource situation, never became established.

EDUCATIONAL AND ECONOMIC INTERDEPENDENCIES

Much of the previous reasoning is based upon an underlying, but unstated, model of rational analysis and decision-making. According to this, the DES (for its part) overviews the total situation, formulates objectives, organizes co-operation, and then acts in a logical and ordered manner.[13] Similarly, LEA or school staff likely to be affected by DES activities, consider the available alternatives and then, having analysed the merits and disadvantages of each, make a clear choice. The reality is invariably different. Organizations of all types often appear to behave quite irrationally: decisions are made which seem not to be based on logical analysis. Two education examples are not untypical. The first is the resistance some Non-Advanced Further Education (NAFE) colleges have shown towards MSC-financed courses for 16-19-year-olds when this may be their most effective route towards long-term growth. The second, the tendency of certain schools to continue with options which cannot attract sufficient pupils, when the associated resources could be diverted elsewhere in the school.

The key issue concerns the inevitable politicization of every organization, whether it is a school, college or the DES. All consist of individuals working alone and in groups. As individuals they have views, interests and values which become modified as they interact with those of other group members. As a result, the group develops an identity, which it then transmits as its contribution to the organizational identity: but without totally subsuming the characteristics of individual members, particularly the most influential and powerful. Therefore, while it may be convenient to speak of a DES view (about curricular intervention, for example), this disguises the range of interests that have dominated, or compromised, to produce this view. In this situation the Teachers Branch, Financial Services and HMI might all have been involved, each represented by individuals arguing on the basis of their own perspectives within a sectional and organizational setting. If they, or the interests they represent, perceive an unsatisfactory outcome they will press to change the view. There can be no certainty of continuity in a political environment, or agreement over interpretation. Therefore, two members of the same organization (the DES in this case) may describe the official position somewhat differently, both because of interpretative uncertainty and in an effort to influence the reformulation of the position.

Within this frame of reference it would clearly be unwise to explain the growth-to-contraction transition of the mid-1970s as a rational piece of decision-making based on the likelihood of falling numbers and previously unrealized expectations. Even the logic of linking fewer pupils to lower expenditure could be disputed, because of the problems inherent in dealing with declining roll situations. Similarly, there is no irrefutable rationality in reducing provision following shortfalls in achievement. It could be argued, quite reasonably, that a lack of resources was contributing to this underachievement in the first place, and to reduce levels further would only exacerbate the situation. However, so far in this discussion one factor has been deliberately excluded: that is the rapid change in the status of public expenditure. Had it been introduced earlier to explain the changed circumstances of education it could have been both seen as the result of rational decision-making (which is debatable) and dominating the other two factors which in education (compared with other public activities) are particularly significant. Undoubtedly the growth in education was facilitated by a buoyant public economy: not surprisingly as this began to falter towards the mid-1970s, education spending followed. However, even as the change began, total public spending, as a proportion of GDP, still grew from 38 to 46 per cent between 1971-72 and 1975-76: an increase exaggerated by limited growth in the economy and almost stagnant industrial production. During this time, for example, annual expansion rates were little more than 1 per cent, in contrast to public expenditure levels in excess of 5 per cent.[14] Clearly, differentials of this order were not permanently sustainable. Yet up to that time public spending increasing its share of national income was not an unusual feature of economic life in either the United Kingdom or elsewhere.[15]

Two further pieces of information exemplify the growth in public expenditure. In the twenty years from 1955 to 1975 the proportion of the working population (including part-timers) employed by local authorities rose from 6.3 per cent to 11.3 per cent: certainly, towards the end of this time, reducing an underlying increase in unemployment. More significantly, in terms of causal relationships, while the cost of public policy increased by 201 per cent between 1950 and 1974 the average rise in take-home pay of 75 per cent was much less substantial (a pattern repeated in other developed countries).[16] Therefore, to explain public expenditure growth simply in terms of increased affluence enabling individual and group generosity towards public services requires some qualification. Perhaps it was a conscious decision to acquiesce to (or elect) governments and authorities more committed to collectively preferred, rather than individually selected, benefits—an acceptance of a higher social wage through increased public spending on education, as well as housing, social services, etc. More generally the rate of social and economic change after World War II was higher than ever before, and governments found themselves (usually willingly, often as a component of policy) involved in activities which previously were either non-existent or performed by charitable and private organizations, as part of a more general process of converting from informal to formal support. In education, a good example of this evolution was the development of services for children with learning and other disabilities. Those involved, and the interests they represented (parents, teachers, counsellors and so on) generated a lobby for further spending. Practically, a special education pressure group was only one among many, ranging from some parents pressing for new school buildings or an additional teacher, through to the national campaigns which usually preceded, and invariably followed, the major educational reports—Plowden on Primary Education, Robbins on Higher Education, etc.[17]

It is difficult, if not impossible, to ascertain with certainty, using subsequent expenditure figures, the specific effects of particular lobbies. Invariably the relevant decision processes are so diffuse while the appropriate time scales are only rarely definable with sufficient accuracy. Occasionally, with the expansion of higher education after Robbins, for example, definitive evidence to link an explicit decision with a resultant impact does exist, but such a case tends to be exceptional. In contrast, the more pervasive orthodoxy (in education and elsewhere) was an expectation of growth, supported both by a general view that this had intrinsic merit and arguments to favour certain priorities. A successful lobby for a particular item (more expenditure on youth work or a new school) was guaranteed to evoke an additional pressure group for better provision or improved facilities elsewhere. The vital issue of the rationality of the choices, or the criteria used in decision-making, received less attention than the creation of high aspirational levels in virtually every activity, and their sustenance by the successful acquisition of still more resources within a competitive environment. Cyclically, the satisfaction of a particular set of needs regularly produced still more wants: therefore the establishment of secondary education in the 1950s, with the elimination of all-age schools, was a substantial factor in generating increased demands for non-compulsory schooling and resultant expansions in further and higher education during the 1960s.

What began to emerge in the late 1960s, more strikingly in the United Kingdom than other developed countries (because of traditionally low levels of economic growth), was the coincidence of inflation and unsatisfactory increases in industrial output—shortly to be followed by rising unemployment—and the associated notion that public expenditure growth was a contributory factor in this inflation. Later, the circle of culpability was complete with the argument that high levels of public expenditure, both by taking employees from productive work and utilizing too great a proportion of national income, was a cause of static industrial output.[18] Up till the late 1960s, however, disparities between levels of public sector growth and economic expansion had been discounted, largely because of optimistic assumptions about government's role in managing the economy, particularly from a demand perspective, and its ability to promote growth. According to such a view any discrepancies were temporary and correctable. Events continued to disprove this idea, as the economy refused to grow at anything approaching actual or forecast rates for public expenditure, inevitably prompting questions about the size of the public sector relative to the total economy and, more particularly, likely future situations if existing trends were to continue. This debate, especially about the size of welfare services that the productive sector could (or should) support, was further intensified by the onset of world recession after the oil price rises of 1973—further minimizing economic growth—and the heightened influences of monetarist economists. Probably the most striking example of changed attitudes was in relation to the methodologies associated with the PESC projections by programme of future government expenditures. Originally, in the 1960s, these had been little more than a statement of aspirational levels and, as a result, a promotion of these levels, with some attempt to identify and order priorities. With the new environment a drive towards control purposes began to evolve.

The first element in control was the attempt to ensure that programmes remained within projected limits, which in effect became targets. Volume terms, in which the actual level of services is considered—so many teachers employed, etc.—became less dominant: actual money expenditure assumed greater importance, particularly after the introduction of cash limits in 1974. Increasingly, both central and local government programmes had to finance expenditure changes occurring during the financial year caused by wage rises, etc., from a sum specified at the start of the spending period.[19] With cash limits the accusation can be deflected that increases in government spending, automatically sanctioned, are themselves principal contributors to the inflationary effects they are supposed to alleviate. By 1983 all projections occurred in cash rather than volume terms.[20] The second element in this control, with implications well beyond the narrow boundaries of the Public Expenditure Survey Committee (PESC) methodology, concerns the attitudinal and procedural effects of stabilizing and reducing public expenditure. So long as aspirational levels relating to expansion are being met, at least partially, the discussion and the competition is about additional resources. The current state of affairs, the activities which have already been financed in previous years, receive far less scrutiny. There is an expectation they will continue with few changes, and given the scarcity of attention orthodoxy pervading all organizations—only limited time can be awarded to any problem—this skewed perspective becomes more understandable, if not defensible. In contrast, without expansion, new interests and different perspectives evolve, for in the context of resource allocation, scarcity of attention never produces nil attention, as the outcomes are so pervasive and important. Existing patterns of resource usage, previously accepted without question, become subject to scrutiny, even in a no-growth situation, because the school or LEA invariably finds itself committed to a number of expansion items (a new course or project) and therefore reductions have to be found somewhere. Obviously, when an overall contraction is sought the numbers and scope of reductions has to rise, with several items and activities needing to shrink or stop. Quite naturally, the many interests threatened try to ensure that the totality of the expenditure scheme receives detailed attention.

A main factor in this greater scrutiny concerns the effectiveness with which resources are utilized. Up to the late 1960s there were few objectives and systematic attempts to evaluate the performance of public services.[21] In general terms, if there were insufficient adverse comments about a school, local authority or whatever, it was assumed, on this basis alone, to be successful.[22] That perspective accurately reflected circumstances in which public expenditure growth was anticipated and achieved. For when aspirational levels are satisfied, the demand for evaluation is minimal both from users concentrating on the competition for extra resources, and external critics, where attention diverts to the distribution and spending of these additional funds. In contrast, reductions are planned and any activity which can demonstrate its effectiveness with resources already received is advantaged. It would be quite misleading to suggest a surge of evaluatory procedures accompanying the pursuit of less public spending. For example, the recommendation of 1972 on the management of the new local authorities,[23] that they should each have a performance review subcommittee, has only been formally adopted by a minority of authorities.[24] More generally though, as public spending moved away from growth expectancy, the stridency of calls to demonstrate what is being sought and achieved with resources, and the need of activities to answer these calls, has increased. The fact that the underlying motive of many criticisms was to reduce spending is, in the changed circumstances of public expenditure, less important than their existence. As a more evaluatory-conscious environment develops, it seems highly probable that education will be disadvantaged compared to most other public services. Regularly the participants are in dispute about aims and objectives, the time scales are long, usually the outcomes are diffuse and intangible, and it is rare for the processes themselves to be well understood. To take one simple example, if a school uses public funds to produce mature adults (as a defined aim), then what definition of maturity is accepted, when should it be assessed, by which method, and how have the committed resources contributed to any achievement? Clearly, evaluatory situations of this type, and they abound in education, are exacerbative factors in any attempt to dispel accusations of reduced standards and concerns for erosion in public confidence.

In more general terms, however, education has followed the pattern of public expenditure in moving from expansion to retrenchment over a period of a few years in the mid-1970s. Only in terms of the size of the move, from the most rapid expander within a growth environment to shrinkage within overall contraction, is education any different to other major public activities. Priorities have changed with time. In retrospect, education grew most quickly from the late 1950s as spending on personal social services displaced that on defence. In the late 1970s defence again began to achieve a higher priority, along with law and order, but increasingly, following high unemployment and low output, spending directed towards industrial regeneration received more support. For education the likelihood of a marked change in priority, as compared to the other main programmes, during the mid- and late 1980s appears improbable. Unlike social services, for example, which in terms of spending requirements benefits from an ageing population,[25] it must cope with a continuing reduction in the numbers of its main clients—schoolchildren. For all programmes the critical item in assessing expenditure prospects remains the rate of economic growth. If relatively high levels can be achieved—perhaps 3 or 4 per cent annually—then all programmes, including educational spending, will benefit. By comparison with negligible growth, the economic, political and social motivations to minimize and further curtail expenditure will be undeniable: placing education, disadvantaged by demographic factors, lacking in public confidence, and without acceptable methodologies to demonstrate effectiveness in a still less favourable situation.

NOTES AND REFERENCES

1. Dennison, W.F., *Education in Jeopardy*, Basil Blackwell, Oxford, 1981, pp. 6–22.
2. CMND 5174, *Education: a framework for expansion*, 1972, pp. 48–49.
3. CMND 8789, *The Government's Expenditure Plans 1983–84 to 1985–86*, 1983.
4. CMND 7439, *The Government's Expenditure Plans 1979–80 to 1982–83*, 1979.
5. CMND 8789, 1983.
6. DES Report on Education, *Pupils and School Leavers: future numbers*, Number 97, May 1982.
7. The comments in the education press at the time (*Times Education Supplement* and *Education*, for example) are highly significant. Also see CMND 6869, *Education in Schools: a consultative document*, 1977.
8. For example, *Times Education Supplement*, 23 January 1976, p. 2.
9. Cox, C.B. and Boyson, R. (eds.), *Black Paper 1975: the fight for education* (Dent, London, 1975).
10. Ashford, D.E., *Policy and Politics in Britain: the limits of consensus*, Basil Blackwell, Oxford, 1981.
11. *Bacie Journal*, May/June 1983, p. 81.
12. *Bacie Journal*, September/October 1983, p. 147.
13. Allison, G.T., *Essence of Decision: explaining the Cuban missile crisis*, Little Brown, Boston, 1971.
14. Wright, M. (ed.), *Public Spending Decisions*, Allen & Unwin, London, 1980.
15. Wagner, R.E., *The Public Economy*, Markham Publishing, Chicago, 1973.
16. Wright, M. (ed.), op. cit.
17. Central Advisory Council for Education (England), *Children and Their Primary Schools: a report*, HMSO, London, 1967, and CMND 2154, *Committee on Higher Education: Report*, 1963.
18. Bacon, R. and Eltis, W.A., *Britain's Economic Problems*, second edition, Macmillan, London, 1978.
19. Department of the Environment Circular 129/75 (DES Circular 15/75), *Rate Support Grant Settlement 1976–77*, 1975.

20. CMND 8789, 1963.
21. Hawley, W.D. and Rodgers, D. (eds.), *Improving the Quality of Urban Management*, Sage Publications, London, 1974, p. 39.
22. Keeling, D., *Management in Government*, Allen & Unwin, London, 1972, p. 116.
23. The New Local Authorities, *Management and Structure*, HMSO, London, 1972.
24. Norton, A. and Wedgewood-Oppenheim, F., The concept of corporate planning in English local government—learning from its history, *Local Government Studies*, Vol. 7, No. 5, 1981, pp. 55–71.
25. Central Statistical Office, *Social Trends*, No. 13 1983 edition, HMSO, London, 1982, pp. 11–22.

SECTION 2
Some Perspectives on Policy-making

3

Educational Politics
a model for their analysis

MARGARET S. ARCHER

The term 'educational politics' could be used to include all the social interaction which influences education. It would thus embrace the whole gamut of influences impinging upon education, from the repercussions of the world system at one extreme, to the effects produced by individual parents in sending their children to particular schools at the other. Hence it would incorporate direct and indirect influences as well as intended and unintended consequences. As a result it would take on board processes which are not intrinsically 'educational' and actions which were not conceived of as being 'educational' let alone 'political'. For any practical purpose such a definition is useless, since by it 'educational politics' become almost coterminous with the relations between education and society. Nevertheless, the latter is precisely what we want to capture in sociological analysis. Therefore the task is to differentiate analytically between different types of educational politics, which together cover the field but which individually have high utility in conceptualizing important processes within it.

Such conceptual distinctions are necessarily plural and their relative utility depends upon the problem in hand. I make a threefold distinction which seems appropriate, given my concern to explain the workings of educational systems. The 'educational politics' with which this paper deals are the attempts (conscious and organized to some degree) to influence the inputs, processes and outputs of education, whether by legislation, pressure group or union action, experimentation, private investment, local transactions, internal innovation or propaganda. These 'broad' educational politics are held to

Source: From Broadfoot, P., Brock, C. and Tulasiewicz, W. (eds.), *Politics and Educational Change*, Croom Helm, London, 1981, pp. 29–56.

be essential for explaining (a) educational operations at any given time, and (b) the dynamics of educational change over time, at the systemic level. They are both essential and central because influences from other parts of the social structure work through them: they are the major mechanisms articulating education and society.

The educational politics with which I am concerned must be distinguished from 'high' educational politics, that is the analysis of interpersonal relations at government (and in our decentralized system, local government) level(s). The two are obviously closely interrelated, for 'high' politics specify the human agents who actually do many (though not all) of the jobs to which 'broad' politics lead. In one sense 'high' politics can be seen as an executive agency (though not the only one) of 'broad' politics. (In this sense the former must clearly not be restricted to officialdom or government.) However, 'high' politics are not confined to this passive role. Their partial autonomy allows of modification, initiative or negation in policy matters: all kinds of things can go right or wrong or differently in the clash of personalities and spontaneous affinities which are part of these working relationships.

It is this relative autonomy, in conjunction with the completely different methodology required for their analysis, which justifies treating the 'high' politics of education as analytically distinct: distinct, but entirely compatible with and an essential supplement to the 'broad' politics of education. Furthermore, interesting questions are raised about the relations between the two levels (about the degrees of freedom of the 'high' politicians, the uses to which these are put and their consequences for subsequent 'broad' educational interaction), which is one way in which analytical distinctions earn their keep.

On the other hand, the educational politics with which I am concerned must also be distinguished from the 'politics of aggregation', those sums of individual decisions—to leave school, to drop maths, to apply to university —which constitute the environment of 'broad' educational politics and a changing one at that.[1] Elsewhere I referred to this[2] as the 'dumb pressure of numbers', meaning by this that educational demography is shaped by the sum of unorganized individual actions (which may nonetheless display great collective regularity along lines of class, ethnicity, etc.). In other words, the aggregate properties developing from the micro-level form the macroscopic demography of the educational system from which 'interest groups' are born and with which they and 'politicians' must contend. The word 'dumb' was also intended to convey that this is the main way in which the majority of any population exerts an educational influence at any time. Some were uneasy with this word, and perhaps with reason for when, say, a parent sends a child to an independent school there is little doubt that he knows what he does in rejecting public instruction and in inviting élitism or social differentiation.[3] Nevertheless, the impact of such actions on the system depends on their direction and scale. The system remains untouched by individual decisions of this kind unless they cumulate into collective properties, rather than dissipating themselves or cancelling out one another.

Certainly there are micro-level dynamics involved in the generation and reproduction of the aggregate properties. Bourdieu has now provided a theory[4] which specifies precisely how the individual receipt and management of cultural, social and economic capital leads to the emergence and perpetuation of collective (i.e. group) regularities. This is invaluable, but it is also distinct from 'broad' educational politics, though complementary in nature. It explains how the educational system reproduces its demographic characteristics over time in collaboration with the strategic transactions of individual members of social classes or groups, but it does not account for the structure of the educational system itself or the processes by which it changes—this is where 'broad' educational politics are needed.[5] Here again the distinction between 'broad' and 'aggregate' politics pays its way by raising some of the most important questions—those about the interplay between the micro- and the macro-levels and about the relationship between statics and dynamics in educational systems.

From now on I will use the term 'educational politics' to refer to the 'broad' variety. To accord this process central importance in explaining the structuration and operation of educational systems automatically entails rejecting any kind of 'correspondence theory'. These assume that education universally, necessarily and therefore unproblematically corresponds to either the requirements of a particular social institution (e.g. the capitalist economy) or the interests of a specific class or group. The complex jargon in which this simple idea is expressed conceals the fact that it basically begs the question—namely what is it that first brings about and then maintains this 'complementarity'?[6]

Equally the significance here accorded to educational politics is inimical to any theory or approach which treats the boundary of the educational system as unimportant by holding that any kind of social factor or force penetrates education directly. Instead concrete processes of social interaction are what cross the boundary between education and society. Outside influences do not flow into the system by an equivalent of osmosis (this would be to abandon human agency for holistic metaphysics). They have to be transacted. The rest of this paper is concerned with these transactions which make up educational politics-and with presenting a model for their analysis. In doing the latter I will try to show the utility of some recent developments in sociological theory, in particular exchange theory and general systems theory.[7]

It should be underlined that the following discussion deals exclusively with educational politics in state educational systems, their form being quite different prior to the emergence of national systems of education.[8] Since the concept of an 'educational system' has been used with negligence in the literature, the following definition is provided to make clear how it is being used here. A state educational system is 'a nationwide and differentiated collection of institutions devoted to formal education, whose overall control and supervision is at least partly governmental, and whose component parts and processes are related to one another'.[9] In accordance with this, England's system emerged in 1902 as did Denmark's; France consolidated hers in the first decade of the nineteenth century, Russia in the 1880s, Japan after 1870, and so forth. The main thing that this definition stresses is that the political and systemic aspects must be present together before education is considered to constitute a state system.

I will begin by breaking educational politics down into three different types of negotiation[10] taking place between different groups. All three processes are held to be universal in state systems although their relative importance varies greatly with the structure of the national educational system. It will become clear that I see one of these as being vastly more important than the others in centralized systems, whilst I view the three as having a rough parity of importance in decentralized systems. This is an argument which I have developed in detail elsewhere[11] and it will not be recapitulated here because the utility of the model presented for the analysis of educational politics is independent of it.

The first type of negotiation is 'internal initiation' and it involves the introduction of change from inside the system by educational personnel, possibly in conjunction with pupils or students. It includes small-scale personal initiative in a particular establishment and large-scale professional action. Although an endogenous source of change (and stability) it necessarily involves negotiations with official authorities and external interest groups.

The second form of negotiation, 'external transaction', involves relations between internal and external interest groups. It is usually instigated from outside education itself by groups seeking new or additional services. As before, the profession is one of the groups involved in these negotiations, but the other party opts into the transaction of its own accord. It is this which distinguishes 'external transaction' from 'internal initiation': in the latter the parties engaged in negotiation are given and their interaction is inescapable, in the former the external parties vary and their interaction with professional groups is voluntaristic.

It is probably clear from the foregoing that 'external transaction' is a form of negotiation which is open only to those groups which have considerable resources at their disposal. Thus both processes of change discussed so far involve relations between education and rather restricted parts of the social structure. The same is not true of the third kind of negotiation, 'political manipulation'. On the contrary, this is the principal resort of those who have no other means of gaining satisfaction for their educational demands—despite the fact that they may also be the least successful at manipulating the political machine. This form of negotiation arises because education now receives most of its funds from public sources. In turn, a whole series of groups (depending on the nature of the regime) acquire formal influence over the shaping of public educational policy. It is this, of course, which encourages popular groups of various kinds to use the political channel in the absence of alternatives.

In sum the three forms of negotiation add up to a complicated process of change. To analyse it involves examining group interaction at the levels of the school, the community, and the nation, and the interrelations between them. For these different types of negotiation do not take place in isolation from one another. 'Political manipulation' influences negotiations between government and the profession, thus affecting the amount and type of 'internal initiation' which can occur. It also helps to determine the nature of 'external transactions', partly because of the power of veto and partly too because it helps define which groups engage in such negotiations, i.e. those whose demands are not well served by public policy. In turn, 'external transactions' conducted with the profession increase the surplus resources of the latter and thus influence the scope and sometimes the character of changes brought about by 'internal initiation'. Together, the changes introduced in these two ways modify the definition of instruction independently of the political centre. This alters the services available in ways which will be favourable to some groups and detrimental to others, thus affecting their policy orientations and the goals they subsequently pursue through 'political manipulation'. Thus each form of negotiation and the changes to which it gives rise has repercussions on the others. This then is the complex network of interaction and change which must be unravelled in order to explain the transformation of educational systems. The object of the subsequent discussion is to conceptualize and theorize about educational interaction in a way which will help to explain and understand the real events taking place in educational systems.[12] <u>The starting point must be the changing interrelationship between the structure of the resource distribution and the structure of educational interest groups.</u>

The principal task ahead is the conceptualization of these general relationships. However, before proceeding with it, the manner in which the three processes of negotiation all involve the exchange and use of resources needs to be spelt out more explicitly in order to show why the analytical framework adopted is apposite. This approach is derived unslavishly from both exchange theory and general (i.e. non-organic) systems theory.

From the former is taken the basic notion that exchange transactions and power relations are inextricably linked with one another. They jointly account for the emergence of either reciprocity or control in the educational interaction between different groups: if a party is not sufficiently endowed with the appropriate resources to reciprocate for those it needs to receive from another, then the other can make such supplies dependent upon the compliance of the former in the educational issue which is at stake between them. Exchange theory assumes that the resources which are exchanged are varied (which is what distinguishes the decentralized from the centralized system), but not that these resources have an exact price in terms of a single medium of exchange. This is not a methodological problem, it is a matter which is unspecific to the actors involved.[13] They have no conversion table in front of them from which to read off constant prices, for example, to be paid by industry for obtaining a particular form of technical training from public education. On the contrary, rates of exchange are socially determined and thus vary over time. Indeed, one of our principal theoretical problems is to account for the particular rates of exchange which are established upon the emergence of educational systems and their modification through subsequent interaction.

From general systems theory we take the notions that the overall distribution of resources provides the context within which all transactions occur and that negotiations completed in one quarter have repercussions in another. This is quite a different statement from the vague Parsonian assumption that every part of the social structure affects every other. Instead, general systems theory is concerned with establishing the existence, the weight, and the precise effect of particular repercussions. Indeed the positive effects of feedback, as influences which amplify change within the system itself (morphogenesis or structural elaboration), are its problematic and what makes it of relevance here. Finally, this type of systems theory insists that exchange transactions and power relations must be examined in their own right, and not just via the norms restraining them and the values reinforcing them, if the dynamic aspect of the social structure is to be understood. This is an equally fundamental assumption as will be seen as we now turn to an initial examination of the various types of negotiation.

INTERNAL INITIATION

The principal resource commanded by the educational profession[14] is its expertise. This includes the specialist knowledge possessed by teachers, their capacity to impart skills, and their techniques for inculcating values. Expertise, therefore, refers to their command of teaching material and teaching methods. Basically internal initiation involves the profession exchanging the expert services it can offer for other kinds of resources which it needs in order to achieve its own goals. These goals are various but their attainment always depends on the profession obtaining the financial means and legal rights to translate them into reality. To do this depends on getting a good rate of exchange for educational services against the financial resources supplied, in return, by external interest groups. But these transactions themselves may be subject to political veto so the profession also has to increase the value of its expertise to the political authorities in order to prevent their imposing such embargoes. The latter is merely one aspect of a broader negotiation with the polity in which expert services are exchanged against increments in autonomy (the legal rights to do x, y and z). Only if the profession succeeds in improving its wealth and autonomy in these ways will it be able to increase the amount of educational change produced by internal initiation and ensure that its direction coincides with professional interests. Thus the main task, on whose accomplishment internal initiation depends, is the exchange of expertise for financial resources and legal rights on favourable terms.

EXTERNAL TRANSACTION

The principal resource commanded by external interest groups is their wealth, or more strictly their liquid assets, which can be devoted to the quest for educational services of various kinds. External transactions fundamentally consist in the exchange of financial resources for educational expertise—for example, a professional undertaking to receive certain pupils, provide a particular form of instruction, or produce a specific kind of output in terms of the knowledge, skills or values of those completing the course of study. The financial resources offered against expert services have to be sufficiently attractive to the profession to overcome their inertia (unwillingness to add new teaching burdens, devise new curricula or invent novel methods of assessment), and any repugnance or reluctance felt towards performing and providing the services required (if, for example, they involve a distraction from research, an extension of teaching hours, a collaboration with non-professionals, an alteration of teaching locale, a diminution of entry standards, or a limitation on the knowledge to be inculcated and assessed). Simultaneously the external interest group must be able to evade or overcome any political resistance to these transactions taking place; for only if it does both will it be able to instigate those educational changes needed to service its particular institutional operations. Thus the main task, on whose completion external transactions rely, is the successful exchange of financial resources for expert services.

POLITICAL MANIPULATION

The principal resource commanded by political authorities[15] (both central and local) is their legal authority and capacity to impose negative sanctions. This includes their ability to pass laws and impose regulations, to withhold benefits and recognition, as well as to penalize irregular practices and offending parties. Political manipulation, therefore, consists in those groups who dominate the central or local decision-making arenas using their official powers to extract the educational services desired and to preclude undesirable outputs. At either level it involves the exchange of politico-educational privileges (ranging from salary increases to teachers, through the institutionalization of professional advice, to the recognition and regularization of internal initiatives) in return for increased educo-political services. Alternatively it can involve the application of political sanctions, in other words the withholding of certain rights or requirements in order to overcome professional resistance or to veto unwanted transactions. The services extracted or suppressed in this way are used to keep educational activities in line with political requirements. Thus the main task, on whose execution political manipulation rests, is the exchange of power resources for expert services.

Obviously the designation of these 'main tasks' involves a considerable oversimplification, because in fact each of the groups concerned (be it professional, institutional or political) possesses more than one type of resource which comes into play in processes of negotiation. Professional groups not only command expertise but also enjoy certain powers (particularly the autonomy they retain and enlarge in the decentralized system), and possess some financial resources of their own (again more pronounced in the decentralized system where they were preserved during, or acquired through, the use of this very autonomy to conduct direct transactions with the community. Similarly, external interest groups not only have wealth, but also status (that is the capacity to confer reflected glory or disrepute on the profession with which it seeks to deal), and power (through the positions its members may occupy on central and local authorities, the coalitions they may form with political élites at various levels, and the sanctions they may be able to exercise on educational outputs, like refusal to employ certain kinds of school-leavers or to recognize certain qualifications). Even clearer, of course, is the ability of political authorities to manipulate wealth and status as aspects of power itself. Power partly consists in the capacity to withhold benefits, and two of the most important of these as far as education is concerned are the financial resources it receives from central and local government, and the status conferred on its practitioners, processes and products through formal public approbation. The significance for interaction of each group possessing all three resources, to some degree, will be taken up a little later.

The point of highlighting 'main tasks' above was to show that different kinds of resources are involved in the negotiations which produce educational change. Thus it follows that their distribution is of great importance in determining who can participate in the processes of change and how they can go about it. These qualifications were inserted here simply to stress that the distribution of all resources was not so uneven as to be a question of total monopoly or complete deprivation on the part of any of the three groups involved. Thus it follows that each type of negotiation is a complex multidimensional process, whatever its superficial appearance.

THE AVAILABILITY OF RESOURCES IN SOCIETY

Access to resources affects which groups will be able to negotiate change. Resource distributions change over time, largely in response to non-educational factors, and thus while they are introduced here, they cannot themselves be explained within the framework of the present analysis: all that can be done is to trace through changes in the availability of resources over time in conjunction with corresponding changes in educational interaction. Resources are considered as inaccessible according to the degree to which socially significant parties do not possess them and cannot make use of them, and the extent to which other social groups can employ them to exclude these parties, their interests, and issues from processes of educational negotiation. The overall availability of each resource (as opposed to its availability to any particular group) varies with the shape of its distribution, i.e. distributions differ in terms of concentration from time to time and from place to place.

The significance of this assumption here is that the greater the concentration of resources, the fewer the number of parties who will be able to negotiate educational change. In other words, the degree of concentration affects two basic aspects of educational interaction. Firstly, it influences the steepness of the gradient between élites and masses and hence their respective opportunities to participate effectively in processes of negotiation. Secondly, it follows that the degree of concentration also helps to determine the volume and kinds of educational demands which can be negotiated from different parts of society.

RELATIONS AMONG RESOURCE HOLDERS

Such relations cannot be conflated with nor derived from the fact of concentration alone, but they are of great importance for the nature of educational interaction and change. Resource holders may be superimposed, homogeneous and united, or they may be unlike one another, mutually antagonistic, and in pursuit of independent goals. The extent to which the distributions of the different resources are superimposed is the crucial variable—for this determines whether one is referring to the same group of people or section of society when talking about those who command most financial resources or political power or expertise. Even if there is a high degree of superimposition, the second question remains—namely, how far do élite members get on with one another and pull together to attain joint or mutually compatible goals?

Elsewhere[16] I have argued that there are no logical reasons for assuming that the class, status and power dimensions of social stratification are superimposed on one another, rather than significant discrepancies being found between the positions of given groups on the three hierarchies. Instead it is maintained that superimposition is a matter of contingency and degree, which have to be established in each particular case and place. The same approach characterizes the treatment of resource holders: they are neither presumed to be a single élite whose privileges extend over all that is scarce and socially valued, nor to consist of a plurality of élite groups which are distinct from one another in terms of the resources upon which their privileged positions are based. Thus the analytical framework employed here is not committed in advance to either a unidimensional ruling class model or a pluralist picture of multiple élites. Moreover, it is neutral in the sense that if one of these models holds universally, or works well for any particular country examined, this will show through the analysis presented. Thus the degree of superimposition amongst resource holders is to be established empirically, and it is this which then determines how far educational interaction approximates to a uni- or multi-dimensional affair.

Here brief reference must be made to an important difference between centralized and decentralized systems. In the centralized system, the greater the superimposition and unity among the relevant élites, the more standardized are the educational changes introduced or the existing practices which are defended. This is because political manipulation is the most important process of negotiation there, so if a solitary governing élite dominates the political arena, the measures introduced reflect its restricted interests. However, in the decentralized system standardized measures are infrequent because those seeking change do not have to accommodate their goals with others, thus diluting their precise requirements in order to be able to exert greater political pressure. Because there are three equally important channels through which demands can be negotiated and satisfied, the structural conditions encouraging the convergence of demands are greatly weakened. Secondly, this means that there is a lower premium on the unity of élites in the decentralized system, since different resource holders can obtain the educational services they want through independent transactions. Indeed, united inaction (in repulsing the educational ambitions of the resources-less masses) is probably the most important form of concerted action, for where positive changes are sought, the sub-élites will tend to pursue their specific institutional requirements. Finally, this does indeed imply that the less the unity among resource-holders, the greater the diversity of educational changes introduced. Unlike the centralized system where all protagonists cluster in and about the political arena often blocking one another and producing overall immobilism, the fact that the three processes for negotiating changes have a rough parity of importance reduces the extent to which groups cancel one another out and contribute to stasis.

THE STRUCTURE OF EDUCATIONAL INTEREST GROUPS

Clearly the social distribution of resources and the structure of educational interest groups can change independently of one another. Educational interaction itself will bring certain interest groups into a better position *vis-à-vis* resources and partly because their distributions are constantly changing in response to various independent factors, thus increasing and decreasing the resources available to particular interest groups. At any given point in time the contemporary distribution of resources places limitations on three basic aspects of exchange negotiations:[17] (1) the nature and number of people admitted to educational transactions; (2) their initial bargaining positions; (3) the volume and kinds of demands which can be negotiated at first. Any analysis of educational interaction over time would follow through the constraining influences exerted by the changing resource distributions on negotiations between educational interest groups.

At all times every educational interest group will have a place on the hierarchical distribution of each of the three resources considered, wealth, power and expertise. Methodologically it is impossible, at least at the present time, to express these general positions in precise mathematical terms. I have discussed the reasons for this in more detail elsewhere,[18] but the basic obstacles are:

(a) doubts about the national character of any hierarchy which is highly dependent on the subjective attribution of prestige—here this is particularly relevant to 'expertise';
(b) difficulties in specifying and ranking all positions on a hierarchy—this is significant for the power dimension where it is desirable to include its more informal and intangible aspects (influential power) as well as official power positions;
(c) problems of commensurability between the three hierarchies, in the absence of a common denominator to which all resources can be reduced. In view of this we are forced to work in rather gross terms, merely designating groups as having high or low access to particular resources, and are constrained to avoid detailed comparative statements about the relative availability of different resources to given groups.

However, working within these limitations, it is possible to advance three propositions which link groups and resources to educational interaction:

1. groups with low access to all resources will be in the weakest negotiating position;
2. groups with differential access to the various resources will be in a stronger negotiating position;
3. groups with high access to all resources will be in the best negotiating position.

A fourth proposition concerning educational change follows from the above, namely that groups are likely to receive educational services in reverse order. Therefore, it is groups in the latter position who will tend to be responsible for the majority of changes, whereas those in the first position will probably not be able to introduce significant educational modifications. It must be remembered, however, that the crucial overall relationship is between the position of the educational interest groups and the availability of the resources themselves. In other words, the less concentrated the distribution of resources, the fewer the number of parties who will find themselves in position (1), and the greater the proportion of groups who will be able to participate profitably in educational transactions. The opposite is equally true; a very high concentration of resources places a very restricted section of society in position (3). Along the same lines, a differential concentration of the three resources maximizes the number of interest groups finding themselves in position (2).

However, these propositions deal only with one side of the equation, because when an interest group commands a resource(s) this represents a necessary, but not a sufficient, condition for successful negotiation. The very meaning of the term 'negotiation' involves two parties, so it is inadequate to concentrate upon what one of them alone brings to the relationship. The propositions advanced above concern the relative bargaining positions of different groups, but this is a unilateral concept. For such a group to have real negotiating strength it must stand in a particular relationship to the other party involved. This concept is a bilateral or relational term, it is not a generalized capacity, possessed by some groups but not by others, but pertains to interaction itself. Negotiating strength arises in exchange situations, i.e. where group X commands resources which are highly valued but lacking (or lacking in sufficient quantities) by group Y, when Y in turn possesses resources of a different kind which are sought by X. It is a matter of degree, which ranges from the ability of X to make Y utterly dependent on the resources it supplies, through a balanced situation of reciprocal exchange between X and Y, to the opposite pole of imbalance, where X is totally dependent on the resources supplied by Y.

With this in mind we can now turn to the structure of educational interest groups, in relation to effective negotiation, and here again we have to note a significant contrast between centralized and decentralized systems. It has already been argued that the most crucial factor is the relationship between the social distribution of resources and the national distribution of those seeking educational change. Now we are concerned with relationships among the latter and whether any particular combinations or characteristics of interest groups improve their prospects of goal attainment. In the centralized system it seems that maximal effectiveness occurs when those experiencing educational grievances are superimposed and well organized, for this enables the greatest leverage to be exerted on the political centre. However, in the decentralized system, where three processes of negotiation operate simultaneously with greater parity, superimposition and organization are not necessary for effective transactions.

For example, a quiet informal transaction may be more productive than a publicly organized one which might alert hostile counter-pressures—a series of local firms working independently may be able to gain the services they seek from the colleges in their vicinity much more readily than if an industrial confederation sought the transformation of colleges of further education *en bloc*. It is also probable that the innovations introduced independently are much more satisfactory to their recipients, because of their specificity, precision and relevance, than the more general changes likely to stem from organized action. Furthermore the superimposition of grievances may do little to help their alleviation. For instance, the overlap between the Catholic population and certain working class and immigrant groups does not improve the position of church schools, decrease class discrimination, or advance the educational rights of migrants. On the contrary, limited resources are spread too thinly in seeking to negotiate improvements on all these fronts, whereas one can speculate that if only the religious issue were at stake, confessional schools would be better defended.

These considerations lead to an important conclusion, namely that the superimposition and organization of interest groups are only advantageous in decentralized systems to the extent that they increase collective resources. The increase can be purely quantitative, such as rich groups getting together to found high quality private establishments, or it may involve spreading the type of resources available to the collectivity, as for instance when a prestige group adds respectability to the financial resources of another, and improves their joint negotiating strength. Unless this condition holds, collective action carries no automatic bonus in processes of negotiation. There is, however, one particular process—political manipulation—for which this condition nearly always does hold. The greater the intensity of organized pressure, whether at the level of voting in elections, shaping party policy, or influencing decision-making, the stronger the impact—because numbers, commitment and organization are the stuff from which power is made. And this of course is why superimposition and organization are always advantageous to interest groups in centralized systems, for to them political manipulation is the main process of negotiation available. Another way of looking at this is that the centralized system is a special case where collective action always increases resources. However, it is only a particular case of a more general rule, whose full workings are only displayed in the decentralized system, with its three equally important processes of negotiation, namely that combination only promotes effective transactions when it enhances the bargaining position of educational interest groups.

PROCESSES OF NEGOTIATION

Earlier we described the 'main tasks' involved in each of the three kinds of transactions which bring about educational change, but these were discussed in the abstract and were not related to real processes of social interaction. At a formal level it was seen that interaction consists in using resources to transact exchanges with others in order to attain goals, whose target may be either educational stasis or change. However, although the importance of the initial bargaining positions of groups was stressed (i.e. the amount of resources at their disposal), no indication was given of even the most general conditions under which negotiations were likely to be successful, or of the type of interaction which would be involved. These two questions will be the concern of the present section and they are inextricably linked to one another. To specify the conditions under which educational changes are transacted is to indicate what, in addition to their initial bargaining position, gives a group negotiating strength. Since negotiating strength is a relational term, this means that the answer is necessarily phrased in terms of the relationships between groups. Automatically this implies examining the interaction between educational interest groups.

Let us start this analysis by isolating three crucial elements of any given piece of educational interaction, namely

1. the participants, (at least) two educational interest groups, X and Y;
2. the resources they respectively command, X^{r1} and Y^{r2}, which constitute their bargaining positions;
3. the exchange (or non-exchange) of r1 and r2, which expresses the relative negotiating strengths of X and Y.

These elements determine the degree of change, if any, occurring in this particular case. They also decide who exercises educational control in this situation; it can be X, if Y finds r1 irresistible, or Y if X cannot do without r2, but control is not necessarily a zero-sum matter, for a reciprocal exchange of r1 and r2 gives X and Y shared control and joint responsibility for the changes introduced.

We can now begin to consider the nature of the relationship between these two groups and what will give one high negotiating strength *vis-à-vis* the other. It has been argued that an interest group has the best chance of concluding an educational transaction in its favour the more irresistible are the resources it supplies to the other party involved. In his discussion of exchange and power in social life, Blau has provided[19] a useful classification of the situations in which such irresistibility arises. X will have the highest degree of negotiating strength when it supplies resources to Y under four conditions. These are when Y cannot reciprocate, cannot get the needed resources from elsewhere, cannot coerce X to supply them, and cannot resign itself to doing without them. From these can be derived the strategies required to attain or sustain educational control on the part of X in relation to

Y. X must try to establish rates of exchanges which are highly favourable to itself; bar Y's access to alternative sources of supply through monopolizing the resource or legally controlling the processes of exchange; discourage any attempt at coercion on Y's part; and prevent Y from being indifferent to the benefits it offers. Equally Y's defensive strategies, aimed at keeping up its own negotiating strength, can be deduced by corollary. It must do everything it can to avoid being reduced to complete dependence on X. This involves a constant effort to prevent the exchange rate from becoming too unfavourable, by increasing the desirability and exclusivity of its own resources or services to X. It must work at keeping alternative supply lines open and accumulating supplies, thus increasing independence from X; developing strong organizations to compel X to behave differently; and propagating counter-ideologies which undermine X's right to use resources in the way it does.

In combination, these aggressive and defensive strategies which are deployed in negotiation draw attention to the four basic aspects of educational interaction:

1. the possibility of reciprocating benefits points to the importance of the initial resource distributions, to subsequent exchange processes, and to resulting change in the resource distributions over time;
2. the possibility of alternative suppliers of the same resource points to the importance of legal, normative and competitive features of the (changing) exchange structure;
3. the possibility of coercive power being used points to the significance of the general political power struggle, the formal organization of power positions and of opposition parties, coalitions and alliances, *vis-à-vis* education;
4. the possibility of resignation to the loss of a resource points to the importance of educational values, the formation of new ideologies, and of conflicts between systems of ideas.

All of these will play their part in the multiplicity of transactions which we seek to describe and explain. However, their precise significance will become clearer if we now look at the three processes of negotiation in turn—political manipulation, external transactions and internal initiation—and at the particular groups involved and their 'main tasks'.

POLITICAL MANIPULATION

As far as pressures on the polity are concerned, these include the articulation, accumulation and organization of interests, and where political control is concerned, they involve the formation, implementation and regulation of policy. Beyond such universals, differences in institutional structure produce diverse patterns of interaction. For example, the less unified nature of the decentralized system means that the very political decision-making arena, officially concerned with educational matters, is broader and embraces central government organs and local authority bodies. This illustrates the fact that the initial distribution of resources (here power), upon the emergence of the system, affects the extent and nature of persons admitted to transactions. In the decentralized system those in official political positions of educational control are a more extensive group, they are found locally as well as centrally, and are of a more varied character ranging, for example, from local councillors to the Minister of Education. Relations between these levels of decision-making is a whole dimension of interaction which is lacking in centralized systems.

In turn the relations between these levels of decision-making affect how those who have acquired official positions in the administrative framework (i.e. have accumulated power resources *vis-à-vis* education) go about influencing or impeding educational change. In the decentralized system, political acts of this kind are negotiated actions, and not merely in the universal sense in which every parliamentary or politburo policy is shaped by the manoeuvrings of those concerned. Here a much broader set of transactions are involved, beyond those directly responsible for the formal introduction of legislation or regulations. These include negotiation with professional interest groups to ensure the implementation of regulations, and with external interest groups to prevent the vitiation or evasion of legislation.

In centralized systems it is possible to concentrate almost exclusively on interaction which culminates in the passing of legislation, decrees, or instructions because their implementation is relatively unproblematic. Educational interest groups, both internal and external, have little alternative but to accept these measures because the polity has continuously been in an unassailable position since the emergence of these systems. In terms of our earlier notation, the polity (X) supplied resources to education under the four conditions which made the professional groups (Y^1) completely dependent upon it, and unable to increase their autonomy through dealings with other interest groups (Y^2). The rates of exchange between X and Y^1 consistently favoured the former, the profession having neither the finance nor the freedom to alter its service and thus manipulate a more reciprocal rate; X's political veto on direct transactions between Y^1 and Y^2 prevented resources from being acquired elsewhere; whilst neither Y^1 nor Y^2 could resign themselves to the situation. The profession, both as a body morally committed to providing educational services for the community and as individuals with vested interests in job security, could not dispense with centrally provided resources. Equally, and this became truer over time, few external groups could remain indifferent to the receipt of educational services. The only weak point in the polity's control was its capacity to contain counter coercion on the part of Y^1 and Y^2, precisely because the negotiating strength of X itself generated so much discontent and opposition. Hence, of course, the pattern of intermittent explosions directed against X, which are a distinctive and major source of change in centralized systems. In the emergent decentralized systems, however, the very different distribution of resources did not leave the polity in an unassailable position, and made its 'main task' of exchanging power resources for educational services considerably more complicated.

In view of this the polity's 'main task' of translating power resources into expert services is made more difficult. Over time the central authority seeks to strengthen its educational control through educational interaction in order to be able to attain its own goals. It does so in the following four ways, all of which, it should be noted, are hedged by the initial and subsequent distribution of resources. In the context of the present paper these can be viewed as four general strategies used/usable by any polity at any time in an attempt to increase its control over the educational system.

1. The first strategy is to try to reduce the capacity of education to reciprocate for the resources supplied to it by the State. The aim here is to attain the educational equivalent of the State's position in a command economy, where it controls the rate of exchange, prices, production and distribution. Education would be unable to reciprocate because everything it had to offer would itself depend on public resources, as in extreme examples of centralization. Since the polity's main educational leverage consists in its ability to withhold benefits and impose penalties, the success of this strategy hinges on both being substantial. Hence the constant readiness of the State to increase its investment in education, even when it has become the majority supplier. Given a steady growth in the proportion of Gross National Product (GNP) commanded by governments, higher rates of absolute investment in education have been the rule, whilst economic recessions have not damaged the relative position of the State since they have had similar effects on other suppliers. As a strategy, however, this can prove double-edged, for to invest generously may be to allow the internal accumulation of surpluses with which the profession can pad itself against political prods whose thrust derives from the withholding of resources. The financing of English universities would prove a fascinating study from this angle. However, if tactic 2 is successful, then dependence on the State can be coupled with a low rate of exchange.

2. The effectiveness of the first strategy is also clearly dependent on the success of the second, namely barring access to alternative suppliers. This cannot be achieved by monopolization of the resources used by education even in the centralized system—the best the State can do is to become the majority supplier, for the initial resource distribution endows others with significant reserves. What it can do is to seek to limit the processes of exchange, via its control of legal machinery. Here it will refuse legal recognition to certain diplomas, establishments, personnel or courses, thus reducing the attractiveness of the services that the profession could offer to external groups. This discourages external transactions by damaging the professional bargaining position, but it is only one branch of a two-pronged

attack. The other involves the imposition of legal vetoes and the refusal to authorize certain negotiations at all. The crucial element in this respect is the degree to which the external interest group is itself politically influential (and can deflect projected embargoes) or is capable of marshalling legal defences (to repulse or lift such vetoes). Ironically this means that the polity's strategy will be most effective against the weaker suppliers, who have least to offer the profession and have little power and status in addition to their financial resources, but who also present least threat to the educational ambitions of governing élites.

3. Political strategies for containing counter coercion all hinge on blocking the access of educational interest groups to political power. Although in some respects a decentralized system is at an advantage in this context (for example, student unrest remains localized and focused on the particular university authorities concerned and does not confront the polity directly), in other ways it promotes the insertion of interest groups at the various levels of decision-making. Since the main problem for the governing élite is resistance to its policies, its strategies are concerned with undermining the autonomy which makes this possible. Thus legislation can reduce local and institutional autonomy, making the system more responsive to central directives, if the governing élite is strong enough to deploy the whole battery of central sanctions to this end. But two things may stand in its way: the political influence and positions already acquired by educational interests and the hostility of opposition parties (who may indeed accept state intervention in principle, but fear the consequences of placing this instrument in the hands of its opponents). This is a parallelogram of forces which results in few education acts and few educational explosions in the decentralized system.

4. Nevertheless, most political élites will promote ideologies favouring political intervention, often justified on totally different grounds but sharing the self-righteous assumption that it would be justly used in their hands alone. Thus the Left will stress the need for increased state control to ensure equal opportunity and the end of social discrimination in education, whilst the Right usually underlines that it is needed to guarantee efficiency, order and value for taxpayers' money. The former seeks to identify State intervention with avoiding unfairness and class perpetuation; the latter with abolishing wastage and anarchy. Both strands are met by opposing ideological cross-currents from amongst their own supporters, i.e. educational interest groups broadly aligned with Left or Right, but supporting autonomy because it advances their aims.

Thus in the decentralized system political manipulation involves a struggle, not only on the part of those wanting to influence governmental policy, but also in order to translate official policy into educational practice. Because of the initial distribution of resources, the polity is not in an unassailable bargaining position, and since the enduring aim of interested parties is to defend if not to improve their own positions of influence, this tends to keep it that way. In this context, parts of the system continually escape political control and introduce changes independently, thus creating new problems for government: whilst with equal pertinacity the polity struggles to contain such developments and to keep education in line with governmental policy. It will be recalled that the next two types of negotiation, though not absent in the centralized system, are much more important where decentralization prevails.

EXTERNAL TRANSACTIONS

The 'main task' of translating financial resources into the expert services required involves direct negotiation with professional groups. The political aspects of such transactions have already been discussed in the previous section, so here we will concentrate on the factors determining the relative negotiating strengths of external and internal groups when they face one another in interaction. Obviously the bargaining positions of the various external interest groups differ according to the resources at their command, and this will be subject to change over time. Although wealth of resources is usually translated into a high level of negotiating strength, it will be extremely rare for any external interest group actually to reduce education, or a particular part of it, to a position of total dependence. Instead, when transactions occur they are more likely to be of a reciprocal nature because the profession is in a good strategic position to defend itself and to bid up the value of its expertise.

1. The fact that a professional group has been approached for services means that it has something of value to offer in the eyes of those making the advances. This it can play upon in negotiations—possibly by proffering a tailor-made package—and can thus make its contribution even more attractive to the purchaser who will improve on his original terms, thus inflating the value of expertise.

2. Any particular external interest group which approaches the profession in this way is one among several as far as the latter is concerned. Given that State funding provides for the majority of educational overheads, few professional groups are ever completely dependent on their outside earnings (except of course in the private sector). Thus as they are not desperate, they can pick and choose among these alternative suppliers of resources, bidding up the rate between them and only settling on advantageous terms.

3. External interest groups cannot force the profession to supply services it does not want to provide (on normative grounds) or does not think are worth providing (at the price offered). On the contrary, the onus is upon the external group to make its terms as attractive as possible to the educational institutions involved.

4. Finally as far as any particular transaction is concerned, the profession may resign itself on normative grounds, on calculative grounds (not putting

off a better supplier), or because it considers the additional effort unworthwhile, to rejecting this specific offer.

Given this good defensive position on the part of the profession, what the external interest group must try to do is to ensure that a transaction takes place at a price which is reasonable to it. It will be most likely to succeed when four conditions hold: firstly, when the external group has considerable resources at its disposal and thus can propose an exchange rate which is not considered cheeseparing by the profession (i.e. leaves the latter a substantial surplus over the actual cost of providing the services required); secondly, when the offer it proposes compares favourably with those made by other interest groups. However, in relation to both of these points it must not be forgotten that such offers are not made exclusively in financial terms. If the profession believes that it gains reflected glory or promotes its own goals through association with a particular group, the cash element will play a smaller part in the transaction. On the other hand, if the profession feels it is degrading itself or jeopardizing its governmental supplies through sailing too close to political veto, the financial inducement will have to be considerably greater. Nevertheless, the two above conditions hold good because wealth always enables an interest group to transact with the private sector, even if it makes no headway with public education. Thirdly, we have argued that it will rarely be possible to coerce educational services from an unwilling profession, but if a group can 'square' a deal in advance with the polity, through the political influence or favour that it enjoys, the educators are more likely to get down to the negotiating table for fear of future political reprisals. Additionally the more attractive the external group makes itself, through tactics like the recruitment of prestige figureheads, the greater its appeal. Fourthly, the more convinced a group is that it cannot dispense with educational services, the more likely it is to obtain them—partly because it will devote a greater proportion of its available resources to getting them, and partly because it will strive to meet the above conditions if it did not do so in the first place.

If the final condition holds, yet the group in question fails to bring about a direct transaction, it can still pursue its educational goals through political manipulation; indeed many groups will be engaging in both forms of negotiation simultaneously. However, it is important to note that repeated repulsion by the profession can lead some groups to resign themselves to doing without educational services altogether. These will be the poorer groups whose lack of resources had given them weak bargaining positions with the profession, and especially those whose political influence was equally low. For minority groups in particular, their failure in one kind of negotiation may produce general discouragement and mean that the profession has played a part in organizing certain issues and problems out of educational politics. This is unlikely to be the case for large lower class groups with strong collective organizations which will champion their cause politically, although certain enclaves within the working class may find themselves in this position, e.g. workers in declining areas, agricultural labourers, those with handicapped children, etc. On the whole, however, the consequence of professional rejection will be greater among poor minority groups, such as immigrants, migrant workers, members of smaller religious sects, or ethnic groups, and those whose mother tongue is not an official language.

INTERNAL INITIATION

Here, where the main task is the translation of educational expertise into other kinds of resources (which increase autonomy and internal self-determination), different sections of the profession find themselves in different bargaining positions. The distribution of resources, vertically among the various educational levels and horizontally among different kinds of institutions, gives certain groups of teachers and academics better starting points in terms of wealth, prestige and autonomy. This needs to be borne in mind when recalling the points made about professional negotiating strength in the discussion of the other two processes. Rather than repeating these again, we can extract from the earlier analysis the conditions under which the educators are most likely to succeed in transactions, and express these in such a way that they can refer to the profession as a whole or to particular parts of it.

From the foregoing discussion it appears that professional groups will do best in negotiation, and in turn be able to introduce more of the internal innovations they desire, when they can do the following:

1. offer services which are attractive in terms of their inputs, processes and outputs. One of the most important aspects of this is professional upgrading through which a higher quality of service is made available. By raising expertise itself, a higher exchange rate can be asked, thus increasing the market value of professional skills. However, all this depends on teachers and academics possessing adequate financial surpluses and sufficient autonomy in the first place or acquiring them through subsequent negotiations;
2. control the certification of expertise, both in terms of the quantity and quality of those admitted to the profession, so as to create a *de facto* if not a *de jure* closed shop which bars alternative supplies of 'teachers' or 'lecturers', or so raises the prestige of the certificated professional that the latter are at best 'instructors' or 'trainers' and at worst 'crammers' or 'unqualified';
3. participate in official processes of educational control and administration in order that they themselves play a part in moulding official policy rather than being reduced to modifying, resisting or sabotaging it at the stage of implementation;

4. reinforce and legitimate the above activities, as well as encouraging the need for expert services, through disseminating appropriate educational values. In this the profession alone can make direct use of the learning situation to spread its values, and also by its very nature it can make good use of public media.

This completes the analytical discussion of the three processes and the parties involved, except in one important respect. So far, in the interest of clarity, attention has been focused on each kind of negotiation in turn. The very fact that cross-references were continually made to other processes of interaction serves to indicate that only in the most artificial ways can one forget the fact that all forms of negotiation proceed simultaneously and their consequences have implications for one another. Finally then, these mutual influences must be examined, in their own right, by taking an overview of the interrelations between the three processes.

INTERACTION AND NEGOTIATIONS

There are two important respects in which the different types of negotiation are related to one another in terms of interaction; one direct and the other indirect. Firstly, it is indeed many of the same people who engage in the three kinds of transactions: some members of the population may only participate at the lowest level in one of them (e.g. by voting), a much smaller number will participate in all three (e.g. an active member of a political party, a parent-teacher association, and a Chamber of Commerce), whilst between these extremes there are varying degrees of participation and of overlap between participants. It seems common sense that experience gained in one context influences behaviour in another—indeed we have presented one example of how discouragement may become generalized, but it is equally important to allow for the reinforcing effects of experiences of successful negotiation. Above all the existence of overlap points to the actors' own knowledge of the fact that what happens via one process then has an influence on others, and that there is more than one way of getting what they want.

This is related to the second and indirect relationship, namely that the consequences of one kind of transaction influence subsequent interaction in the other kinds of negotiation. In other words, each transaction brings about a shift in educational control and the definition of instruction which alters the context in which other transactions occur, and these effects may be cumulative. This can be pictured most graphically by presenting different hypothetical scenarios, in which one of the three processes of negotiation was consistently more effective than the other two over time.

1. The greater the effectiveness of political manipulation, the more educational change is polity-directed and educational activities are politically

controlled. Consequently, the lower will be the autonomy of the profession to introduce internal changes and the lesser will be the volume of external transactions which are allowed. Because of both, the financial resources earned by the profession will fall, thus lowering the attractiveness of the services which can be offered to external groups, above and beyond the political embargoes which might be placed on these anyway. As education becomes increasingly dependent on the polity for supplies, the rate of exchange falls and hence there is a decrease in surplus resources, as well as of professional freedom, which will reduce the amount of internal initiation possible. The end result in this scenario is one in which the relations between education and society become like those in the centralized system. This is because, as in those systems, educational control rests on political power, and negotiations are largely confined to this single medium of exchange. This has come about through a string of transactions, in which power resources have been progressively revalued (because the polity has pursued successful strategies in negotiation), whilst professional expertise and private finance have been correspondingly devalued (because their bearers have adopted less satisfactory tactics in negotiation). The last fifteen years in England have witnessed some shift towards such *étatisme*: this is not irreversible, it has happened before, but reversal now seems to depend on an end to economic recession and the consequent recovery of alternative suppliers of resources to education.

2. The greater the effectiveness of external transactions, the more educational operations are responsive to other social institutions and the control of change is in the hands of their élites. It follows that the polity has a declining ability to monitor or maintain a given definition of instruction. Instead, as external transactions proliferate, instruction becomes increasingly diversified and differentiated and moves outside the orbit of state control. (Hence this is the exact opposite of the case above, where education became progressively more standardized and unified.) Simultaneously, however, as education becomes more dependent on external supplies, it may well be less possible to protect professional expertise or to defend academic values. True, the existence of a multiplicity of external suppliers would offer some protection, but in an increasingly open educational market it would be more difficult for educators to maintain the other three conditions which keep rates of exchange up—they would tend to lose control over the certification and training of teachers (for if the end-product of instruction is externally determined, so to some extent is the nature of its producers)—they would be less able to insert themselves into positions of educational control (which would now be situated in company boardrooms, union headquarters, church hierarchies, commercial offices etc.)—and would have less capacity to propagate 'pure' academic values (since these would contradict many of their current activities and the piper has little love of that tune). As exchange rates fall, so too does the profession's capacity to introduce internal innovations,

and it may finally come to regret the protection it derived from the political control in dealings with the community. These then are the consequences of transactions in which expertise and power are devalued in relation to wealth. Some Marxists presume that this has taken place, but this assumption leaves them unable to account for past, present and future variations in the degree of control exercised by the economic infrastructure over the educational system.

3. The greater the effectiveness of internal initiation, the more the profession itself becomes master in its own house. Its progressive gains in autonomy free it from political tutelage and allow educational change to be introduced in accordance with professional values, whether this involves simple self-serving or response to (acceptable) external demands. Resources earned in this way not only strengthen teachers against threats of state re-intervention, but also underwrite various activities which increase their standing—for example, upgrading of professional skills, increasing academic specialization, improved facilities and conditions of work. This is part of a reinforcing cycle in which the refinement of expertise then increases professional prestige, which in turn raises the exchange rate for educational services supplied to external parties. As interest groups pay more, professional surpluses accumulate and are used for new forms of internal innovation. These increments in self-determination lead to a less unified educational system and a more specialized, but also a more academic, definition of instruction. This endstate will only occur if expert resources have been well defended and advantageously exchanged against political power and private wealth. In many Western European countries advances in professional autonomy have stimulated parental demands for participation in the belief that education is too important to be left to the teachers.

Each of these scenarios, crudely sketched in, is merely meant to bring home how the results of one kind of transaction alter the context in which other kinds subsequently take place. The three processes go on simultaneously, and the continuation of each of them represents an important vested interest to particular social groups. These they will tend to defend, by bringing additional resources to bear, if the balance tips too far in favour of the other processes which give advantages to different groups and interests.

However, there is nothing automatic about the maintenance of parity between the three processes in a decentralized system—this depends upon interaction, and thus upon how strongly the groups involved feel, how far they are prepared to extend themselves, and how much of their resources they are willing to invest. Indeed, at any one time the chances are that the balance does favour the greater effectiveness of one process of negotiation over the other two. Also over a period there is nothing logically which precludes this balance from shifting sequentially to render political manipulation, external transactions or internal initiation the most important process in determining educational control and the definition of instruction. All that is universally the case is that the three forms of negotiation always have consequences for one another, and that each of them shapes the action contexts in which the others take place.

Perhaps one of the most interesting questions which comparative education could explore is the relative importance of these three processes for negotiating educational stability and change in different countries with different systems at different times. I hope this paper has at least served to indicate that recent developments in sociological theory can contribute to conceptualizing and theorizing about educational politics, for these are what ultimately determine the three major issues in education—who gets it, what it is, and what they do with it.

NOTES

1. In cases like this example it might appear difficult to assign them unambiguously to either 'broad' or 'aggregative' educational politics. Analytically, however, such cases present few problems and empirically they are rarely intractable. The action of a parent in sending a child to an independent school is part of aggregative politics, but if he joins an association of parents of independent school pupils, he is simultaneously engaging in 'broad' politics. If he supports his child's school (e.g. by a gift), any systemic impact again depends on aggregation. However, the distinction is not absolutely watertight. If his support consists in praising his child's school to others, we enter the groundwork of 'broad' politics—the flux of educational attitude formation—but much has to be built on these footings before the system receives positive endorsement or a prod to change from subsequent political interaction of the broad variety.
2. Archer, Margaret S., *Social Origins of Educational Systems*, London and California, Sage, 1979.
3. Craig, John E., On the development of educational systems, *American Journal of Education*, forthcoming.
4. Bourdieu, Pierre and Passeron, Jean-Claude, *Reproduction*, London, Sage, 1977.
5. I have developed this argument in much greater detail in *The neglect of the educational system by Bernstein and Bourdieu*, forthcoming. In relation to this paper I would argue that Bourdieu's theories make a massive contribution to our understanding of the politics of system inaction, but practically none to the politics of structural elaboration in education.
6. These ideas are examined in more detail in my *The sociology of educational systems*, Presidential Address to the International Sociological Association's (Research Committee on Sociology of Education) Conference on The origins and operations of educational systems, Paris, August 1980, and forthcoming.
7. The main works drawn upon are: Blau, P.M., *Exchange and Power in Social Life*, New York, Wiley, 1964; Buckley, Walter, *Sociology and Modern Systems Theory*, Englewood Cliffs, New Jersey, Prentice Hall, 1967; Buckley, Walter (ed.), *Modern Systems Research for the Behavioral Scientist*, Chicago, University of Chicago Press, 1968.
8. See *Social Origins of Educational Systems*, op. cit., chapter 5, State systems and educational negotiations.
9. Ibid., p. 54.
10. Ibid., pp. 239–244.
11. Ibid., especially pp. 244–268. This is followed up in chapter 6, Interaction in the centralised system, and chapter 7, Interaction in the decentralised system, which also set out what are taken to be the defining characteristics of the two sorts of system.
12. Largely taken from *Social Origins of Educational Systems*, op. cit., chapter 7.
13. Blau, P.M., *Exchange and Power in Social Life*, op. cit., especially chapter 4, Social exchange.
14. The term 'educational profession' will be used to refer collectively to teachers and lecturers.

However, all the general propositions can be reformulated, as appropriate, to refer to particular parts or levels of the profession.
15. From now on the term 'polity' will be used as shorthand.
16. Archer, Margaret S. and Giner, Salvador (eds.), *Contemporary Europe: Class, Status and Power*, London, Weidenfeld and Nicolson, 1971, pp. 1-28.
17. As Eisenstadt argues, 'the institutionalisation of exchange .... sets normative and organisational limits to some of its basic properties and elements, such as the rates of exchange, the initial bargaining positions, and the extent of persons admitted into the exchange'. Eisenstadt, S.N., Review of P. M. Blau's Exchange and power in social life, *American Journal of Sociology*, Volume LXXI, Number 3, 1965, p. 334.
18. Archer, Margaret S. and Giner, Salvador (eds.), *Contemporary Europe: Class, Status and Power*, op. cit., pp. 14-19.
19. Blau, P.M., *Exchange and Power in Social Life*, op. cit., chapter 5, Differentiation of power. See also Buckley, Walter, *Sociology and Modern Systems Theory*, op. cit., pp. 202f.

4

The Politics of Administrative Convenience:
the case of middle schools

ANDY HARGREAVES

Broadly speaking, there are two contrasting traditions in the study of educational policy: pluralism and Marxism. These differ greatly in the theoretical and methodological approaches they adopt, to the extent that they are professionally embedded in distinctive kinds of discourse and in separate, relatively insulated communities of academic exchange.

In this article I want to sketch out a provisional framework which might allow these two approaches to be brought more closely together. This will not simply be an occasion for 'free-floating' theoretical speculation, but will also provide an opportunity to ground the framework in a detailed empirical analysis of one particularly illuminating case of postwar educational policy—the origin of English middle schools.

EXPLANATIONS OF EDUCATION AND THE STATE

Pluralism

Until very recently the study of educational policy was virtually monopolized by a tradition of 'administration and management' studies not especially renowned for their theoretical sophistication. These studies document the nuts and bolts of the educational decision-making process in rich detail; pointing to the relative influences exerted by a plurality of interest groups in the control and administration of education; to the complex

Source: From Ahier, J. and Flude, M. (eds.), *Contemporary Education Policy*, Croom Helm, London, 1983, pp. 23–58.

interactions, negotiations and mutual influences between political, administrative, professional and lay groups in the educational decision-making process at local and national levels. But while writers in this tradition have been admirable sticklers for empirical detail, and while to their credit they have sifted through the apparent messiness of educational politics and administration with great precision, it would also be fair to say that on occasion they have been less meticulous with theory, leaping to rash and premature conclusions that such messiness effectively discredits the false prophets of Marxism and their crude doctrines of economic determinism (Bell, 1981).

To pluralists, then, the superficial appearance of immense political and administrative variety in educational decision-making has a strong ideological appeal. As a result, their accounts are usually permeated by a sense of their being an almost limitless diversity of influences within and upon the decision-making process; a diversity which is matched only by the apparent elusiveness of the whole process, its seeming capacity to confound systematic analysis within an overall theoretical framework. The consequence is that while the study of educational policy abounds in elaborate taxonomies of different kinds of pressure groups and different modes of exerting political influence, it is weak on any kind of integrating theory. In Glennester and Hoyle's words (1976, p. 196), 'these studies are often useful at the level of description but lack explanatory power'.

Marxism

The weakness or absence of theory in the administration and management tradition has been more than compensated for in recent Marxist writings on education, the state and capitalism. This interest of Marxists in the state and its educational system marks their brave and ambitious progression beyond earlier rather simplistic explanations of the relationship between schooling and capitalism (Bowles and Gintis, 1976) in an effort to understand the complex political processes of modern capitalist societies and the dynamics of educational policy-making as part of those processes.

The aim of dealing with current political and educational complexities while still retaining allegiance to the concepts and framework of Marxist analysis has not been achieved without cost, however—mainly to intelligibility and coherence. This is apparent in the frequent juxtaposition of different, apparently contradictory, assertions about the relationship between education, the state and capitalism. These include the following:

—that the state maintains the conditions for capital accumulation and thereby protects the long-term interests of capital by reproducing a skilled, adaptable and compliant work force; by averting social unrest either through policies of law and order or ones of social and educational

amelioration; and by direct intervention in the management of the economy (Scase, 1980).
—that the actions of the state are not, however, directly determined by the needs or demands of the capitalist economy: the state, that is to say, has its own *relative autonomy* or *political specificity* (Poulantzas, 1973).
—that while the state is an instrument of class domination, it is also a site of class struggle and resistance (Corrigan, 1979).
—that the state is a site of contestation among a number of groups (political and professional as well as class ones) and that state policies are a product of 'the balance of political forces' in any instance rather than a direct consequence of economic influences (CCCS, 1981).

While individually, perhaps, few of these statements would arouse vigorous objections, the inclusion of many or all of them often within a single account of educational policy (e.g. CCCS, 1981; Dale, 1982) makes it extremely difficult to assess their relative importance in any particular case, or indeed to deduce whether or not economic factors *are* the major determinants of educational policies in those cases, and if so, to what extent. In other words, while, in the name of theoretical openness, an important role for political, professional and other influences as well as class and economic ones is allowed, the additional insistence that economic factors rooted in the nature of the capitalist mode of production are nonetheless somehow ultimately determinant *in the last instance*, seems to owe less to measured scholarly judgement and analysis than to unexamined belief and political commitment.

My purpose in the rest of the article is to explore two very different yet broadly compatible interpretations of the determination of educational policy in order to identify different possible relations and strengths of connection between education, the state and capitalism. This will be done with reference to an empirical analysis of the emergence of English middle schools. This evidence is deliberately selected in order to highlight complexities and variations in the politics of educational change. By pursuing such a course, I hope to contribute to the understanding of the establishment of middle schools, to sketch out possible relations between political and administrative complexities of educational decision-making and the broad structural context in which such processes are located, and to illustrate areas of possible compatibility between Marxist and pluralist analyses of educational policy.

THE CASE OF MIDDLE SCHOOLS

In legal terms, middle schools were made possible by the Education Act of 1964. This allowed, for the first time, transfer between primary and secondary education at ages other than 11. But it was an Act of more mature vintage—Butler's Education Act of 1944—which created the problem to which middle schools would eventually provide an answer. From the point of view of postwar educational reorganization, this Act left two important legacies: a system of educational provision which included a sizeable collection of relatively small but architecturally sound secondary modern schools; and a firm legal distinction between primary and secondary education fixed at 11. When several local authorities began to push hard for comprehensive schooling during the late 1950s, these legacies jarred awkwardly with one another.

The reason for this was the Ministry of Education's insistence that unless new school building was warranted by population expansion or urban renewal, local authorities who wished to reorganize their secondary education systems should do so within the existing stock of school buildings. But one of the most manageable ways of doing this—a three-tier system of 5–9, 9–13, 13–18 schools—was then illegal and was therefore either ruled out by most LEAs after the briefest of enquiries (Marsh, 1980), or not really seriously considered by them at all.

The following account explores some of the detailed negotiations that took place within just one LEA—the West Riding of Yorkshire—which attempted in some of its 28 regional divisions to grapple with this difficult issue.[1] When those particular divisions elected to go comprehensive, the West Riding's Chief Education Officer, (now Sir) Alec Clegg, mindful of the limited money that the Ministry was prepared to make available for school building purposes, drew up plans for effecting the various reorganizations within existing premises. In very many cases, this entailed a system of junior (11–14) and senior (11–18) high schools. The fortunes of this proposal in *three* separate divisions or part-divisions, will be analysed in order to illustrate the range of outcomes that can follow from a single policy initiative such as this.

In two of those divisions, the junior high school proposal was rejected—leading in one instance to the eventual establishment of all-through 11–18 provision (Ecclesfield—part of the Wharncliffe division), and in the other to one of the country's first sixth-form colleges (Mexborough). In the third division (Hemsworth), the junior high school proposal was accepted but only to meet with subsequent resistance from the Ministry of Education. It was as a result of this impasse that Clegg came up with the middle school formula, Hemsworth eventually being one of the first two areas to receive ministerial approval for the middle school experiment, and to host the opening of the first such schools in 1968.

In empirical terms then, this article seeks to explain the conditions which led to the framing of that middle school proposal, while also sketching out a provisional theoretical framework of two different kinds of determination through which the genesis of those conditions might be more completely understood.

STRUCTURAL LIMITATION—THE ROLE OF ADMINISTRATIVE CONVENIENCE

When we think of how one thing is determined by another, we usually have in mind some kind of direct pressure, or immediately observable process of cause and effect. In this respect, educational changes might be seen as the outcome of such things as political sponsorship as with the Labour Party and comprehensive schooling (Parkinson, 1970), or pressing economic demands as with the rise of the Manpower Services Commission (CCCS, 1981). However, the idea of exertion of pressure provides only one sense (albeit an extremely important one) of the meaning of 'determination'. As Williams (1976) points out, the original meaning of the term was very different from this, referring, in fact, to the setting of bounds or limits to possible actions. Wright (1979) calls this boundary-setting process, *structural limitation*. This, he argues,

> constitutes a pattern of determination in which some social structure establishes limits within which some other structure or process can vary, and establishes probabilities for the specific structures or processes that are possible within those limits. That is, structural limitation implies that certain forms of the determined structure have been excluded entirely and some possible forms are more likely than others. This pattern of determination is especially important for understanding the sense in which economic structures "ultimately" determine political and ideological structures: economic structures set limits on possible forms of political and ideological structures, and make some of these possible forms more likely than others, but they do not rigidly determine in a mechanistic manner any given form of political and ideological relations (Wright, 1979, pp. 15-16).

Structural limitation, therefore, is what makes the autonomy of education and politics *relative* rather than *complete*.

For writers such as Dale (1982), it makes no fundamental difference which particular educational policy options are considered within the capitalist state. The important thing is that all viable options *must not and cannot be inimical to* the capital accumulation process. What is interesting for Dale and other contemporary Marxist writers is not so much whether this or that particular change occurs in educational policy-making; why middle schools are established in one LEA, sixth-form colleges in another and 11-18 schools in another, for instance. Rather, they are much more fascinated by the negative case; by what *doesn't* happen, the educational changes that *don't* take place, the radical social transformations that *fail* to come to fruition. The reason for these absences, they argue, is to be located in the limits to change set by the capitalist mode of production; in particular its need for the reproduction of a skilled and flexible labour force and an acquiescent citizenry.

Action, change and conflict in educational policy-making, then, is a remarkably diverse and, in many respects, an unpredictable process. However, the extent of unpredictability in educational change is not infinite; the range of policy options not without limit. As Williams puts it, citing Engels in support, 'We make history ourselves, but, in the first place, under very definite assumptions and conditions' (Engels). What this recognizes,

Williams continues, 'is the idea of direct agency: we make history ourselves. The "definite" or "objective" assumptions and conditions are then the qualifying terms of this agency: in fact, "determination" as "the setting of limits"' (Williams, 1978, p. 85). Conflicts and struggles about education may very well be based on or organized around all kinds of non-economic considerations—those of race, gender, religion and professional status, for instance. But at the end of the day, the scope of these multifaceted conflicts is significantly limited by factors rooted in the capitalist mode of production and the logic of its development.

Assumptions

There are, to recall Williams's statement, two aspects to such structural limitation: assumptions and conditions. Assumptions about the naturalness and legitimacy of the existing order are deeply influential upon the educational policy process. Alec Clegg, for instance, though an eminent proposer of many educational innovations, was no great critic of the capitalist economic order, being a keen public supporter of the expansion of such a system and of the preparation and deployment of labour to this end. Thus, commenting in 1958 on the problems of educational underachievement in the South Yorkshire coalfield he remarked that,

> in the last 40 years vast new industries have arisen dealing with plastics, non-ferrous metals, aeronautics, radio, radar, television; not to mention the nationalised industries and the welfare state all of which have to be manned and serviced by people who are much more highly trained than those who manned the 19th century economy. In these circumstances, it appears to be the height of national folly to waste ability as we are wasting it in South Yorkshire.[2]

These remarks were not unusual for the time, being duplicated in a string of education reports such as those of Newsom, Robbins, Plowden and Crowther (to which Clegg made a contribution). Together these displayed a taken-for-granted support of the existing economic order, urging not large-scale change, but certain adjustments to improve its efficiency. To have argued otherwise would have given an impression of being altogether bereft of reason, being *against* growth and prosperity, rather than opposed to the specific economic system in which such growth occurred (Tapper and Salter, 1978). Whatever particular educational changes they favoured and sponsored, therefore, educational policy-makers such as Clegg invariably assumed that schooling would contribute to or at least, in Dale's words, *not be inimical* to capital accumulation, and the schemes and proposals that were presented by them reflected those limiting assumptions.

Within British society such assumptions have been given a particular inflection through a dominant style of educational and political reform by piecemeal and pragmatic means. As Gramsci (1971, p. 372) put it, such 'pragmatism cannot be criticized without taking account of the Anglo-Saxon historical context in which it was born and developed'. The origins of that tradition lie deep rooted in the intellectual and social fabric of eighteenth- and nineteenth-century Britain, but the approach is best epitomized in the long-standing political orientation of the British Labour Party, especially in its Fabian branch.

This orientation persisted through to the First and Second World Wars when, even in its most apparently radical phase of postwar reconstruction,

> Labour sought to improve the existing social order, not to change it. However much the party might remain symbolically committed to the achievement of a socialist commonwealth, its behaviour in the coalition of World War II was suggestive of a commitment to amelioration, not to radical transformation (Howell, 1976, p. 118).

There was no abatement of this approach in the 1950s and 60s; indeed the Conservative Governments of that period were themselves increasingly drawn into the broad educational and social concerns of economic expansion and amelioration through educational and social reform which characterized the era of social democracy (Finn, Grant and Johnson, 1977; CCCS, 1981). In other words, educational change has for a long time taken place according to a principle of gradualistic reform and amelioration within the parameters of existing institutional arrangements. Innovation has therefore moved slowly, building incrementally on past changes, adapting to local circumstances, and utilizing limited resources (see Robinson, 1977).

Conditions

Educational and social assumptions of this kind, however, are not simply indicative of the unenlightened outlook of educational administrators, but are themselves rooted in a set of deeply constraining economic conditions in which educational policy has been developed and implemented. This can be seen most clearly in the phenomenon of administrative convenience. Administrative convenience had a powerful effect on patterns of educational reorganization in the West Riding and elsewhere. In Ecclesfield, for instance, the West Riding Education Committee noted that school buildings were generally of high quality. The one existing grammar school contained some excellent postwar extensions, three of the secondary modern schools had been built since the 1944 Act, and of the remaining three one was an attractive prewar school, another required some improvements which had already been incorporated into the school building programme, and only one required much larger scale alterations. In these circumstances, the Committee felt it most unlikely that any proposed scheme for 11-18 schools would be accepted by the Ministry, given the amount of rebuilding involved.

> The Committee must ... realise that the accommodation does completely limit what can be done. It is inconceivable that when children are so excellently accommodated, this or any future Ministry would allow any bids for Comprehensive adaptations until the more squalid old buildings elsewhere have been replaced or improved.[3]

The story was the same in Mexborough. In the third division, Hemsworth, the conditions arising from administrative convenience were more restrictive still. 'The difficulty about the Hemsworth division', Clegg wrote, 'is the existence in it of a large number of small secondary schools, which means that there is no easy or obvious solution to the problem.'[4] He later stressed that given the buildings available a programme based upon 11–18 comprehensive schools would be utterly impractical.[5] His solution, yet again, was a junior high school system where all pupils would be transferred at ages 11 and 14.

But the proposal, practical though it seemed, became caught between two competing forces. While the existence of many small secondary modern schools meant that any new scheme would have to make use of at least some of the buildings in which those schools were housed, at the same time, a considerable proportion of those schools were regarded as inadequate and as needing replacement.

In view of the 'very considerable capital expenditure' which would be involved in any scheme, the Committee decided to press in the first instance for reorganization in the southern part of the division only, proposals for Hemsworth being shelved until later.[6] Even this plan was not sufficiently persuasive, though, and the Ministry withheld their approval and, despite repeated pressure from the West Riding, had still not granted it by late 1963.

The difficulties were becoming almost insuperable. Clegg was being pressured by his Divisional Executive to force through a scheme of comprehensive schooling, yet the building limitations restricted the feasible proposals to a Junior High School scheme only. Furthermore, while the scattered provision of small secondary schools certainly prevented 11–18 schools being established, the poor physical condition of many school buildings meant that virtually *any* scheme including one involving junior high schools would entail considerable expenditure on new premises which the Ministry would not be prepared to sanction.

In large part it was this highly restrictive set of conditions which pushed Clegg to 'float' the middle school idea with the Ministry in May 1963, naming Hemsworth as one of two possible areas where such a plan might be implemented. For as Clegg later confided to Councillor Palmer in March 1964, 'It is more likely that we shall be able to use and adapt existing premises if we can have 9–13 schools than if we have to make the transfer at 14.'[7] Certainly, figures for the new middle school scheme presented to the Ministry in October 1964 did not appear to exceed those already agreed for its Junior High School predecessor.[8] Indeed, their relative cost-effectiveness greatly impressed the Schools Branch at the Ministry of Education, Hemsworth eventually being the first area to be granted ministerial approval for a middle school scheme.[9]

Middle schools, then, offered an administratively expedient way of going comprehensive, and because of that fact were eventually legalized through the 1964 Education Act which gave cautious approval to middle schools as an interesting though limited educational experiment. Indeed, Edwards (1972, pp. 64–65) suggests that the middle school was surreptitiously sponsored by the Department of Education around 1964

> since it was seen as a useful experiment which would be an economic method of going comprehensive and which would also relieve considerably the pressures on secondary school accommodation which would follow the projected raising of the school leaving age.

It is tempting simply to agree with Doe's (1976, p. 22) rather cynical observation that middle schools 'were created for the best of all educational reasons—because they were cheap'—to dismiss them, in effect, as a mere administrative convenience and end the analysis there. In fact, most accounts of the emergence of middle schools which explain them primarily in terms of expediency do just this (e.g. March, 1973; Bryan and Hardcastle, 1978). They view administrative convenience either as an irritating preoccupation of educational politicians and administrators which fouls up the process of school reform (as in Edwards, 1972), or they imply that economic expediency is an irremovable feature of the policy-making process; an unavoidable, though somewhat irksome constraint which all those who work in the education system have to confront (as in Stone, 1978). As they stand, however, such interpretations are insufficient for three reasons:

—they treat 'administrative convenience' as an adequate explanation in itself without locating it in the economic and political conditions of modern British society;
—they fail to account for the diversity of supposedly convenient arrangements between and within LEAs;
—they overestimate the importance of administrative convenience, at times even implying it is the only causal factor of any significance. Other equally important determinants of the middle school thereby tend to get neglected.

To some degree, of course, a certain amount of administrative convenience is unavoidable. It is part of the global problem of scarcity. Only in imaginary utopias are there enough resources to satisfy all human needs, be they ones of health, education or whatever. While this is true enough, the problem takes on an additional dimension in capitalist societies, for here the economic system is not primarily geared to the satisfaction of human need at all, but in order to guarantee its own survival, to the maximization of profits. In such circumstances, continuous efforts are made, if not always successfully, to tailor human fortunes and ambitions to the needs of capital. The effect of this upon education in the 1960s was to encourage growing state involvement in and expansion of educational provision in order to produce a technically equipped, socially compliant labour force; and to 'buy' broad social and political consent by accommodating educational demands (Adams, 1979;

Dale, 1981). Much of the official support for comprehensive schooling can be explained in terms such as these (Bellaby, 1977).

But herein lies a crucial dilemma. For while comprehensive schooling was in part introduced to maintain and enhance the process of capital accumulation by providing a suitably adaptable and acquiescent labour force, and while it was to some extent also the price paid for securing broad social consent, the investment could not be too costly, the price not too high. If it was, if state expenditure on education reached an apparently exorbitant level, investment in the business of social reproduction would seriously threaten to exhaust the fruits, the surplus value realized from production. It would become a drain on society's resources rather than a crucial investment in its seeming well-being. Educational expenditure, therefore, was limited; and the sums channelled into the programme of comprehensive school reform were, as a result, remarkably meagre.

Viewed in this light, 'administrative convenience' as it has been experienced in modern British society takes on a broader significance than that which has conventionally been accorded it. It highlights, in fact, a central and endemic tension within modern capitalism between the actual and perceived requirements of industrial production and the direct accumulation of wealth on the one hand, and those of reproducing the conditions in which such wealth creation can continue on the other. This tension places firm limits on the policy options for social and educational change within such a society. Administrative convenience in educational policy-making is therefore part of a broader set of tensions and contradictions generated by the capital accumulation process and is thus a vivid example of what Habermas (1976, p. 46) calls the *rationality crisis* in modern capitalism 'in which the administrative system does not succeed in reconciling and fulfilling the imperatives received from the economic system'.

It is here, in the explanation of how educational policy options are structurally and hegemonically contained, that Marxist thought has a crucial role to play which must not be underestimated. In this respect, Marxism deals exceptionally well with important aspects of educational policy-making that have been sadly neglected in other traditions such as political pluralism.

For all that, though, it cannot explain the whole story. Many things are possible within the limits: policies vary greatly from one LEA to the next; the same policy is often adopted for widely varying reasons, even in the same LEA; and nationally generated initiatives are frequently resisted at the local level and vice versa. When it comes to explaining these kinds of complexities, Marxist theory with its rather loose talk of the impact of 'balances of political forces' and the like, within 'relatively autonomous trajectories' of educational change (CCCS, 1981, p. 176), is much less helpful. It is at this point that we must turn elsewhere for firmer theoretical support and more precise empirical assistance.

WITHIN THE LIMITS: VARIATIONS IN EDUCATIONAL POLICY

Multicausality

In examining the determination of educational policy and practice, most non-Marxists, particularly those drawn to pluralism and to the writings of Max Weber, are rightly anxious not to reduce all aspects of educational conflict and negotiation to forces implicated in the capitalist mode of production and the means of its preservation. Education, as other social processes, rather, is viewed as a diversely determined process and detailed empirical study is advocated and undertaken in order to establish who is most influential in the control of education in any particular instance and to ascertain which goals have been realized through the exercise of that control (Archer, 1979).

The struggle for and implementation of comprehensive schooling provides a good example of such many-sided conflicts and oddly composed alliances in the process of educational change; for invested in that single educational reform were many of the different hopes and aspirations of a wide range of social groups (Marsden, 1971). For certain sections of the working class and the Labour Party, for instance, comprehensive schooling stood for radical and egalitarian social reform (Parkinson, 1970); elsewhere, it was seen to hold out the prospect of greater all-round educational opportunities within a truly meritocratic educational system; and at the highest levels in particular, among politicians and their advisers, comprehensive schooling promised the realization of economic growth and prosperity. Moreover, these varying and differently grounded justifications were often skilfully run together by policy-makers in their pronouncements on the comprehensive issue. Such convergences of disparate interests and justifications and their diverse consequences for educational policy can be seen in the case of the West Riding at the time when junior high schools were being discussed.

Labour councillors in Mexborough rejected Clegg's suggested junior high school scheme with transfer at 14, because for them it had too many selective connotations. In particular, it called to mind the Leicestershire Plan—a scheme where children were only allowed to transfer to the senior high school at 14 if their parents agreed to them staying on beyond the minimum leaving age (Mason, 1964).

Meritocratic arguments were also broadly influential on the attempts to reorganize secondary education; perhaps even more so. The Ecclesfield subdivision provides a good example of this. Here, while junior high schools offered definite administrative advantages in going comprehensive, Clegg was worried that such schemes did not allow pupils to be prepared sufficiently for external examinations at 16 plus. Moreover, in a letter to the Divisional Education Officer, Clegg argued that the junior high school proposals for Ecclesfield ignored what he rather misleadingly called 'the purely educational problem'.[10]

By this, Clegg meant access to Oxbridge. In the 1950s and 1960s, this was dependent upon an examination qualification in Latin. To get around this problem, a solution was tentatively advanced for itinerant teachers based in the senior high schools to devote four or five periods a week to teaching in the junior highs. Although Clegg was less happy about this, he felt constrained into putting it forward because 'We have to face that fact that Oxford and Cambridge demand it (Latin) for all students, and almost every Arts Faculty in every red-brick University also demands it.'[11]

In the event, this arrangement proved too difficult and the junior high school proposal was dropped. Nevertheless, the very reason the scheme was rejected and comprehensivization in Ecclesfield subsequently delayed was because the divisional education committee along with Alec Clegg himself only wanted a system of comprehensive schooling if it was compatible with efficient grooming of the tiniest proportion of pupils for a privileged Oxbridge education.

The interesting thing about the junior high school proposal, therefore, is that while it suffered rejection in both Ecclesfield and Mexborough, it was, in fact, turned down for very different reasons. This interesting contrast is indicative of the fact that the very same educational change may be supported or rejected by very different groups and for strikingly different reasons. It rather depends who is pursuing what goals and with what effect in each case.

In this sense, educational change is undoubtedly a 'multicausal' process in the way claimed by many contemporary Weberians (e.g. Collins, 1979; King, 1982), education being an important cultural resource through which different groups pursue their own ends, be they ones of an economic, political or status-related kind. It is not uncommon for the ends these different groups pursue to be opposed to one another, this leading to situations of intense and protracted political conflict. But equally, they may at times be rendered compatible within a single educational proposal such as comprehensive schooling. Within the broad limits to educational change, then, policy-makers like Alec Clegg virtually *have* to exercise strategic dexterity in order to devise proposals for change which are acceptable to the various groups who voice their competing educational demands in any particular locality.

But we must also not forget, of course, that they do so in such a way as to realize social and educational goals which are distinctively their own. Though there is not the space to document such goals in detail here, in Clegg's case these mainly concerned the maintenance of manageable school communities. These concerns were expressed in his opposition to 11–13 schools where all pupils were entrants or leavers; to split-site schools which divided the school community; to conventional Leicestershire Plan 11–14 schools whose tone would be set by the 'truncated group' of less able 15-year-olds who had elected not to move on to the senior high; and to 11–18 schools where young boys and girls would be mixed with men eligible for the services and women 'of marriageable age' (*sic*). To these concerns Clegg later added the extension of innovative primary school regimes to older pupils in the middle school. And later still, he suggested that middle schools were institutions with their own distinctive ethos and identity (Hargreaves and Tickle, 1980).

Greatness as a highly innovative and influential educational administrator, therefore, is as much thrust upon the individual as it is his or her own unique accomplishment. Here I would concur with Carr (1964, p. 55) when he asks us 'to recognize in the great man an outstanding individual who is at once a product and an agent of the historical process'; someone, we might add, who in this case is burdened with the educational dilemmas and constraints of his time, assailed by a multiplicity of educational demands emanating from numerous political and social groups and yet who, from all this, manages not just to cobble together an unsatisfactory administrative compromise, but actually succeeds in forging a major new educational initiative that secures broad social support.

Administrative complexity

The multifaceted nature of educational change is complicated still further by the fact that variations in outlook, interpretation and social support occur not only between different localities, but also at different levels of the educational decision-making process, each level having the capacity to generate proposals of its own and to frustrate or obstruct the implementation of proposals framed at other levels. In other words, when the state acts as a determinant of schooling, it does not do so as a unitary force. There are important divisions between national and local state (Cockburn, 1977)—in education, between the DES and LEAs for instance—which often make themselves felt in marked differences over policy.[12]

In the case of Hemsworth, for example, where both local and county council were agreed upon the necessity for a junior high school scheme as the only apparently feasible way of going comprehensive, the Ministry of Education would not sanction the necessary building changes. Partly, this was for reasons of economic expediency of the kind discussed earlier, but also because of a set of unspecified objections to the idea of junior high schools hinted at in correspondence between Clegg and the Ministry, though never fully revealed by them.[13] Indeed, it was because of this resistance at the highest level to secondary school reorganization in Hemsworth, that Clegg's hand was effectively forced into the craftsmanlike shaping and skilled marketing of the middle school idea; a proposal which appeared to be cheaper still than its junior high school predecessor and therefore better suited to the economic constraints of the Hemsworth division. In addition, of course, middle schools, unlike their junior high school counterparts with their later age of transfer at 14, would not undermine the preparation of pupils for external examinations. They would, that is to say, be very much compatible with the meritocratic, examination-dominated interpretation of comprehensive schooling which Harold Wilson once saw as offering 'grammar schools for all'.

The involvement of the State in the determination of schooling is therefore a multilayered one: there are important degrees of autonomy *within* the State, as well as *between* it and the mode of production. To speak of 'relative autonomy' in this sense is therefore not to talk of properties of educational systems or the State in general but of much more precise relations between specific sets of institutions within society.

One effect of such degrees of autonomy between different parts of the State can be seen in the remarkable diversity of educational provision that came about under the auspices of comprehensive reorganization.

The point is that what is convenient in one area may not, because of the condition of local buildings, the extent of population expansion or contraction and so on, be convenient in another. For instance, while middle schools were cheaper than junior highs in the early yet crucial case of Hemsworth, the position was completely reversed in Gateshead which, on the grounds of sheer expediency, threw out a middle school scheme for one based on junior and senior high schools. As the authors of a study of educational policy-making in that borough remark, 'ultimately, the age of transfer was settled on the grounds that only 14+ was possible, given the existing school buildings' (Batley, O'Brien and Parris, 1970, p. 68). In some cases at least, then, though not in others, the claim made by Clegg and others (WRYECR, 1965, p. 4; Halsall, 1971, p. 193) that 14+ was a more convenient age of transfer than 13+ can be upheld.

The really important issue, however, is that in an internally differentiated or decentralized state system, the restrictions of expediency lead not to uniformity but to diversity of educational provision; a state of affairs which is further compounded by the many-sided nature of the conflicts and negotiations concerning education that are played out, with different results, in each locality.

Historical lags

In a 'perfect' capitalist world, the state, its policies and ideologies would respond swiftly and appropriately to the shifting demands and pressures of the labour market, technological change and social unrest. It would equip the future workforce with new skills and shape its most basic wants so that its members would wish to become scientists instead of technologists, mothers and housewives rather than competitors in a contracting male job market, and so on. In the normal course of events, though, the response is, for a number of reasons, sluggish rather than swift, and if it comes at all, from the point of view of capital, it often comes too late. Why should this be so?

In part, in the sphere of schooling, these lags take the form of persisting ideas and beliefs about education which are inappropriate to a changed economic and political context. An example here are those middle-aged, career-blocked secondary modern school teachers who tenaciously clung to the aims and ethos of the secondary modern school even when they had been redeployed to work within a meritocratically-oriented, academically pressured comprehensive system (Riseborough, 1981). But the failure to undo the old tripartite system is not only a result of entrenched beliefs and conventions among those for whom educational reform offers no obvious advantages. It is also a product of past policy commitments making themselves felt in harsh and intractable material realities; in the very bricks and mortar of schooling.

To that extent, the failure of the postwar Labour government to establish comprehensive schooling, choosing instead under the Education Minister, Ellen Wilkinson, to endorse the tripartite system as outlined in the Spens and Norwood reports which preceded the 1944 Act, must be seen not just as what Marsden (1971) calls 'an opportunity lost', in postponing large-scale comprehensive reorganization for two decades; but also it must be viewed as effectively restructuring the future possible ways in which any reorganization of secondary education might be managed. Small secondary modern schools designed for a fading educational tradition severely restricted the possibilities for bringing about comprehensive school reform.

To sum up, much of the inefficiency of state responses to economic change is a result of historically induced restrictions, of commitments to past policies and beliefs not well suited to the demands of the present. Partly, of course, these lags are reinforced in decentralized educational systems such as that in Britain where the negotiation of educational change is often a long, involved and broadly-based process. But equally, once a restriction has been recognized and confronted, as with the tripartite legacy of buildings unsuited for the purposes of comprehensive schooling, decentralized systems may actually *accelerate* the devising of practical solutions since they make it possible for the circumstances of each locality in which change is to take place to be appreciated and responded to: hence the variety of institutional structures—middle schools, sixth-form colleges, etc.—in which comprehensive schooling came to be established.

CONCLUSION

Multicausality, pluralistic conflict, administrative complexity and historical inertia can therefore tell us a great deal about the dynamics of educational policy-making, its determinants and its outcomes. And careful documentation of these processes can tell us more about the complex nature of educational decision-making and state policy than mysterious invocations of concepts like 'relative autonomy' which simply tend to gloss over these differences and subtleties. But saying this does not amount to a refutation of the Marxist thesis. For all these administrative and political complexities, immensely important as they are, are nonetheless still confined within broad limits to educational change which are set down by factors rooted in the nature of capitalism as a mode of production and the logic of its development. We have seen this not only in the enduring and pervasive assumptions of policy-makers which tacitly endorse the existing economic order, but also in the phenomenon of administrative convenience—an example in the educational sphere of much more extensive and deep-seated irrationalities in the administration of the capitalist order as a whole.[14]

It is difficult and perhaps futile to argue that one-half of this two-sided problem is more important or more politically and educationally 'fundamental' than the other: to propose that the limits to change are more significant than the different possibilities contained within them, or vice versa. This is the trap, however, in which Marxists and their enemies have been caught; one in which a dialogue of the deaf prevails; each side falsely assuming that the one who wins the argument will be the one who shouts longest and loudest.

Studying the limits or what goes on within them are therefore complementary, not competing ventures. Choosing between the two options is a matter of value choice, not one of theoretical correctness. The more complete explanation, however, will attempt (with unavoidable difficulty) to combine them in a theoretically open and empirically grounded way. This is as true for the analysis of current educational issues where, arguably, the limits to change have been drawn in by the strengthening of central government control over curriculum and examinations in the context of deepening economic recession (Salter and Tapper, 1981) as it is for the social-democratic era of educational policy-making with which this paper has been concerned. Indeed, the more crucial that education and political issues become for the lives of ourselves and our children, the more we must try to ensure that we get the analysis of them right. In this sense, theoretical openness and empirical rigour are not the nit-picking enemies of a policy-relevant sociology of education, but its closest allies.

NOTES

1. The data on which this account is based consists of the correspondence and memoranda of the West Riding Authority at the time prior to and during that Authority's consideration and implementation of the middle school system. I am grateful to Paul Sharp of Leeds University School of Education for drawing the existence of these records to my attention in the late 1970s. A fuller account of the whole history of the West Riding LEA is provided in Gosden and Sharp (1978). Sharp has also subsequently written a short account of the development of middle schools in that authority.

2. The education of the gifted child in the comprehensive school of the Yorkshire coalfield, presented to Policy and Finance Sub-Committee, 9 December 1958.
3. The request for comprehensive schools or a comprehensive scheme of education—Ecclesfield Area, Policy and Finance Sub-Committee, 9 December 1958.
4. Letter to Mr. Cockell, Divisional Education Officer for Hemsworth, 19 June 1959.
5. Further letter to Mr. Cockell, 22 September 1959.
6. Hemsworth Division—organization of secondary education, memorandum to Policy and Finance Sub-committee, 8 March 1960.
7. Letter to Councillor Palmer, 4 March 1964.
8. As Clegg recorded in a memorandum to the Policy and Finance Sub-Committee (13 October 1964),

> The future organization of the Hemsworth Division was under discussion at the time the Department of Education and Science was compiling the 1966/67 (Building) Programme and for this reason a specific project could not be included for Hemsworth. Some new secondary provision for Hemsworth was however included on the understanding that whatever projects the Authority did put forward (e.g. for middle schools) ... would be financially comparable to the proposals (for junior high schools) already made.

9. Such a demonstration was offered in relation to the establishment of middle schools in the Castleford Division where Clegg was asked by Miss Small at the Schools Branch of the Ministry to document the relative costs of junior high and middle school schemes respectively for that division. Clegg seized this opportunity to stress the economic advantages of the middle school scheme. Replying to Miss Small (26 November 1963), he wrote:

> May I emphasize that if approval were to be given to our present suggestion (for middle schools), all these developments could take place without the provision of major new building, whereas the situation described in the Public Notices (in terms of a junior high school proposal) referred to the future and depended on new buildings being provided.

10. Letter to S. Wright, Wharncliffe Divisional Education Officer, 20 August 1958.
11. Ibid.
12. Of course, these are not the only important differences. The DES itself is by no means in uniform agreement about educational policy, HMI often presenting an important source of polite but firm dissent in this respect (Salter and Tapper, 1981).
13. Letter from Clegg to L. R. Fletcher, Schools Branch, Ministry of Education, 15 May 1963.
14. An important question worth pursuing, however, is that these limits, while having a powerful economic component, may not be entirely constituted by factors to be located within the mode of production. Feminist writers, for instance, have pointed to the limits to educational change set by patriarchal relations (e.g. McDonald, 1980) and it would be difficult to conduct a research project in Northern Ireland without being aware, possibly on pain of death or serious injury, of the limits to change set down by religious factors (e.g. Jenkins et al., 1981). These problems are currently unresolved in the sociology of education, but a serious treatment of them must lead us not only to reassess our understandings of educational change, but also to place in honest doubt the superior explanatory power of Marxist analysis even at this level. On this matter, my own position is not yet resolved.

BIBLIOGRAPHY

Adams, P. (1979) Social control or social wage: on the political economy of the 'welfare state', *Journal of Sociology and Social Welfare*, Vol. 5.

Archer, M. (1979) *Social Origins of Educational Systems*, Sage, London.

Batley, R., O'Brien, O. and Parris, H. (1970) *Going Comprehensive*, Routledge & Kegan Paul, London.
Bell, R. (1981) Institutions of educational government, Unit 8, E200 *Contemporary Issues in Education*, Open University, Milton Keynes.
Bellaby, P. (1977) *The Sociology of Comprehensive Schooling*, Methuen, London.
Bowles, S. and Gintis, H. (1976) *Schooling in Capitalist America*, Routledge & Kegan Paul, London.
Bryan, K. and Hardcastle, K. (1978) Middle years and middle schools: an analysis of national policy, *Education 3-13*, Vol. 6, No. 1.
Carr, E.H. (1964) *What is History?*, Penguin, Harmondsworth.
Centre for Contemporary Cultural Studies (CCCS) (1981) *Unpopular Education*, Hutchinson, London.
Cockburn, C. (1977) *The Local State*, Pluto Press, London.
Collins, R. (1979) *The Credential Society*, Academic Press, New York.
Corrigan, P. (1979) *Capitalism, State Formation and Marxist Theory*, Quartet Books, London.
Dale, R. (1981) The state and education: some theoretical approaches, Unit 3, E353 *Society, Education and the State*, Open University, Milton Keynes.
Dale, R. (1982) Education and the capitalist state: contributions and contradictions, in Apple, M. (ed.), *Cultural and Economic Reproduction in Education*, Routledge & Kegan Paul, London.
Doe, B. (1976) The end of the middle, *The Times Educational Supplement*, 28 September.
Edwards, R. (1972) *The Middle School Experiment*, Routledge & Kegan Paul, London.
Finn, D., Grant, N. and Johnson, R. (1977) Social democracy, education and the crisis, in Centre for Contemporary Cultural Studies, *On Ideology*, Working Paper 10.
Glennester, H. and Hoyle, E. (1976) Educational research and education policy, *Journal of Social Policy*, Vol. 1, No. 3.
Gosden, P.H.J.H. and Sharp, P.R. (1978) *The Development of an Education Service: the West Riding 1889-1974*, Martin Robertson, Oxford.
Gramsci, A. (1971) *Selections from the Prison Notebooks*, Lawrence & Wishart, London.
Habermas, J. (1976) *Legitimation Crisis*, Heinemann, London.
Halsall, E. (1971) *Becoming Comprehensive*, Pergamon Press, Oxford.
Hargreaves, A. and Tickle, L. (1980) *Middle Schools: origins, ideology and practice*, Harper & Row, London.
Howell, D. (1976) *British Social Democracy*, Croom Helm, London.
Jenkins, D. *et al.* (1981) *Chocolate, Cream, Soldiers: final evaluation report on the Rowntree Schools Cultural Studies Project*, New University of Ulster Education Centre.
King, R. (1982) Organizational choice in secondary schools, *British Journal of Sociology of Education*, Vol, 3, No. 1.
McDonald, M. (1980) Schooling and the reproduction of class and gender relations, in Barton, L. and Walker, S., *Schooling, Ideology and the Curriculum*, Falmer Press, Lewes.
Marsden, D. (1971) Politicians, equality and comprehensives, Fabian Tract 411, Fabian Society, London.
Marsh, C. (1973) The emergence of the English middle school, *Dudley Journal of Education*, Vol. 1, No. 3.
Marsh, C. (1980) The emergence of nine-thirteen middle schools in Worcestershire, in Hargreaves and Tickle, op. cit.
Mason, S. (1964) *The Leicestershire Experiment and Plan*, Council and Education Press, London.
Parkinson, M. (1970) *The Labour Party and the Organization of Secondary Education 1918-1965*, Routledge & Kegan Paul, London.
Poulantzas, N. (1973) *Political Power and Social Classes*, New Left Books, London.
Riseborough, G. (1981) Teacher careers and comprehensive schooling: an empirical study, *Sociology*, Vol. 15, No. 3.
Robinson, P. (1977) *Education and Poverty*, Methuen, London.
Salter, B. and Tapper, T. (1981) *Education, Politics and the State*, Grant McIntyre, London.
Scase, R. (ed.) (1980) *The State in Western Europe*, Croom Helm, London.
Stone, J.A. (1978) The age of transfer, in Department of Education and Science, *Comprehensive Education*, report of a conference held at the invitation of the Secretary of State for Education and Science, University of York.

Tapper, T. and Salter, B. (1978) *Education and the Political Order*, Macmillan, London.
West Riding of Yorkshire Education Committee Reports (WRYECR) (1965) *The Organization of Comprehensive Schooling in Certain Areas of the West Riding.*
Williams, R. (1976) *Keywords*, Fontana, London.
Williams, R. (1978) *Marxism and Literature*, Oxford University Press, Oxford.
Wright, E.O. (1979) *Class, Crisis and the State*, New Left Books, London.

5

Social Policy and the Theory of the State*

CLAUS OFFE

CONTROVERSIES CONCERNING A SOCIAL SCIENTIFIC THEORY OF THE STATE

In the liberal social sciences, the study of the state and social policy is guided by *formal* concepts. Liberal definitions of the sociological nature of the parliamentary-democratic constitutional state generally refer to the forms, procedures, rules and instruments of state activity, and not to state functions, their consequences and the contending interests within the state. For example, the Weberian definition of the state as the 'monopoly of physical violence' refers to the ultimate formal authority of sovereign acts, but reveals nothing of the direction of the relation of violence, i.e. by whom and against whom it is deployed. The concept of politics, understood as the solitary, decisive deeds of 'leaders' unconstrained by reason, becomes irrational, and renders such questions meaningless. The methodological concept of democracy prepared by Weber, and later applied by Schumpeter, has made his work the high court of liberal democratic and pluralist theory: as Weber says, democracy is a 'state-technical' and particularly effective mechanism of generating order, but theory can predict none of its outcomes.

This form of argument—which first posits content as contingent (i.e. as dependent on the will of great individuals, on empirical processes of coalition and bargaining or, finally, upon the variable, scientific-technical 'force of

---

* This essay, co-authored with Gero Lenhardt, was first presented as a paper to the opening plenary session of the Eighteenth Convention of the Deutsche Gesellschaft für Soziologie, Bielefeld, September 1976. It is here translated (and slightly abridged) from the version later published as Staatstheorie und Sozialpolitik—politische-soziologische Erklärungsansätze für Funktionen und Innovationsprozesse der Sozialpolitik, in Ferber, C.V. and Kaufman, F.X. (eds.), *Kölner Zeitschrift für Soziologie und Sozialpsychologie*, special issue, **19**, 98–127, 1977 and also in Offe, Claus, *Contradictions of the Welfare State*, Hutchinson, London, 1984, pp. 88–109.

circumstances') and subsequently disregards it theoretically—also prevails in related disciplines like constitutional law and administration theory.

* * * * *

Similarly, in the science of administration, strategies not determined by content or practicable, normative alternatives—the 'incrementalist' (Lindblom), 'opportunistic' (Luhmann) treatment of problems—are characterized as the empirically predominant form of administrative rationality.

In contrast, what we understand by the theory of the state may be described as the totality of attempts to expose this formalistic blind spot by means of social-scientific research. The reduction of the state and democracy to categories of *procedure*—a persistent and increasing tendency since the First World War—has permeated the flesh and blood of the liberal social sciences so thoroughly that not only do the marked systematic *gaps* in knowledge (of the content and *results* of procedures) go unnoticed as such, but scientific attempts by the respective professions to fill them are as a rule abandoned to official ignorance.

* * * * *

The point of departure of this kind of substantive investigation is not the establishment of particular modes of procedurally regulating state activity (for example, the constitutional state or democracy) but, rather, hypothetical notions about the functional connection between state activity and the structural problems of a (capitalist) social formation.

* * * * *

Normative investigations are also considered to be the specific concern of sociological research into social policy. The problem, of course, is that the ought-value inputs are more or less directly drawn from the social conscience of the researcher. The research demonstrates that the practice of social policy fails to meet the politically progressive criteria of criticism that the research itself has adopted. Thereby, normative research projects are open to the objection, first, that they are incapable of sustaining the validity and necessity of their normative presuppositions, and, second, that they habitually overestimate their capacity to induce at least some unease among those political and administrative actors to whom proof of the discrepancies between 'ought' and 'is' is presented (and who, as a rule, have the power to finance—or refuse to finance—such research). In any event, any theoretical conception of social policy that seeks to 'stimulate... long-term, relevant, and continuous research into welfare-state interests'[1] must find a way to escape this twofold—methodological and political—dilemma.

Despite their opposition to formalistic (particularly economic and juridical) accounts of social policy, the normative[2] approaches actually confirm, rather than overcome, the unreconciled duality of spheres into which social reality is sundered by liberal social science. In both cases, procedural rules are counterposed to needs, 'facts' to 'values', formal to material rationality. It seems to us that both the formalistic and normative approaches to the study of social policy avoid the question that is of central importance within recent social-scientific discussions of the theory of the state, especially those stimulated by authors of a Marxist persuasion. How does state policy (social policy in this case) arise from the specific problems of an economic and class structure based on the private utilization of capital and free wage-labour, and what *functions* does this policy perform with regard to this structure?

Speaking generally, this question can be reformulated as follows: how does a given historical society reproduce itself while maintaining or altering its identity? What structures and mechanisms engender its continuity and identity or bring about breaches in that continuity? It is easy to show that the insight that this continuity is problematic, or at least is not guaranteed by any meta-social factors (for instance, human nature) is at the heart of any effort, whether by Comte or Marx, to formulate a *theory* of society. It is with this insight that sociology first becomes possible. Sociology masters this original, undiminished, central and ever-present problem to the extent that it is able to identify the *structural problems* that make the cohesion and historical continuity of society problematic rather than self-evident, and identifies the means of social 'integration' through which a given social system overcomes, or fails to overcome, its specific structural problems. In the theoretical tradition of historical materialism, the reference to the state regulation of bourgeois society has always played a role in hypothetically answering this latter question. Clearly, this hypothesis must be measured against evidence concerning both the specifically repressive, regulative, ideological and other functions of the state apparatus and its unique organizational components and policies. In what follows, we shall adopt this approach with respect to the domain of social policy.

ON THE SOCIAL FUNCTION OF SOCIAL POLICY INSTITUTIONS AND THE PROBLEM OF FUNCTIONAL FRAMES OF REFERENCE

Any analysis of social policy that seeks to answer such questions is well advised to begin with the hypothetical construction of a functional frame of reference, which must then prove its worth as the key to the explanation of empirical political processes.³ We suggest that one such hypothetical point of reference for the functional explanation of social policy is: social policy is the state's manner of effecting the lasting transformation of non-wage-labourers into wage-labourers. This hypothesis is based on the following consideration. The process of capitalist industrialization is accompanied—and by no means only at its historical origins, when the phenomenon is especially evident—by the disorganization and mobilization of labour power. The spread of relations of competition to national and then world markets, the continual introduction of labour-saving technical changes, the undermining of agrarian labour and forms of life, the impact of cyclical crises: these and other factors effectively destroy, to a greater or lesser extent, the hitherto prevailing conditions of the utilization of labour power. The individuals affected by such events find that their own labour capacities—whose conditions of utilization they control neither collectively nor individually—can no longer serve as the basis of their subsistence. But this, of course, does not mean that they automatically hit upon the solution to their problems by alienating their labour power to a third party in exchange for money. Individuals do not automatically enter the supply side of the labour market. To assume such an automatism would be to tailor the historical norm to something that seems sociologically self-evident, thus losing sight of the mechanisms that must exist if the 'normal case' is to actually occur.

A distinction between 'passive' and 'active' proletarianization may be helpful in presenting this problem more precisely. It should be uncontroversial that massive and continuous 'passive' proletarianization, the destruction of the previously dominant forms of labour and subsistence, has been an important socio-structural aspect of the industrialization process. Sociologically speaking, however, there is no reason why those individuals who find themselves dispossessed of their means of labour or subsistence should spontaneously proceed to 'active' proletarianization by offering their labour power for sale on the labour market. To assume this would be to regard the consequences of 'passive' proletarianization—hunger and physical deprivation—as factors of sociological explanation.

* * * * *

Given that the structural problem of proletarianization, of the incorporation of labour power into a labour market, is not resolved 'by itself' in any serious social-scientific sense, what component social structures in fact functionally contribute to its effective resolution? We propose the thesis that the wholesale and complete transformation of *dispossessed* labour power into active wage-labour was not and is not possible without *state policies*. While not all of these policies are conventionally considered part of 'social policy' in the narrow sense, they do perform the function of incorporating labour power into the labour market.

Our central problem—that 'active' proletarianization does not follow naturally from 'passive' proletarianization—may be sub-divided into three component problems.

1. If a fundamental social reorganization of the kind that did occur in the course of capitalist industrialization is to be possible, then dispossessed potential workers must in the *first* place be prepared to offer their capacity for labour as a commodity on the market. They must consider the risks and burdens associated with this form of existence as *relatively* acceptable; they must muster the *cultural motivation* to become wage-labourers.

2. Socio-structural preconditions are necessary for wage-labourers to function as wage-labourers. Because of their special living conditions, not all members of society could function as wage-labourers unless certain basic reproduction functions (especially in the domain of socialization, health, education, care for the aged) are fulfilled. A range of special institutional facilities is therefore required, under whose aegis labour power is, so to speak, exempt from the compulsion to sell itself, or in any event is expended in ways other than through exchange for money-income (the housewife is a case in point). The functional indispensability of such non-market subsystems as family, school and health-care facilities may be considered less problematic than the answer to the question of why these forms of organization must fall within the province of *state* policy. Two points may be offered to support the thesis that forms of existence outside the labour market must be organized and sanctioned by the state if the transformation of labour power into wage-labour is to be possible. To begin with, those subsystems that dealt with living conditions in the pre-industrial and early industrial phase (particularly the family, but also private and church charity, as well as other primary-group forms of social welfare) lose their ability to cope in the course of industrial development and have to be replaced by formal political regulations. Second—this point is quite compatible with the first, and probably no less important—only the 'statization' of these flanking subsystems makes possible ruling-class control over the living conditions of that segment of the population who are permitted access to that special form of life and subsistence that stands outside the labour market, and who are, therefore, temporarily or permanently exempt from the compulsion to sell their labour power on the labour market. The nub of this second argument is that the 'material' preconditions of reproduction and, equally, of ruling-class control over wage-labourers, make it necessary to *politically* regulate who is and who is not a wage-labourer. Without this argument, it would be hard to explain why nearly everywhere the introduction of a common educational system (i.e. the replacement of family forms of training and socialization) was accompanied by the introduction of a general and definite period of *compulsory* education (which amounts to the obligatory organization of

certain periods of life outside the labour market). The reliable and permanent incorporation of 'additional' labour power into the wage-labour market can be guaranteed only by strictly regulating the conditions under which non-participation in the labour market is possible (and where purely repressive measures like the punishment of begging and theft do not suffice). The choice between a life of wage-labour and forms of subsistence outside the labour market must accordingly not be left to the discretion of labour power. When, and for how long, individuals remain outside the labour market, the decision whether someone is too old, sick, young, disabled, or has a valid claim to be part of the education system or to social provision must be left neither to individual needs nor to the momentary chances of subsistence outside the market. These choices must be positively regulated through politically defined criteria, for otherwise there would be incalculable tendencies for wage-labourers to evade their function by slipping into the flanking subsystems. This is why a precondition of the constitution of a class of wage-labourers is the political institutionalization—and not merely the *de facto* maintenance—of various categories of non-wage-labourers.

3. Finally—this is the *third* component problem—there must be, in the long run, an approximate quantitative balance between those who are 'passively' proletarianized (whether through enforced flight from agricultural forms of reproduction, dismissal as a result of recession or technological change, etc.) and those who are able to find employment as wage-labourers given the volume of demand on the labour market.

The first of the component problems mentioned above is dealt with by all those state policies emanating from the 'ideological' and 'repressive' sections of the state apparatus (to use the terminology of the French structuralists).

This deep-seated problem of the 'social integration' of wage-labour must be dealt with by mechanisms of social control that are not reliably engendered by the labour market itself. Examples of this include the criminalization and prosecution of modes of subsistence that are potential alternatives to the wage-labour relation (from the prohibition of begging to repressive acts like the Bismarckian Socialist Law) and the state-organized procurement of norms and values, the adherence to which results in the transition to the wage-labour relation. Only the long-term application of these two mechanisms of state policy produces a situation in which the working class 'by education, tradition, and habit looks upon the requirements of that mode of production as self-evident natural laws'. This transformation of dispossessed labour power into wage-labour is itself a constitutive socio-*political* process whose accomplishment cannot be explained *solely* by the 'silent compulsion of economic relations'.[4]

* * * * *

It is precisely because the 'anarchic' fluctuations of the supply and demand sides of the labour market are socially generated but not socially controlled, that 'social "catchment areas" outside the process of production are required to ensure the reproduction of labour power even when no actual employment within the production process results'.[5] This problem of the institutional 'storage' of that portion of the social volume of labour power which (because of conjunctural and structural changes) cannot be absorbed by the demand generated by the labour market becomes acute as traditional forms of caring for such labour power become ineffective. This thesis may be substantiated more closely through the results of a social history-oriented study of the sociology of the family,[6] and through studies of the loss of function of private welfare and charity institutions.

Our conclusions so far may be summed up in the following way. The dispossession of labour power generates three structural problems: the incorporation of labour power into the supply side of the labour market; the institutionalization of those risks and areas of life that are not 'subsumed' under the wage-labour relation; and the quantitative regulation of the relationship between supply and demand on the labour market. These structural problems are by no means resolved automatically by the 'silent compulsion of economic relations', whose participants are somehow left no choice but to submit to the ineluctable imperatives of capitalist industrialization. If 'economic relations' compel anything, it is the invention of social institutions and relations of domination that in turn are not at all based on *mute* compulsion. The transformation of dispossessed labour power into 'active' wage-labour does not occur through the market alone, but must be sanctioned by a political structure of rule, through state power. The owner of labour power first becomes a wage-labourer as a citizen of a state. Thus, we understand the term social policy to include the totality of those politically organized relations and strategies that contribute to the resolution of these three structural problems by continuously effecting the transformation of owners of labour power into wage-labourers.[7] A more thorough analysis would probably confirm our impression that, while these three basic problems—the *willingness, ability* and *objective 'sales prospects'* of labour power—can be precisely delineated at the analytic level, 'multi-functional' devices nevertheless prevail at the level of the corresponding social policy measures. These devices are constructed so that, simultaneously and in shifting combinations, they seek to control motives, adjust labour capacities and quantitatively regulate the labour supply. From a strategic-conceptual point of view, the predominance of such social policy devices, which may be characterized as 'broad band therapy' for these structural problems, makes it appear somewhat unwise to exclude from the concept of social policy the rather repressive measures of social control (or the problem-solving strategies of education, housing and health policies), especially since the connections between these individual measures are clearly recognized today within the state administration itself. The scope of state activities designated as part of social policy therefore should not be deduced from their departmental allocation. These activities should instead be determined on the basis of their functional orientation to that objective structural problem to whose treatment the various state institutions, departments and intervention strategies contribute: the problem of the constitution and continuous reproduction of the wage-labour relationship.

APPROACHES TO THE EXPLANATION OF PROCESSES OF POLITICAL INNOVATION IN THE FIELD OF SOCIAL POLICY

The goal of state-theoretical investigation into the historical and contemporary forms and changes of social policy is to explain this policy on the basis of its substantive functions. The functional linking of state social policy to the structural problems of the socialization of labour proposed in the previous section offered only preliminary indications of this goal. Questions concerning the driving forces or crucial influences determining the historical development of the instruments and institutions of social policy remain open. Indeed, the institutions of social policy are not fixed, but are subject to constant development and innovation. We have, so far, only outlined and illustrated a theoretical frame of reference for state-theoretical research on social policy, one that seeks to examine and understand the 'existence' of social policy institutions in relation to the structural problem of the 'integration of labour power into social production in the form of wage-labour'. But even if these institutions have completely fulfilled the three functions discussed above, they do not do so once and for all. It is also necessary to explain the regularity of the changes in their existence, the 'laws of motion', so to speak, of the development of social policy. In discussing this 'dynamic' aspect we shall base ourselves *inter alia* on the theoretical perspectives and conclusions of a case study of the development and implementation of a special field of legislation in the domain of the labour market and social policy—a domain whose pattern of development requires political and sociological clarification.[8]

In reply to this question concerning the driving forces of policy development, two forms of argument have been offered in the political science literature. Each of these has its specific difficulties. They may be distinguished as follows.

Explanation of the genesis of state social policy in terms of interests and needs

We said earlier that wage-labour could be successfully established as the dominant organizational form only if the specific risks faced by the owner of the 'commodity' labour power were made acceptable, and only if any 'escape' from the wage-labour relation—whether in the form of regression to pre-capitalist or progression to socialist forms of organization—was simultaneously prevented. This suggests the hypothesis that the further development of the institutions and operations of social policy are impelled by the actual risks of the process of capitalist industrialization, and also by the organizational strength of the working class, which raises and enforces appropriate *demands* on the state. Developments in social policy may thus be analysed as the result of objective risk-burdens and the political implementation of demands.

The obvious problem in this explanatory approach is that it presupposes that the system of political institutions is constituted so that it actually concedes the demands of working-class organizations in exactly the measure and combination corresponding to the prevailing conditions of objective risks and the political strength of these organizations (workers' parties and trade unions). But the achievement of this type of correspondence is itself an open question. Those who seek to explain social policy developments with reference to interests or needs, or to demands for various changes must therefore provide additional explanations of how it is that the system of political institutions is, first, sufficiently responsive and reactive to become aware of such demands so that they are accorded the status of political 'issues'; but, second, not *so* responsive and reactive that these 'inputs' might be significantly registered and dealt with in ways that are not *necessarily* linked with either the level of objective risks facing wage-labour or with the political strength of organized workers. This consideration leads at least to the conclusion that policy development cannot be fully explained by needs, interests and demands alone, and that the process of the conversion of 'demands' into 'policies' is always refracted and mediated through the internal structures of the political system, which is what determines whether or not 'needs' are acknowledged as themes worthy of treatment.[9]

Explanation of developments in social policy by 'objective' imperatives of the process of valorization of capital

The explanatory approaches that may be grouped under this type of argument maintain that the causal variables of developments in social policy are not 'demands' of the working class, but functional exigencies of the capitalist valorization process. A crucial characteristic of this process is its 'extravagance' in devouring labour power, the consequence of which is the wholesale destruction of labour capacities and, therewith, the foundations of future accumulation.[10]

State social policy is thus explained by capital's long-term self-interest in the maintenance of the 'material' substance, the level of skill and availability of labour power, and in its protection against short-sighted and excessive exploitation. Apart from the fact that this explanatory approach must exclude any measures of social policy that cannot be unconditionally related to the maintenance of the material substance of labour power (or must bracket them under the perplexing concept of 'non-system-specific social policy', as do Funke et al.),[11] methodological objections, or at least queries, can also be raised. First, this approach must clarify the extent to which it can be assumed that state agencies command the requisite foresight and analytical capacity for diagnosing the functional exigencies of capital more accurately than the bearers of the valorization process themselves. And second, even if the state administration were staffed by veritable super-sociologists, this approach is forced to clarify under what circumstances state agencies are in a position to freely respond to the perceived exigencies with suitable measures and innovations in social policy.

A more complex and less problematic model of explanation may be obtained by combining the two approaches. There are two different ways to do this, the first of which—an extrapolation, it seems to us, of Marx's analysis of the determination of the normal working day—predominates in a good part of Marxist analysis on the subject.[12] This first argument may, without too much simplification, be condensed into the following thesis: when the (existing) organizations of the working class propose and politically enforce demands for security through social policy from the state, they only ever bring about conditions that are necessary—in the long run, at any rate—for the interests of capital and a cautious modernization of the relations of exploitation.[13] The organizations of the working class thus merely force capital to 'concede' what then turns out to be in the latter's own well-understood interests. At least, this is said to be true in the sense that capital, in exchange for the costs it must pay for concessions in social policy—costs that are possibly burdensome in the short term but tolerable in the medium term—is compensated in the long run with the advantages of a physically intact and properly skilled workforce, as well as a secured social peace that an increasingly ideologically immunized working class will willingly observe. Such hyper-functionalist constructions imply that the state apparatus, or rather the parties and trade unions that effectively function as its components, have at their disposal fine-tuning and balance mechanisms of colossal complexity and unerring accuracy. If the suggested hypothesis is to be plausible, these mechanisms must be able to ensure that all those, or only those, demands that lead to social policy measures and innovations *at the same time* have the effect of satisfying the long-term functional exigencies of accumulation.

In contrast to such markedly 'harmonistic' interpretations of the genesis and function of social policies of the state, we seek to defend the thesis that the explanation of social policy must indeed take into account as causal factors both 'demands' and 'systemic requirements', that is, problems of 'social integration' and 'system integration' (Lockwood),[14] the political processing of both class conflict and the crises of the accumulation process. As the reaction to *both* these sets of problems, social policy development can never deal with these problems consistently. The solution to one set of problems in no way coincides with the solution to the other; they are mutually contradictory. Accordingly, we maintain that the pattern of development of the strategies and innovations of state social policy is determined through treatment of the 'meta-problem' that may be summed up by this question: how can strategies of social policy be developed and existing institutions modernized so that there can be a satisfaction of *both* the political demands 'licensed' in the context of the prevailing political rights of the working class *and* the foreseeable exigencies and labour and budgetary prerequisites of the accumulation process? The crucial functional problem in the development of social policy and, thus, the key to its social-scientific explanation is that of the *compatibility* of the strategies through which the ruling political apparatus must react to 'demands' and 'systemic requirements' in the framework of existing political institutions *and* to the relationship of social forces channelled through them.

This thesis proposes that particular social policy measures and innovations should be conceived as 'answers' to neither specific demands nor perceived modernization imperatives generated by the problems of the valorization of capital. As is manifest in the themes and conditions of the formation of social policy innovations, social policy instead consists of answers to what can be called the *internal* problem of the state apparatus, namely, how it can react *consistently* to the two poles of the 'needs' of labour and capital—in other words, how to make them mutually compatible. The problem to which state policy development in the social policy domain reacts is that of the precarious compatibility of its own institutions and performances.[15] Our functional reference-point for the explanation of innovations in social policy is therefore the problem of the *internal rationalization* of the system of performance of social policy; in this view, the corresponding *pressure* for rationalization results from the fact that the conflicting 'demands' and requirements faced by the political-administrative system continually call into question the compatibility and practicability of the existing institutions of social policy.

ADMINISTRATIVE RATIONALIZATION AND THE IMPLEMENTATION OF INNOVATIONS

This view of the 'compatibility problem', we contend, depicts the causal condition and driving force of innovation in social policy, and is quite accessible to empirical sociological analysis. Accordingly, it would be possible to test the thesis that those actors (in the ministries, parliaments and political parties) who are responsible for social policy institutions and innovations within the state apparatus actually do find themselves constantly faced with the dilemma that many legally and politically sanctioned demands and guarantees remain unreconciled to exigencies and capacities of the budgetary, financial and labour-market policy of the capitalist economy. They are brought into conflict with this policy by uncontrollable environmental factors. The initiatives to innovate in matters of social policy are chronologically and substantively tailored to the specific parameters of this dilemma. If this thesis were confirmed, we would be entitled to assert that such state policy innovations do not 'serve' the needs or exigencies of any particular social group or class, but instead react to the internal structural problems of the welfare state apparatus.

This thesis would be incomplete and misleading, however, unless it was added that the state's efforts at political innovation, though 'goal abstract' and related solely to its own internal problems (namely, the integrity of its legal, physical and institutional organizational resources), have effects that are not at all *limited* to these internal spheres of state organization. On the contrary, every measure of internal rationalization—whether technical, medical, administrative-organizational or fiscal—always entails more or less far-reaching 'external effects' upon the level of wealth and power resources of social groups. This is quite obvious in cases in which social policy innovations—new laws, decrees and institutional procedures—explicitly and manifestly modify the balance of burdens and benefits among particular categories of people. A (comparatively trivial) sociological example would be the raising of taxes or the cutting of services in the course of efforts to balance the budget. The connections are less transparent (and therefore require sociological explanation) if the external effects of social policy innovations are not regulated explicitly but are enacted wholesale as a more or less indeterminate and latent function of the process of administrative rationalization. An instance of this would be the organizational changes in the management of municipal youth, or social services. However such measures of administrative reform are enacted in a given case, it is certain that there is no such thing as an administrative reform that is *nothing but* an administrative reform; it always entails changes in the quality of the available social services, their accessibility to clients, the composition of the clientele, and so on.

Finally, of the greatest interest to sociological investigations of social policy developments and rationalization strategies are political innovations of a third type. In this case, the real social effects ('impact') of a law or institutional service are not determined by the wording of laws and statutes ('policy output'), but instead are generated primarily as a consequence of social disputes and conflicts, for which state social policy merely establishes the location and timing of the contest, its subject matter and the 'rules of the game'. In these cases of extra-political or 'external' implementation of social policy measures state social policy in no way establishes concrete 'conditions' (for example, the level of services, specific insurance against difficult living conditions). Instead, it defines the substance of conflict and, by differentially empowering or dis-empowering the relevant social groups, biases the extent of the specific 'utility' of the institutions of social policy for these groups. An illustration of this relationship is the function of youth labour protection laws, which do not entail effective protection and security for young employees at all, but merely define the framework within which the relevant power positions of suppliers and buyers on the labour market are brought into play. Thus, the legal regulation of particular quality standards relevant to the jobs of young people can, as often happens, become a serious handicap to their job prospects, whose possible violation of the legal requirements may, in turn, be tolerated as necessary. As this example indicates, between the legal and social realities of state social policy lie power processes that direct the transformation of 'output' into 'impact'. It is not only suppliers and buyers on the labour market who are involved in these power processes; depending on the particular social policy issue being legally regulated, these processes also include administrative personnel, members of the (medical, educational, legal, etc.) professions, organized interests and the mass media. What is important to us here is only that aspect that concerns research strategy: the developments and innovations of state social policy can be conceived not as the *cause* of concrete social conditions or changes, but only as the initiator of conflictual interactions, the outcome of which is open and ambivalent precisely because it is determined by the structural relationship of power and the constellation of interests. From this observation we draw the conclusion that the task of any specifically sociological investigation of social policy cannot be the prescriptive development of 'policy designs' and 'policy outputs', but is pre-eminently that of offering an explanatory description of the conditions of socially implementing policy regulations. It is only this knowledge that supplies the foundation for the expression of political recommendations in non-normative and non-voluntaristic ways.

The considerations and hypotheses developed so far yield a schema of sociological analysis of social policy development that comprises three steps. First, it must be shown that, when the modalities of the generation, financing and distribution of social policy activities are altered, the actors in the state apparatus actually find themselves in the dilemma of reconciling 'licensed' demands or recognized needs, on the one hand, with the perceived 'exigencies' or tolerance of the capitalist economy for 'unproductive' social policy expenditures, on the other hand. The pervasive relevance of this basic problem, only hinted at here, may be tested by establishing whether the timing of the appearance, issues and effects of social policy innovations are linked to such concrete 'compatibility problems'. If this is the case, then the second step is to identify the solution strategies that—aside from the specific themes and tactics of political self-representation that tend to accompany such innovations—are applied within the administration itself to the consistency problem—a problem that is usually not designated as such. Finally, in the third step, there must be an uncovering of the 'external effects' of such solution strategies, their more or less latent benefits and burdens, the consequent increases and decreases of power, together with the pattern of conflict that strategically guides the process of socially implementing social policy innovation.

These processes of social implementation may be categorized according to whether (at one extreme) they result in the essentially undistorted attainment of the goals declared in the official 'policy outputs' of administrators and legislators, or whether (at the other extreme) they encounter more or less organized acts of obstruction by social power groups, which in turn pose fresh consistency problems within the state apparatus and which may possibly require actual repeal of the innovations. It would be of great theoretical and practical interest to be able to locate concrete social policy innovations at particular points along this scale of 'implementation consequences', as well as to identify the relations of social power and conflicts responsible for the given result. But in view of the limited theoretical and empirical foundations of current sociological policy research, it seems inevitable, for the time being at least, that such investigations will be retrospective rather than prospective; abandoning any intention of producing advice and 'improvement', their goals will be empirical-analytic rather than normative-analytic. Their aim will be that of empirically reconstructing the social 'history of effects' of past innovations in social policy.

We may thus expect sociological investigations of this type to elucidate questions like: what immediate benefits, burdens and business prospects were generated by a new programme in social policy? What categories of 'persons affected' were placed in relations of competition and/or co-operation by this programme? To what extent were those affected really able to claim advantages, or to counter or obstruct regulations disadvantageous to them? From whom and to whom can the group-specific burdens be shifted, and which social power groups are able to block the administrative implementation of the programme? The answer to such questions is not only not deducible from the texts of the relevant laws and decrees: it also cannot be known with certainty by state policy-makers themselves. The material effects of social policy innovations will be forged only in the course of their social implementation, and the ambivalence of new measures and agencies will be resolved into unambiguous 'impacts' only when the socio-structurally conditioned relations of power and conflicts have bestowed this unambiguity upon them.

The thesis that these social policy innovations with which the state apparatus responds to its own inherent consistency problem are ambivalent in principle, and the accompanying thesis that official 'outputs' are converted into factual 'impacts' outside the state, may be clarified by a few examples. Here our analysis is based on a few models of rationalization that represent, as it were, the strategic common denominators of more specific innovations in social policy. Although a more exact analysis cannot be provided here, these schemata highlight the ambivalence within the respective rationalization strategies, and therefore the need for these strategies to be completed 'outside' the state. At the very least, we may expect these schemata to challenge the widespread supposition that state social policy by itself produces such conditions as the 'quality of life', 'social security', and so on. In contrast to that supposition our thesis is that the function of 'shaping society' of state social policy is limited to the definition of the themes, times and methods of conflict and, thus, to the establishment of the political-institutional *framework*—and not the *outcome*—of processes of social power.

NOTES AND REFERENCES

1. Tennstedt, F., Zur Ökonomisierung und Verrechtlichung in der Sozialpolitik, in Mursweick, A. (ed.), *Staatliche Politik im Sozialsektor,* 1976.
2. There should be no need to insist that our critical argument against the normative approach is only *methodological,* and makes no mention whatsoever of the question of the political-moral correctness of posited ought-norms. The treatment of this question would require political argumentation.
3. In this regard, one should note Goldthorpe's reservations and objections concerning any overestimation of the analytical capacity of a functionalist explanation of social policy: 'It is hard to see how one could ever demonstrate that particular social processes are essential for the actual physical survival of a society in the same way as one can demonstrate the necessity of particular biological processes for the survival of an organism'. There is the danger of an 'explanation of a metaphysical and entirely uninformative kind to which an unthinking and uncritical functionalist approach is likely to give rise' (Goldthorpe, J., The development of social policy in England, 1800–1914, *Transactions of the Fifth World Congress of Sociology,* 4, 53ff., 1962). However, a functional analysis guided by historical materialism can take this reservation into account with comparative ease since, unlike functionalism, it proceeds from the idea that the functional imperatives that a social system 'must' follow are not simply *given* 'objectively' (for sociologists), but are registered and established in class struggles; in other words, it is *social actors* that make these imperatives problems. It therefore takes care of the question of why the given functional imperatives of a social system *'tend to be regarded as imperative'* (ibid., p. 54, emphasis in original). Goldthorpe's second methodological proviso, that functional analyses tend to unfold at a relatively high level of generalization and thereby fail to explain the choice between functionally *equivalent* solutions, would have to be reckoned with to the extent that the given alignments and processes of conflict and consensus arising from concrete actors and situations were not minimized and ignored as 'surface phenomena', but were seen—both theoretically and politically—as quite unavoidable components of processes through which societies resolve their structural problems and face the choice between equivalent systems of resolution. (See Offe, Claus, *Berufsbildungsreform, Eine Fallstudie über Reformpolitik,* Frankfurt, 1975, pp. 45ff.)
4. Marx, K., *Capital, I,* Penguin Books, Harmondsworth, 1976, p. 899.
5. Böhle and Sauer, Intensivierung der Arbeit und staatliche Sozialpolitik, *Leviathan,* 3, 64, 1975.
6. See, for example, Heinsohn, G. and Knieper, R., *Theorie des Familienrechts,* Frankfurt, 1975.
7. This conceptual framework avoids both the formalism criticized earlier and the complementary defect that seems evident in the normative and 'critical' positions. Instead, the foundation of this conceptual framework is shaped by *definite structural problems,* the reality of which then becomes evident whenever, for any reason, there is a failure of the mechanisms whose function is to deal with these problems—and therewith make them imperceptible *as* structural problems.
8. Offe, Claus, *Berufsbildungsreform, Eine Fallstudie über Reformpolitik,* Frankfurt, 1975.
9. Cf. Standfest, E., Die Kostenentwicklung in der Socialen Sicherung, *WSI-Mitteilungen,* 29, 7, 396, 1976. In view of such innovations as parliamentary systems and social democratic

parties, it is difficult to ignore the problem of 'optimal' (for capitalist social structures) responsiveness by regarding it as solved once and for all. In other words, the possibility of an infringement of functional harmony, and therefore of the presumed 'optimalness', must always be reckoned with, either in the direction of a curtailment of the political rights of the organizations of the working class or of an enlargement of these rights to the point where they are no longer compatible with the organizational form of wage-labour. The political system's supports for either *free* wage-labour or (as the case may be) for free *wage-labour* would thereupon crumble.

10. Cf. Böhle and Sauer, Intensivierung der Arbeit und staatliche Sozialpolitik, loc. cit.
11. Funke, R. *et al.*, Theoretische Problemskizze für eine Untersuchung der Entwicklungstendenzen im Bereich staatlicher Socialpolitik, Manuscript, Max-Planck-Institut, 1976, p. 11 and *passim.*
12. See, for example, Müller, W. and Neusüss, C., The illusion of state socialism and the contradiction between wage labour and capital, *Telos*, **25**, 13–90, Fall 1975.
13. Thus, for example, Talos, E. Zu den Anfängen in der Sozialpolitik, *Österreichische Zeitschrift für Politikwissenschaft*, **2**, 151, 1976:
 'The necessity of state action (in the legislative domain concerning the protection of labour and security) is doubly based:
 —on the development of the workers' movement ... which constitutes a threat to social and political relations alike;
 —on the danger to the physical existence of workers generated by an unrestricted valorization of labour power. The interest in the maintenance of the valorization of capital compels measures that serve to preserve the existence of workers through guaranteeing their reproduction possibilities.' 'The securing of labour power's reproduction possibilities objectively serves the self-interests of capital' both because of the consequent maintenance of the physical subsistence of labour capacities and also because of the consequent 'appeasement and integration of social contradictions' (ibid., p. 157). Similarly, Funke *et al.*, Theoretische Problemskizze, pp. 23–24: through 'innovation thrusts in state social policy ... the social integration of workers, which had been temporarily endangered, is guaranteed anew (!).... This is the price of social innovations.' In such constructions, of course, it remains mysterious how the process of policy formation, which is characterized on the level of *action* by 'conflicts between social classes' and by a 'plethora of political controversies' (Talos, Zu den Anfängen in der Sozialpolitik, p. 146), is to lead to results whose *objective function* is to establish, as perfectly as possible, a class harmony. It must at least be explained why this insight has not been communicated to the political organizations of the ruling class, which instead continue to suspect and combat every rise in pensions as creeping socialism, etc. In our view, this is a hyperfunctionalist (or even vulgar Hegelian) blind alley that resembles the maxim, 'Whatever was necessary' (cf. Goldthorpe, The development of social policy in England, 1800–1914, *op. cit.*, p. 56).
14. Lockwood, C., *The Blackcoated Worker*, Allen & Unwin, London, 1958.
15. In this respect, we would *in general* defend an explanatory model of processes of social policy innovation which Funke, R., Zur sozialpolitischen Entwicklung in der Bundesrepublik, Manuscript, Max-Planck-Institut, Starnberg, 1976, p. 14, emphasizes as only a *particular* feature of the social policy documented in the 1976 *Sozialbericht* (Bonn, Ministry of Labour and Social Affairs): 'At the centre of interest ... stand not new tasks but the preservation of the status quo within the output and financing systems of social policy.'

SECTION 3

The Collapse of Consensus?

6

Changing Relations between Centre and Locality in Education

STEWART RANSON

I

Education has perhaps been the most complex and burdened of services. As the keystone of public policy-making and social reform in the postwar period, education has been expected to fuel economic growth, facilitate equality of opportunity and afford some social justice to the deprived: to educate has been to bring a new world out of the old. To accomplish this burdensome collective vision, education has had to manage the most complex network of relationships which cuts across communities, services, authorities and levels of government. A rising birth-rate, economic growth and political will coalesced in the expansion of the education service during the 1960s and early 1970s. But education now occupies a changed and more fragmented world: the confluence of forces has altered. Demographic and economic contraction, eroded beliefs about the contributions which education can make and the disquiet of parents and politicians have combined to produce a more severe and pessimistic context for education. This changing context is having enormous implications for the management of the service. Its vision and objectives are being questioned and simplified, while the complex, often ambiguous, traditional framework of decision-making—with its assumptions about *who* should be involved, *whose* values should count, *how* decisions should be arrived at—is being clarified, concentrated and centralized: in short, the traditional balance of autonomy, power and accountability in education is being redefined.[1]

Source: From *Local Government Studies*, Vol. 6, No. 6, 1980, published by Charles Knight.

II

Education is described conventionally as a national service locally administered. Even if those general assumptions are acknowledged, the description rather oversimplifies administrative and political relationships in the service. Yet it is arguable, for example, that the service is complex and ambivalent enough to allow a teasing but plausible antithesis which proposes that education is more accurately described as a local school service occasionally administered from differential central positions such as the LEA and the DES (John Stewart likes to provoke this argument). The education service thus incorporates much contradiction and ambiguity (cf. Glatter, 1979).

There is an important sense in which these ambiguities were endemic to the 1944 Education Act which intentionally created a division of powers and responsibilities between 'partners' to the service. The centre was to be given very general duties and responsibilities: 'to promote the education of the people of England and Wales and the progressive development of institutions devoted to that purpose and to secure the effective execution by local authorities under his control and direction'. But the Act offered the centre only very specific powers to carry out such broad responsibilities: for example, to approve the establishment, closure or reorganization of individual institutions, to approve the building programme of LEAs, to settle disputes between LEAs, and between LEAs and school managers or governors, to arbitrate between LEAs and parents over admissions, to exercise default powers if the other partners have acted 'unreasonably', and so on. The Local Education Authorities were charged, for example, with providing schools 'of sufficient number, character and equipment' and with the control of the 'secular instruction' in those schools. The managers and governors of schools would be given responsibilities of general oversight. The 1944 Act, therefore, created 'a complex web of interdependent relationships among the manifold participants' (Weaver, 1976). The distribution of responsibilities in practice worked out rather more schematically than all this suggests, with the centre acting as broad policy promoter and controller of overall resource volume and distribution. The LEA built, staffed and maintained institutions, while the curriculum and teaching methods remained largely under the control of the teaching profession in schools. The upshot is what Professor Briault (1976) chooses to call a distributed system of decision-taking and responsibility so as to form essentially a triangle of tension, of checks and balances.

Although in the literature some consensus may surround the notion of a distributed system of duties and responsibilities there remains more disagreement over the extent to which we may attribute power and influence between the partners. Fowler and his colleagues (1973) talk of a diffuse, devolved system, while Vernon Bogdanor suggests that we cannot sensibly identify a 'controlling voice':

the 'efficient secret' of the system, to adapt Bagehot, was that no *one* individual participant should enjoy a monopoly of power in the decision-making process. Power over the distribution of resources, over the organisation and content of education was to be diffused amongst the different elements and no one of them was to be given a controlling voice (Bogdanor, 1979).

Recent Ministers at the DES have concluded that their powers were very much circumscribed (see Weaver, 1979): thus Shirley Williams believed that 'there isn't much direct power in the hands of the Secretary of State except in a number of rather quirky fields; there is (however) a lot of indirect influence'; Gerald Fowler as Minister of State for Education agreed that Ministerial power was constrained but that influence could create or change a 'climate of opinion'.

Some authors may be unwilling to generalize about the overall relative powers of the education partners but suggest that it makes more sense to pinpoint influence in relation to specific controls available or in relation to the kind of educational task (for example, extending opportunity, shaping curricula, distributing resources, etc.) that is being discussed. Sir Toby Weaver (1979) reserves judgement on attributing a dominating influence but argues that it is 'in the sphere of individual and social *opportunity* that the Secretary of State's control over the education system, through "provision" and "access", may be said to be at its greatest', while over the *curriculum* the power of the teachers is at its greatest and that of the Secretary of State at its most limited. The influence of the centre upon *resources* 'remains one of the strongest controls', but influence on *organization* is circumscribed allowing LEAs considerable scope and initiative.

A number of writers have, however, been more prepared to chance generalization. Some have characterised an essential role or function for the centre and therefore, by implication, the extent of control. Griffith (1966) in his classic study produced a classification of central government departments which distinguished between *laissez-faire* departments (e.g. the old Ministry of Health), *'regulatory'* departments (e.g. the Home Office) and *'promotional'* departments such as the DES. Regan (1977) confirms this characterization of the centre in education and therefore its assumption that the centre is the strongest partner standing in a relation of deep involvement to the service although not in a relation of hierarchy or dictatorial determination. Other commentators are prepared to be more direct about the powers of the centre within the partnership. Saran (1973) ascribes to the DES various fatherly roles, 'advising, moderating, pleading, cautioning and ultimately wielding the big stick of refusing its approval to any proposals from the LEA which offend against national policy as interpreted by the Ministry'. Kogan (1975) concluded that the only certainty in the complex structures of educational policy-making was that 'the DES wields determinant authority and great power'. Previously, in 1974, a small team of investigators from the OECD (Organization for Economic Co-operation and Development) were appointed by the DES to review educational planning in England and Wales and concluded that 'although the powers of government with regard to educational planning are formally limited ... the central Department of Education and Science is undoubtedly the most powerful single force in determining the direction and tempo of educational development' (OECD, 1975).

This paper wishes to take the argument a stage further and suggest that it is appropriate to identify partners who have been more powerful in a complex educational system but that the balance of influence and power has varied over time. The attribution of dominance requires to be located historically. The paper will argue that three approximate periods of dominant influence can be identified since the Second World War: an early post-war period until the mid-fifties specifies a period of central dominance; a middle post-war period until the early seventies identifies a period of local dominance; while the present period witnesses a gradual acceleration towards the restoration of central control. Each period will be discussed in turn.

EARLY POSTWAR PERIOD[2]

In the early postwar years it is arguable that the Ministry of Education was clearly the dominant partner. This can be supported by an interpretive account of the 1944 Act which it is suggested intended to give the Minister *directive* powers. This interpretation is grounded not in a reading of section 1 alone (which as we have already seen laid on the Minister the duty 'to secure the effective execution by local authorities under his *control and direction* of the national policy...') but in association with sections 11–13 and section 100:

- Section 11 required every LEA to produce a development plan for the whole LEA,
- Section 12 enshrined the plan in a development order which the LEA had to follow and from which it could not depart,
- Section 13 specified how an LEA could tinker with its system (clearly there would have to be occasional changes) by submitting proposals to the Minister,
- Section 100 stated that the Minister would pay grant to LEAs directly in the form of specific grants.

The 1944 Act 'was aimed at radical change' (Halsey *et al.*, 1980). Sections 11 and 12 were only meant to last a time, but they were about transforming secondary education. We talk glibly about secondary education before the war, but the 1944 Act through these sections was the revolutionary change to introduce secondary education. Sections 13 and 100 were further key directive controls. Those who drafted the Act, which was to be the instrument of these radical changes, clearly saw the Minister as absolutely central to the educational system and gave him important powers to direct the other partners.

Things did not quite work out as the drafters of the Act intended. A number of LEAs produced a development plan, but not a single development order was ever made. The reason lay in the rapidity of economic and social change. The gap between the world as conceived by the framers of the Act and the world as it was (early postwar austerity, sluggish growth, substantially expanding birth rate) began to grow. The world was too fluid, too under-resourced, to allow the plans any *overall* relevance. For some years, however, this lacuna between plans and reality did not undermine the power and influence of the centre in education. The Department continued to use the plans to monitor in some detail the development of individual LEAs, while the control of recurrent education expenditure of particular authorities through the specific education grant enabled officials of the Department to scrutinize LEA expenditure in detail and disallow particular items for grant purposes if necessary. Moreover, the Minister gave detailed advice through administrative circulars and issued elaborate codes of guidance.

This strong lead from the centre was supported by two further factors. Firstly, a broad consensus amongst the partners on education policy and, secondly, the strong central leadership of the two main other partners. Bogdanor (1979) expresses the process of elite determination nicely:

> this process of elite accommodation reached its apogee during the post-war period when, so it was believed, many policy decisions in education were taken over lunch at the National Liberal Club by a troika consisting of Sir William Alexander, secretary of the Association of Education Committees, Sir Ronald Gould, the general Secretary of the National Union of Teachers, and the Permanent Secretary of the Department of Education. If these three agreed on some item of educational policy, it would more often than not, be implemented.

MIDDLE POSTWAR PERIOD

The balance of power began to shift as the years passed and the local authorities gained power at the expense of the centre. In 1958 the grant funding arrangements changed with the introduction of General Grant (later to be superseded by Rate Support Grant (RSG)) thus ending the close scrutiny by the Department of LEA recurrent expenditure. In the face of opposition from the local authorities and their associations, the centre also ceded detailed control of capital expenditure. Guidance, too, in the form of circulars and administrative memoranda, became less detailed.

The shift in the balance was a gradual process, however. Studies (for example, Davies, 1968; Byrne, 1974; Pyle, 1976) began to show that however concerned the centre may have been to produce an equal distribution of resources so as to ensure 'a national service', there was enormous scope for LEA autonomy and discretion:

> not only on matters of style—for example, type of secondary education provided, the content of the curriculum and the age of transfer from primary ... but also in terms of the

amount of resources used in the education service, for example, teaching staff, age and standard of buildings, equipment and facilities (Pyle, 1976).

It is, however, in studies of comprehensive secondary reorganization that the shifting balance of power has become clearly apparent (cf. Saran, 1973; David, 1977; Pattison, 1980; James, 1980). Reorganization has illustrated a number of key issues about the centre-local relationship. Firstly, that important policy initiatives are often made by local rather than central government:

> in fact, a number of LEAs had either reorganised or were seriously considering doing so well before central government was committed to such a course of action. Indeed until 1965 the role of central government whether Labour or Conservative controlled, was usually to inhibit and delay local initiative in this area... When national government introduced its own plans in the mid-sixties it drew heavily on the experience of those authorities (James, 1980).

The Department, therefore, may be seen not so much as a policy-maker as a promoter and catalyst of policies around which there is a growing consensus. Thus government did not legislate for comprehensivization but rather issued a circular (the famous 10/65) which, it believed, rested on a bedrock of common agreement: government required to do no more than encourage and exhort. The role of delayed-promotion-given-consent may be forced upon the centre given the means available to it—section 13. This provision is the statutory means for controlling the change of structure or character of schools, but as such it is a statutory provision which allows the Secretary of State the powers of objection rather than initiation. *When* LEAs wish to initiate change they publish notices of their intentions allowing parents and the centre to object. From the point of view of the Minister, section 13 is an essentially negative instrument: the centre's contribution must await local initiative. Circulars 10/65, requesting LEAs to submit full plans for reorganization, and 10/66, asserting that building project funds would be reserved for plans compatible with comprehensivization, both added weight to the centre. But initiative still lay with the LEAs, and, at times, the DES was relieved:

> we were working flat out at the DES; circular 10/65 asked for plans, but we had all the reorganization work we could cope with until the seventies to complete the task. Time, limited organizational manpower, scarce financial resources meant that the world could not be changed overnight.[3]

The second important feature of the centre-local relationship in this period which reorganization illustrates is that LEAs were able to negotiate considerable discretion to suit local circumstances. David (1977) concluded from her study of reorganization that although the DES has the powers to set the value framework, to control resources and monitor LEA activity—and takes these powers seriously—it did not operate with any general guidelines or rules of procedure:

> it certainly did not have a notion of the appropriate planning process when the changes investigated were mooted and it was struggling to define its position throughout. In fact the

DES operated on the basis of *discretion*. Its civil servants chose by professional judgment which LEAs to encourage or inhibit.

LEAs thus had considerable opportunity to exploit a vague situation. Saran (1973) and James (1980) confirm that LEAs were able to bargain discretion for themselves:

> considerable leeway was allowed local authorities in drawing up their plans and the DES was throughout very conscious of local conditions and resources (James, 1980).

Comprehensive reorganization, therefore, illustrates in centre-local relations the locus of policy initiative, sources of local discretion and, thirdly, the ability of the LEA to win out in a test of power—that is, to achieve objectives in the face of opposition and resistance. Comprehensivization began on a wave of consensus, but the process began to accumulate political opposition. Pattison's (1980) study of conflict between the DES and the London Borough of Sutton describes the limitations of central control in the face of a determined LEA:

> in this study the 'softer' control mechanisms, such as persuasion through circulars or bargaining over new buildings, appear to be useful as long as central government's initiatives coincide with the consensus within the issue network. Cooperation and compliance is also aided when the multiplier effect is operating in the local government system, which in turn is more likely if the reform originated at the local level. However, if local opposition develops these softer controls may be turned to the lower tiers' advantage. When overt conflict is produced and the 'tougher' central controls such as legislation and financial penalties are contemplated, limitations on their use and effectiveness become apparent. Coercive measures are probably sufficient to block change—for example the refusal to approve changes to schools or to provide money for alteration to buildings—but in a competitive central government.

An election prevented the Sutton conflict reaching the courts, but the cases of Tameside and Enfield illustrate the ability of an LEA (in the case of the former authority) and a local action group (in the case of the latter authority) to frustrate the intentions of the Secretary of State in the courts and win (cf. Kogan, 1978; Griffith, 1977). In short, the comprehensivization experience pinpointed the essential weakness of the centre when confronted with resolute opposition.

The financial and educational changes we have discussed demonstrate the diminishing power of the centre. A number of other, broadly political, factors contributed to the process over time. First, the teacher unions became more militant in pursuit of their professional claims (cf. Coates, 1972); second, the rapid growth of political organization and, occasionally, of corporate management in many local authorities contributed to an increase in the centralization and concentration of decision making so that the dialogue that central departments, such as the DES, had with local services came increasingly to be mediated by the local authority in general at a political and an official level; third, the voice of the consumer came to be articulated more clearly and vociferously and was represented in the Taylor Committee's considerations upon an enlarged role for parents and community on governing bodies. The body politic of education in particular and local government in general became more organized and aggressive in pursuit of sectional claims. But, at the same time, it became more fragmented and therefore more difficult for the centre to connect with and control.

LATE POSTWAR PERIOD

The balance of power between the partners in education had at the end of the sixties and early seventies swung very much towards the local authorities and to heads and teachers in schools (for whom the Schools Council, the influential Plowden Report and the CSE exam had enhanced professional control of curriculum and assessment). But the context was beginning to change. The economy was moving into recession, the political climate was sharpening, and the scrutiny of public expenditure in general and education's performance in particular was growing. With tighter RSG settlements and reduced capital programmes, the DES could exert even less influence and had limited success in reinforcing its policy initiatives such as in-service training. The centre, bereft of funds and the necessary statutory instruments, had become manifestly unable to secure policy implementation through persuasion alone. The Secretary of State and the DES moved to arrest the decline in its influence and reassert control.

Initiatives begun in 1975 by the Secretary of State and the Department (the *Yellow Book*, 1976) to review standards and the curriculum in education were given Prime Ministerial support in a speech at Ruskin College, Oxford, in October of 1976. Lawton (1980) charts these developments which culminated in the Green Paper, *Education in Schools* (1977) and points to some of the underlying themes: that education is a national service which must attend to the legitimate needs of the world of work, and, therefore, that the Secretary of State in order to ensure such accountability had a central responsibility for standards and the curriculum. A senior civil servant has commented[4] that 'education is a national service (it is the first thing we teach our Secretary of State) and there are therefore legitimate concerns about education which are too great to allow to continue the extent of local control and discretion. The other partners must accept the recent centralizing initiatives because the Secretary of State is the public embodiment of national expectations of central control and accountability.' Patricia Broadfoot (Broadfoot, 1979) reviews central initiatives in assessment—for example, the APU and recommendations for a new examination at 16+—and interventions in the curriculum—for example, circular 14/77, *A Framework for the Curriculum*—and concludes that the centre 'has been more or less consciously arrogating to itself more and more responsibility for the direction of the education service'.

Teachers, therefore, are beginning to lose some of their traditional professional control of the 'secret garden' of the curriculum. But other areas of professional autonomy are equally under challenge. Appointments, conditions of service, promotions, deployment, in-service training, etc., which have been strongly influenced by the teaching profession in schools, are increasingly subject to the determination of LEA managers. In the face of falling rolls and economic contraction, the management of the teaching profession has become one of the service's critical problems. The teachers may have to come to terms with altered career expectations, role definitions, and professional status, but if LEAs are to plan educational provision rationally within their areas then a much more interventionist role in the planning, deployment and training of the teaching force is to be expected.

An overview of the curriculum, assessment and the service's key professionals seems to indicate a distinct attempt to shift the balance towards the centre. This movement towards the restoration of central control will be given a powerful and perhaps conclusive thrust if the key provisions in the Local Government Bill—especially the new Block Grant—become law. The radical implications of the block grant arise from the proposed power for the centre to fix for each authority a 'standard expenditure' (now called 'grant related expenditure') and then to determine its share of the total grant available according to the extent to which its actual expenditure is related to standard expenditure.

Other implications of the block grant system may give LEAs more cause for concern. It may be possible for the Secretary of State and the DES to make the link between an authority's grant share and actual expenditure a basis for influencing more directly an LEA's pattern of expenditure. This might involve the centre in an ongoing dialogue with LEAs about the broad thrust of their educational policies. The new system, therefore, may incorporate a potential for the centre obtaining more information about, and thus influence over, the policies of individual LEAs. Should this occur over time it would indicate a major shift in the balance of power in the 'partnership'. Many commentators believe such a centralizing thrust to be inherent in the new machinery and have been explicit and vociferous in condemning the new Bill. Professor Stewart (1980) argues that the block grant will be a significant change because it indicates the centre's shift in concern from the general to the particular: local authorities will increasingly be judged by national standards and the centre will acquire powers of intervention to correct deviations:

> Central government has moved from a concern with the aggregate level of local government expenditure to a concern with what happens in a particular authority in a process—the budgetary process—which is the heart of the local political process. The change of principle is emphasized by the fact that central government is taking the power to penalize individual authorities in accordance with the relationship between actual expenditure and standard expenditure (Stewart, 1980).

III

The previous section of this paper has provided an historical account of changes in the relationships between partners to the education service. But how is such an account to be understood and interpreted? This paper wishes to argue that an adequate interpretation of such changes requires us to undertake theoretical rather than merely descriptive work so that we can *explain why* events have taken the course that they have. Narrative without explanation is not vacuous (cf. Runciman, 1972) but necessarily incomplete. Yet, with some notable exceptions, much of the literature in educational administration as in public administration generally (cf. Greenwood *et al.*, 1980; and Dunleavy, 1980 for critical comments) eschews analytical work and is preoccupied instead with description of the legal and administrative framework within which services must operate, or with empirical accounts of the way services may vary. The study of public sector services and institutions is an undernourished area theoretically. This section wishes to begin to outline a theoretical framework that will account for changes in centre-local relations in education.

What we can expect from theory is the discovery of an underlying pattern which has previously been inaccessible to everyday experience and which therefore illuminates the relations of causal dependence between institutions, activities and events in ways which will allow us to explain why such and such has occurred. Theory exposes the social mechanisms which account for events (cf. MacIntyre, 1969, 1971; Keat and Urry, 1975). Central to such activity is abstract, conceptual analysis isolating the crucial dimensions and constituents of the social arrangements that we wish to explain. This may simplify some of the rich description contained in narrative but it has the advantage of highlighting central connections and interdependencies: it makes explicit the crucial axes around which the narrative revolves (cf. Gellner, 1974).

What methodological criteria identify an adequate theory? A cogent theory, it is argued, should be adequate at the levels of meaning and causality (cf. Weber, 1948) so as to embrace three integrated modes of analysis: phenomenological, comparative, and temporal.[5] Adequacy at the level of meaning presupposes certain *phenomenological* procedures which provide an interpretive account of the meanings that actors create to make sense of their worlds. By focusing upon the ways actors reflexively monitor their experience and thus remake and recreate that experience, this mode of analysis illuminates the agency that lies behind social arrangements. Yet if an adequate explanation is to be developed we must break with this level of experience to begin an analysis that will involve a more detached abstraction and systematization of events in order to reveal underlying regularities and connections of which actors may be unaware. This requires a *comparative* analysis of the contextual constraints upon institutional decision-makers and so an examination of, for example, the regularities that derive from the environment.

If, however, we are to establish clearly the degree to which actors in fact construct their worlds, if we are to provide a causal explanation that goes beyond statistical uniformities, we must conserve but transcend both previous levels of analysis and lock our explanation into a *temporal* mode which focuses on the historical development of structures. The derived propositions at this level are neither day-to-day negotiated practices, nor reified uniformities, but the discovery through time of underlying structures of social relationships whose constitutive political processes account for the structural relationships that we wish to explain (cf. Bourdieu, 1971, 1977; Giddens, 1976, 1979).

With such criteria in mind we can evaluate two of the main theoretical frameworks that can be advanced to explain changes in relations between the education partners since the Second World War: the resource dependency theory and the neo-systems theory. The first constructs an explanation around the agency of the key actors in a social network, while the second identifies the key functional problems and dilemmas of the social system as the central explanatory axis.

EXCHANGE, POWER AND ACTORS

This theory conceives the relations between levels of government as forming a complex network of institutions, organizations, agencies and interest groups. These 'actors' live in an environment of uncertainty produced by the scarcity of resources necessary to ensure survival. They can pursue their interests and acquire the strategic resources necessary for managing uncertainty only by escaping or creating dependencies amongst the other actors. Autonomy and power provide the critical bargaining levers to manipulate exchange relationships in the network. The powerful actor can win more resources and so ensure the delivery of its services, implement its policies as well as protect and extend the boundaries of its influence and domination.

The operation of the intergovernmental network is shaped by the pattern of resource ownership and the structure of dependencies. Resources are defined broadly (often too broadly) as: *finance*—capital, revenue, manpower; *authority*—hierarchical position, political access, legitimation, status; and *work and services*—tasks, expertise, information, markets, etc. To monopolize the ownership of such critical resources is to create dependencies, exact compliance and accrue power. Emerson (1962) defined dependence (and thus potential power) as the commitment to goals which are mediated by limited others: 'the dependence of actor A upon B is (1) directly proportional to A's *motivational investment* in goals mediated by B, and (2) inversely proportional to the *availability* of these goals to A outside the A–B relationship'. The potential power of A over B is actualized if A can overcome B's potential resistance. Blau (1964) sought to articulate further the conditions which actors must meet if they are to maximize autonomy and bargaining power in an exchange relationship. First, possess strategic resources which others may desire; second, ensure that these resources are scarce and unavailable elsewhere; third, have the capacity to use coercive sanctions if necessary; and, lastly, be indifferent to the resources possessed by other actors. A further qualification to the theory has been added by others (cf. Mindlin and Aldrich, 1975; Salancik, 1979) to the effect that dependency may be a characteristic of a relationship which lies latent until one of the parties seeks to exert pressure and to impose demands.

This theoretical model of exchange and power (known as the resource dependency theory) has acquired much analytical status and leverage in the study of organizations and inter-organizational relations (cf. Aldrich, 1976, 1979; Benson, 1975; Aiken and Hage, 1963; Pfeffer and Salancik, 1978). It derives primarily from American studies into the problems of achieving coordination amongst social welfare organizations, employment service agencies, community organizations, etc. But the theoretical developments in the model have allowed greater empirical range, particularly into intergovernmental relations (cf. Crozier and Thoenig, 1976; Hanf and Scharpf, 1978). The resource dependency model has, for example, been adopted by the SSRC to form a framework for a series of studies they have commissioned to examine relations between central and local government (cf. Rhodes, 1979; Jones, 1980; Hinings, 1980). The fruit of that model will be evaluated in due course but the theory already has one excellent and relevant application in the monumental comparative study of Margaret Archer (*Social Origins of Educational Systems*, 1979).

The framework can be used to account for the changes that have been described earlier in centre-local relations in education since the war. The local parties to the partnership were able to expand their power and discretion because they monopolized the ownership of critical resources that were unavailable elsewhere while possessing the sanctions necessary to reinforce such scarcity. The teachers were the sole owners of the complex professional expertise required to give effect to a curriculum designed to fulfil diverse individual needs. To underpin this critical resource the teachers organized, inserted themselves at all levels of the decision-making process and increasingly undertook militant sanctions that were effective in winning concessions to economic and professional goals (Coates, 1972; Locke, 1974). The LEAs, for their part, were able to consolidate and expand their area of discretion by possessing the legal resource of 'gatekeeper' to policy implementation as well as possessing alternative sources of finance (in many cases) should the centre take retributive action. The LEA could, if it chose, remain indifferent to the values of a nationally defined partnership and, if necessary, impose its own sanctions on government: delay central initiatives, deny information and, ultimately, claim redress in the courts. When necessary the teachers and the LEAs, as Archer (1979) nicely describes, exchanged alliances to reinforce localist causes and frustrate the centre: 'the NUT and the Association of Education Committees (AEC) played a mutually supportive role in protecting their extensive autonomous powers of decision-making'. The movement to extend parental participation can also be interpreted in resource dependency terms: the key resource of legitimate membership of the partnership (reinforced by Plowden) was supported by effective organization [for example, Campaign for the Advancement of State Education (CASE), Advisory Centre for Education (ACE), National Association of Governors and Managers (NAGM)] and typical pressure group tactics and sanctions. The response of the Secretary of State and the DES to such aggrandisement of disparate local powers conforms to the model. The centre's privileged access to law-making and the control of financial resources—using the former to reinforce the latter in the case of the Local Government Bill and the block grant—will finally ensure the reluctant compliance of hostile local authorities: he who pays the piper will call the tune. The (alternative) resources possessed by local authorities are therefore undermined, while in the case of teachers the centre begins to articulate goals for the system (simpler purposes and basic skills) which may enable it to be indifferent to complex professional expertise.

Here is a plausible theoretical framework which will account for the changes in centre-local relations in education that we are searching to explain. Actors who monopolize resources which are critical to the network accrue power, ensure the compliance of others and survive. In terms of the criteria outlined at the beginning of the section to identify theoretical adequacy, the resource dependency theory goes some way to meeting them: it is adequate at the level of meaning—working out from the interpretive and strategic activity of actors—it specifies an abstract comparative model and, in the hands of a few (notably Archer), possesses an historical dimension. An underlying social mechanism of competitive self-interest constrained by power relations has been exposed in a way which lends order to, and makes causal sense of, complex everyday experience.

Yet, there are deficiencies in such a theoretical framework; a number of its assumptions are problematic. The first is the *assumption about the nature of the actors*. The framework is shaped by its cultural source: American studies of coordination problems amongst competing welfare agencies, etc. The organizations being studied were relatively equal. Such assumptions are inappropriate when the focus becomes the relationships between the state and other organizations: the relationship is different in kind. Secondly, a different understanding of the actors involved would undermine the *assumptions of exchange*. All actors, it is supposed, have the possibility of renegotiating their position with a little shrewd politicking. Such assumptions will not do. Transactions with the state are by definition likely to be unequal and as a last resort it will usually find the powers and resources to win most games. Thirdly, the *assumptions about the notion of meaning* are arguable. The orientations of actors as defined solely by sectional interests and the purposive pursuit of resources and autonomy is too limiting. Values and beliefs (cf. Evetts, 1973; Taylor, 1978; Kogan and Becher, 1980) are not subordinate epiphenomena and may tie the network of actors together in a domain consensus, thus undermining the basic assumption in this model of competitive, instrumental rationality. Finally, the *assumptions about the environment* are equally limiting theoretically. The significant environment, so the argument goes, is only made up of other 'organized' actors but this may be begging the question as to what are the significant features of the environment: what of deeper seated functional dilemmas surrounding, for example, the economy, or what of the significance of more amorphous environmental actors—the social class interests that lie behind 'the actors' we have considered?

The resource dependency theory is a plausible theoretical framework. But the social mechanisms it unearths are situated quite close to the surface. The analysis it reveals of purposively interested actors is close to our experience. The explanation is close to being a good story. This theoretical account may require supplementing and rounding out, if not recasting.

ECONOMY, POLITY AND SYSTEMS

This theoretical framework overcomes some of the deficiencies of the previous model by raising the level of analytical abstraction and mapping the social arrangements we wish to explain as a complex system. Rather than focusing upon actors, this theoretical model identifies fundamental functional problems and dilemmas as the dynamic of all social systems. The traditional systems theory invited us to examine the ways differentiated subsystems mutually reinforced each other so as to maintain the system and favour stability. Contemporary models drop some of these assumptions while retaining the basic framework: the system will survive to the extent that the constituent parts are systematically oriented to maintaining and supporting the most important subsystem—the economic infrastructure. But in place of stability and equilibrium, this interpretation typically identifies contradictions between the parts and inconsistencies in the extent to which they satisfy the functional prerequisites of the economic infrastructures: such contradictions tend to favour conflict and change.

With the deepening economic crises of the 1970s the State (of this and other countries) has become increasingly preoccupied with re-examining the bases of economy-polity-social system relationships searching to clarify and redefine points of control. Habermas (1976) has argued that such crises create 'steering problems' for social systems if they are to maintain control and integration. To protect and restore system integration the state responds by progressively extending its boundaries, its tentacles of political leverage, into the economic and social subsystems. The extension of steering capacity, however, presupposes the emergence of new modes of rationality, 'new technically utilizable knowledge about subsystems' and their operation.

A number of writers have indicated what the new modes of rationality might look like. Blau and Schoenherr (1971) suggest that new forms of power are emerging which rely less on the exercise of command and more on indirect forms of control—such as the use of technically efficient rules and procedures. Offe (1975) extends the argument. The state, in order to maintain its functions of system integration, is increasingly driven to develop new forms of intervention. The minimalist role of central control of overall aggregate resources is increasingly inadequate and the state is constrained to adopt a productive mode to sustain and develop the system's economic infrastructure, progressively intervening in 'education, skills, technological change, control over raw materials, health, transportation, housing, the structure of cities, physical environment, energy and communication services'. What is significant, however, is less the matter of new fields of intervention than the mode of intervention—that is the decision rules the state adopts to operate in this new situation. The traditional decision rules of the state, adequate for the purposes of legislating the system's broad inputs and boundary rules, become inappropriate and have to be replaced by decision rules which determine policy formation itself. This new mode of intervention calls 'for stricter controls of objectives, outputs and outcomes by such techniques as program budgeting, cost-benefit analysis and social indicators'. To ensure system maintenance and the development of infrastructures the state is driven into progressively detailed planning of service activities.

Both Blau and Schoenherr and Offe are aware that what is crucial for an understanding of the new state systems of policy planning is their form and mode rather than any particular content of policy. Here they do no more than extend Weber's (1968) formulation of contemporary rationality. Specifically modern rationality, he argued, denoted not only means-end instrumentality but, more importantly, the pervasive application of formally abstract procedures based upon increasingly specialized and technical concepts. The convergence of purposive and formal rationality ensured maximum precision, calculability and control of decision processes. Implicit in the rules were the ends to be pursued and the interests served. Offe is particularly articulate on the matter:

> the formal rules that give structure and continuity to the operation of the state apparatus are not merely instrumental procedures designed to carry out or implement political goals or to solve social problems. They do determine themselves, in a hidden and unexplicit way, what potential goals are and what problems have the chance to come up on the agenda of the political system. Thus it is not only true that the emergence of a social problem puts into motion the procedural dynamics of policy formation, program design and implementation

but, also, conversely, the institutionalized formal mode of operation of political institutions determines what potential issues are, how they are defined, what solutions are proposed, and so on (Offe, 1975).

Confronted by problems of control and integration, the state develops new policy planning processes as modes of rationality that are particularly appropriate to system strains and contradictions yet may work to reproduce them as the erosion of subsystem autonomy leads them towards conflict.

We may be witnessing the way the education subsystem may be conforming to such an analysis. Its place in social systems and in relation to the infrastructures of economy and work has always been an ambiguous one and is the focus of an increasing literature. Education has always been shaped by ambivalent purposes seeking to fulfil the complex needs of individuals as well as striving to fulfil social functions of control and reproduction—shaping the skills and dispositions which the system requires. Bourdieu and Passeron (1977) argue that education, though possessing relative independence from the economy, plays a critical role in reproducing the 'cultural capital' necessary for maintaining the structure and relations of the economic system. Bernstein (1973) equally does not see any necessary subordination of education to the requirements of production, but suggests that the mode of production is anterior to the mode of education and that the stronger the systemic relations between the two the stronger the grip of the modes of production on the codes of education. Dale (1980) believes that we may be witnessing an attempt of the state increasingly to articulate such systemic relations, to centralize control and to effect a qualitative change in the modes of control in the ways which Offe was indicating above.

The systems analysis we are developing here invites us to explain the state's reappropriation of control in education as a concerted attempt to reintegrate subsystems and ensure the integrity of infrastructure. Contributions to this discussion have charted the manifold ways the centre is both increasing its intervention and changing the mode of its intervention, progressively mapping educational arrangements with formal and technical procedures. The new financial systems of the block grant will permit detailed intervention in local budgets and therefore policy making and, in other areas, we are witnessing a resurrection of technocratic planning (cf. Williams, 1979) to cope with the problematic of contraction: the DES is asking management consultants to produce technical unit-cost manuals to help LEAs manage falling rolls, close schools and influence policy on provision for the 16–19 age group. Rules, codes and manuals will also increasingly circumscribe the teachers and thus the management of a profession. Subtle changes in curriculum, pedagogy and assessment will produce the required shift in cultural capital necessary to restore education to a primary functional role in a time of crisis.

The systems theoretical framework of economy and polity provides a plausible account of the changes in educational relations that we are searching to explain. It has the advantage of locating the analysis at a deeper level of functional dilemmas for social systems, as well as meeting the criteria of comparative and temporal dimensions to satisfy notions of theoretical adequacy. Yet this theory's manifest inadequacy lies at the level of meaning: the framework is bereft of actors whose purposive agency would make sense of contradictions and conflicts. The theory seems inherently mechanistic and deterministic with subsystems inexorably adapting to meet the functional requirements of others. The theory, equally, seems in danger, in some of its formulations, of the logical flaw—of teleology—that erodes most systems theories: that is, effects, the adaptation of one subsystem to perpetuate another, become treated as causes.

An adequate theoretical framework seems to require some dovetailing of the advantages of both the theories we have considered (cf. Flynn, 1978; Saunders, 1979). Such a theory would be rooted in the agency of actors indicating the way social arrangements are continually produced and reproduced, yet a theory which is aware of the deep seated constraints of 'system requirements'. Such a theory has yet to be elaborated.

IV

We have sought to account for the changing relationships between the central and local partners in education. Analysis, hopefully, can pinpoint the direction for effective action—in the words of Auguste Comte, 'savoir pour prévoir, prévoir pour pouvoir'. A plausible interpretation of the past can more adequately guide the future.

Analysis has suggested a beleaguered education service. On the one hand, the partners are revealed in an internecine struggle, with central powers reappropriating control. If such an account is pursued we might discover the centralization of control being concentrated beyond the DES in the DoE and the Treasury. On the other hand, a systems analysis may indicate that the needs of one sector are being subordinated to another, with education required to support more directly the infrastructures of economy and work.

For a service which has been accustomed to privileged status, such an account portrays a rather gloomy prospect. Some of those committed to the service blame new management styles in local government and point to the solution of withdrawing education into new independent structures that would better protect its integrity. Others debate the degrees of centralization or decentralization that would best serve its interests. Both 'solutions' focus upon structures and constitutions. Yet, it is arguable that such a focus is either mistaken or inappropriate at this time.

The critical importance that one of the explanatory models places upon the *meanings* which actors transact (as well as resources) and the other upon the *interdependence* of system parts can assist the discussion here. Education *has* been challenged—and justifiably so—but it has been held to account at the level of meaning and purpose informing the service rather than at the level of structure: the scrutiny has focused upon the place of education and what it is reasonable to expect it to accomplish. Those arguments have not met serious challenge or qualification. Decisions about structures would better await the actors clarifying and renegotiating the meanings and purposes of the service: the ascription of roles presupposes conceptions for those roles. The work of the political philosopher, the sociologist and the economist may be required before that of the constitutional lawyer. The way the partners stand in relation to each other, it is being argued, must depend upon clarification of the place education holds in the system as a whole. But education has lost the sense of its necessary location within the social structure: its significance must follow from the way its *inter*dependence is articulated.

Education *had* such a structural location and relevance. Its vision and purposes embraced economy, polity and society. Essentially, as one chief education officer put it, education was an instrument of social reform. The attack upon the service has eroded such beliefs and undermined confidence —leaving disenchantment without the despondency within. If the purposes of the service are to be renegotiated, which of the earlier expectations can be rescued? Such an assessment ideally requires much research, but there may already be sufficient indication that a summary dismissing of education's contribution would be premature even according to some of the terms of its original vision. (The long time spans required for education to unfold its task, and the slow processes of social change which it may have initiated, demand ultimately a more detached historical perspective.)

The 1944 Act inaugurated the radical change of universal secondary education. The consolidation of this massive quantitative expansion of educational provision may itself in time be regarded as an extraordinary social achievement. But what of education as an instrument of reform? What of the hopes of one respected CEO who confided that 'class privilege is very deep in our society: and although education often works to reinforce privilege it can slowly undermine it and increase life chances'? The most important research, in this country, into the impact of education upon class and social structure points to slow but significant change:

> the hierarchy of classes is transformed by egalitarian expansion into a moving column with the service class in the van and the working class in the rear, passing points of consumption, or in any case educational welfare, which had been reached by the more advantaged classes at an earlier point in history (Halsey *et al.*, 1980).

It is an irony perhaps that the partnership which has been the focus of this paper and the early consensus on which it was founded, developed around this great radical change in education (the 1944 Act) and the social reform it initiated. We may be approaching slowly a further major juncture of historical change—the mass extension of post-16 education which could have implications for the whole of the service. That change too could be the basis for the foundation of a new partnership between the education powers if the internal bargaining is tempered by external realization that 'expansion can bring us higher standards more fairly shared. Education has changed society in that way and can do more. It does so slowly against the stubborn resistance of class and class-related culture. But it remains the friend of those who seek a more efficient, more open, and more just society' (Halsey et al., 1980).

NOTES

1. For further elaboration of this contextual change see David (1977), Regan (1977), Kogan (1978) and Maclure (1979).
2. This section draws on research undertaken as part of the SSRC (Social Science Research Council) centre-local policy planning project.
3. An SSRC project interview.
4. An SSRC project interview.
5. Elaborated elsewhere in Ranson et al. (1980).

REFERENCES

Aiken, M. and Hage, J. (1963) Organisational inter-dependence and intra-organisational structure, *A.S.R.*, Vol. 33.
Aldrich, H.E. (1979) *Organisations and Environments*, Prentice Hall.
Aldrich, H.E. (1976) Resource dependence and inter-organisational relations, *Administration and Society*, Vol. 7.
Archer, M. (1979) *Social Origins of Educational Systems*, Sage.
Becher, T. and Kogan, M. (1980) *Process and Structure in Higher Education*, Heinemann.
Benson, J. (1975) The interorganisational network as a political economy, *Administrative Science Quarterly*, Vol. 20.
Bernstein, B. (1973) *Class, Codes and Control*, Volume 3, Routledge and Kegan Paul.
Blau, P. (1964) *Exchange and Power*, Wiley.
Blau, P. and Schoenherr, R. (1971) *The Structure of Organisations*, Basic Books.
Bogdanor, V. (1979) Power and participation, *Oxford Review of Education*, Vol. 5, No. 2.
Bourdieu, P. (1971) The thinkable and the unthinkable, *Times Literary Supplement*, 15 October 1971.
Bourdieu, P. (1977) *Outline of a Theory of Practice*, Cambridge.
Bourdieu, P. and Passeron, J.C. (1977) *Reproduction in Education, Society and Culture*, Sage.
Briault, E. (1976) A distributed system of educational administration: an international viewpoint, *International Review of Education*, Vol. 22, No. 4.
Broadfoot, P. (1979) *Assessment, Schools and Society*, Methuen.
Burgess, T. and Travers, T. (1980) *Ten Billion Pounds*, Grant MacIntyre.
Byrne, E. (1974) *Planning and Educational Inequality*, NFER.
Coates, R.D. (1972) *Teachers Unions and Interest Group Politics*, Cambridge University Press.
Crozier, M. and Thoenig, J.C. (1976) The regulation of complex organised systems, *Administrative Science Quarterly*, Vol. 21.
Dale, R. (1980) Education and the capitalist state: contributions and contradictions, in Apple, M. (ed.), *Cultural and Economic Reproduction in Education*.
David, M. (1977) *Reform, Reaction and Resources, The 3 Rs of Educational Planning*, NFER.
Davies, B. (1968) *Social Needs and Resources in Local Services*, Michael Joseph.
Dunleavy, P. (1980) *Urban Political Analysis*, Macmillan.
Emerson, R. (1962) Power-dependence relations, *American Sociological Review*, Vol. 27.
Evetts, J. (1973) *The Sociology of Educational Ideas*, Routledge and Kegan Paul.

Flynn, R. (1978) The state and planning, *Public Administration Bulletin*, No. 28.
Fowler, G., Morris, V. and Ozga, J. (eds) (1973) *Decision-Making in British Education*, Heinemann.
Gellner, E. (1974) *Contemporary Thought and Politics*, Routledge and Kegan Paul.
Giddens, A. (1976) *New Rules of Sociological Method*, Hutchinson.
Giddens, A. (1979) *Central Problems in Social Theory*, Macmillan.
Glatter, R. (1979) *An Introduction to the Control of Education in Britain*, Open University Press.
Greenwood, R., Walsh, K., Hinings, C. and Ranson, S. (1980) *Patterns of Management in Local Government*, Martin Robertson.
Griffith, J. (1966) *Central Departments and Local Authorities*, Allen & Unwin.
Griffith, J. (1977) *The Politics of the Judiciary*, Fontana.
Habermas, J. (1976) *Legitimation Crisis*, Heinemann.
Halsey, A., Heath, A. and Ridge, J. (1980) *Origins and Destinations*, Oxford University Press.
Hanf, K. and Scharpf, F. (1978) *Interorganisational Policy-Making*, Sage.
Hinings, C.R. (1980) Policy planning systems and central-local relations, in Jones, G.W. (ed.), *New Approaches to the Study of Central-Local Relations*, Gower.
James, P. (1980) *The Reorganisation of Secondary Education*, NFER.
Jones, G. (ed.) (1980) *New Approaches to the Study of Central-Local Relations*, Gower.
Keat, R. and Urry, J. (1975) *Social Theory as Science*, Routledge and Kegan Paul.
Kogan, M. (1979) Different frameworks for educational policy-making and analysis, *Educational Analysis*, Vol. 1, No. 2.
Kogan, M. (1978) *The Politics of Educational Change*, Fontana.
Kogan, M. (1975) *Educational Policy Making*, Allen & Unwin.
Kogan, M. and Becher, T. (1980) Patterns of change, *Times Higher Education Supplement*, 2 May 1980.
Lawton, D. (1980) *The Politics of the School Curriculum*, Routledge and Kegan Paul.
Locke, M. (1974) *Power and Politics in the School System*, Routledge and Kegan Paul.
MacIntyre, A. (1969) On the relevance of the philosophy of the social sciences, *British Journal of Sociology*.
MacIntyre, A. (1971) *Against the Self-Images of the Age*, Duckworth.
Maclure, S. (1979) The endless agenda: matters arising, *Oxford Review of Education*, Vol. 5, No. 2.
Mindlin, S. and Aldrich, H. (1975) Interorganisational dependence, *Administrative Science Quarterly*, Vol. 20.
O.E.C.D. (1975) *Educational Development Strategy in England and Wales*, Paris.
Offe, C. (1975) The theory of the capitalist state and the problem of policy formation, in Lindberg *et al.*, *Stress and Contradiction in Modern Capitalism*, Lexington.
Pattison, M. (1980) Intergovernmental relations and the limitations of central control: reconstructing the politics of comprehensive education, *Oxford Review of Education*, Vol. 6, No. 1.
Pfeffer, J. and Salancik, G. (1978) *The External Control of Organisations*, Harper & Row.
Pyle, D. (1976) Resource allocation in education, *Social and Economic Administration*, Vol. 10, No. 2.
Ranson, S., Hinings, B. and Greenwood, R. (1980) The structuring of organisational structures, *Administrative Science Quarterly*, Vol. 25.
Regan, D. (1977) *Local Government and Education*, Allen & Unwin.
Rhodes, R. (1979) Research into central-local relations in Britain: a framework for analysis, SSRC.
Runciman, W. (1972) *A Critique of Max Weber's Philosophy of Social Science*, Cambridge University Press.
Salancik, G. (1979) Interorganisational dependence and responsiveness, *Academy of Management Journal*, Vol. 22.
Saran, R. (1973) *Policy Making in Secondary Education*, Clarendon Press.
Saunders, P. (1979) *Urban Politics: A Sociological Interpretation*, Hutchinson.
Stewart, J. (1980) The Bill and central-local relations, in *The Local Government Planning and Land Bill*, INLOGOV, collected essays, May 1980.
Taylor, W. (1978) Values and accountability, in Becher, T. and Maclure, S. (eds.), *Accountability in Education*, NFER.

Weaver, T. (1976) Tenth Report from the Expenditure Committee 1975–76, HC621 p. 379.
Weaver, T. (1979) *Department of Education and Science: Central Control of Education?*, Open University Press.
Weber, M. (1948) *The Theory of Social and Economic Organisation*, Glencoe.
Weber, M. (1968) *Economy and Society*, Bedminster.
Williams, G. (1979) Educational planning past, present and future, *Educational Policy Bulletin*, Vol. 7, No. 2.

7

Distributing Resources

W.F. DENNISON

The characteristics of the relationship are too complex to dismiss either as a partnership (government and local authority working together as equals) or a principal-agent, central control model (a hierarchy with government handing down instructions, rules, etc., to local authorities).[1] The more useful perspective is of a mix of dependencies and local independencies. Local authorities exist and derive their duties and powers from Statutes passed by Parliament: often these confer on government ministers the duty of monitoring the exercise of local authority powers. Education ministers, for example, oversee LEA primary and secondary school provision in some detail, with regard to facilities, teacher qualifications, etc.[2] In addition, through performing these tasks, local authorities must rely on government for grants to cover about half their spending. As the sums involved come from general taxation, ministers remain accountable to Parliament for their distribution and use. Taken together, these elements present a formidable dependency, and a perception of local authorities implementing national policy, with some interpretation, according to local needs, under the supervision of ministers and civil servants. Such a view, however, overlooks the independent stance local authorities are able to take because of their status as locally elected councils accountable not to the centre, or particular government departments, but to local electorates. The two main interrelated components of this accountability being, first, a knowledge of local needs, beyond that available centrally, and how best these might be satisfied: and, second, a responsibility for raising and spending the rates (an independent taxing power) in pursuit of these needs.

So far this discussion of local dependency has implicitly assumed a single centre and a typical local authority. In practice the relationship consists of a series of government departments communicating with appropriate local

Source: From Dennison, W.F., *Educational Finance and Resources*, Croom Helm, London, 1984.

authority agencies (DES with LEA, DHSS with Social Services, etc.). Each of these links has certain features. In the mid-1960s, for example, the DES was seen as the most promotional of government departments in relation to LEAs:[3] now it would be categorized as more interventionist. That, however, describes the general situation, but as secondary school reorganization has demonstrated, the alacrity with which individual LEAs accept DES policy leads and interventions, even when supported by legislative provision, varies enormously. More generally, numerous relationships and associations have evolved, covering the full range of authorities, services and government departments. The local authority associations provide a unity when representing all authorities, for example in grant negotiations, and add a new dimension to the total relationship, but do little to hide inter-authority and inter-service differences in approach to central government. As a result of the uniqueness in the link between central and individual local departments, not to mention that involving local departments within their own authority setting, it is more profitable to view the relationship as a web of interaction between ministers, civil servants, councillors and officers. Implicit in this network are a series of dependencies, without them the network would not exist, but the main characteristics of the relationship are consultation, negotiation and bargaining between separate organizations, each functioning in its own political environment. For every local authority is itself a political system with parties and factions representing various ideologies and pursuing certain objectives, usually at variance, and sometimes clashing, with those nominated centrally. Conflict must, therefore, be added to the other characteristics.[4]

The extent to which that conflict is realizable has been clearly shown during retrenchment since the mid-1970s. Although there is a powerful element of interdependency, the reliance of local authorities on a central grant introduces a significant bias. Sufficient evidence has appeared over time to confirm that government would not change that situation. For example, the Royal Commission on Local Government (1969) considering structure and functions had finance excluded from its terms of reference,[5] even though a preceding White Paper (1966) on local government finance reported that there was no prospect of reform within existing arrangements, while the desirability of change was given by government as an additional reason for the Royal Commission.[6] More specifically, much of the interest in modifying financial arrangements has centred, in recent years, on supplementing local authorities' solitary tax source—the rates. In this respect, British local authorities are exceptional by international standards, and while the Layfield Report (1976) suggested Local Income Tax (LIT) as the only feasible addition or alternative to rates,[7] progress towards offering local authorities a broader tax base lacks impetus. The idea of LIT is not new, but has always been opposed by central government, particularly if involving local autonomy in fixing tax levels.[8] In fact the impression, increasingly in recent years, has been of government reluctance to accept local freedom in determining rate poundages. Autonomy remains, but has in effect been gradually constrained by elimination of the right to raise a supplementary rate, the various penalty clauses (to be described later), and the probability of legislation to limit rate rises. The whole notion of rates as a form of taxation has, simultaneously, been criticized, because of unfairness in its imposition and impugned unpopularity. The idea that rates, on account of their lack of buoyancy (a slow rate of growth, unaffected by inflationary boosts, as compared to income tax or VAT) provide an unsatisfactory tax base, and the advantages of the rating system (local in character, cheap to administer) have received much less attention.[9] In the foreseeable future, therefore, a rating system modified so as to reduce local freedom—will continue exaggerating central resistance to any measures which might reduce local authority financial dependence. By giving local authorities statutory responsibilities without the complementary financial infrastructure, government implies that local authority reliance on grants for a main share of resources is a desirable and necessary component in consultation, negotiation, bargaining and conflict.

Although central grants to local authorities have a long history, it was with the introduction of the Rate Support Grant (RSG) in 1967 that much of the detail in the current arrangements emerged. A block grant (a sum paid to each authority which then determines its distribution) supplemented by specific allowances (grants paid for nominated activities), it contains two main equalization elements, as well as a domestic rate relief component to reduce the rate bills of local residents. The intention with the resource equalization element is to reach a situation in which each local authority can raise the same revenue with identical rate poundages. For example, a 1p rate in Sutton would raise £297,000, while a similar rate in South Tyneside, with a similar population, would only raise £154,700.[10] In other words, to achieve the same revenue South Tyneside would have to impose a rate in the pound almost double that of Sutton. Needs equalization, in contrast, attempts to eliminate the differences which arise because expenditure requirements across authorities are not consistent. The necessary fiscal equity happens when each local authority spends the same proportion of resources on a service to achieve equal levels of performance: in practice assessed relative to input costs. In simple terms, an authority with a high proportion of children will need to spend highly per capita on education. From 1967/68 to 1980/81, therefore, RSG included three separate elements. Domestic (constituting around 9 per cent of total grant): resources (about 30 per cent), with grant paid to each authority which fell below a 'standard' rateable value per head set by government, although without a compensatory attempt to reduce those authorities above to this average level: and needs (approximately 60 per cent) in which the grant payable to each authority every year was the result of complex calculations based on local parameters, with the particular choice of variables being determined annually by government, based after 1974/75 mainly on past levels of expenditure.

A number of factors explain the modification to RSG introduced in 1981/82, following the Local Government, Planning and Land Act, 1980. The calculation of the needs element, in particular, was becoming increasingly complex and readily subject to political whim. Up to 1974 the detail of the calculation was specified in regulations, but the Local Government Act, 1974 gave the Secretary of State for the Environment much more flexibility in nominating variables and determining the allocation. Therefore, on an annual basis, adjustments could be made to favour inner cities, rural areas, or London authorities, depending upon the current priorities of the government. However, the main defect, as perceived by the Conservative administration of 1979, was that the method of implementing RSG frustrated their attempts to control public expenditure. In particular, the needs element, by concentrating on previous expenditures as a determinant of need, favoured high spending authorities and offered few inducements to lower expenditure. The new RSG that emerged consisted of two elements. Domestic rate relief grant replaced the domestic element, but was otherwise unchanged: while a new block grant, directed towards the simultaneous pursuit of resource and need equalization, was substituted for the separate resources and needs element.

As might be expected, the two main components of the grant still reflect need and resource considerations. An assessment of the Grant Related Expenditure (GRE) of each authority has first to be made.[11] Equivalent to the needs element, the intention is that by estimating the expenditure requirements of an authority, dependent upon its characteristics (population, number of children requiring education, recreational facilities, miles of road, etc.) weighted by an evaluation of the unit cost of each service it provides, rate poundages can be equalized across authorities for the same standard of provision. More directly, GREs are supposed to supply an objective assessment of what authorities ought to spend on each service. It cannot, though, be a simple calculation, because of the numerous variables involved, and any claim that the mechanism for calculating GRE is more comprehensible than that for needs elements remains unproven. In fact, GRE now includes a much higher number of factors, as a result of having to assess the size of the client group, and the unit cost of each group, while simultaneously making allowance for particular features in a local area (the number of non-white children, say) which influence expenditure. In education, for example, actual size of group (number of children or students) is used in nursery education and NAFE: but for schools an additional factor appears to allow for the age distribution of pupils. In this respect education seems comparatively straightforward because the client group is relatively well defined. In social services or planning that is not the case: more obviously with parks, for example, the need to spend depends upon levels of provision previously determined, and for all of these services past expenditures enter the calculation. However, once the size of the client group or its equivalent has been determined, its product, and the cost of supplying one unit, represents the GRE for that service. The outcome of a GRE for each service (including education) aggregates to give a GRE for the authority. When the new arrangements were introduced, opposition to the notion of publishing service GREs emerged, mainly because the resultant grant was not subdivided. Significantly, DES led the way to the publication of education GREs with figures for each service in all authorities readily available, although they do not appear until after rates have been fixed so as to minimize their potential influence on decision-making.[12]

In terms of one of its objectives, the elimination of rewards to high spending authorities, GRE offers more potential than the needs element. By concentrating upon the size of the client group, and the costs of supplying each service in relation to a direct payment to each providing authority, government has clarified the link between grant acquisition and service provision while minimizing the financial incentive to retain high expenditure. In fact, authorities which reduce spending on some discretionary services can be relatively advantaged by the calculation. With those modifications, however, the criticisms of complexity and influences of political whim levelled at the needs element remain. The rationale may be clearer but, intentionally, by adding so many additional factors to the calculation understanding has not been assisted. In addition, by adjusting variables and dominating the whole process of calculation, government retains control and is enabled to pursue its political objectives. Indeed, that was a powerful motivation when initiating the change. Perhaps this is most clearly demonstrated with discretionary services. Authorities have both statutory duties and discretionary powers but in the latter, for example with social services, a number of authorities (particularly those Labour controlled in metropolitan areas) have established a high level of commitment. GRE calculations, however, because they tend to use average costs, and on occasion overlook the actual number of clients receiving services, penalize those authorities. Yet some authorities have built up what they would regard as irrevocable commitments, such as social workers in employment, as well as heightened aspiration levels among recipients. When potential client numbers (possibly the whole population) replace actuals the benefits of this GRE component effectively transfer from authorities which offer services widely to those with few actual participants. In the limit, an authority can be credited with a GRE for a discretionary service it does not offer. Although, in expenditure terms, education organizes comparatively few discretionary activities, and would appear exempt from such effects, as the grant to each authority deriving from GRE is general, any deficiency, even arising from non-educational factors, can still have considerable implications for resource availability.

More fundamentally, however, GRE introduces an additional dimension into central-local grants. For the first time some form of itemization of what ought to be spent, authority by authority, service by service, is made. Of course, an authority does not have to comply with the specified figures, but their existence is potentially significant at both levels. Centrally, they provide a framework for much tighter control, if required: locally, they can be used as nominated national norms by particular groups in the authority to argue for preferred spending patterns. However, GRE is only one element in the calculation of grant and its combination with the second main component, Grant Related Poundage (GRP) must now be considered. As for the 'standard' rateable value per head of the resources element, the main intention involves equalization necessitated by the different tax bases of authorities: but on this occasion, by using GRP in conjunction with GRE, the aim is to satisfy both resource and needs requirements simultaneously. The initial step involves the calculation of a GRP for all authorities (134.42p in the £ for 1981-82, 151.34p in 1982-83). That is, were the country considered as a single authority, this figure would represent the rate levy to cover expenditure equal to GRE not met by the block grant. The national GRP has then to be disaggregated, in terms of the range of services an authority has to provide, by use of an average GRE for different groups of authorities (metropolitan districts, non-metropolitan counties, etc.). The outcome is a percentage allowance for each authority in the same area. In non-metropolitan areas, for example, during 1982/83, county level took 86.6 per cent of GRP and district the remaining 13.4 per cent: giving respective GRPs of 130.99p in the £ and 20.35p. GRP and rateable value per head are then combined and deducted from GRE, in the equation which determines the size of the block grant payable to each local authority.

Block grant received = GRE − (GRP × rateable value per head)

In other words the higher the *per capita* rateable value (that is wealthy authorities) the more the grant received is below GRE.

By telescoping needs and resource elements into one grant, a full equalization of tax bases for all authorities is made possible. This did not occur previously, as authorities with low tax bases were only raised to a standard level, for to offer all authorities a base equal to that of the wealthiest authority would have proved too costly. Also, unless all authorities had been similarly placed to those with the lowest required expenditure per head, a complete needs equalization would have been impossible. In effect, with the new grant, tax rich authorities (high r.v. per head) with low expenditure needs (small GRE) are effectively penalized to the advantage of poor authorities with high spending requirements. Politically, this part of the change was acceptable because the great majority of authorities continued to receive some grant, while government had achieved inter-authority equalization at a relatively low level of grant. However, most appealing of all to a

Conservative administration determined to reduce public expenditure by devising arrangements in which a standard rate levy across all authorities should lead to a uniform level of provision (in theory at least), a route towards increased central control over total spending had been arranged. This possibility was already foreseen with the inclusion in the 1980 Act of 'thresholds' and 'tapering multipliers'. The idea, basically, is to penalize those authorities which overspend in relation to their GRE. When expenditure goes above a threshold (for 1981/82 and 1982/3 10 per cent above the GRE for the authority) a tapering multiplier is introduced so that an increased proportion of the spending above the threshold has to be met by local ratepayers (a 25% rise in rate poundages to support excess expenditures was used during these years). In terms of the equation for calculating block grant, the GRP for an authority becomes dependent upon deviation of actual spending from GRE.

These developments proved inadequate, as far as government was concerned, in limiting increases in local spending. Apart from the difficulties it encountered with high expenditure authorities, more general problems arose from the transition to the new block grant, particularly the assessment of GRE associated with discretionary services. Owing to under-development of these activities some authorities were actually encouraged to increase expenditure and this, combined with the normal tendency to over-budget, produced anticipated spending nearly 6% above GRE. To some extent because of these factors even though they were probably transitional, government still found it necessary to introduce more long-term measures to further restrict what it would assess as overspending. As well as the elimination of local authority power to levy a supplementary rate (Local Government Finance Act, 1982) an additional threshold based on volume assessments was introduced during 1981-82, affecting those authorities which were more than 5.6% above their 1978-79 figures. By 1982-83 the volume and GRE thresholds were combined so that not only were overspending authorities subject to tapering of block grant, but they could actually lose part of their grant through abatement. When this notion was first introduced during 1981-82 government concern was directed towards a small number of authorities (invariably Labour controlled) who despite exceeding thresholds, and being subject to tapering, refused to lower planned expenditures to levels closer to GRE or volume targets. When threatened with abatement (or holdback) of some block grant most agreed to lower anticipated spending, but despite this government still introduced, for 1981-83 and later years, a complex system of target expenditure for each authority largely based on spending in the previous year.[13] Spending above the target allows government to abate grant by means of a penalty. With these developments the whole basis of the relationship is changed. Through determining targets, and the other items of thresholds, multipliers, GRE and GRP, as well as nominating the factors which influence their determination (such as predictions about the effects of price changes) government has not only introduced a new grant system, but also sponsored a major increase in central control over local decision-making.

Undoubtedly, any transition from needs and resource elements to a block grant would have introduced uncertainty for authorities. Had it occurred at a more favourable time economically, there would still have been need for 'safety nets' to protect some authorities from individually disadvantageous aspects of changeover: that is losing substantial grant through the different base for calculation. However, the pursuit by government of its own objectives of reduced local spending has introduced complexity far in excess of anything experienced with the original system. More confusing still, further modifications and details often emerged as government itself discovered by experience the intricacies of the arrangements it was initiating. Familiarity with the new arrangements will eliminate some uncertainty, but as the final assessment of actual expenditures, and their effects on tapering multipliers and penalties, etc., will have to take place some time after the year in question, it seems that the processes of local resource management and planning will be hindered by a considerable time lag before the exact total grant is known. It might be argued that some measure of uncertainty is intentional to assist a government imposing its own view of preferred spending. On this basis local authorities are more likely to comply with GRE figures, or not exceed thresholds, when not fully aware of the precise effects of doing otherwise. Yet within this framework of increasing centrality procedures for consultation remain largely undisturbed, particularly before the start of the year. The impression to an external observer can still be of two equal partners (local authority associations and government) considering spending requirements and tax.

Actual discussions for each year, involving authority officers and civil servants, begin up to twelve months before its start. A framework exists with PESC expenditure projections (which are not yet firm for the year in question) and the foci are both the expenditure plans of local authorities, and the arrangements for grant distribution. Negotiations about the actual grant system occur in the Grants Working Group, while expenditure groups (including one covering education) consider actual and projected spending in each of the main service areas. Outcomes from the groups are used by an 'Officers Steering Group' feeding into the Consultative Council on Local Government Finance, a mix of politicians and officials—both central and local, representing all major interests and chaired by the Secretary of State for the Environment. To an outsider, therefore, it is easy to create an image of continuing negotiation and bargaining, even following the changes, with the same three pieces of main information emerging a few months before the start of the year: an estimate of relevant expenditure in the coming twelve months (£21.76 bn for 1982–83), the proportion of this total to be met by a central government grant (57.1 per cent in that year), and the actual distribution of the grant to individual local authorities.[14] Not all of the total sum transferred from central to local authorities (£12.43 bn in that year) is distributed as block grant: first specific grants, most prominently to urban aid and the police (nearly £1.7 bn in 1982–83) and supplementary grants to transport and national parks (nearly £0.5 bn): and second, almost £0.7 bn to achieve the 18.5p in the £ relief for domestic ratepayers, have to be subtracted. The remaining money (£8.7 bn for 1982–83) is then allocated through the block grant mechanisms, although clearly, some authorities will receive more and others less than 57.1 per cent of their relevant expenditure, depending upon individual circumstances.

Up to 1981–82 central efforts to reduce the aggregate level of local spending had two intersupportive components. First, by dominating the negotiations with local authorities (both on account of the resource dependencies which the discussions were intended to satisfy, and the possession of a more sophisticated information base) government views about aggregate expenditure, and the percentage it would support, provided the framework within which local decision-making had to take place. In minimizing increases in exchequer grant, for example, it forced many local authorities into simultaneously reducing services and increasing rate poundages: in effect it raised the visibility (and unpopularity) of their accountability to the local electorate. The most effective mechanism of achieving this minimization was by lowering the percentage of total relevant expenditure government was willing to support from 66 per cent in 1975–76, to 57.2 per cent in 1982–83, and then to 52 per cent in 1984–85. Second, government could try and persuade, or perhaps cajole, local government as a whole, and individual authorities, to restrain spending within centrally determined guidelines. However, up to that time spending both in total and relative to priorities (provided all statutory objections were met) was solely a matter for local autonomy. In fact, given this dual approach, government efforts to restrict local authority expenditure had been remarkably successful, certainly in relation to government efforts to restrict its own spending. Between 1975 and 1981, for example, local government expenditure as a proportion of GNP fell from 16 per cent to 14 per cent, and as a proportion of total public expenditure from 32 per cent to 28 per cent; for central government the equivalent figures were increases from 33 per cent to 35 per cent and 68 per cent to 72 per cent.[15] Were the main component of unplannable central spending ignored, that associated with unemployment and social security payments, government was still less effective in containing its own expenditure than local authorities.

It is within a framework of increasing constraints since the mid-1970s that efforts from 1981–82 onwards to further reduce and control local authority expenditure must be judged. According to some central government perspectives, no reason exists why local spending should not be planned and controlled in detail and to effect, both to restrain aggregate expenditure and facilitate the pursuit of policy objectives, but this will happen far more readily if most decisions are made centrally rather than within 400 or so local political systems. Extending this view, arrangements involving low level control through resource dependency, coupled with persuasion, proved inadequate not so much relative to an intention of lowering local authority spending, but more as a mechanism to contest with those authorities who either decided it was impossible to keep to, or were determined to ignore, guidelines. Clearly, the introduction of the block grant encompassed a number of government objectives: an ability to be more specific in circumventing the expenditure plans of some authorities was one, but so were more effective control over aggregate expenditure, greater emphasis on centrally determined policy objectives, and the development of a fairer system of distributing grant. Naturally with retrenchment, and in a political environment, the emphasis in any consideration of the efficacy of the new system has been on the adverse effects of less grant, and the conflicts between government and a few authorities to which it is opposed politically. More generally it seems improbable that, with hindsight, local authorities would have accepted the Local Government Planning and Land Act with so little concerted resistance.[16] Yet, following all the modifications the situation still continues for the time being at least, that a local authority is accountable to its electorate for the total level of spending and the decisions about priorities among its services. Thresholds, tapering multipliers, targets and grant abatements have not altered that fact, although they make it certain, that spending well in excess of target will force authorities to impose intolerable rate poundages. Some authorities may try to retain previous freedoms by raising rate levels, or even continuing to spend when they have no balances, but government will always retain ascendancy because of the nature of the dependency and its ability to introduce new legislation, in this case by limiting the right of authorities to increase rate poundages.[17] The risk, of course, from a government perspective (on the assumption that it wishes local authorities to continue) is that eventually the notion of local autonomy will be reduced to a meaningless level. It has always been circumscribed and its continued erosion must produce circumstances in which those elected (and eventually the electorate) will perceive that no choices remain open to them. Undoubtedly, that would mean a major constitutional change with no further place for local government, as duties could be performed by central officials working locally. In the case of education, a 'national service locally administered', the government has views and policies, but has made little attempt to translate these directly into financial decisions in such a way as to affect the detail of activities. Changes in the grant mechanism, and the abolition of rate-raising autonomy, could alter that situation. If this were to result in few opportunities for the determination of local needs and limited decision-making about optimum means for their satisfaction, the logical outcome would be a national service nationally administered.

LOCAL EDUCATION AUTHORITY

The overlap between LEA and local authority decision-making, although exaggerated by corporatism, has always existed. A discreteness and a hierarchy still pertain, of course: the local authority as a whole makes a series of inter-service decisions and fixes the rate, at the same time the LEA must distribute resources among schools, etc., with both the distribution and the total expenditure subject to Council control. However, the authority cannot sanction education expenditure without a clear plan of what is to be spent. As a result, the production of a budget for education (and simultaneously in other services) constitutes an integral component of resource distribution. Probably the most effective way of considering the influence of the processes in budget construction on the disbursement of resources is through the outcome—a typical budget document (Table 1). Essentially a spending plan, completed just before the start of the financial year, its formulation combines both technical detail with political and educational priorities. However, once an item appears in the final budget that represents permission to spend up to whatever level is specified. Therefore, the main thrust is towards the demands of fiscal accounting, which is well suited by the object of expense approach: so much to be spent on a whole series of items—teachers' salaries, books and equipment, heating, lighting etc.[18] The requirements of fiscal accounting (that money should only be spent in categories, and up to levels, as agreed) are also demonstrated by the precision of the forecast expenditures. Clearly, it is impossible to estimate spending on salaries, for example, involving several million pounds, to the nearest hundred pounds, given the variations and unanticipated events likely to happen during the year. Instead, the specified figure for each item is best perceived as an expenditure target, which can be used to monitor the rate of spending during the year to strengthen the control element sought by the document. In the same way, categorization of planned expenditure facilitates fiscal accounting by enabling the separate scrutiny of spending on each item, although making virement procedures—the transfer of expenditure between sub-heads after the document has been confirmed—more difficult.

In such a document there are two outstanding, but potentially conflicting, features. The first, and more obvious, concerns the detail, implying that construction demands considerable technical expertise and knowledge about the system. Second, and less clearly, the document contains within that detail the most important statement of LEA policy. Priorities as between primary and secondary education, teaching and non-teaching staff, etc., are established and pursued, not perhaps in ways which can be readily understood from the document. Nevertheless, by committing itself to certain expenditures, the LEA has specified its preferences. The budget, therefore, is not a neutral document, although the technicalities involved in its construction can sometimes make it appear as such, and all parties—politicians and officers

Table 1. LEA budget document for 1983-84

A. Estimated net cost of current levels of service*

	Employees Teachers	Employees Others	Running expenses	Debt charges	Total expenditure	Income†	Net expenditure
Administration and inspection	—	2,480,620	1,435,560	—	3,916,180	286,320	3,629,860
Nursery education	36,890	56,270	28,220	—	121,380	—	121,380
Primary education	17,560,320	3,072,660	5,172,600	1,872,640	27,678,220	278,980	27,399,240
Secondary education	21,462,240	2,207,630	7,254,720	2,073,190	32,997,780	254,390	32,743,390
Special education	2,576,310	867,320	1,974,460	250,740	5,668,830	490,320	5,178,510
FE: Colleges	5,024,810	1,032,680	1,674,980	258,960	7,991,430	2,587,260	5,404,170
Adult education	100,760	2,750	16,720	—	120,230	86,790	34,440
In-service training	—	—	68,960	—	—	—	68,960
Teachers Centres	25,280	18,960	37,490	—	81,730	4,820	76,910
Community education	56,110	112,720	190,190	96,390	455,410	59,780	395,630
School meals	—	3,172,660	2,452,100	59,280	5,684,040	1,710,390	3,973,650
Youth service	—	382,920	310,290	62,280	755,490	49,240	706,250
Outdoor study centres	112,920	149,610	225,740	6,280	494,500	280,620	213,930
Careers advisory	—	690,780	170,120	20,220	881,120	292,480	588,640
AFE pooling	—	—	5,220,420	—	5,220,420	820,340	4,400,080
						Total	84,935,040

*For the sake of conciseness only the main categories have been included.
†Including specific government grants.

Table 1 (cont'd)

B. Secondary education proposed gross spending 1983–84 (in cash terms)

	1983–84 Proposed	1982–83 Proposed	1982–83 Probable
Teachers' salaries	21,462,240	20,876,520	21,004,760
Non-teaching salaries	572,280	528,690	532,280
Other salaries	1,635,350	1,592,740	1,608,710
Building maintenance	1,006,780	970,620	960,480
Building alterations	124,320	136,220	140,480
Grounds maintenance	637,690	620,110	630,470
Heating, lighting	1,976,450	1,896,720	1,884,630
Furniture and fittings	125,160	131,720	129,640
Rent and rates	2,176,430	2,080,340	2,146,720
Books and equipment	826,970	834,720	836,410
Printing, stationery and telephone	196,980	198,740	195,370
Insurance	58,720	61,220	59,470
Aid to pupils	125,220	110,590	108,160
Debt charges	2,073,190	2,001,420	1,964,110
	32,997,780	32,040,370	32,201,690

particularly, other interest groups less directly—have a stake in production. Particularly during contraction it is relatively easy to depict the whole process as entirely incremental, in the sense that the current budget represents no more than an extension of the previous year. A view strengthened by the object of expense format which places previous and proposed expenditure on each item alongside, in a way that directs attention towards possible changes in spending. Essentially, each line appears as

NAME OF ITEM   A   B   C

where A and B represent previous or current expenditures (during the year in which the document is being prepared) and C the proposed spending on the item. Even during expansion, however, there is usually a powerful measure of sameness about an organization's budget over time. Two types of reasoning can be used to explain this situation. The first, and more negative, utilizes the limitations of all decision-makers. They are attempting to maximize needs satisfaction in circumstances of resource shortage, and although an infinite number of solutions exist, the constraints on time and limits of knowledge concentrate attention upon a few. As a result, when changes are possible during budget production, modifications to current arrangements dominate.[19] Second, this argument can be developed from a positive stance. In effect, the latest budget represents an investment by the organization in obtaining a resource allocation scheme which has been accepted as a compromise, in addition to providing a spending pattern already being used and as a result supplying experience in this use. In many sectors, quite possibly, circumstances hardly change from year to year, and therefore arguments for a comprehensive review of resource distributions gain little support.[20] More practically, the budget of every organization consists of a base to which, because of shortages of time and knowledge and as existing distributions appear to be adequate, it is already committed before budget-making starts, and a series of increments. Obviously, it is to these that attention switches in decision-making, for they represent the allocative freedom available.

The notion that budget choices take place entirely at the margins is not an over-simplification. It would be to imply that a clear divide exists, visible in the budget document, between those items which constitute the base, and those at the margins: or that all organizations of the same type functioning in similar circumstances perceive the same base-increment relationship.[21] To take two cases: one authority will, by having a 'no-redundancy' policy, erect a larger staff salary base than another willing to reduce teacher numbers, while a LEA deciding, irrespective of other factors, to maintain school capitation allowances in real terms sustains a high base for that item. What, however, these examples also illustrate is both the clarification necessary in the concept of incrementalism, especially with contracting or static conditions, and the impact of organizational factors. An increment is that part of the planned spending where decision-makers could induce a change if they wished. Clearly, with expansion this component of potential spending grows, although as a result the organization, as happened with schools and colleges, may increase the base by entering into new and irrevocable commitments. Conversely, during a time of retrenchment there may still be opportunity for incrementalism provided the planned spending, determined as the base, is less than the total expenditure allowed. Essentially, the problem faced by LEAs during contraction was to ensure that, with a high level of committed expenditure through organizational arrangements and statutory requirements, the base spending was below that likely to be permitted. Indeed, some LEAs argued that a base to total spending deficit, in their perception, was sufficient grounds to make a case for extra resources. In doing so, however, they overlooked two important issues. The size of a base can always be challenged as it is not an objective entity, and by accepting that no gap between base and spending exists, they risk turning budget-making into a wholly technical exercise in which the previous document converts into the next budget.

There has, of course, to be a powerful technical component in LEA decision-making. The complexity of the organization would not permit otherwise. A typical LEA is distributing tens of millions of pounds to several main sectors and hundreds of discrete items. The starting point for budget preparation, several months in time before the year, can only be the previous document. By any standard the base must be large, because of the labour intensity and the high level of fixed costs, and therefore the first task, performed by professional staff, is to extend last year's figures either into the potential cost of irrevocable commitments or, more likely, an estimate of spending if present patterns of provision were continued in the likely circumstances of the new year. That is attempting to make allowances in expenditure terms for changes in pupil and student numbers, increases in salaries and prices, and other foreseeable variables: essentially, a cash determination performed in volume terms. Although these procedures occur at officer level, the political dimension is provided by both national and local parameters. Central government as a whole, and DES in particular, publicize expenditure expectations on their part, but it is not until these are converted into individual RSG settlements (four months, or so, before the start of the year) that authorities know with any degree of certainty their potential financial situation. Up to that point, the assembly of the education budget, and those for other services, is influenced by no more than general guidelines from the main Council or Policy and Resources Committee, produced as a result of their interpretation of government policy and the likely circumstances of the next year. Perhaps a standstill budget is suggested, in real terms, by the authority, or a 2 per cent reduction or a 1 per cent increase in level of services. Often, at this stage, these guidelines will be consistent across services, but it is with the receipt of a RSG figure that the authority begins to balance likely income (from rates, grants and charges) against expenditure it will permit. From an educational perspective, the spending estimates have then to be converted into a detailed plan. Practice varies among authorities, but in general terms this process is sanctioned by sub-committees and the main education committee. As they assemble the estimates, education officers are liaising with schools and with colleges (who will be producing their own budgets in most cases) and officers in the finance department, while working with more detailed contraction or growth parameters established by the authority, alternatively a total aggregate expenditure to be allowed might be specified. The separate outcomes for the various sectors of further education, schools, etc., are then presented to the appropriate further education or schools sub-committee. After adjustment, perhaps, these separate components are used to prepare a full budget document for the Education Committee. Following approval it proceeds to the Policy and Resources Committee, and after agreement there, normally by 'rubber-stamping', to the main Council before becoming the spending plan.

It is, however, much more than a series of technical procedures, and the accompanying determination of local priorities, as expressed through the political processes of the authority, demand attention. In the first place the statement by the authority of growth rate guidelines to be used in early budget preparation represents local intentions relative to national priorities. Although enormously curtailed by targets and penalties, authorities still determine aggregate expenditures. Government may suggest a 'no-growth' situation from one year to next across all authorities, for example, but that does not prevent some aiming for a measure of expansion, either because they are willing to impose large rate increases or as some aspect of the grant calculation is working in their favour. Similarly, the specification by government of expenditure priorities between and within services, in PESC and other statements, does not prevent a LEA exercising its own and different prerogatives. A government view that the RSG settlement allows some increase in books and equipment expenditure, for example, does not commit a LEA to any extra spending. Such adjustments, at variance with government policy, can only occur with increasing difficulty, and at the margins of expenditure, but in an activity like education, with a high level of spending inflexibility, that is the area on which much budget decision-making centres. So that when a sub-committee is presented with draft estimates there are few major choices likely to be available. In the circumstances of a standstill budget, for example, some potential savings could be listed alongside the possible priorities that might be sought if total spending is to remain constant in real terms. As can be seen from Table 1, the sums involved are minuscule as compared to total spending, but by deciding which expenditure reductions to sanction, and determining whether extra remedial teaching staff in employment should take priority over an increase in capitation allowances, for instance, the overt inclusion of political interests has been accommodated. More drastic change, such as increase in Parent/ Teacher Ratio (PTR) to generate more flexibility, is usually circumscribed by covert political pressures, as all of the processes, including the construction of the estimates, occur within the local political environment. To take the example of a proposed rise in PTR, which almost certainly will create job losses: the teacher unions, once alerted, must pressurize for alternative spending patterns, even if this involves spending reductions elsewhere with still less flexibility and fewer choices. As a proposal, therefore, it is unlikely to come before a sub-committee without prior discussion. For except in the case of apolitical authorities (of which there are very few) or those with no overall control, the ruling group will have arranged a majority throughout the committee structure so as to sustain a political consistency.

It is very easy to go on from this fact and portray budget decision-making in a local authority as a series of technical procedures performed by professional staff, within a framework established in private by the main political party, leaving a small number of relatively minor decisions to the public arena of education and other service committees. In some authorities this description will be close to reality, yet even in such circumstances there are several elements which require consideration because of their centrality to distributive outcomes. Clearly, if decisions about aggregate expenditures, and spending priorities among departments, occur within the controlling political group, the relationship between senior members of Policy and Resources, and Education Committees, most especially at chairman level, becomes of crucial importance to education spending. At any time, but particularly with contraction, inter-service competition for resources cannot be resolved other than by the exercise of political power. Without rational arguments to prove that one suggested expenditure is better than another, perceptions by committee chairmen about the potential benefits of rival spending proposals provide, in the limit, an arbitration. All that happens in these cases, as opposed to a discussion in full committee, is that bargains are struck beforehand, but in either case only incremental expenditures reach the agenda. At the same time, in such a political environment, the relationship between the education committee chairman and the chief education officer assumes considerable significance. Between them they are responsible for combining technical details with the interpretation of educational and political priorities for the establishment of the budget. Within this framework they co-ordinate the conversion of estimates into a final document as it moves through sub-committee to education committee and main Council. Also, as happens with contraction, when reductions are demanded by Policy and Resources they must organize opposition to ensure that the cutbacks are minimized and arrange that whatever retrenchment has to be made is accepted, however grudgingly, by the various lobbies within, and impinging upon, the sub-committee and committee structure.

The LEAs' need to compete for resources with other services has been exaggerated, not only by contraction, but also through the provisions of the Local Government Planning and Land Act, 1980, in relation to capital expenditure. Previous to that, central government permission to spend (essentially allowing the authority to raise a capital sum subsequently repaid through revenue expenditure) was strictly categorized between, and within, services. Under the changed arrangements each LEA, and the rest of the authority, presents a case about the capital expenditure they would choose to make on major projects and minor works, separated into basic needs and improvements, and phased over more than one year, if necessary. The Department of the Environment, having received bids from each authority, then converts these into a series of maximum cash expenditures (again through a permission to raise capital) for every authority. The process of conversion, although obviously related to aggregate government spending intentions, is little understood at local level. Although categorized by service, and within education into nursery education, schools and further and higher education totals, authorities are allowed to vire expenditures, i.e. transfer money between different budget heads.[22] Ultimately, the only restriction is on individual authority levels of total spending. Therefore, during contraction, and reduced need for buildings, not only is education's case diminished, but it cannot be sure of its capital spending allocations. Of course, sustained virement on a large scale might prejudice authorities' subsequent bids for spending permission: but the issue of enhanced inter-service competition remains. Whatever the causes—reduction in resource levels, modifications to the main thrust and some of the detail of government policy, variations in demographic factors—the potential for rivalry between education and other services has risen, paradoxically during a time when many authorities have been pursuing corporate management approaches.

Some evidence that education has been disadvantaged by such changes exists, for example, since the first year of the new local authorities (1974-75) until 1981-82 the total of net local authority expenditure by the education service has declined from 51.9 per cent to 50.3 per cent.[23] In absolute terms this deficiency, had education remained at the higher figure, involves considerable and significant sums of money, particularly as they would have represented expenditures at the margins where decision-makers can exercise some autonomy. However, the circumstances of the two years are not exactly comparable. For example, the number of clients in education has declined while those in social services (another main spending department) have increased: central policy towards school meals and milk has reduced expenditure on these items, and overall government intentions during the intervening time has been to lower educational spending disproportionately to other expenditures. Unsurprisingly, education's percentage of total spending commitment has dropped, but the key yet unanswered question, from an objective perspective, concerns the rate of decline and its appropriateness. Whether there should be any decline is an issue which has been pre-empted by direct, but unsubstantiatable, political parameters. In the same sense, projections about the implications of the existence of items like GREs governing each service, target expenditures etc. for educational spending may suggest that these procedures will in themselves produce a further decline, but it will be extremely difficult, if not impossible, to prove the extent to which they are contributory factors. For example, a knowledge of GREs relative to decisions being sanctioned, even when there is an awareness of them,[24] may have little effect, because of the numerous other factors that impinge upon, and in fact constitute, the political processes in each local authority. These define the base and determine incremental expenditures in education and other services.

NOTES AND REFERENCES

1. Hartley, O.A., The relationship between central and local authorities, *Public Administration*, **49**, 439–456, 1971.
2. Mainly through regulations: see, for example, SI 1086/1981, *The Education (Schools and Further Education) Regulations*, 1981.
3. Griffith, J.A.G., *Central Departments and Local Authorities*, Allen & Unwin, London, 1966, p. 522.
4. Jones, G.W. and Stewart, J.D., The Treasury and local government, *The Political Quarterly*, **54**(1), 5–15, 1983.
5. Cmnd 2923, *Local Government Finance: England and Wales*, 1966.
6. Cmnd 4040, *Royal Commission on Local Government in England 1966–1969*, 1969.
7. Cmnd 6453, *Committee of Enquiry into Local Government Finance*, 1976.
8. Bennett, R.J. The local income tax in Britain: a critique of recent arguments against its use, *Public Administration*, **59**, 295–311, 1981.
9. Cmnd 4741, *Future Shape of Local Government Finance*, 1971, and Cmnd 6813, *Local Government Finances*, 1977.
10. *The Education Authorities Directory 1983*, School Government Publishing, Redhill, 1983.
11. Bennett, R.J., *Central Grants to Local Governments*, Cambridge University Press, Cambridge, 1982, pp. 103–130, describes the arrangements in detail.
12. Marslen-Wilson, F. and Crispin, A., How much influence does the GRE have on LEA attitudes?, *Education*, 16 September 1983, pp. 232–233.
13. For example, their effects as reported in *Education*, 17 December 1982, pp. 483–484.
14. See the overall perspective in *Education*, 12 December 1982, pp. i-iv.
15. Jones, G.W. and Stewart, J.D., op. cit., **54**(1), 5–15, 1983.
16. Travers, T., Local Government, Planning and Land Act 1980, *Political Quarterly*, **52**, 355–361, 1981.
17. Cmnd 9008, *Rates—Proposals for Rate Limitation and the Reform of the Rating System*, 1983.
18. Hartley, H.J., *Educational Planning—Programming—Budgeting: A Systems Approach*, Prentice Hall, Englewood Cliffs, N.J., 1968, pp. 129–137.
19. Danziger, J.N., Assessing incrementalism in British municipal budgeting, *British Journal of Political Science*, **6**, 335–350, 1976.
20. Down, A., *Inside Bureaucracy*, Little Brown, Boston, 1967, pp. 249–251.
21. Greenwood, R., Hinings, C.R. and Ranson, S., The politics of the budgeting process in English local government, *Political Studies*, **25**(1), 25–47, 1977.
22. Department of the Environment Circular 14/81, *Capital Programmes* (1981) and 7/82 *Capital Programmes* (1982).
23. Department of the Environment, *Local Government Financial Statistics 1981-2*, HMSO, London, 1983.
24. Marslen-Wilson, F. and Crispin, A., *Education*, 16 September 1983.

8

The DES

BRIAN SALTER and TED TAPPER

The origins of the Department's shift from 'holder of the ring between the real forces in educational policy-making' (local authorities, the denominations, teachers and parents) to 'enforcer of positive controls, based increasingly on knowledge which the department itself went out to get' (Kogan, 1971, p. 30) can be traced back to changes in the DES-LEA relationship in the 1950s. During this period it became obvious that certain basic processes of resource allocation within the educational system could no longer be subject to the whims of decentralized administrative procedures without complete confusion resulting. In particular, more effective centralized influence was seen to be necessary over capital spending on buildings and the prediction and supply of teachers. This led to the setting up within the department of the Architects and Building Branch, and the Teachers Supply Branch. Referring to major developments in the Department's forward planning capacity in recent years, Sir William Pile (1979, p. 59) noted that 'These changes reflect the growing recognition that an essential function of the Department, over and above the performance of specific practical and administrative duties deriving from the education Acts, is that of resource planning for the education service as a whole.' He elaborated:

> that is, the formulation of objectives, the framing of national policies best calculated to meet these objectives, the undertaking of long term costings of policies in a way that enables ministers to choose their priorities, and the task of effectively presenting the consequential resource needs within central government.

Now there can be little doubt that, given the Department's final responsibility for the administration of education and the increasing demand for education and expenditure on it, the emergence of these more sophisticated kinds of planning mechanisms was inevitable. The question

Source: From Salter, B. and Tapper, T., *Education, Politics and the State*, Grant McIntyre, London, 1981, pp. 100–114.

which concerns us is how far the theme of 'administrative necessity' was used to justify the enclosure of the policy-making process; how far the planning process has been internalized within the Department on the grounds that the Department alone has the planning know-how and that, within this, projections about capital expenditure and teacher manpower, for example, have an objective and unchallengeable validity of their own. As Woodhall (1972, p. 63) puts it,

> The real weakness of manpower forecasts is not that they are inaccurate, for all long-term forecasting tends to be inaccurate, but that they have been treated as though they are accurate, as though opportunities for substitution, flexibility, or alternative use of resources, did not exist.

The attraction of 'projectionism' is principally that the arithmetic behind it is simple, though there tends to be a lot of it, and that the conclusions which stem from it are easy to comprehend (see Armitage, 1973, pp. 214–16). So it is not entirely surprising that the methodology of the Robbins Report (1963) was based on projected numbers of students in higher education and that it envisaged a system of rolling planning based on projections made for ten years ahead. In effect, the prestige of Robbins further legitimated the use of projections in DES planning as well as extending the range of its use to include students as well as teachers.

Official government confirmation of the Robbins method for estimating future provision required in higher education appeared in 1970 with the publication of Educational Planning Paper No. 2. This claimed that it was 'a working document intended to assist discussion ... and carries no implication whatever for future Government policy or finance' (DES, 1970c, p. iii), a highly dubious claim in view of the fact that it did not see fit to explore more than the single policy option implicitly contained in its projections. It dismisses the possibility of considering other options in terms which by now have a familiar ring:

> There are a considerable number of factors, both internal to the higher education system and external to it, which may have a significant impact on its future development. *In many cases it is not practicable to assess their impact in quantitative terms* [our stress] (ibid., pp. 8–9).

In other words the capacity for quantification becomes the key criterion, as in corporate planning, for inclusion as a possible policy option. Behind it lies the confident but dubious assumption that the past is capable of an unambiguous interpretation and that on this sure foundation planning for the future can be built.

The more that official estimates dominate the context in which policies are made, the more these estimates are likely to become self-fulfilling prophecies and, conversely, the more that opportunities to develop the system in different ways will be neglected. Official command of the type of information input for the consideration of policy makers (as in the case of a heavy reliance on the extrapolation of existing trends) will naturally prescribe the parameters of possible policies. There is also an easy symbiosis between the use of projections of student and teacher numbers by the DES and the financial procedures governing department spending organized under the Public Expenditure Survey Committee (PESC). This requires that early each year government departments submit estimates of what they expect to spend over the next five years of each of their programmes to PESC. Given that departments compete with each other for a share of the expenditure cake, the DES is naturally not going to lose the opportunity of supporting its case and its financial projections with parallel figures concerning student and teacher population trends. The 'hard' data culled from the latter thus have considerable political appeal for the DES in the annual round of interdepartmental budgeting warfare, and until it can find an equally authoritative substitute it is not likely to downgrade the importance of projections in the face it presents to the rest of Whitehall.

As a means of estimating the financial implications of existing government programmes the Public Expenditure Survey system obviously suffers from the weakness that it does not cost and compare alternative policy options, as the White Paper 'The reorganization of central government' (The Cabinet Office, 1979, para. 50) pointed out. In an attempt to remedy this problem, an output budgeting technique called Programme Analysis and Review (PAR) was introduced into government planning in 1970, and the DES (1970b) has been one of the first departments to try and develop it. Like corporate planning, PAR seeks to systematize the process of policy analysis and policy formation along lines which place a premium on being able to assess the budgetary implications of different policy developments. The objective is to take a particular programme area such as nursery education and then to set out in a logical and informed fashion the alternative policies and their alternative costs.

Again it has that rational quality with immediate ramifications for the delimitation of the policy-making process. Firstly, some educational policies are going to be more easily costed than others and these are likely to be those already tried and tested and those which can be linked to trend data. Newer and less quantifiable policies are bound to appear experimental and hence more of a gamble. Secondly, the more confident that officials and ministers become that this management technique supplies them with the information required to make rational policy choices, the more policy formation will be internalized within the DES and the more outside interest groups will be excluded from it. Or, to put it another way:

> The stronger are formal systems for policy analysis and evaluation in the government of education, the more doubtful becomes the autonomy of teachers and academics in deciding what they shall do, and how. The development of sophisticated management systems in government and in the DES is of interest not just for its own sake, but for its effect upon the balance of power in the education system—even the concept of 'partnership' between DES, the LEA, and teachers (OU, 1974, p. 43).

Consultation with outside groups may take place, therefore, but in the context of choices already defined. Such consultation is consequently likely to be confirmatory rather than initiating in its objectives. However, what this argument does not deal with is the possibility that no matter how systematic the administration of PAR may be, and the indications are that it is not that systematic, room still exists for the injection of values not sanctioned by the DES into policy-making in the form of the education minister's role. How real is this possibility?

The most detailed evidence relevant to this question is Maurice Kogan's conversations with ex-DES ministers Edward Boyle and Antony Crosland in *The Politics of Education* (Kogan, 1971). His general conclusion (p. 41) is that the 'ability of even the most able Minister to create, promote and carry out policies is limited'. Both Boyle and Crosland emphasize the constraints under which a minister operates in terms of policies already in train or being explored, the amount of information to be digested and the continually evolving nature of educational policy. Crosland calculated that it takes about two years to fully master a department but that even so, within these two years 'there will be chunks of the Department and of Department policy which you have not really had time to look at at all' (ibid., p. 158). Similarly Boyle felt that he did not have control over the vast range of policies of the DES—partly because he did not have time to understand all the various parts of education (ibid., p. 137). This feeling is reinforced by the arguments of Lord Crowther-Hunt (a former Minister of State in the DES) concerning the gathering of influence by the bureaucratic élite. Crowther-Hunt maintains that the continual turnover of ministers of education (he estimates that in recent years their stay has averaged 17 months) means that they are rarely in the position of having sufficient independent knowledge to challenge the details of the policy agenda advanced by their civil servants. So when one of the Whitehall official committees (which ministers do not attend) or PAR reports (which are not published) produce their recommendations, it is increasingly difficult for a minister not to accept them (Crowther-Hunt and Kellner, 1980).

Probably the most influential role one can ascribe to a minister, therefore, is that of arbitrator of competing policies within the DES rather than the initiator of completely new ones and the imposer of foreign values. This does not deny of course that department policies are heterogeneous rather than homogeneous. What Toby Weaver, ex-Deputy Secretary at the DES, has described as the 'dialectic within the office' ensures that such choice is available (ibid., p. 123). However, it is our contention that the procedures on which the policy-making process is founded increasingly circumscribe the nature of its possible content and hence the range of choices available to a minister.

For those continually concerned with the generation of those choices, the civil servants of central government, it would seem that there would be little to object to in the enclosure and limitation of policy formation. Indeed, if Locke (1974, p. 71) is correct in his belief that the 'dedicated professional thinks of himself as fair and able to avoid self-interest in a way which representatives of localities or particular interests are not' then there would apparently be much to gain. The OECD report *Educational Development Strategy in England and Wales* was very forthright on this issue:

> The feeling exists strongly within the Department that when it comes to planning leading to policy decisions for which resources have to be secured and allocated, such informal methods, utilised by sensitive and fair-minded government servants, are superior to highly structured formal procedures which invite half-baked and politically sectarian opinions, and encourage demagogy, confrontation, and publicity battles, leading to a considerable waste of time (1975, p. 31).

If Birley's (1970) opinion of CEOs (protectors of democracy) and OECD's opinion of the DES are correct, then local and national managers of education have at least their self-esteem in common. But if the enclosure process means that the civil servant is seen by others to be the initiator of educational policy then his own conception of his role will have to shift accordingly. For although there is little doubt that the professional administrator regards himself as rightly influential in policy formulation, he is accustomed also to being supplied with protection by the cloak of democracy around him. Visibility is really not the name of the game for the civil servant and neither is direct public accountability. In the long term, however, he cannot expect to have both increased power and the same degree of anonymity. Those formerly included in policy formation are bound to demand that the new breed of expert managers be seen and held to be responsible for their actions.

The more activist definition of the educational administrator's role is a necessary corollary of the interventionist DES prepared both to take the lead in policy making and to prescribe its acceptable limits. Although the traditional conception of the department as aggregator and synthesizer of pressure group demands, responsive to the movement of the consensus, is still much beloved by many writers on education including the public self-presentation of the DES itself (see OECD, 1975, pt. 1), it is a conception rapidly being rendered obsolete by the march of events. And just as the Department shrugs off its passive policy stance so must those who administer it. But while shrugging off a self-conception is one thing, rearranging the relationships with others to fit that new conception is quite another and depends, firstly, on the amount of control the DES can exercise over its environment in the construction and execution of policy and, secondly, on its capacity to legitimize new policy. Changing the state apparatus can be a dicey affair.

CONTROLS

Until recently, the department has been engagingly modest in its estimation of its own power. In its contribution to the 1975 OECD report, for example, it argued that the powers of the Secretary of State under the 1944 Education Act and subsequent Acts 'though important are not extensive' and that he 'relies heavily on non-statutory means of implementing his policies, by offering guidance and advice through the issue of circulars and other documents' (pp. 8–9). Phrases such as 'adequate consultation', 'foundation of assent' and 'general consensus' are scattered liberally throughout the DES section of the report as the Department insists that it is reflecting an aggregate of existing opinion rather than seeking to mould a new one. Its view of its controls are here fully consistent with its consensus model of educational policy making. This passive public face of the DES has changed considerably in the last few years in recognition of its search for more controls to service more adequately its burgeoning planning function. As it happens the Department's earlier promulgation of a public image where its powers were presented as limited and mainly non-statutory was in any case something of a false modesty.

All LEAs operate within an established network of national policies: the length of school life, salaries paid to teachers, minimum building standards and maximum building costs and pupil-teacher ratios. Any consideration of departmental control must in the first instance recognize that this framework exists and itself sets limits upon an LEA's capacity to deviate too far from central guidelines. Similarly, the much vaunted autonomy of the classroom teacher is regulated by the national system of curriculum control, namely the General Certificate of Education Examination at Ordinary and Advanced Levels, and the Certificate of Secondary Education Examinations in their various modes. Although the actual examinations are administered by autonomous examining bodies (eight GCE and fourteen CSE) the Secretary of State decides what changes will occur in the system after listening to the advice of an intermediary body, the Schools Council. Beyond this framework of controls, the DES has its financial controls, whatever overlap exists between local and central administrator values on policy making and, last but not least, Her Majesty's Inspectorate.

Although the Department does not directly control the capital finance used by LEAs for educational building, it does decide (according to building regulations and cost limits developed by the Architects and Buildings Branch and the annual building programme allocated to each educational sector— schools, further education and teacher training, etc.) which LEA projects will be given the go-ahead and which ones refused. The fact that local authorities must submit educational building plans to the Department for approval means that the DES can not only apply the standing administrative requirements to the plans but can also use the opportunity, if it so wishes, to exercise political control over changes in local authority provision. The most notable clashes recently in this respect have been those over LEA plans for comprehensivization which have failed to meet DES standards, flexible though these are, on what precisely constitutes a comprehensive system.

Given this method of financing the physical context in which education takes place, it is obviously in the interest of LEAs to remain sensitive to developments in DES policy both by keeping a close watch on the numerous circulars issued by the Department and by consultation with its local liaison officer, the HMI.

Even recognizing this ultimate control of capital investment by the DES, it would not do to conclude as a result that LEAs are the easy and obedient servants of the Departmental will. For although Crosland 'was very struck by how much influence, control, power, or whatever the right word is, the Department has' (Kogan, 1971, p. 169), Boyle pointed out (ibid., p. 124) that 'there can't be a straight, single control here for the very simple reason that the Ministry directly controls so very little money'. Boyle was referring to the fact that the majority of the expenditure on education by local authorities, that is recurrent as opposed to capital expenditure, comes to the LEA as part of the annual Rate Support Grant (RSG) from which the government finances all local authority services. The RSG is a block grant within which, until very recently, no funds were separately labelled for the use of the education service alone: education had to compete with the other services for its share. At first sight this system may appear to have given LEAs substantial discretion in terms of what they spend on education and how they spend it but, bearing in mind the national guidelines within which LEAs must operate, the true situation is much less clear cut and the arguments continue (see Boaden, 1971; Byrne, 1974). The picture is further muddied by the 1980 Local Government Planning and Land (No. 2) Act which replaces the single block grant with one awarded on a service by service basis. Precisely what effect this will have on the DES-LEA relationship it is as yet too soon to say. What is, nevertheless, clear, is that considerable variation exists in LEA provision of books, equipment, furniture, in-service training of teachers, school transport, etc., indicating that although the DES may control the broad parameters of education so far it does not substantially influence the quality of the day-to-day provision within these parameters (see Taylor and Ayres, 1969).

Nor are its financial controls integrated so as to form an efficient basis for the policy-making process. Reporting the reactions of local authority associations to the 1969 Public Expenditure White Paper, the Education and Arts Sub-Committee of the House of Commons Expenditure Committee stated:

> The associations were also anxious about the effect of the [annual] PESC predictions on the biennial Rate Support Grant settlements. They complained that the PESC figures and the Rate Support Grant figures were on a different price basis and could not therefore be related to one another in their present form. The association wished ideally to see a Rate Support Grant and PESC as parts of a single interrelated exercise rather than as two separate and, as they suspected, conflicting operations (Armitage, 1973, p. 39).

Add to this the particular problem of higher education where the responsibility for financial provision lies both with the LEAs (polytechnics), and the University Grants Committee (universities) with its own quite distinct planning procedures and relationship with the DES, and you have a less than coherent financial framework within which to form policy. Recent reorganization of the DES Higher and Further Education Branches responsible for financial planning into a single new 'super-branch', FHE 1, is an attempt to mitigate the problem by bridging the binary divide and reducing the power and isolation of the University Branch. As yet it is too early to know what effect this will have on the co-ordination of DES policy on the universities and polytechnics.

At present, then, the fragmentation of the financial procedures on which the DES relies in its attempts to construct policies leads to tensions between the local authorities and the Department. However, it is worth noting that both would agree on the diagnosis of the reasons for the problem, that is the inefficiencies of the financing mechanisms, and the need for more systematic co-operation. Whether this also means that they would agree on who has what say in a more integrated planning system is open to doubt. For our previous analysis suggests that the DES has already defined what it means by more efficiency in central policy making and it will be a question of how far local authorities are prepared to go along with this definition once its structural implications begin to percolate through. Despite the common professional concern that long-term planning in education should be rationally organized the traditional central-local differences are bound to pose problems. Thus Mrs Thatcher's rather abrupt withdrawal of Circular 10/65 enforcing comprehensivization and its replacement with Circular 10/70 allowing LEAs to decide against comprehensivization if they so wished drew unanimous protest from the local authority associations. As Kogan (1975, p. 100) points out, 'it was not what she did but the way that she did it that was objectionable'.

If there is doubt this far about the Department's ability to orchestrate policy change, where does that leave its territorial force, Her Majesty's Inspectorate? How far can HMI be regarded as the willing tool of the DES in its attempts to impose central definitions of desirable policy shift and how far is HMI an independent body with opinions and values of its own? Its position in the educational system as authoritative supplier of information both to the LEAs and schools on the one hand, and the DES on the other, is undoubtedly critical. At the local level, HMIs have the functions of inspectors of schools and colleges, interpreters of Department policy to the LEAs, and are members of numerous committees such as examination boards and regional advisory councils for further education. (The latter is particularly important since HMIs have the singular power to accept or reject new courses.) At the central level, they act as professional advisers to the DES, drawing on their network of local contacts, contribute to Department publications and staff Department courses for teachers. Any move by the

DES to systematize further the process of policy construction is therefore dependent upon HMI to acquire and to disseminate the right information at the right time. This would imply that from the Department's point of view the closer the ties between itself and HMI the better.

Writers on Her Majesty's Inspectorate are frequently at pains to point out that HMIs are independent-minded people if occasionally idiosyncratic. With some pride Blackie (1970, p. 53; and see Edmonds, 1962), an ex-HMI himself, argues that,

> An inspector's essential independence is professional. In all educational matters he is free to hold and to express his own opinions, and no departmental control can be exercised upon them. This means that what he says to a teacher or writes in a report is what he really thinks, and is not in any way trimmed to suit government or departmental policy.

More realistically he subsequently admits that the 'Department could not tolerate a situation in which one of its employees was openly and explicitly hostile to a policy which it was implementing at the behest of Parliament' (ibid.). Other sources tend to confirm this image of HMIs operating within very severe constraints set by the Department and only exercising or voicing their personal judgement in situations not likely to offend. Thus the Select Committee on Her Majesty's Inspectorate (1968) concluded that the Department and the Inspectorate are in fact a very integrated body and the DES in its pamphlet *HMI Today and Tomorrow* (1970) also down-played the significance of HMI autonomy:

> HM Inspectors are a body of men and women who are ultimately answerable to the Secretary of State for Education and Science. They may well be given direct instructions by him. Their appointment is made on his recommendation.... It is the duty of the Inspectors, as of other civil servants, to assist the central government in discharging the responsibilities that successive parliaments have laid down (1970a, p. 9).

As the DES moves further in the direction of policy-making enclosures, so it must rely more on its internal means of information collecting rather than on information supplied by external groups. In this respect the role of HMIs as the field representatives and data collection agents of the DES is bound to be crucial in its efforts to sustain this move. This role is likely to be eroded in response to the requirements of the new style of policy making; though the myth of autonomy may well be retained as long as possible since it enhances the supposed objectivity of the information on which the Department rests its policy proposals.

THE LEGITIMATION OF THE STATE APPARATUS

The OECD report (1975, p. 28) on British educational development bravely stated that 'the evolution of education in the United Kingdom cannot be charted without placing the planning function of the Department of Education and Science at the centre of the story'. It summarized DES policy formation as characterized by attempts to:

minimize the degree of controversiality in the planning process and its results; reduce possible alternatives to matters of choice of resource allocation; limit the planning process to those parts of the educational services and functions strictly controlled by the DES; exploit as fully as possible the powers, prerogatives and responsibilities given to the DES under the 1944 Education Act; understate as much as possible the full role of the Government in the determination of the future course of educational policy and even minimize it in the eyes of the general public (ibid., p. 42).

Our own analysis of the bureaucratization of educational power in Britain has so far reached similar, though probably less emphatic conclusions. However, our theoretical perspective leads us beyond the recognition that bureaucratic change has and is taking place in the management of education and takes us on to the further question of what ideological change is necessary to support these bureaucratic shifts in the state apparatus given education's central ideological function in society. Our theory insists that if educational change is to be acceptable to the populace at large it has to go through an ideological stage. There are, analytically speaking, two aspects to this stage: (a) the way in which policy is produced and (b) the policies produced. Both require ideological legitimation and, in practice, the nature of this legitimation may overlap the two aspects. Nevertheless, as we will show, the overlap is not so complete as to undermine the importance of the analytical distinction itself.

In the past the process of educational policy production was legitimated by the Department's claim that it aggregated and reflected the existing educational consensus. The major instrument reinforcing this claim was the work of the educational committees appointed either by the Central Advisory Council (CAC) on education, a standing statutory body, or by the DES itself. Major shifts in educational policy have, until recently, always been heralded by reports from such committees (e.g. Robbins, Crowther, Plowden) and their public hallmark has been their independence from the Department, the eminence of their membership, their sensitivity to the broad sweep of educational opinion, their increasing use of 'objective' social science, and, stemming from these others, the authority of their pronouncements. To a large extent these qualities are in fact illusory and the committees are, as Kogan documents, 'far more "in-house", far more a part of official review, than the outward forms seem to suggest' (Kogan and Packwood, 1974, p. 23). Committees generally have their terms of reference and membership determined by the Department and their secretariat and research data supplied by the Department (Robbins being a notable exception to the latter). This has meant that, up to now, they have performed the latent functions of enabling the Department to use them both as a jury against which Departmental policies could be tested as they emerged and as a centre for negotiations on policies which had, in any case, to be discussed with the main educational interests before reaching the public stage (ibid., p. 23).

Nor is the DES in any way obliged to accept the policy implications of a committee's conclusions, though public opinion may force its hand. In his examination of the influence of prewar advisory councils on the Board of

Education, Graves (1940, p. 89) cites the example of the report *Books in Elementary Schools* which was widely read, reprinted, yet comprehensively ignored by the board. He concludes that this well illustrates the impotence of an advisory body once it has reported: 'Unless the education authorities are willing to take the matter up, or public opinion is strong enough, a first-class report may disappear almost without trace. And the Department is only likely to take the matter up if it fits a prior policy decision made internally.'

Yet if education committees and their reports are such malleable material, to be promulgated by the DES as policy-legitimating instruments as and when it thinks fit, why are such committees used less now than before? Why did Crosland deem it appropriate to disband the CAC after the publication of the Plowden and Gittins reports in 1967 particularly since, as Kogan (1978, p. 135) underlines, 'since then there has been discontent at the way in which the recently created planning system within the DES seems to feed on its own expertise and knowledge rather than bringing in wider circles of expertise and knowledge', as it had done previously? Crosland's own explanation is revealing: he argues that there is a danger of too many and too lengthy reports—'And they can slow up action, as Plowden would have done on comprehensivization if I hadn't been very firm' (Kogan, 1971, p. 174). In justifying the phasing out of the CAC, Sir William Pile (1979, p. 38) observed that if committees of inquiry are to be used then *ad hoc* ones which reach speedy conclusions are increasingly preferred by ministers. The difficulty with placing this premium on decision-making efficiency, however, is that the legitimating function of the committees is neglected. While it is one thing to take a decision swiftly, it is quite another to get it accepted by the rest of the educational system.

As the Department adopts a more positive stance towards the rest of the education system, gathers its own information, internalizes its planning procedures and shrugs off its old service image, it has to face the fact that since policy can no longer be deemed to 'emerge' (like those Conservative party leaders of old) by some hidden but natural process of evolution, neither can the ideology necessary to support both the policy-making framework itself and the policies produced. At present the tendency is for the DES to attempt to legitimize its own dominance of the formation of policy by arguing that the planning techniques which it employs are in some sense 'objective' and 'scientific' and allow ministers a fair choice between a full range of policy options. This can be characterized as a low profile approach which will work so long as major educational interests are not unduly offended by the policy biases inherent in the Department's use of these techniques. Even so, the fact that the policies which are produced are directly the DES's responsibility alone, rather than that of a vague consensus, will increasingly place the Department in an exposed position.

If questions are raised about the legitimacy of the means of policy formation employed by the educational state apparatus, this is bound to have an effect in turn upon the DES's ability to manage the tensions between education's social control and economic functions. For these functions to be performed effectively by the educational system, it is essential that any change in their operation (i.e. any new educational policy) is both cloaked with the suitable ideological apparel and viewed as having been produced by legitimate policy-making machinery. As the forum in which these underlying pressures are politically negotiated, along with the inputs from demographic shifts and party policy, the Department undoubtedly comes under considerable institutional stress as it seeks to reconcile the policy implications of these demands with its own bureaucratic needs and ambitions. To relieve this stress, though not to remove it, the DES needs ideological protection: in order to implement successfully its social control and economic functions and to legitimize its policies. Merely claiming that the policies were produced by 'rational' planning techniques is not going to be good enough. We do not live in a rational world. What the CACs and the other committees were good at, and what the DES is still learning, was that assembling of broad societal values into patterns which carried authority—i.e. they were good at producing ideology. Until the Department acquires the art of developing ideological positions to match the policies it sponsors, it will not have fully worked out the implications of its own bureaucratic changes and education's social functions and will remain exposed to attacks such as that of the OECD report.

REFERENCES

Armitage, P. (1973) *Planning in Practice*, in Fowler, G., Morris, V. and Ozga, J. (eds.), *Decision-making in British Education*, London, Heinemann, 1973.
Birley, D. (1970) *The Education Officer and His World*, London, Routledge & Kegan Paul.
Blackie, J. (1970) *Inspecting and the Inspectorate*, London, Routledge & Kegan Paul.
Boaden, N. (1971) *Urban Policy-making: influences on county boroughs in England and Wales*, London, Cambridge University Press.
Byrne, E. (1974) *Planning and Educational Inequality: a study of the rationale of resource allocation*, Slough, Bucks., National Foundation for Educational Research.
DES (Department of Education and Science) (1970a) *HMI Today and Tomorrow*, London, HMSO.
Crowther-Hunt, Lord and Kellner, P. (1980) *The Civil Servants: an inquiry into Britain's ruling class*, London, Macdonald & Janes.
DES (Department of Education and Science) (1970b) *Output Budgeting for the Department of Education and Science: Report of a Feasibility Study*, Education Planning Paper No. 1, London, HMSO.
DES (Department of Education and Science) (1970c) *Student Numbers in Higher Education in England and Wales*, Educational Planning Paper No. 2, London, HMSO.
Edmonds, E.L. (1962) *The School Inspector*, London, Routledge & Kegan Paul.
Graves, J. (1940) The use of advisory bodies by the Board of Education, in Vernon, R.V. and Mansergh, N. (eds.), *Advisory Bodies*, London, Allen & Unwin.
Kogan, M. (1971) *The Politics of Education*, Harmondsworth, Penguin.
Kogan, M. (1975) *Educational Policy-making*, London, Allen & Unwin.
Kogan, M. (1978) *The Politics of Educational Change*, London, Fontana.

Kogan, M. and Packwood, T. (1974) *Advisory Councils and Committees in Education*, London, Routledge & Kegan Paul.
Locke, M. (1974) *Power and Politics in the School System: a guidebook*, London, Routledge & Kegan Paul.
OECD (1975) *Educational Development Strategy in England and Wales*, Paris, OECD.
OU (Open University) (1974) *Decision-making in British Education Systems*, E221, Units 5–7, Walton Hall, Milton Keynes, Open University Press.
Pile, W. (1979) *The Department of Education and Science*, London, Allen & Unwin.
Robbins Report (1963) Report of the Committee appointed by the Prime Minister under the chairmanship of Lord Robbins, *Higher Education*, Cmnd 2154, London, HMSO.
Taylor, G. and Ayres, N. (1969) *Born and Bred Unequal*, London, Longman.
The Cabinet Office (1970) *The Reorganisation of Central Government*, Cmnd 4506, London, HMSO.
Woodhall, M. (1972) *Economic Aspects of Education*, Slough, Bucks., National Foundation for Educational Research.

9

Competition ... and Competence?
education, training and the roles of DES and MSC*

D.L. PARKES

INTRODUCTION: THE EUROPEAN CONTEXT

The provision of education and training for post-16-year-olds has been subject to changes in content and structure for most industrialized countries from the early 1970s. In these countries debates on the curriculum (and on vocationalizing it) would be very familiar to a UK academic.

As far as initial skill training, vocational preparation and recurrent education are concerned, an OECD study (1974, 1984; Parkes, 1979) pointed out that in most countries initial skill training (apprenticeship) had become less a separate system and more part of a larger integrated national training programme. This included specifics such as vocational education in public sector institutions, non-apprenticeship training by employers and government training programmes. Most European OECD countries have a common dialogue between education and employment ministries providing programmes which create competition and conflict as well as collaboration and co-operation.

In most OECD countries technological and organizational changes have shifted the preferences of younger age groups to full-time vocational education. Economic and technological changes and high youth unem-

---

* A number of colleagues have made suggestions on the thrust of the text. In particular, my colleague, Russ Russell, has made invaluable contributions to the structuring of the section on 'Control of curriculum policy'.
Specially commissioned article. © 1985 The Open University.

ployment have made it difficult to sustain a balance between employer and employee needs. Training has been made to correspond more closely with employee and longer-term employment needs than those of the immediate employer. Governments have intervened structurally most commonly along the following lines:

1. Delay in specialization by introducing:
   (a) Skill groups or clusters.
   (b) A broad introductory year.
   (c) Modular structures of training.
2. Standardized off-the-job training.
3. Reduction of the apprenticeship period.
4. Revision of syllabus and improved instructor training.
5. Government intervention for special purposes, e.g. for:
   (a) Low academic achievers.
   (b) Minority groups such as the handicapped.
   (c) Girls.

Also, as Morgan (1980) points out for the 'job corps' in the United States, full-time vocational preparation acts in a custodial role, a kind of holding phase equivalent to national service or raising the school-leaving age.

The Manpower Services Commission (MSC) draws a good deal of its moneys from the European Community's Social Fund. The fact that the Commission is devoting this money is indicative that the problems of the United Kingdom are following a pattern that exists across Western Europe and for which common criteria for access to funds have been laid down. In a sense a good deal of what the MSC does is Community directed.

THE UK PICTURE

In the United Kingdom, participation rates for 16–19-year-olds under schools or FE regulations, full or part time, have until recently been less than 40 per cent. In terms of full-time equivalent students, occupancy of places has been 2 to 1 in favour of schools over FE colleges, although the ratio is more balanced if one counts individuals (FT or PT) attending each type of institution, and there was a 'drift' of FT students to colleges throughout the 1970s. Table 1 (below), collated from various statistical bulletins, gives some indication of changes by mode of attendance in non-advanced FE. These figures exclude those on YOP and similar schemes and conceal shifts between different kinds of qualification *within* the FE sector (e.g. 240 per cent increase in SCOTEC full-time ONC students). Hollyhock (in Parkes, 1982) suggests the sector has had to reflect:

(a) Declining numbers of courses for the more traditional manufacturing industries accompanied by a wide range of courses to cope with training in new technologies.

(b) An increased demand for vocational education in areas of business and service sectors particularly in the public sector.
(c) An increased demand for general and continuing education.
(d) Pre-employment (vocational preparation) courses reflecting youth unemployment.

Table 1

	England 1972–82	Scotland 1980–83	N.I. 1978–82
Full-time/sandwich	+81%	+22%	+34%
Part-time day release	−34%	−2%	−9%
Other part-time day	+78%		
Evening	−16%	+34%	−3%

During the last decade the Technician and Business Education Councils, now integrated as BTEC, have rationalized the provision of courses and certification from the jungle of pre-1970s accrediting agencies and professional bodies. The City and Guilds of London Institute has refocused on craft courses. At the same time the Manpower Services Commission has had an increasing impact. In 1980 MSC programmes accounted for only 6 per cent of expenditure on non-advanced further education. By 1984 it was twice that figure and its impact was correspondingly greater. 1984 also saw a fall in the *school* staying-on rate at 16+, perhaps reflecting different levels of student financing in different sectors.

Concern with the contribution of schools and colleges to economic prosperity in general and industry and commerce in particular was the focus of the Callaghan speech at Ruskin College in 1976, commonly referred to as the opening of the 'Great Debate' and the Green Paper, *Education in Schools* (DES, 1977). The Prime Minister argued that it was 'vital to Britain's economic recovery and standard of living that the performance of manufacturing industry is improved and that the whole range of government policies, including education, contribute as much as possible to improving industrial performance and thereby increasing national wealth'. From this impetus has followed a series of initiatives shared, and creating a debate between the DES and the MSC under the aegis of the Department of Employment.

The post-16 curriculum now has four streams:

- The 'A' level route for those intending to proceed to higher education and the professions.
- The technician route for those generally above average attainment.
- Residual craft studies for those of average ability and below either in employment or part time education.

- The MSC-sponsored programmes for a growing and increasingly alienated body of the young unemployed.
  (Farmer, in Parkes, 1982)

The documentation and reports providing the structures for the last two streams have centred first on the debate set up by the publication of *Proposals for a Certificate of Extended Education* (DES, 1979) and *A Basis for Choice* (FEU, 1979). The proposals of ABC, as it became known, were incorporated in the design of a Certificate in Pre-Vocational Education (CPVE) scheduled to start in 1985 with an integrated curriculum, not a single subject base as had CEE. The victory in this debate merely started another battle between the ABC curriculum and that of the Youth Training Scheme (YTS) implemented by the MSC in 1983 as part of the New Training Initiative (NTI) (MSC, 1981).

The aims of the scheme are laid down in the Youth Task Group Report (MSC, 1982, para. 4.3).

(a) To provide all young people participating in the scheme with a better start in working and adult life through an integrated programme of training, education and work experience, which can include work in and for the community, and a record of achievement, which can serve as a foundation for subsequent employment or continued training or relevant further education.

(b) To provide for the participating employer a better equipped young work force which has acquired some competence and practical experience in a range of related jobs or skills, thus enabling him to operate more productively and effectively in an increasingly competitive trading environment and a period of often rapid and far reaching technological and market changes.

(c) To develop and maintain a more versatile, and readily adaptable, highly motivated and productive work force which will assist Britain to compete successfully in the 1980s and beyond.

The major difference between the YTS and the CPVE is in the design base.

> The design base for 17+ is a general education process with a vocational bias and *where possible* a short period of work experience. MSC programmes will focus on work-based learning which will include the promotion of broad objectives, some of which might be called general education (Levy, 1982).

So the impetus and impact of the MSC upon vocational preparation at 16+ has been in terms of emphasis on *employer based* rather than *college based* schemes. Two other centrally determined initiatives complemented the NTI and YTS and further challenge traditional policy and administrative structures. The Technical and Vocational Education Initiative (TVEI) for 14–18-year-olds introduced in 1982 is school-based but funded by the MSC, not through existing LEA modes. The White Paper, *Training for Jobs* (DE, 1984), proposed a major incursion into the role of the local authorities by removing 25 per cent of the rate support moneys of the local authorities for work-related FE and allocating it to the MSC. Authorities and colleges would have to submit schemes of work to MSC Area Offices.

All this was accompanied by a new rhetoric from Ministers:

> Pupils needed to be given an understanding of the economic base of our society and of the wealth creating process. (Neil McFarlane, Parliamentary Under-Secretary of State, 1982.)
>
> If we fail to provide today's young people with the basic skills for employment they are likely to be permanently unemployed. (William Shelton, Parliamentary Under-Secretary, 1982.)

For the period 1975–85, then, the rhetoric of vocationalism was accompanying a movement away from part-time provision for students in work to provision for full-time students either prior to work or not in work. From 1979 there were increasing measures to cope with youth unemployment and to establish a climate and structures for work related or orientated training and education.

Within the common trends of Western countries, specific issues and differences in the United Kingdom give rise to anxiety and some have led to action (whether effective or ineffective) from central government. These concerns are that: the participation rate of the 16–19 cohort in full- or part-time education and training is low; there is an overlapping of two separate sectors (i.e. a mixed provision) of school and FE; the industrial and commercial contribution to training is minimal; the relationship among the contributing parties (education institutions/private sector/local authorities/examining and validating bodies/professional bodies/governmental agencies) is complex enough to be virtually incomprehensible (Parkes, 1976, 1982) even to those who work in the network. There appears to be a lack of coordination and coherence among the partners.

Beryl Pratley's *Signposts* (1980), a map of 16–19 educational provision, sets out comprehensively the dilemmas of fragmentation: 'piecemeal and retrospective course design', '169 pages listing the courses in FE establishments leading to work', 'the implementation of TEC by lecturers without teacher training', 'feverish activity taking place all over the country', '70 professional bodies who award qualifications'. Pratley reinforces the view that provision tended to focus on the more able and on industries' needs: a reactive rather than proactive response from FE colleges traditionally associated with a minority of the middle ability range of the 16–19s.

These factors are not new. Corelli Barnett (1975) puts them into a medium-term historical perspective by recalling similar debates in Victorian England on vocationalism and the need for a rationalized system with more state intervention, culminating in the report of the Samuelson Commission of 1884.

A hundred years on, however, we had still in the 1970s and 80s an FE service in a complex environment: growing at the margins of a traditional response to middle level industrial, commercial and community needs;

rationalizing its technician provision (albeit reluctantly) and caught by resource and developmental constraints, with unreliable or inadequate manpower and forward planning. The resource constraints expressed themselves throughout the decade in terms of staffing norms which, attempting to maximize lecturer class contact and class size and minimize student class contact, had negative impacts on manoeuvrability for new teaching methods.

From what 'value' standpoint can one perceive English FE? In what, if any way, does it reflect society at large? Its evolution, from mechanics' institutes on, reflects an administrative mode of providing for training needs unmet elsewhere; its incremental growth reflects no central thrust, no coherent policy. Its diffusion, its incapacity to become 'a development force', reflects the diffusion, lack of integration and coordination in the United Kingdom as a country.

We do not have the corporate identity of American colleges accompanied by a higher level of independence and accountability and more appraisal. Likewise, we do not have the service station approach of the French: curriculum, resourcing and staffing decisions taken by highly trained administrators outside the institutions. We sit in the middle, weighed down with middle managers—entrepreneurial or otherwise: our institutions are complex because of the delegation of curricular freedoms; shallowly independent; each level of independence checked by another—course tutor, head of department, dean, vice-principal, principal, LEA adviser and administrator, HMI, DES—a system which allows financial and growth checks as each college acquires an identity and ethos apparently in tune with a set of minority local needs. The locality is, in its turn, difficult to define, since it represents British industry: its tradition of self-training on the job, rather than a coordinated systematic system of training.

The NEDO Report *Competence and Competition* (1984) updated the criticisms. Like Samuelson, it compared the provision of education and training in the United Kingdom unfavourably with the Federal Republic of Germany, the United States and Japan. Despite the fact that the substance of the evidence from these three countries, however interesting, bears little relation to the Report's recommendations, it caught a mood of public anxiety. In the same year the MSC produced a new action plan based on the recommendations for a greater volume of provision more intensely focused and better structured. The latter two factors were the more highly stressed, however.

CONTROL OF CURRICULUM POLICY

There can be some debate about the nature of the curriculum in FE colleges since they reflect responses to a wide variety of needs otherwise unmet, i.e. varied institutional responses to a mixed market demand. There is a claim, however, to interface with the employment sector both at college level, professional body level and at that of examining and validating body. The major bodies—BTEC, City & Guilds and RSA—have variously local and central consultative committees with private sector representation. There is also an issue of process rather than content. Where and how should learning take place: for example, in projects/case studies or as with the MSC/YTS in the work place itself?

A major influence on the tertiary curriculum since 1977 has been the Further Education Unit funded directly by the DES with a brief to make possible a more coordinated and cohesive approach to curriculum development in FE. Its most persuasive influence on FE has been the philosophy of *A Basis for Choice* (FEU, 1979) which argues for an integrated basis for 17+ students, together with a common core offering vocational preparation and transition from adolescent to adult life. The FEU has been active in carrying some of the burden of its patron, the DES, in promoting an alternative to the DE proposals in the debate on 16–19 provision. In the 1980s it was moving also into adult provision as the MSC also grew more active in its interest in this group.

We must also examine interaction and influences among other categories, including:

1. The curriculum bodies.
2. Central government departments and agencies.
3. The institutions.
4. The market place.

Russ Russell, reviewing major styles of curriculum design in FE (Russell, 1981), examines the modes of operation of ten key bodies which provided a wide spread in terms of relationships to central government, of subject and vocational areas, of levels of student entry requirements and of relationships with colleges. Russell categorized types of bodies into:

examining—firm control over syllabus and examinations, little intervention into learning situations and less on content (e.g. City & Guilds);

validating—initiative in syllabus and examination from the college with monitoring from the central body (e.g. CNAA and BEC higher courses);

controlling—central body maintaining firm control over the syllabus and attempting firm control elsewhere (e.g. TEC, BEC).

However, given the relative financial and educational separateness of such bodies from central government and the lack of the firm legislative framework which binds the constituent parties together in, say, France and Germany, relations with government, industry, colleges and LEAs are ambiguous.

This ambiguity is partly due to the mode of establishment of such bodies.

The DES, historically, has chosen to exercise its responsibility by establishing, monitoring and occasionally regrouping them. They are separate from central government because of the older ideologies of the former of not dominating in a pluralist society and DES reticence in matters of curriculum which it saw as a professional domain. Central government thus set up a series of mediation points where educationalists, industry and providers can meet.

As a consequence, there is a necessity to negotiate with these parties rather than to exist in an authority relationship: influence and possibly power rather than authority. The outcome is a substantial machinery for consultation with representation on a plethora of committees both national and local, both general and curriculum specific. The various locations for negotiation (central/LEA/college) allow considerable manoeuvre for re-interpretation in the process of policy implementation (Challis et al., 1984). The claim of all, therefore, is that curriculum control and design is never decided without extensive reference, both informal and formal, to employers. The curricula of courses are closely linked to vocational objectives, but not necessarily with total clarity, leaving colleges a capacity and the need to reinterpret and maintain their own elaborate consultative machinery with the private sector.

The apparently decentralized nature of the English systems, the relative independence of the parts and the lack of legislative framework suggest, as above, that it is the examining and validating bodies that have been established as the mechanisms for coordination, failing other structures for determining ends between central and local government, between industry and unions, between education and industry.

Stewart Ranson has argued (Ranson, 1981, 1983a, 1983b) that this situation is changing in face of an increased centrist role from the DES. He examines the fluctuations post-1944 in central and local influence and argues that post-Ruskin and the Green Paper there has been an attempt not merely to clarify and redefine points of control but to reappropriate it. This is not only a reflection of education and training but of the wider and much publicized attempts by central government to 'curb' local authorities.

Ranson argues that 'steering' occurs on three fronts: vocationalism, rationalization and stratification. The last he argues as a complement to vocationalism—that is the encouragement of manpower planning within a context of social control. The approaches are, first, not to encourage unreal job expectations and, second, to establish a firm hierarchy of provision: the 'modern' stream—MSC-YTS-17+; the 'technical' stream—TEC-BEC-TVEI; the 'advanced' stream—'A' level-HE. With the MSC to the forefront in the first and the DES in the latter, the battle for control between the DES and the MSC is at the middle level. The instruments effecting this strategy of the DES may be seen as: the establishment of a new values climate by the rhetoric of reports, fora and public speeches; the imposition of resource rationalization; the establishment of tighter regulating procedures.

Competition... and Competence? 167

Ranson admits that the processes towards the achievement of the strategy are slow, uneven and incremental and the outcomes still uncertain, but he argues that the price of success is the erosion of the principles of common citizenship, equality of opportunity, fairness. What he omits to justify is the previous complexity with its failure to provide for 50 per cent of the 16–19 cohort. We have to ask whether the three types of provision he identifies as stratifying are not better than the traditional provision of the top two layers with nothing for the rest; that some degree of coordination is better than none, although the nature of that coordination may remain questionable.

MSC AND DES: COMPETITIVE OR CO-OPERATIVE?

Ranson also fails to elaborate the relations between the MSC and the DES. The rise and rise of the former around the New Training Initiative is arguably a more powerful instrument of vocationalism and centrism than the DES can muster.

In examining the MSC/DES dialogue one has to be careful, particularly in identifying the protagonists. Ministers at the DES use the rhetoric of corporate responsibility: 'if one is in central government then provided the initiatives conform to overall policy it doesn't matter who takes the credit' (Peter Brooke, 1984). At administrative level there is no DES or MSC except as bureaucratic stereotypes, but there exist factions within each body who vary in numbers and influence. There may be stronger affinities across the boundary than within each organization. There is some anecdotal evidence that *Training for Jobs* was redrafted at the DES to reduce its original rather more draconian thrust, but also that it was not entirely unsupported there.

Training for Jobs is *the* major instrument for centrism and vocationalism outside the traditional pattern. It argues the three objectives of NTI. It rehearses TVEI and the vocationalism of the school curriculum. It justifies work-based YTS. It makes the case for coherence.

> The wider aim must be to open up access to training and to jobs through a coherent system of training standards and certificates of competence, covering achievement in vocational education and training, both initially and throughout working life.

Most significant, however, are the proposed new arrangements within vocational education. Emphasis is placed on the need for the public sector to provide training and that vocational education must become more responsive to employment needs at national and local level.

The MSC is to be given 'important new responsibilities by enabling it to purchase a more significant proportion of work-related non-advanced further education provided by local education authorities'. By 1986/87 the Commission would account for 25 per cent of non-advanced further education with consequent reductions for the local authorities in rate support grant.

The reaction from the local authorities, both Conservative and Labour, was to resist. The implications were interesting; at the beginning of 1985 it was likely that the scheme would be implemented over their heads. Colleges of FE and local authorities would (a) have to bid for moneys for particular schemes and (b) shape their bids against MSC criteria; not an unusual market situation for the colleges—but a severe diminution in local authority influence. With the YTS, the MSC provides training allowances to all participants in lieu of social security; LEA discretionary awards or educational maintenance allowances for students in non-advanced FE are fairly small.

The rhetoric, the financing and the structures in education and training —all reflecting anxiety from central government—are shifting. The likely significance of these shifts—will they make any difference and to whom? are still open questions and therefore worth exploring, particularly as to whether it is the DES or the MSC which is in the process of changing the rules.

THE PROBLEMS OF POLICY IMPLEMENTATION

Implementing policies is subject to two major difficulties. First, initiatives may be the outcome of political anxieties that reflect perceptions rather than realities. These perceptions may not be shared by all the bodies from whom consensus is required before action can be half-way effective. Second, within the English system there are a wide variety of levels and types of agencies responsible for carrying out central initiatives; these bodies are capable of reinterpreting and thus diffusing the impact of policy at the point of implementation.

The first difficulty is illustrated by the reaction to the White Paper *Training for Jobs* of both Labour and Conservative local authorities who refused, throughout 1984, to co-operate with the MSC in working the suggested new structures.

The White Paper rhetoric began:

> Successful training is a continuing investment in the most valuable of all our national resources—the energies of our people. We have not sufficiently recognized its importance in the past. This we must now remedy and ensure that the skills of our people are fitted for the challenge of the years ahead.

While accepting the general premise (the words are not so different from those of a century ago) the local authorities were less willing to accept the analysis that their own FE provision had failed to fulfil national and industrial requirements, and gained some support from an HMI report which suggested that employers were vague about their requirements and often deficient in their own training provision. That report's title, *Education for Employees* (DES, 1984), provides an elegant debating counterpoint to that of the White Paper.

The LEAs continued to put forward an alternative scenario to the criticisms in the White Paper which ran roughly that during the previous decade there had been a wholesale shift from part-time to full-time courses, partly caused by the decline of apprenticeship and partly by professional body (and parental) preference for full-time courses. TEC, for example, had been moved by market forces to offer the full-time version of traditional part-time courses. The City & Guilds position was similar. In fact the rich, part-time vocational tradition of FE remains in outline but the market pressures are towards full-time LEA provision based on the conversion of traditional examining body syllabuses. Such provision reflected accurately employer needs and market conditions. In criticizing the provision the White Paper had got its analysis wrong.

The second major point is the capacity for reinterpretation of policy by the implementing bodies. Challis, Mason and Parkes (1984), in a work on the local authorities and YTS, make the case:

> first, that the agencies delivering YTS disagree not only among but within themselves as to what the objectives of YTS are. These agencies include colleges, managing agents, employers, MSC national and area representatives, Careers Service, the local authorities themselves. The interpretation of YTS objectives varies widely from primarily social to primarily vocational, from 'custodial' to job recruitment;
>
> second, in terms of control and maintenance of empires, in the implementation of YTS there are winners and losers but these vary from area to area: within an authority—education or personnel department, community section or college; outside the authority—Chamber of Commerce or consortia of managing agencies. Control of the curriculum may stay firmly with colleges or shift to the education department. Control of accredited centres for staff training across the public/private sector boundaries may rest with either party depending on the area. Despite an apparently tight bureaucracy MSC area offices have, within limits, varying interpretations of central office policy.

A national scheme locally delivered allows local interpretation within the ambiguities of whether the YTS is about havoc or recruitment, i.e. stirring up the system and inducing employers to take on youngsters; alleviating unemployment figures; providing the potential for a trained workforce against a cyclical pick-up in the economy; providing a broad base for life without paid work. The YTS may merely be providing a mini-forum for a longer term debate about who 'owns' 16–19 rather than the nature of the curriculum, and the generous funding of TVEI may be a gift like the Trojan Horse allowing 'alien' access to the schools and pupils from 14+.

PROBLEM OR OPPORTUNITY?

There seems little doubt that the British economic and industrial situation has been in decline for more than a century. The volume of post-16 provision, whether education, vocational preparation or training, is of a lower order than all other EEC countries except Greece; since 1944 we have continued to neglect up to 50 per cent of school-leavers. Industrial commitment to training, in the round, has been negligible compared with most Western technological democracies. Structural relations among the parties concerned (local authorities, government agencies, curriculum bodies, industry and commerce, colleges, unions) have been diffuse. There are compensations—on a longer time scale diffused social and political structures have given the United Kingdom greater political stability and relatively less social unrest than say France and Germany in the period 1920 to 1950. Social mobility in the United Kingdom has been and is still higher than in those two countries.

Nevertheless, there appears to be something to gain from international comparison. For example, the German model appears to tell us something about training structures, particularly in relation to political consensus towards agreed outcomes (Parkes and Shaw, 1983).

What seems significant about the German system is that 85 per cent of those who leave German schools at the minimum school-leaving age gain apprenticeships within a dual system. This requires compulsory day release until the age of 18 (a provision of the 1918 Education Act in Britain which still awaits implementation!) and work experience from curricula laid down from central government. At the technician and post-apprentice business levels the usual route forward is from those who have finished craft apprenticeship and spent two years in industry. It is only then that they go on to a technician level training; either a two-year full-time or a four-year part-time route.

The apprenticeship structure is a prerequisite of what follows and this prerequisite involves industrial commitment of both employers and employees to training; legislation and regulations laying down common curricula across the whole country for in-firm training; local industrial involvement in testing standards; co-operation between public sector schools and private sector training; creating a qualification linking the right to be an employer and the right to be an in-firm trainer; full involvement of employers and trade unions at all levels.

In framing the regulations there has to be political agreement among central government, the Länder, employers, the unions, the education system, as to what, eventually, outcomes will be. Very often these are imprecise, but there is sufficient measure of agreement to move forward to a detailed curriculum and for everybody to be pointing in a similar direction.

The Germans have a front loading system which creates coordination among the various competing and conflicting interests in the system. The English do not have such coordination. They have semi-autonomous institutions, with shallow freedoms over curricula, method and resources. They have many different local authorities warring with central government. They have a wide variety of examining and validating bodies established by central government but without legal authority. Germany is an example of a decentralized federal country creating an effective training programme which appears, at least at a distance, to be more successful than ours. Content and method from secondary to further education sectors seem well behind English experiment and development, but there are structures which support an integrated approach to basic training between various factors in society.

However, structures are a reflection of much more difficult abstract issues. It is difficult to transfer solutions between systems and the 'we don't start from there' reaction is pertinent. Nevertheless, we have to ask: 'Where do the West Germans actually start from?' One tends to tease out, from very difficult discussions, rather less a new structuring after the war than the clear commitment to the application and development of existing structures. While the heart of the German training system (apprenticeship and the development of master craftsmen) can be traced back to a medieval root, it is, however, the will to make the structures work, the will to co-operate and relate the various parts of the system that seem critical. The implication, however crude, is that the *discontinuity* provided by the material collapse of Germany after the Second World War created the motivation either to make existing structures work or to mould them in such a way that they were more likely to work, in terms of co-operation rather than conflict within structures with perceived outcomes.

It is possible to argue that there is *now* in the United Kingdom a discontinuity or a potential discontinuity where restructuring is possible. But structure alone is not the answer. It is the intangibles of motivation and will, the desire to make things work, that are at the heart of the differences between West Germany and the United Kingdom. What does seem probable is that both intangible and structural factors are necessary for successful training and desired economic outcomes and that neither is yet evident in the United Kingdom. The opportunity window, however, may now be here.

There are prices to be paid for central interventions whether DES or more substantially MSC's New Training Initiative. The fabric of society may be torn by social engineering of the kind described by Ranson. On the other hand, the diffuse nature of United Kingdom institutions may enfeeble all such initiatives. However, many an HMI now says from behind his or her hand, 'We may not like the source or even the motives—but what is coming from MSC is what many of us have been advocating for a long time.'

REFERENCES

Barnett, C. (1975) Further education and the development of an industrial society, *Coombe Lodge Report*, Vol. 8, No. 14.

Brooke, Peter (1984) Parliamentary Under Secretary, DES, speaking at the Further Education Staff College, June.

Challis, R., Mason, C. and Parkes, D. (1984) *The Local Authority and YTS*, Interim Report, MSC, Sheffield.

Department of Education and Science (1977) *Education in Schools: a consultative document*, HMSO, London.

Department of Education and Science (1979) *Proposals for a Certificate of Extended Education* (the Keohane Report), HMSO, London.

Department of Education and Science (1984) *Education for Employees—an HMI survey of part-time release for 16–19-year-olds*, HMSO, London.

Department of Employment (1984) *Training for Jobs*, Cmnd 9135, HMSO, London.

Further Education Unit (1979) *A Basis for Choice*. Report of a Study Group on post-16 pre-employment courses, FEU, London.
Levy, M. (1982) Education and training at 17+, in *Coombe Lodge Report*, Vol. 15, No. 9.
Manpower Services Commission (1981) *A New Training Initiative: a consultative document*, MSC, Sheffield.
Manpower Services Commission (1982) *Youth Task Group Report*, MSC, Sheffield.
McFarlane, N. (1982) Education for 16–19-year-olds, *Coombe Lodge Report*, Vol. 14, No. 7.
Morgan, D. (1980) Vocational objectives within the US educational system, *Comparative Papers in Further Education*, No. 6, Blagdon, Further Education Staff College.
NEDO/MSC (1984) *Competence and Competition*.
OECD (1974) *Policies for Apprenticeship*, OECD, Paris.
OECD (1984) *Policies for Post Compulsory Education and Training*, Draft Report, OECD, Paris.
Parkes, D.L. (1976) Further Education in Italy and England: a community of interests, *Education Administration*, Vol. 6, No. 1.
Parkes, D.L. (1979) Craft apprenticeship in Europe, *Comparative Papers in Further Education*, No. 5, Blagdon, Further Education Staff College.
Parkes, D.L. (ed.) (1982) *The Changing Face of FE*, FEU, London.
Parkes, D.L. and Shaw, G.K. (1983) Britons take a Meister class, *THES*, No. 616, 24 August 1983.
Pratley, B. (1980) *Signposts*, FEU, London.
Ranson, S. (1981) Towards a tertiary tripartism: new codes of social control and the 17+, in Broadfoot, P. (ed.), *Selection, Certification and Control*, Falmer Press, Falmer.
Ranson, S. (1983a) 16–19 policy, differentiated solidarity in the DES, *Institute of Local Government Studies*, September 1983.
Ranson, S. (1983b) Changing relations between centre and locality in education, *Local Government Studies*, December, 1983 (reprinted in this volume, article 6).
Russell, R. (1981) *Curriculum Control*, FEU, London.
Russell, R. and Parkes, D.L. (1983) Measures to deal with youth unemployment in the FRG, *Studies in Vocational Education and Training in the FRG*, Blagdon, Further Education Staff College.
Shelton, W. (1982) Education courses and examinations at 17+, *Coombe Lodge Report*, Vol. 15, No. 9.

The British University Grants Committee 1919–83

changing relationships with government and the universities

MICHAEL SHATTOCK and ROBERT BERDAHL

SECTION ONE: THE UGC AS BUFFER (1919-1963)

Although *ad hoc* advisory committees had been called together for this purpose at irregular intervals since 1889, the establishment of the University Grants Committee in 1919 reflected the need for some new and effective mechanism for channelling funds to universities which had suffered severely through neglect and lack of government funding during the war. The UGC was created from above by politicians, most notably Lord Haldane, and by civil servants as an aid to government, not by pressure from below by universities, by vice-chancellors or by academic opinion. It was primarily a mechanism for resource allocation, for the division of a given sum amongst a group of needy institutional claimants. It was not a planning body, although from time to time it was called upon to advise on where certain facilities or departments should be located. Essentially its role was reactive to the universities and colleges amongst whom it was charged to distribute government subsidies. Government funds made up on average no more than 30 per cent of institutional recurrent income. In terms of capital grants the UGC's contribution between 1923 and 1929 was only £500,000 against endowments of £3,320,000 (Owen, 1981). In these circumstances planning and development was an institutional function rather than the UGC's.

Source: From *Higher Education*, Vol. 13, No. 5. Published by Elsevier Science Publishers, Amsterdam, The Netherlands, 1984.

The financial circumstances were to change sharply during and after the Second World War. First, as in 1919, the depredations of war required an immediate capital outlay estimated by the UGC in 1944 to amount to some £28 million at 1938-39 prices: many university buildings had been used for wartime purposes and those that had remained in university use had built up a substantial maintenance backlog. Some had been damaged by enemy action. More important, the social and educational aspirations built up during the war years set a requirement for support which the vice-Chancellors' Committee (CVCP) rightly said was 'nowadays beyond the resource of private benefaction' (CVCP, 1957). The UGC was clearly required to take on a wider role than it had done previously. The Barlow Committee on Scientific Manpower reported in 1946: 'it is clear that the UGC was originally intended to be a somewhat passive body whose main function was to criticize proposals put forward by the universities and which was not itself expected to make any attempt to suggest possible developments involving expenditure to university authorities... we think that circumstances demand that it should increasingly concern itself with positive university policy'. The CVCP, in its *Note on University Policy 1947-56,* 'entirely accepted the view that the government has not only the right but also the duty of satisfying itself that every field of study which in the national interest ought to be cultivated in Great Britain is in fact cultivated in the university world... and they will be glad to have a greater measure of guidance from the government than, until quite recent days, they have been accustomed to receive'. It went on to support the view that the UGC 'should enlarge the range of its activities and concern itself with the promotion of any necessary developments in the university system' (CVCP, 1957).

Government responded by broadening significantly the UGC's terms of reference. In 1919, when the UGC had been established as a committee reporting direct to the Treasury, its terms of reference were laid down as:

> To enquire into the financial needs of University education in the United Kingdom and to advise the Government as to the application of any grants that may be made by Parliament to meet them.

In 1943 the following words were added:

> To collect, examine and make available information relating to university education throughout the United Kingdom.

and in 1946 the Chancellor of the Exchequer announced a further addition:

> and to assist, in consultation with the universities and other bodies concerned, the preparation and execution of such plans for the development of the universities as may from time to time be required in order to ensure that they are fully adequate to national needs.

Nevertheless the style of the committee's operations seems not much to have changed. The committee envisaged its new relationship with universities as a 'form of partnership' (UGC, 1948) and pursued its policies 'in a tactful and measured manner' (Owen, 1980). Indeed the changeover to an enlarged sphere of operations seems to have been accomplished almost imperceptibly under the chairmanships of Sir Walter Moberly and Sir Keith Murray.

Thanks to co-operation and joint planning with the CVCP, the UGC was able to present the Treasury in 1945 with outlines for a ten-year university development plan which required substantially enlarged government grants. The Chancellor of the Exchequer agreed to an immediate doubling of grants and promised further increases after the reports of a series of committees of enquiry appointed by various government departments to investigate the national need for certain types of professional specialists. Building on the Education Act of 1944, which promised to increase greatly the number of students qualified for university matriculation, a range of specialized manpower study committees reported between 1943 and 1946, in each case recommending an expanded supply of university-trained professionals. For the quinquennium 1947–1952 nearly 30 per cent of the grants allocated by the UGC were in the form of funds earmarked to support special fields of study. These fields (medical and dental education, agricultural and veterinary studies, teacher education, the social sciences, Oriental and African studies, Slavonic and East European studies) had all been the subjects of specialized enquiries and the UGC justified the earmarked grants as a temporary expedient. By 1951–52 the committee had reverted to the full acceptance of the block grant principle.

During the 1950s the UGC was also involved in basic government decisions dealing with the role of technology in national life. In 1954, following the canvas of the universities by a UGC Sub-Committee on Technology, the government announced that the universities of Glasgow, Manchester, Leeds and Birmingham were to be the main centres for a proposed higher technological expansion. Later in the decade increased sums of both recurrent and capital grants were expressly channelled by the UGC into buildings and facilities for, and attracting the students to, the study of advanced technology.

Finally, during this period the UGC also endorsed a major expansion in the number of universities. Earlier in 1949 the UGC had supported the establishment of the experimental University College of North Staffordshire, this over the considerable opposition of the CVCP. But by the later 1950s it was becoming clearer that the demographic pressures for expansion in the next decade were going to exceed the number of additional places that the existing universities were willing to create. The UGC took the lead in bringing to government's attention the need to provide more university places and was extremely active in selecting the sites for new universities and in advising on the membership of the Academic Advisory Committees which were established.

During this period the UGC operated with very broad support from both government and university circles. Nevertheless, there were two indications of future difficulties. On several occasions during this period there was some pressure for a fresh look at higher education by a body other than the UGC. For example, Lord Lindsay, an influential Labour Party figure as well as the Master of Balliol College, Oxford (and shortly to become Principal of the University College of North Staffordshire), suggested that the UGC was not capable of thinking of 'revolutionary change'. 'I have the uneasy suspicion,' he said in a House of Lords debate, 'that if only the UGC or even that other great body... the Vice-Chancellors' Committee, were asked to report on this matter, you would find how surprisingly satisfactory everything was' (14 May 1947). He was supported by the editor of *Nature* and some other senior academic figures, but neither the existing Labour nor later Conservative governments offered support. In 1953 the Prime Minister, Winston Churchill, in response to a request for a Royal Commission on the role of the universities, 'saw no reason to be dissatisfied with the way in which the needs of society have been met by the universities', and put an end to any question of a further government initiative (House of Commons, 19 June 1953). In Section Two, however, we shall describe the creation of the Robbins Committee eight years later in 1961 and point out that its very establishment seemed to indicate the need for a broader look at higher education than the UGC was apparently thought to be able to render. This preoccupation with a narrow conception of university activities was to become a more serious criticism of the later years of the UGC.

If the earlier pressures for a Royal Commission indicated some doubts about the breadth of 'the buffer's' vision, the Henry Brooke affair in 1962 was a direct challenge to the effectiveness of 'the buffer's' advice to government. The Conservative government then in power regarded its austerity and 'Pay Pause' programmes as having priority over full-funding the university expansion (Boyle, 1978). By itself, a Treasury decision to cut the total level of grants available might be thought to be nothing out of the ordinary. What was unusual was that Mr. Henry Brooke, Chief Secretary to the Treasury, insisted that, even with grants significantly reduced below recommended levels, universities would still be held to expansion targets with no expectations of lowered academic standards. Until then it had been the long-standing tradition that UGC advice to the government on university needs was confidential, but, in this case, Mr. Brooke felt obliged to add that:

> ... considerations of economic policy, which are of course right outside the scope of the [UGC's] responsibility, have made it necessary to depart from the Committee's recommendations. This in no way alters the Government's confidence in the Committee's judgement in the whole field of university matters on which they are responsible for giving the advice (House of Commons, 14 March 1962).

University and parliamentary opinion erupted in a barrage of criticism both over the fiscal cuts and the rejection of the UGC's advice that, to protect academic quality, expansion targets should be reduced if funds had to be cut. According to Sir Edward (later Lord) Boyle, a Treasury minister alongside Mr. Brooke in 1962, the government's guilty conscience over this incident led it not only to increase university recurrent grants and academic salaries within the next year, but also to give an immediate public acceptance to the Robbins Committee recommendation in 1963 for major university expansion during the remainder of the decade (Kogan, 1971). While most of the fiscal damage had been reversed within a year and the UGC's position apparently vindicated, the Brooke affair illustrated the fragility of the UGC's 'buffer' role.

SECTION TWO: THE UGC AND THE POST-ROBBINS ERA (1963-1979)

When Sir John Wolfenden took over the chairmanship of the UGC he was faced with Robbins's recommendations for a tripling of student numbers in universities by 1980-81 and major structural changes in the administration of higher education. Wolfenden, however, inherited machinery which did not match up to this situation. His predecessor had chosen not to expand its staff in line with the growing scale of the university system. Under Wolfenden's chairmanship, the staffing of the UGC, which had stood at 22 in 1953 and 50 in 1963, rose to 112 in 1968. Wolfenden's period of chairmanship marked an important transitional stage in the life of the UGC. Partly, this reflected quite simply the impact of the Robbins Report and partly the change of style in the UGC's operations. Wolfenden himself described the latter process as follows:

> Over recent years the UGC has gradually but visibly moved from being a buffer to becoming the strategist.... If through ... dramatic and rapid changes the former relationship between Government and the universities was to endure, if, that is, there was not allowed to develop a direct control by the Government of the activities of the universities, then the passive buffer must come to life and undertake some positive and planning initiatives (Wolfenden, 1970).

In the UGC's Quinquennial Report for 1962-67 (UGC, 1968) it argued that its function, earlier described by Labour Chancellor of the Exchequer, Hugh Dalton, as 'to act as a buffer or shock absorber between the government and the universities', had become more positive and that its role had been extended by the need to advise on the creation of new universities, on the establishment of new medical schools, and on new subjects generally, and on the closure of three schools of agriculture. 'It no longer makes sense,' the report continues, 'if it ever did, that each university should seek to develop its own range of offerings with no regard to the intentions and practices of sister universities. Increasingly there has been recognized the need for at least the outline of a central strategy if only because of this notable increase in the size of the university family.'

The period 1963-67 marked a high point in the public esteem for higher education both in the government and the country at large. The arrival of a Labour government certainly led to no reduction in financial support. Nor was there anything but praise for the UGC as a piece of machinery. The

Estimates Committee of the House of Commons stated its support for the principle of 'a committee independent of politics and not subject to ministerial direction' (1965) and the Public Accounts Committee (PAC, 1967), even while urging a change in arrangements for the Comptroller and Auditor General to have access to UGC records, described the UGC as 'the accepted source of expert advice on university affairs' and as 'an eminently successful example of administrative ingenuity'.

The UGC as the strategist for university development

The impetus provided by the Robbins projections of student numbers and the public support for the expansion of higher education provided the background to the UGC's first public steps to play a more positive role in the planning of university development. It is important to note the word 'public' because the chairman of the UGC had long been understood to deliver 'private' advice to the various vice-chancellors, most often over *tête-à-têtes* at the Athenaeum. But as this 'advice' became more extensive, vice-chancellors felt the need for it to become public in order to convince their Senates and Councils of the strength of UGC convictions.

The major innovation was the General Memorandum of Guidance which was henceforward to accompany the quinquennial planning process. The first such memorandum was issued in 1967 to accompany the 1967–72 allocation of the quinquennial grant to the universities. In spite of Wolfenden's bold words quoted above, this first memorandum was couched in modest style, reflecting the UGC's unwillingness to encroach on university autonomy. The memorandum denied 'it was intended to be a comprehensive blueprint of university activity and development', but stated that its purpose was rather 'to call attention... to a certain number of areas which from the national point of view would seem to offer special opportunities' (UGC, 1967).

The next memorandum was issued in 1970 as a Preliminary Memorandum of General Guidance to assist universities in their preparation of their 1972–77 quinquennial submissions. But its guidance was largely negative since it took 'as a starting point the capacity of the buildings which will be available on completion of the building programmes up to 1971–72' and based its expansion target for each university on such criteria as building capacity, availability of sites, unit costs and only lastly 'relevant academic factors' (UGC, 1970). The actual 1972–77 memorandum issued in 1973 contained 34 paragraphs of macro-university statistical material about overall numbers and costs and only a sketchy eleven about individual subject areas. It emphasized the UGC's wish 'that each university should be left to manage its affairs with the minimum of detailed directions' (UGC, 1973). By 1977 the UGC's horizon was so dominated by economic constraints that its guidance was minimal and may be summed up by the following abdication of its role as a positive strategic body: 'With resources severely limited and any costs for new developments having for the most part to be found from savings from existing activities, any progress is primarily a matter of universities' own priorities and choices' (UGC, 1977). These memoranda do not suggest that 'the buffer' came to life or that the UGC was willing or perhaps able to undertake significant 'positive and planning initiatives' (Wolfenden's earlier expression).

One result of the growth of the university system, and particularly the number of institutions, was the enlargement of the UGC's machinery, by the increase and importance accorded to discipline-based advisory sub-committees. These sub-committees were expected to advise the main committee on the development of the subjects falling within their remit and increasingly to rationalize existing provision. Analysis of university developments in the light of subject committee recommendations reveals that the UGC did not systematically monitor the extent to which its subject rationalization proposals were carried out. In Russian Studies, for example, warnings were issued about the excessive proliferation of courses and departments in three successive memoranda without effect, and when in 1979 the UGC at last launched an enquiry it was forced to recommend the discontinuance of programmes and departments in six institutions and consideration of the phasing out of Russian Studies in seven more (UGC, 1979).

The UGC and government policies in higher education

In 1964 responsibility for the UGC was transferred from the Treasury to the newly constituted Department of Education and Science (DES). Prior to this critics of the UGC could have argued that the UGC had a special responsibility for recommending policy initiatives because the Treasury, its parent department, could hardly have been expected to exercise educational leadership. After the transfer the UGC might have expected the Secretary of State for Education, or the minister responsible for higher education within the department, or the department itself through its higher education policy groups, its planning unit, its universities branch or even the deputy secretary responsible for further education, to play a significant role in assisting the UGC to interpret 'national needs'. There is no evidence, however, that the DES had any real capacity for this or that it saw its role as other than simply quantifying student numbers as successive parliamentary enquiries revealed (cf., in particular, *Policy Making in the DES*, Expenditure Committee Tenth Report, 1976). Even in the field of student numbers the major public documents Planning Paper No. 2 (DES, 1970), the White Paper *Education: A Framework for Expansion* (DES, 1972) and *Higher Education into the 1990's* (DES/SED, 1978) were to prove seriously awry in their projections.

The period 1963 to 1966 was crucial in establishing the modern structure of British higher education culminating in the creation of the polytechnics. Once this burst of decision-making was over, neither major political party seems to have had a policy on higher education. Lord Crowther-Hunt, on being appointed Minister of State responsible for higher education, recalled seeking guidance without success from the Prime Minister Harold Wilson and his Secretary of State, Mr. Reg Prentice, as to what was the government's policy on higher education (Crowther-Hunt, 1983). Indeed, the two major reports on substantive policy issues affecting university education, the Todd Report on Medical Education (1968) and the Finniston Report on Engineering Education (1980), were sponsored by departments other than the DES.

Thus neither the DES nor UGC, nor, it must be said, for the most part, the universities were inclined to launch new policy initiatives. The Robbins recommendations accepted by the government were essentially quantitative in character and the planning that derived from their acceptance was based on student numbers and how the system could be expanded to meet a quantified demand. By 1972 a concern about numbers was beginning to be replaced by a concern about costs. The dominant themes of the period 1963 to 1974 both in the UGC and in the DES were initially student number targets and, later, concepts of 'productivity', 'efficiency', rationalization and financial control. A single exception was the creation of the polytechnics, and the enunciation of the binary line philosophy. Once created, however, there was little attempt on the DES's part to ensure that the new polytechnics remained consistent with the philosophy that created them. From 1972 onwards the chief concern within the DES was more the achievement and maintenance of parity of student numbers between the university and the public sector of higher education than any clear differentiation of their roles.

Throughout, without the pressure to make hard choices, the hard choices were not made. No tests of academic quality or potential were applied to the colleges of advanced technology, which, in 1963, were in widely different stages of development from their technical college past, to decide which should be granted university status as recommended by Robbins. We have seen no evidence to suggest that the UGC raised any critical voice at the wholesale incorporation of these institutions into the university system. Eighteen years later, as a group, they were to suffer more severely from the cuts than any other, and only two, Bath and Loughborough, seemed to have been accorded the seal of UGC approval. Within the UGC itself, decision-making and resource allocation seems not to have favoured a differentiation of institutions. The constraints imposed by the priority given in the planning process to the existence of building space led to a passive policy of allocating additional student science places to universities more on the basis of filling all the existing science buildings than on the quality of the departments concerned. The UGC's resource allocation model itself was largely mechanical.

The Barlow Committee in 1946 had stressed the importance of the university expansion for the output of science graduates. Robbins recommended that the balance of science:arts based students should be 60:40, yet in successive Memoranda of Guidance this figure was whittled down to 55:45 (1967), to 53:47 (1973) and eventually to 50:50 (1979). When questioned in the early 1970s about their acceptance of the drift away from science, both the chairman of the UGC and the deputy secretary in charge of higher education in the DES referred complacently to an OECD report which was alleged to show that Britain had a higher proportion of scientists and technologists in the labour force than other industrialized nations. There is no public evidence that until 1981 the priority accorded to the expansion of the medical intake up to the level recommended by the Todd Commission in 1968 was ever seriously debated and the UGC appears simply to have accepted figures handed down by the Department of Health and Social Security (DHSS). Nor, in spite of the high cost, which in 1981 the UGC estimated as being six times more than the training of an arts graduate and three times more than a science graduate, is there evidence that the UGC initiated any inquiry as to alternative, less expensive methods of meeting medical manpower needs.

The most substantial failure however lay in the UGC's narrow conception of the role of universities and of university education. Only once, in the 1967 General Memorandum of Guidance, were universities urged to make 'a further and determined effort to gear a large part of their output to the economic and industrial needs of the nation'. Although the UGC was able to swallow the transfer of the CATs to university status, because they came as a package from Robbins, it would not take over the Royal College of Art or the Cranfield Institute of Technology because it said their roles were distinct from the traditional university model. In 1964 it advised the government against allowing the universities to take over the administration of the colleges of education, which Robbins had recommended, although the universities were keen to do so; it discouraged the new universities of Sussex and Warwick from merging with or developing special collaborative relationships with local colleges of technology; and, much later, it showed little enthusiasm for bringing the Open University under its auspices. In 1978 *Higher Education into the 1990s* urged that one of the future options for higher education to avoid the worst effects of the demographic downturn was to move more extensively into continuing education. It was five years before the UGC got around to setting up a working party to devise a policy on what all political parties saw as a key element in a future higher education system.

The UGC could argue that the essential basis of its partnership with the universities was that the initiative for instigating change lay in their hands, and that the pressure on resources post-1972 was such that the UGC was constrained from commending departures from the existing pattern. The fact remains that after 1963 the UGC chose to stand aside from the changes that were taking place in education and society and took no significant initiatives to bring either itself or the universities into the growing debate about the wider relationship of the universities and the needs of society.

The UGC chose to plan at the margin only, approving small developments here and not approving others there, and when the economic and other constraints began to bite, it chose a policy of more or less equal misery, seeking to preserve the system at a broadly common level rather than building on exceptional academic strengths and running down elsewhere in compensation. Resisting any widening of institutional differentiation had the benefit of maintaining the appearance of system-wide academic standards, but left some institutions vulnerable to the nemesis that was to befall them after 1979 when more serious scrutiny revealed a lack of substantive strengths to sustain equal treatment status. Moreover, by not encouraging attempts to break out of the traditional university model, it left the whole system vulnerable to changes in the political climate and to the charge that it was no longer in tune with the needs of the times. It may be argued that the UGC was in no position to initiate policy when a policy vacuum towards higher education existed in government itself. The fact remains that in spite of calls for more positive approaches in the immediate postwar period, the UGC remained a largely reactive body preferring the system to be tidy rather than innovative.

The UGC's fall in status and loss of power

The UGC's loss of status in Whitehall and its loss of influence in government, and the appropriation of UGC's powers by the DES are two sides of the same coin. Loss of powers led to downgrading; downgrading led to loss of powers. There was no decisive break point, just a steady trend throughout the period from 1964. This was not, however, the result of a persistent DES policy to reduce the status of the UGC, but reflected much more the relative growth in the scale, complexity and centralization of the powers of government, particularly over the public sector of the economy.

The first major change was the transfer of the UGC from the Treasury to the DES. In 1919 the UGC was placed under the Treasury, largely because the Board of Education had no jurisdiction over Scotland and Ireland, so that it had no powers to allocate funds to universities outside England. The UGC's location under the Treasury was an *ad hoc* decision which suited the circumstances of the time. The Treasury relationship was also highly convenient for the UGC because of the political protection it provided and the direct access, without competition with other claimants, to the government's financial decision-making process. When the government finally rejected the Robbins recommendation for a separate Ministry for Arts and Science and transferred the UGC to the new Department of Education and Science, Sir John Wolfenden was able to argue convincingly that at least in the short run the combined weight of the then Secretary of State, Quintin Hogg, and of his Minister of State, Sir Edward (later Lord) Boyle, a former Treasury minister who had a seat in the Cabinet, was at least as good a guarantee of adequate funding as having the Chancellor of the Exchequer as the UGC's minister.

With the progressive reform of the government's resource allocation apparatus through the Public Expenditure Survey Committee (PESC), however, the UGC's distance from the central financial decision making process rendered it increasingly vulnerable as the nation's economy began to slip out of gear. The UGC is able to make a direct appearance in the process but only under a DES umbrella: if rapid cuts in public expenditure are invoked or supplementary bids to cover inflation are required, the UGC is in an exposed position at the extremity of a long chain of government decision making (Shattock and Rigby, 1983). These uncertainties increased after the introduction of the government's 'cash limits' policy in 1979 under which a figure is fixed for government expenditure incorporating a fixed inflation figure.

Not only did the UGC find itself gradually pushed further away from the crucial financial decision points, but higher education, and with it the UGC, lost status in Whitehall. The new department started well under Quintin Hogg and Lord Boyle, but when they departed much of the kudos went with them. Between 1964 and 1970 higher education had its own minister of state within the department but with the arrival of the Heath government the post was downgraded to parliamentary under-secretary. This did not affect the minister's 'clout' within the department, but certainly reflected a changed external view of the importance of higher education. In 1982 the UGC secretaryship was downgraded from deputy to under-secretary. In the staffing cuts which beset the DES in the 1981–83 period, the UGC's staff was cut much more severely than the DES as a whole. Although the Universities' Vote represents the largest element in the DES budget, ministers spend far more time on the more politicized local authority relationships and the role of DES officials *vis-à-vis* the UGC becomes that much more important. One chairman, Sir Edward Parkes, suggests that because DES officials deal direct with the public sector of higher education they tend to have more sympathy for its problems and quoted an occasion where a highly significant UGC response on funding seems simply not to have been transmitted to the Secretary of State (Parkes, 1984).

Simultaneously with this downgrading process, the UGC found itself increasingly constrained in the areas of planning and finance, and had no option but to pass these constraints down the line onto the universities. As expansion gathered pace, the student unit cost became a base line negotiating figure between the UGC and government for total recurrent grant, and the convention was adopted that the government in effect 'bought' an additional number of student places in each quinquennium. Initially this approach worked well. In 1967 the government agreed to fund an expansion up to 220,000 places in universities by 1971–72, but the UGC told universities that their 'figures were not being laid down as precise targets or directives, still less as ceilings', and that 'it is open to any university to admit more than the number of students indicated' (UGC, 1967). By 1972 the DES was exercising much firmer control because it wished to achieve a balance between the university and the public sector of higher education. The significance of this reduction in UGC control was underlined in the UGC's report *University Development 1967-72* (1974) which, in referring to the exercise of DES 'strategic influence' through decisions on student number targets, stated that: 'we should not necessarily agree with and must occasionally regret government's decisions on these matters'. Three years later the UGC admitted that

> the Department defines the quantitative parameters for the university system as a whole, including
> (1) global student numbers forecasts;
> (2) overall balance between science-based and arts-based studies;
> (3) overall undergraduate/postgraduate split (Expenditure Committee Tenth Report, 1976).

In 1981-82 the UGC actually 'fined' universities that had exceeded their UGC targets.

An even more serious constraint on the UGC was introduced in respect to the capital building programme. In the period of rapid expansion the provision of buildings became a more effective determinant of the rate of expansion than the recurrent grant. In 1968-69 the Public Accounts Committee (PAC) summoned the DES, the UGC and the universities of Essex and Keele to account for their under-utilization of science buildings. The DES and the UGC were criticized for providing excess building capacity for these universities which had not achieved their science student number targets. The result was the introduction of an extremely rigid capacity survey and capacity planning exercise which was henceforth to dominate the expansion programme. By 1973 it was clear that, instead of the UGC deciding its own building priorities freely within a capital sum allocated by the DES, the science:arts balance was being decided by the DES. Henceforward, notwithstanding the agreed quinquennial plan, the actual rate of growth of student numbers was determined by capital allocations made annually by the DES.

But the greatest blow to the UGC was the loss of the quinquennial planning system. The quinquennial system represented an integral part of the network of procedures and conventions which had been created to preserve university autonomy within the framework of government funding. In essence, the system reflected a balance of advantage to the funding agency and the bodies funded. The universities were given a five-year promise of funds within which to plan their activities; the UGC, and by implication the government, were given the opportunity to review university development across the board every five years and to set guidelines for the following five. The universities submitted their plans (the quinquennial estimates) to the

UGC, the UGC submitted a plan, 'an expression of overall needs without reference to individual universities' (UGC, 1973), to the government, the government responded with a grant of funds and the UGC distributed those funds amongst the institutions with such general and specific guidance as it thought appropriate.

In its report for 1962–67 the UGC identified three weaknesses in the quinquennial system: its inability to cope with major developments arising during the quinquennium, the eroding effect of inflation on the grant, and the failure to provide adequate overlap between one quinquennium and the next (UGC, 1968). By 1970 mounting inflation, leading to the need for annual supplementary grants, was beginning to undermine the quinquennial system and in 1974–75, with a rapidly deteriorating national economic situation, inflation running at over 20 per cent and the abandonment of the university building programme (thus effectively negating the quinquennial student number targets), the quinquennial planning system was brought to an abrupt end. Looked at from the wider perspective of government, the quinquennial system was an anomaly because it involved a public expenditure commitment further ahead than other areas of government expenditure. To the universities and to the UGC, however, its removal offered the prospect of university expenditure being tied much more closely to the fluctuations of government economic policy as a whole.

Considerable financial constraints were also imposed on the UGC. The first battle to be lost was over the right of the Comptroller and Auditor General (C&AG) to have oversight of the books and records of the UGC and the universities. The introduction of the C&AG into university affairs is sometimes argued to be not significant, because the PAC laid down that the C&AG could not comment on matters of policy. However, subsequent critical PAC reports dealing with universities' ability to hold financial reserves and on the allocation of funds for furniture and equipment had an important impact on university finances. The PAC grew increasingly interested in policy questions and brought pressure to bear on the DES to 'cash limit' student maintenance awards and monitor the size of university intakes (which forced the UGC to initiate a 'fining' system for overshoots). It also pressed the UGC to reconsider the terms of academic tenure and to consider specifying optimum class sizes as a way of controlling staff:student ratios. The UGC resisted these latter pressures, but had no option but to concede to others and to pass new constraints on to the universities.

The UGC's loss of control over academic salaries occurred when Mr. Crosland referred academic salaries for consideration by the National Incomes Commission in 1967. Subsequently, a joint negotiating procedure was established which brought the DES into direct involvement with the universities and which increasingly left the UGC only a peripheral role. This was followed by the universities' voluntarily bringing clerical, technician and manual workers' pay into a national centralized negotiating structure. This again had the effect of bringing the DES into direct involvement with the universities, because successive government national pay policies and the need to maintain alignment with other public sector workers in hospitals, local authorities, etc., meant that the universities needed to have communication directly with the DES both about the actual wage levels and about whether the proposed wage increases qualified for inflation supplementation of the recurrent grant.

Perhaps the clearest evidence of the UGC's loss of influence over the DES has occurred in respect to student fees and overseas student numbers. The power to decide fee levels is clearly set out in university charters and statutes, but prior to the early 1960s the universities had operated a convention not to raise fees except in consort and after due consultation with the UGC. No distinction was ever made between home and overseas students. In 1966, however, Mr. Crosland announced that as from 1968–69 the recurrent grant would be adjusted downwards to assume that a modest fee differential would be introduced for overseas students. The decision was described as 'unilateral action without prior consultation' by the CVCP (1967). Two universities, Bradford and Oxford, chose to ignore what was technically a recommendation to universities (but both fell back into line in time). Demands by the government for a reduction in overseas numbers to limit the financial subsidy being provided to overseas students were passed on by a plainly uneasy UGC, but overseas numbers continued to rise. The new Conservative government in 1979, without consultation with the UGC, decided to require universities to charge full cost fees to overseas students. 'It was a financial decision. That is why it was made and made quickly' the Parliamentary Under-Secretary at the DES told the Foreign Affairs Select Committee (1980). But the fee story was not yet over because in 1981–82 the government proceeded to halve the home student fee under pressure fom the PAC which was afraid that even the modest home student fee of £980 would be sufficient to tempt universities to exceed their UGC imposed student number targets and thus generate a requirement for student maintenance awards that did not figure in the government's estimates.

The unhappy history of student fees illustrates more clearly than anything else the extent to which the UGC could be put into the position of an unwilling but occasionally dictatorial messenger boy for the DES. In practice, neither the fees policy nor the overseas students policy arose from political considerations. Neither Labour nor Conservative governments were opposed to universities taking overseas students. The pressures were entirely financial and were Treasury-led, and because they affected higher education as a whole the UGC became little more than a conduit pipe to the institutions.

By 1979 the UGC system was in serious disrepair. Its planning mechanisms were in tatters, with the chairman being able to do little more than react to the twists and turns of the government's counter-inflation policy. It had sought with some success to keep the universities informed of developments, but there could be little pretence that it remained a body which carried much weight with the DES or in Whitehall. The changed position of the UGC was certainly in part a consequence of the transfer from the Treasury to the DES, which removed it from the protection of the senior department of state and made it just another cog in the machinery of government. The DES exercised much more control over university matters than the Treasury had done, but this was more a product of the increasing controls that the Treasury and the PESC machinery were exercising over the DES as a result of the general worsening economic situation than of encroachment by the DES as a matter of policy. Where this was not true DES interventions came about because of its policy of even-handedness with the public sector rather than from any lack of respect for the UGC itself. The Chairman of the UGC retained his right of direct access to the Secretary of State, but the rapid turnover of secretaries of state over this period made this less useful than it might otherwise have been. The most serious incursions into university affairs were mostly brought about either by the PAC or by the threat that it might comment adversely on some matter. As the all party financial watchdog of the House of Commons, the PAC is one of the few ways that Parliament can control the executive and no minister or civil servant would willingly cross its path. There is no evidence that the PAC was hostile to the UGC, but only that it believed that the DES should conform with the kind of controls over public expenditure which applied elsewhere in government.

SECTION THREE: THE UGC REGAINS THE INITIATIVE (1979–83)

The actions of the incoming Conservative government were to generate a more robust atmosphere. The withdrawal of £100 million from the university system provoked the UGC to announce that it was going to become more *dirigiste*. In October 1979 it embarked on a planning exercise unique in the UGC's history in which universities were asked to prepare three scenario planning documents on the basis of a 2 per cent increase in funding, level funding and a 5 per cent reduction and to engage in 'dialogue' meetings with the UGC to discuss the plans submitted. The UGC made it plain that in order to preserve the prospect of innovation it was prepared to make significant cuts across the system and the subject committees were charged with the task of reviewing each academic discipline. Before this new approach could be tested, however, the government announced a further cut of 8.5 per cent in the recurrent grant spread over 1981–82 to 1983–84, bringing the total cut since 1979 to somewhere between 11 per cent and 15 per cent. Paradoxically, this situation and the implementation of these cuts had an invigorating effect on the UGC; the vigour and snap with which the UGC tackled the task greatly restored its prestige within Whitehall where government departments were wrestling often ineffectually with similar cost-cutting exercises.

The UGC took over the driving seat for the university system in a way it had not been forced to do since 1963. In December 1980 the government announced a reduction of £30 million (3.5 per cent) in the recurrent grant for 1981–82. Between December 1980 and March 1981 the UGC engaged in and won what the chairman called 'a three month struggle' to persuade the government to announce its funding plans over a three-year cycle to enable the return to a longer term planning strategy. From the moment the government announced its second round of cuts, a further 5 per cent for 1982–83 and 1983–84 in May 1981, the UGC made it absolutely clear to universities that although it did not contemplate the closure of any university it certainly envisaged the closure of courses and even whole departments. In addition, in spite of the additional 8.5 per cent cut it still intended to make financial provision for new academic initiatives for the good of the system as a whole. It emphasized that it did not regard academic tenure as a bar to making such recommendations and that large-scale job losses would be an inevitable consequence. It rejected completely any policy of levying an equal percentage cut across the system.

Its standing regained, the UGC proceeded to act up to its promises. It reclaimed, temporarily at least, its power to determine student numbers and imposed a 5 per cent reduction on the system. It halted the planned expansion of medical schools, the target for which had in effect previously been laid down by the Department of Health and Social Security, and set targets for the various university subject groups which provided for a 3 per cent expansion in engineering and increases in the physical sciences and very sharp compensating reductions in the arts and social studies. For the first time since the 1960s the trend towards the arts-based disciplines was reversed, turning a 50:50 arts:science split in 1979–80 to a planned 48:52 in 1984–85. The UGC had not previously sought to follow up its Memoranda of Guidance in any detailed way and its Report on Russian Studies (UGC, 1979) illustrated that universities had not themselves been active in taking tough action voluntarily to deal with problems of overprovision of staff in particular areas. The UGC, therefore, working through its subject committees, took the opportunity in a number of fields to rectify imbalances which the UGC felt had grown up in the system. The resulting allocations of grant to universities showed that the UGC had been highly selective in its approach. The allocations were accompanied by detailed advice on the closure or running down of individual subjects, courses and departments, and the protection or expansion of others, and by a request for a full response on the action the university proposed to take and the staffing implications.

In one important respect, however, the UGC machinery proved to be less than adequate. Since the mid-1960s the UGC had come increasingly to rely on its subject-based sub-committees for detailed advice. These varied greatly in their effectiveness, and in the energy of their chairman who was a member of the main committee. Some exercised their right to make mini-visitations of universities, others occasionally called regional subject-based conferences, others seemed unwilling even to stir from the UGC's offices in Park Crescent. Because of the delay in the government's announcement of the recurrent grant for 1982–83 and 1983–84, the UGC had to rely very much on its sub-committees whose interests were subject, not institutionally, based. 'The UGC are much more interested in subject provision across the whole system, and our interest in institutions is secondary', the chairman told the Parliamentary Science Committee (Parkes, 1982). Indeed, he told the PAC: 'We have made no value judgements about institutions at all' (PAC, 1982). This approach had two consequences: first, the total effect of the UGC's decisions on some institutions was unbalanced and, it was argued, failed to take in local or regional factors; the second was that the apparent ineffectiveness of some of the sub-committees excited justifiable criticism from institutions where the closure of courses or departments in the sub-committees' field was recommended.

The post-1979 period greatly strengthened the UGC's position *vis-à-vis* the universities. The UGC maintained that the change in its role was fundamentally only one of degree. During the period of expansion it said it had had to co-ordinate priorities for development because 'the sum of local aspirations may not form a sensible overall picture for the system' (UGC, 1980) and during the period of contraction the only real change was that instead of adhering to 'a philosophy of laissez faire with regard to the development of all but the most expensive subjects' it now wanted universities to concentrate on their strengths and to cut off support for 'pallid growths which are now never likely to reach maturity' (UGC, 1980). To the universities, however, especially to those hardest hit by the cuts, the 'direct intervention' promised by the chairman had something of the ring of steel about it.

The committee resisted vigorous calls that it should have resigned rather than implement the cuts, calls that echoed similar appeals directed to the academic members of the UGC in 1962, with the answer that it was 'not a fair weather committee', and in spite of the obvious distress in which some universities found themselves, it retained a substantial sum to fund new initiatives, or 'restructuring' projects, rather than distributing all its available recurrent grant to bail out universities in trouble. It thus retained for itself a significant ongoing role to institute change and to reward initiative.

The UGC's relationship with the DES and the government took a similar upturn. After the shock of the overseas student fee decision it persuaded the government to finance a small running down fund for universities suffering from especially severe falls in overseas numbers. When it learnt of the 3 per cent cut for 1981–82 it successfully campaigned to persuade the government to provide a longer term planning horizon up to 1983–84, while at the same time it retained its freedom to condemn the timescale of the cuts which it said created 'disorder and diseconomy' in the university system. Later, in a determined rearguard action, it convinced the government that a generous and expensive government-backed early retirement scheme was essential if the contraction of the university system was to be achieved. Finally, acting together with the Research Councils, it persuaded the government in 1983 to fund 750 'new blood' posts (250 each year) to reinvigorate and restructure the university system. Applications for these new posts together with 140 information technology posts, intended mostly for young scientists, were solicited from universities on a subject specific competitive basis. The UGC, jointly with the Research Councils, awarded posts strictly on research criteria. Perhaps not surprisingly the award list mainly mirrored the qualitative judgements that were implied by the 1981 implementation of the cuts. But this exercise was significant from many points of view. It reflected a major success in persuading government that universities had an important part to play in the regeneration of the British economy, and was clear evidence of the government's confidence in the effectiveness of the UGC's decision-making machinery. But it also took the UGC into a detailed involvement in the universities' internal affairs. Making judgements on individual applications for support for particular posts was a very far cry from a block grant system where the universities made up their own minds on priorities. This was perhaps only a temporary expedient, but it fuelled suspicion that the UGC might have difficulty in ever returning to its former arm's length relationship with the universities.

The UGC's new determination and selective decision-making was not arrived at without exciting a storm of protest and criticism from within and outside higher education itself. Much of the criticism reflected a latent dissatisfaction with the UGC's record through the 1970s. A Labour Party discussion paper stated 'that the UGC is in urgent and radical need of reform. To all intents and purposes it has become an arm of Government—and an extremely inefficient and inept one at that. It is secretive, unrepresentative and totally unaccountable' (Labour Party, 1982). The Social Democratic Party (SDP) (with Parkes's successor Sir Peter Swinnerton-Dyer a member of its education committee) said the UGC had become 'an agency of government' and invited consultation on a series of options, two of which envisaged replacing the UGC either by a new body covering the whole of higher education or simply leaving the distribution of funds to the DES (SDP, 1982). The Institute of Economic Affairs, a right wing research organization closely linked to the views of at least some members of the government, suggested that 'the UGC designed originally to preserve the independence of universities has become an agency for their enfeeblement, a useless quango whose only purpose is to do to the universities what the Secretary of State would not care to do on his own initiative' (Ferns, 1982). For the first time individual universities publicly doubted the UGC's impartiality, and allegations were made that the fact that some of the hardest hit universities did not have members on UGC committees was an important factor in the UGC's eventual decisions.

A particularly strong attack on the UGC for its performance during this period was launched by Maurice and David Kogan who claimed that the UGC 'was both less objective and less consultative than its spokesmen claimed' (D. and M. Kogan, 1983). The Kogans reserved their special criticism for the UGC's decision to require a reduction of student intakes, a decision which 'preserved a hypothetical notion... at the expense of young people's opportunities.... The UGC, of its own will, not the government's, made the currency harder.' Our conclusion is that given the determination of the government to reduce public expenditure, the UGC was right to concentrate on saving the university system rather than indulging in gestures. It was wrong to rely so much on the sub-committee system in the final allocations of grant income, but perhaps the real fault lay in the lack-lustre performance of the UGC in the 1970s when it failed to monitor its sub-committees' performance. We believe that, in all the circumstances, the UGC was right to reduce intakes in order to protect universities.

All of these attacks postdated the UGC's exercise in *dirigisme* and suggested that the UGC's position and its mode of operation might be endangered. The greatest threat to the UGC may, however, have predated the cuts exercise. In 1979–80 the senior civil servant responsible for higher education in the DES was making speeches at conferences and to the select committee about the need for a manpower-orientated higher education policy and the importance of the DES playing a major role in the co-ordination of higher education. He suggested that the DES should make a 'clear proclamation, as it were, from the centre' about national needs (Education, Science and Arts Committee, 1980). This represented a serious potential encroachment on UGC territory. Dr. Parkes's address to the CVCP in October 1980 suggested that in government circles there were serious doubts as to whether a UGC 'composed as it largely is of practising academics, has too cosy a relationship with the universities and is incapable of enforcing change externally', and that there were people who argued that 'the time for peer judgement is past' and that universities should be controlled by 'the government machine' or by a committee of 'hard headed businessmen or trade unionists according to taste'. Dr. Parkes told the Vice-Chancellors' Committee that unless the universities were seen to be managing retrenchment effectively 'we shall cease to control our destiny, because it is at any rate my view that the greatest threat to the United Kingdom universities today is not a financial one' (Parkes, 1980). The UGC's metamorphosis into the 'positive buffer' which it had aimed to become in the 1960s, not only regained the initiative in managing the university system but also ensured that, at least for the immediate future, threats to its survival were averted.

CONCLUSION

The UGC's largely passive role as a buffer seemed to serve both the country and the universities well up until World War II. Its failure after 1946 to exploit more fully its enlarged terms of reference and to take an ongoing comprehensive view of higher education was criticized in some quarters and led indirectly to the establishment of the Robbins Committee. In the second period, 1963-79, the UGC attempted to play a more active role—but the needs of the country for 'more' and 'different' higher education, combined with the increased number of institutions, created the paradox described earlier wherein a more active UGC actually lost power to the government. As the national economic picture worsened, more was needed of the UGC than it was able or willing to deliver. Finally, in the third period, 1979-present, the UGC reclaimed a central role in the awkward and controversial policies dealing with retrenchment in higher education. It is our judgement that it has been better both for the country and for the universities that selective retrenchment should have been undertaken by an intermediate UGC style body, no matter if imperfect, than to have been mandated directly by the government or alternatively left to the workings of the so-called free market in higher education. In practice the British UGC rose to the occasion and undertook both a major restructuring exercise and an investment in new developments which had an invigorating effect on the university system.

However, the continued viability of the UGC is dependent on more than its ability to retain the initiative inside the university world. Higher education faces an uncertain future with the likelihood of continued restraint in public expenditure and the prospect of a demographic-led fall in student numbers. In this situation a number of scenarios can be envisaged. One vice-chancellor has suggested a full cost fees policy for home as well as overseas students, which could considerably reduce the UGC's powers (Hill, 1983). A further range of possibilities revolves around the future of the National Advisory Body for Local Authority Higher Education (NAB) created in 1981-82 to manage the public sector of higher education. The Robbins recommendation for a Higher Education Commission has been raised in a number of forms since 1963 and, if the NAB fails in its efforts to restructure the public sector, could be reintroduced either as a merger of the UGC and NAB or as a wholly new body (Shattock, 1983). If the NAB succeeds, the DES might prefer the two bodies to continue to work side by side, where they can be played off one against the other, or supervised by some kind of overarching body.

Whatever the future holds, the vigour of the UGC's recent performance and its longevity in the face of immense societal and governmental changes since 1919 suggest that there will remain a need for a body suspended between the universities and government. Moodie has suggested that the UGC's power is essentially that of a 'go between' or broker (Moodie, 1983). We believe that this view somewhat underestimates the UGC's position in the immediate postwar period and between 1957 and 1962, and certainly over the last three years. Moreover, we think that in the future it will need to be even more active and more decisive to survive. We agree with Moodie, however, when he argues that in part the UGC derives its role from the standing of its two principals, the government's on the one hand and the universities' on the other. The strength of the government's position certainly set a climate for the selectivity of the cuts exercise though there is evidence that the government was in the event surprised at the disparities in the cuts levied. Nevertheless, we believe that the wide range of its functions—not only acting as broker but also adapting, co-ordinating and reconciling university plans; arguing for funds and then distributing them; assisting institutional development and interpreting national needs—gives the UGC a power base which will prove difficult to erode unless it chooses to do so itself by abandoning the more active role it has pursued since 1979.

REFERENCES

Boyle, Lord (1978) Government, Parliament and the Robbins Report. Address to the Reading Education Society, 9 May.
Committee of Vice-Chancellors and Principals (1957) *A Note on University Policy 1947–1957*, London, CVCP.
Committee of Vice-Chancellors and Principals (1967) *Report on the Quinquennium 1962–67*, London, CVCP.
Committee on Scientific Manpower (1946) *Scientific Manpower* (The Barlow Report) Cmnd. 6824, London, HMSO.
Crowther-Hunt, Lord (1983) Policy making and accountability in higher education, in Shattock, M.L. (ed.), *The Structure and Governance of Higher Education*, Guildford, SRHE.
Department of Education and Science (DES) (1970) *Student Numbers in Higher Education*, Education Planning Paper No. 2, London, DES.
DES (1980) Evidence to the Select Committee on Education, Science and Arts, published in Vol. II of *The Funding and Organisation of Courses in Higher Education, Fifth Report*, H.C. 787-11, London, HMSO.
DES/SED (1978) *Higher Education into the 1990s*, a Discussion Document, London, DES.
Education, Science and Arts Committee (1980) *The Funding and Organisation of Courses in Higher Education: Interim Report on Overseas Student Fees*, Vol. II, Minutes of Evidence, H.C.363, London, HMSO.
Estimates Committee (1965) *Grants to Universities, Fifth Report, 1964–5*, H.C. 283, London, HMSO.
Expenditure Committee (1976) *Policy Making in the Department of Education and Science, Tenth Report*, 1975–76, H.C. 621, London, HMSO.
Ferns, H.S. (1982) *How Much Freedom for Universities?* London, Institute for Economic Affairs.
Foreign Affairs Committee (1980) *Third Report*, Session 1979–80, H.C. 553, London, HMSO.
Hill, Graham (1983) Developing individually, *Times Higher Education Supplement*, No. 552.
Kogan, M. (1971) *The Politics of Education*, Harmondsworth, Penguin Books.
Kogan, M. and Kogan, D. (1983) *The Attack on Higher Education*, London, Kogan Page.
Labour Party (1982) *Education After 18: Expansion with Change*, Labour Party.
Moodie, G.C. (1983) Buffer, coupling and brake: reflections on 60 years of the UGC, *Higher Education*, Vol. 12, pp. 331–347.
Owen, T. (1980) The University Grants Committee, *Oxford Review of Education*, Vol. 6(3), pp. 255–278.
Owen, T. (1981) Financing university education. Unpublished.

Parkes, Sir Edward (1980) Address by the Chairman of the UGC to the Committee of Vice-Chancellors and Principals.
Parkes, Sir Edward (1982) Address to the Parliamentary Scientific Committee, *Science in Parliament*, Vol. 40, No. 73.
Public Accounts Committee (1967) *Parliament and Control of University Expenditure, Special Report 1966–67*, H.C. 290.
Public Accounts Committee (1982) *Report: Department of Education and Science. University Grants Committee. Assessment of universities' grant needs. Relaxation of control over university building projects*, H.C. 175, London, HMSO.
Shattock, M. (1983) *The Structure and Governance of Higher Education*, Guildford, SRHE.
Shattock, M. and Rigby, G. (1983) *Resource Allocation in British Universities*, Guildford, SRHE.
Social Democratic Party (1982) *Education and Training*, Policy Document No. 7, SDP.
University Grants Committee (UGC) (1948) *University Development from 1935–47*.
UGC (1967) Memorandum of General Guidance, 13 November.
UGC (1968) *University Development 1962–67*, Cmnd 532, London, HMSO.
UGC (1970) Preliminary Memorandum of General Guidance on Quinquennial Planning 1972–77, 8 October.
UGC (1973) Memorandum of General Guidance, 15 January.
UGC (1974) *University Development 1967–72*, Cmnd 5728, London, HMSO.
UGC (1979) *Report on Russian and Russian Studies*.
UGC (1980) Planning for 1980–81.
Wolfenden, Sir John (1970) The economic and academic freedom of universities, Jephcott Lecture, *Proceedings of the Royal Society of Medicine*, Vol. 63.

11

School Governing Bodies and the Political-Administrative System

M. KOGAN, D. JOHNSON, T. PACKWOOD and T. WHITAKER

INTRODUCTION

The administrative structure of the English education system is characterized by a lack of clear relationships between the various institutions and bodies. The 1944 Education Act prescribed a diffusion of power and authority between the elements such that no single body was intended to assume a dominant position; instead, partnership and balance were to be the guiding principles determining the style of these relationships. School governing bodies were therefore vested with certain powers in order to provide a point at which the authority of the individual school and of the local education authority could come into balance. However, the values and assumptions underlying their role have changed as new expectations have arisen and systems of control altered. In any analysis of their roles they cannot be treated in isolation but have to be viewed as part of the local political-administrative system dealing with the education service.

THE POLITICAL-ADMINISTRATIVE SYSTEM OF EDUCATION

The assumption underlying the concept of the local political-administrative system is of a network of a number of different organizations and groups

Source: From Kogan, M., Johnson, D., Packwood, T. and Whitaker, T., *School Governing Bodies*, Heinemann, London, 1984.

each fulfilling certain functions in the governance of local educational provision. Because of their common concern with education they engage in interaction with each other. The main institutions and groups involved are illustrated in Fig. 1. The lines between the different bodies indicate possible linkages rather than formal relationship; they are, of course, involved with many entities other than governing bodies and the different networks criss-cross each other.

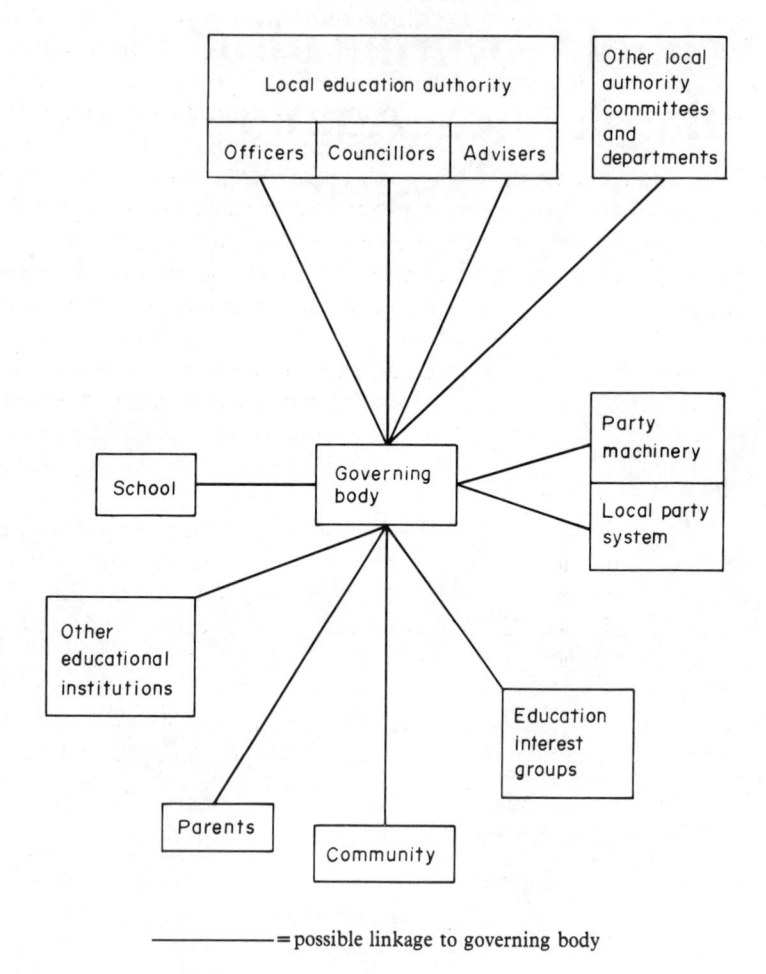

FIG. 1. The governing body's potential links with the local political-administrative system of education

The concept of a policy-making or inter-organizational system is found in the fields of political science, public administration and organizational

School Governing Bodies and the Political-Administrative System 197

theory.[1] It developed as a heuristic and analytical tool to portray 'government' as a series of different groups which impact upon each other and therefore form relationships. Implicit in this approach are, first, multiple linkages involving different types of influence and, secondly, the existence of complexity and at times an ambiguity in these relationships. Although each body may have its own terms of reference, there is overlap between the functions performed and bodies become interdependent.

At the level of the local education system there is the distinction between the responsibility of the local education authority and the strength of the school as a prime institution. This notion of the school as a prime institution is important in understanding the operation of the education political-administrative system. The prime institution, as defined by Kogan, is 'the lowest level of the system with sufficient discretion for the principal resources to be deployed, for judgements to be made by individual practitioners in their relationship to client needs'.[2] The implication of this level in education is that substantive decisions, such as curriculum issues and the organization of teaching, are principally the prerogative of the school. Yet the school does not have unlimited autonomy, for it has to engage in important relationships with the local education authority to gain resources. In formal terms the LEA has the specific tasks of determining the level of overall finance and allocating it between schools, building developments, and setting the staffing establishment of the school. Its role is therefore one of providing a coherent range of education in its area and if necessary to initiate development in policies.

The LEA is also part of a local authority with its own electorate and subject to control by the political system; its autonomy is not unlimited and it has to compete with other services to secure new policies and funding. The LEA also has relationships with national government and is required to implement national policies on education. For the LEA there is the question of the balance between the need to maintain and enhance institutional autonomy and to ensure public accountability. Its difficulties in managing and coordinating the system are perhaps accentuated by financial and demographic pressures, and may lead to the LEA exerting a more centralized style of authority and control in the system.

Included in the local political-administrative system are numerous pressure-groups associated with the provision and consumption of education. These may be groups with a formal organization and established contact with policy-makers such as a Community Relations Council or more informally based groups such as parents' associations. A further distinction may also be made between 'sectional' groups (such as teachers' associations), whose function is to protect a distinct interest in the education system, and 'promotional' groups (such as groups wanting to abolish corporal punishment in schools) seeking to promote a cause. All these types of group may not only exert pressure upon policy-making but may also play a part in the implementation of policies. Their style and strategies will in part depend upon the distribution of power in the political-administrative system.

Within the political-administrative system governing bodies have a place between the LEA and the level of the school. Inevitably they are subject to the pattern of interactions in this system and moreover their role is to a large part determined by the structure of power. This article goes on to analyse the main form of interactions between school governing bodies and the rest of the political-administrative system. At the end, an attempt is made to explain the pattern of relationships.

LEAs AND SCHOOL GOVERNING BODIES: THE FORMAL RELATIONSHIP

In formal terms the school governing body is subordinate to the local education authority because its existence and status are controlled by the LEA. This is important in structuring the potential role of the governing body in the local political-administrative system. The LEA determines whether each school should have its own governing body or whether a single governing body should serve a group of schools. Within this structure the LEA determines the functions and categories of governors.

The formal functions of governing bodies are specified by the LEA in the articles of government for all of its governing bodies. The LEA sets the functions and can decide, subject to the approval of the Department of Education and Science, to amend them. The LEA Articles of Government are based upon the 1945 Model Articles of Government and Management set by the DES. Although articles have a similar format, there are significant variations between authorities in the actual functions given to governing bodies. For example, articles differ in the extent to which governors play a part in areas of concern of school management such as the suspension of pupils, the appointment and dismissal of teaching and non-teaching staff, the finance of the school, and determining the use of school premises. Likewise, the form of participation delegated to the governing body indicates the extent to which management functions, such as the appointment of staff, are centralized or decentralized and delegated to the governing body. This variation may be seen to reflect the nature of political and administrative control in the local education system.

The composition of governing bodies is determined by the LEA in the instrument of government which it draws up. By this instrument the LEA determines those eligible to take part in school government and may determine the manner of appointment of certain categories of governors. Of importance in setting this structure is the LEA view of the balance between the different categories and in particular the proportion of LEA nominated governors. The strength of this latter category may indicate how strong political control is in the local education authority. In formal terms, then, the governing body is subject to LEA control over its functions and balance of composition.

LEA VIEWS OF SCHOOL GOVERNING BODIES

The articles of government provide a formal statement by the LEA on the specific functions of governing bodies which reflect a division of authority in the political-administrative system. This can be supplemented by 'notes of guidance' for governors which provide an interpretation of this role and suggestions about how governors may seek to fulfil their duties. It is likely that notes will reflect a more recent assessment than do the articles of their role and indicate current concerns of the LEA. For example, our research shows that in some authorities the formal responsibility of governors in the appointment of teaching staff has been changed by the LEA as the redeployment of teachers has become more widespread. In such circumstances the LEA redefines the role of governing bodies. Likewise, in three of the authorities in the research, governing bodies were expected to contribute to LEA policy-making, and yet the articles of government did not mention this role. The attitudes and values of decision-makers in the LEA (both officers and councillors) are of key relevance in determining the role of governing bodies. In our research these attitudes reveal more complicated perspectives than those formally conveyed to governors in the articles of government or notes of guidance, and were likely to place more emphasis upon the form of governing body participation in their areas of responsibility.

The LEA's statement of views constitutes expectations which may be continuously reinterpreted to governors. Our research reveals a wide range of possible views, but there are distinct patterns to be found. They indicate what purposes the LEA sees governing bodies as fulfilling in the different areas of concern in the local education system; their role in local education policy-making; their participation in school management and place in mediating interests between the different elements in the system. The main purposes of governing body activity which were found in our interviews with councillors, education officers and advisers are set out in the following paragraphs. Although they are treated here as separate entities they will of course coexist in various patterns in different LEAs.

As an intermediary between school and LEA

The role of intermediary is most frequently stated as a purpose by LEAs; it places governing bodies as a form of contact between the LEA and school. According to this view the governing body enables both councillors and education officers to keep in touch with developments in the individual school. The governing body constitutes a channel of communication with the LEA and provides the school with a forum to articulate its interests to the LEA. Through this link the school can be kept aware of LEA policy and receive expectations from the rest of the local education system. It follows from the intermediary role that the governing body should include both governors nominated by the LEA and school interests.

As an executive body

The executive body role would confer on governing bodies certain statutory functions to perform in school management which it is expected to perform in an efficient and responsible manner. The value of delegating these functions to the governing body is that it is democratic to allow the laity to participate in educational government, and by decentralizing decision-making it ensures that decisions are compatible with local needs. For example, on judging appeals against suspensions the governing body, whilst acting as a quasi-judicial body, is expected to reach a decision based upon its knowledge and assessment of local circumstances. Similarly, in the appointment of staff, the governing body can choose teachers who will respond to the objectives of the school.

As a forum for local accountability

In this approach the governing body is expected to become a forum for the local accountability of the school. The assumption is that the governing body is so composed as to allow the views of the local community to be made known to the school. The governing body aggregates and transmits these different views to the school and provides for a dialogue between the professionals and laity on the governing body. In so doing it may evaluate the school or the local authority and attempt to call either to account for its actions.

As part of the local consultative network

The governing body in this view is able to provide feedback to the LEA on proposed policies, including those that go beyond the immediate interest of the school. It is part of the LEA's network for consultation which includes formal groups and other pressure groups. The governing body, in bringing together different interests, acts as another route for community views to be made known to the local education authority. As will be seen, the purposes behind this consultation vary.

As a system of support

In this view the governing body's main function is as a system providing moral support to the school and other forms of assistance such as relevant expertise to its staff. The assumption is that the governing body will display a strong attachment and loyalty to the individual school. A variant of this view may also be where governing bodies are expected to provide support for the LEA. This might be used to promote the position of the education service within the local authority.

The LEA's perspectives are conditioned by a number of interrelated factors derived from the characteristics of the local education authority. The first and most important is the organization of education policy-making in the authority. A key dimension of this organization is the extent of party political control of policy-making in the local authority. Numerous studies have revealed that the impact of party political activity has increased since the reorganization of local government in 1974.[3] In terms of local authority policy-making structure several changes have become evident. There is the strict organization of policy-making on the basis of party allegiance resulting in increased party solidarity, the use of whipping for voting, party control of co-options to committees, and the majority party control of council business. There is the emergence of the party group composed of senior party members occupying key committee chairmanships which assumes a dominant position in the policy-making process. Associated with this informal arrangement, the policy and resources committee acts as the main committee in the local authority and is able to dominate all other committees. The overall impact of these developments is the production of a more formalized and centralized policy-making system. As one writer has noted with respect to education: 'The policy process for education in local authorities takes place in an increasingly closed system which is characterized by an emphasis on domination and control through party political organization and direction.'[4]

If in practice the extent of party control varies considerably in scope and intensity between authorities, its effect upon policy-making is pervasive. Authorities in the research characterized by a high level of party political control were more likely to have governing bodies with a large number of LEA-nominated governors who are apportioned strictly on the basis of party allegiance. Majority party-nominated governors may be expected to implement LEA policies in the confines of the individual school and be held accountable to the party political machinery which nominated them. For example, in one authority in the research governors nominated by the Labour Party were allocated to schools by a committee of the local constituency party. Regular meetings were organized for these governors by the local party to brief them on party policy and to discuss their role. The governing body in this context is viewed as a political mechanism existing between the LEA and the school. In such partisan authorities there will be variation in how open or closed is the structure of decision-making. In closed systems party political factors will override other independent views, whereas in open systems it is acknowledged that full control over the activity of governing bodies is neither possible nor necessarily desirable.

At the opposite end of the spectrum there are those authorities with a weaker party political alignment. The LEA-nominated governors are not a majority on the governing body and party membership is not a criterion for their appointment. These governors stated in interviews that they did not see their role as party political, and in many cases they were not members of a party but were nominated because of their standing in the local community. Governing bodies are therefore not viewed by the LEA as party political bodies and are more likely to be independent from the policy-making machinery of the LEA. As such, they are not necessarily concerned with the affairs of the local education system, but are attached to their individual schools.

The operation of party political factors upon governing bodies in the LEA is also reinforced by the political culture and style of political activity in the authority. The political culture refers to the predominant way in which demands are expressed and received in the local authority, and the degrees of cleavage or consensus amongst participants. An expression of this is the way the LEA approaches public participation. In certain authorities an open structure of participation is evident where there are numerous pressure groups placing demands upon the LEA. In this context the governing body is more likely to be viewed by the LEA as part of the consultative network of the local education system and a further source of pressure. Likewise, governing bodies may be viewed by interest groups as an alternative channel for articulating demands in the local education system and are subject to such pressures either from outside or from governors who represent these groups.

The third dimension of local education policy-making found in the research with repercussions on the activity of governing bodies is the balance between the views of education officers and councillors. So far in this article the LEA has been treated as a single body, but this ignores the different value positions that exist between officers and councillors.[5] Different views about governing bodies are apparent between these two groups. Education officers may adhere to certain professional standards which define the way that policies should be made and who should be involved. In terms of Alford's terminology they may be seen as a 'challenging interest' to the institutional autonomy of the school by trying to coordinate the local education system and make schools more efficient.[6] The delegation of management functions to governing bodies may limit officers' administrative control. In a similar vein, our research showed that advisers who share the values of teachers tended to be hostile to what they perceived as the intrusion of lay governors into the sphere of the professional control of the curriculum. Likewise, councillors evince values about issues such as representation and participation which have implications for their view of governing bodies. In some authorities councillors stated that the existence of governing bodies as local representative bodies could detract from the representative role of the councillor. Councillors have their own distinct views about educational issues and the relevance of public accountability. The balance between the views of officers and councillors influences the LEA's view of its governing bodies.

The final factor which affects how the LEA approaches school governing bodies is the style of relationship between the LEA and individual education institutions. This 'administrative culture' consists of the whole style and complex of relationships that exist between LEAs and schools and the views about these from the different participants in the local education system. As has been noted, the underlying assumption of the school as a prime institution possessing discretion to maintain its own organization has been entrenched in this relationship, but is susceptible to change. Important elements in this relationship are factors such as administrative procedures on finance and staffing, the nature of accountability, past history, and the existence of multiple channels of contact.[7] For example, in one authority in the research where advisory staff had a strong relationship with schools, the role of the governing body as an intermediary between school and LEA was seen to be limited. Also, in some LEAs the use of meetings of head-teachers as a channel of contact and source of policy advice acted as a constraint upon the possible activities of governing bodies in providing a link between the school and the LEA. Besides such organizational factors, if there is a large number of schools an authority may find it difficult to maintain governing bodies as an efficient channel of contact.

Of increasing significance in these relationships is the administrative complexity of the local authority. Accompanying the development of party political control in some local authorities is the rationalization of policy-making involving the procedures of corporate management. The implication for the education department is that it becomes increasingly linked to other departments of the local authority which provide allied functions such as the control of non-teaching staff.[8] In some authorities, prompted by financial stringency, this has led to a centralization of local authority decision-making in the local education system and particularly the position of the education service in the local authority. A number of governors interviewed felt that on questions of finance, decisions were being taken centrally in the local authority. The implication for governing bodies is that the locus of power may shift from the LEA to the rest of the local authority which makes it difficult for them to exert pressure.

LEA-SCHOOL GOVERNING BODIES: STRUCTURE OF CONTACT

The view of the LEA about the role of school governing bodies and the boundaries set by their composition are reflected both in the tasks they are expected to undertake and the resources made available to them. As has been demonstrated, there are a variety of possible roles for governing bodies which are conditioned by a number of interrelated factors. Within this general framework the most significant influence upon the operation of governing bodies is the contact between governing bodies and the LEA. This determines to a large extent the relationship between individual governing bodies and the rest of the political-administrative system.

In analysing the lines and form of contact there is first the range of tasks given to governing bodies by the LEA. As has been seen, although the articles of government frame responsibilities these do not necessarily emerge as salient but are interpreted and operationalized by the LEA. At this stage an important distinction can be made between those authorities which do not directly seek to influence the work of governing bodies and those which consciously shape the direction by influencing the substance of their work. In the former case governing bodies are seen to be school-centred and their mode of relationship with the school is left to the governing body to establish rather than imposed by the LEA. In the latter LEAs, the use of an authority-wide agenda for all governing body meetings determines the sequence and type of work to be undertaken by the governing body. Normally in case a model agenda is constructed by the LEA which puts forward items to be supplemented by school-initiated items.

Items initiated by the LEA can be of two types. First, specific documents relating to a policy issue may be placed on the agenda in order to consult governing bodies. Examples from our research included such issues as tertiary reorganization plans, multi-cultural education, and the use of school crossing patrols. The intention behind this process is to incorporate the views of governing bodies on changes affecting the level of the whole local education system. The decision on which items of policy governing bodies will be consulted is made either by the Education Committee or Director of Education. Items, too, such as DES documents are introduced in order to prompt governing bodies to consider aspects of educational provision such as curricular changes that might be relevant to the school. Here the LEA is attempting to enable governing bodies to perform their role effectively. In some cases in the research the LEA involved governing bodies in schemes for the self-evaluation of schools, where governors were expected to provide an input to this process.

As has been shown earlier, the range of functions contained in articles of government varies considerably between authorities. In particular, governors may act as committees to consider appeals against suspensions or to appoint staff. Governing bodies thus vary in their discretion and the autonomy allowed them. The LEA, in controlling the work of the governing body, is able to direct the focus of concern, but this may be subject to the requirements of central government. Indirectly the form of the agenda influences the scope for governors to raise demands. For example, in one

LEA a specific item was introduced on the agenda to allow parent governors to have an opportunity to raise issues. In contrast, in another authority some governors stated that the large amount of LEA-initiated items on the agenda of meetings had the effect of reducing the amount of time they had for discussing issues related to their individual school. However, as will be seen, this control over the substance and sequence of work does not automatically lead to the governing body performing the role expected.

The main intermediary between the LEA and governing bodies in most LEAs is the clerk to the governing body. Again there is an important distinction between those authorities which clerk all governing bodies and those which do not provide clerking or which clerk only secondary school governing bodies. The clerk services the governing body in producing and distributing agenda, reports and minutes and communicating with other bodies in the local education system on behalf of the governors, and by providing a linkage between the LEA and governors. The way clerking is organized is likely to influence the type of contact. Some authorities have clerking sections which service governing bodies and consist of specialized governing body clerks. In other cases the clerking is carried out by an education officer, adviser, or even an officer from another local authority department. The administrative status of the clerk is likely to be important in how he is viewed by governors. In two of the case study authorities the clerk was accompanied to meetings by a more senior officer to advise on policies and provide a direct line with the authority. Governors in these cases thought that the presence of these more senior officers meant that their views would carry extra weight.

What then happens to resolutions and minutes depends upon such factors as the view of the LEA concerning the importance of governors' views, and the structure of the education department. In some authorities in the research the clerk sent the specific requests from governing body meetings to particular officers in the department for their attention. Also in some authorities the copies of all governing body minutes were circulated to all senior officers. However the extent to which the requests from governing bodies were made known to councillors varied. In some cases it was practice for members of the schools subcommittee to receive minutes and notification of action on specific resolutions. Similarly on issues of consultation it was practice in some authorities for all responses from governing bodies to be collated by officers and presented to councillors. In turn the clerk reported back to the next governing body meeting on the progress on particular items raised by governors. In those cases where no clerk was provided by the LEA this process becomes less formalized because the clerk was not a full-time member of the education department and not necessarily familiar with the organization and processes of the LEA.

As well as the formal mechanism of transmitting views between the governors and the LEA there are additional informal links which might be used. The LEA-nominated governor can assume a particular significance. The appointment of party-nominated governors is normally in accordance with the party balance on the council. There are a variety of methods of appointment to this category reflecting the nature of party organization in the authority. In some authorities ward parties put forward nominations to the party group on the LEA and the final decision was made by party whips or senior councillors. In other cases it was individual councillors in an area who nominated governors and party membership was not a requirement. Instead it was expected that governors should have similar values or some specific experience or expertise which would benefit the governing body.

The LEA view of the role of these LEA-nominated governors again depends upon the extent of party political organization. In certain authorities it was felt important for councillors and, in particular, members of the education or schools sub-committees to serve as governors. The assumption is that by having a member of council on the governing body a direct link to the LEA is provided and the councillors can aid the governing body. Yet it is important to note that councillors from the minority parties do not see themselves as spokesmen for the authority. In certain cases in the research they used the forum of the governing body to criticize majority party policy.

A further line of contact can be provided by the chairman of the governing body. Before the 1981 Regulations[9] it was customary for the chairman to be a councillor or at least a member of the majority party on the authority. This was seen both to provide contact with the LEA and in some cases ensure that governing bodies acted within the confines of LEA policies. The chairman had a dual role of acting for the LEA and as one of the governors. Since then, in many LEAs it is still assumed that it is best to choose a councillor as chairman. The role of the chairman in all authorities was viewed to be a key one, although there were not any specific guidelines by which to define his role and responsibilities. It may be expected that the chairman is a link with the LEA. In some authorities biannual meetings were held for the chairmen of all governing bodies to discuss issues of common concern. In other cases the chairman had the right to meet with the chairman of the education and schools sub-committee. But, in general, this line of contact was likely to be varied depending upon the individual's own status and sources of contacts. Therefore the structures of contact will vary between authorities both in their range and styles. Of particular importance is the degree to which the role of the governing body is strictly defined by the LEA and has to work within a formal, regulated system for governing bodies in the authority. This will influence the range of activity and style of bargaining of the governing body.

STYLES OF LEA-SCHOOL GOVERNING BODY INTERACTION

The first part of this article has outlined the formal structural relationship between the LEA and governing bodies and has shown that within certain limits the LEA can control the functions of governing bodies. In particular, opportunities for governing bodies to interact with the political-administrative system are structured in different ways. The image is of the governing body as a subordinate body to the LEA and working within defined parameters. The next part of this article explores in more detail the actual relationships that exist and delineates the various patterns of interaction.

Local education authority policy-making

A feature of the policy-making process of many LEAs is the extent to which governing bodies are an element of the consultative process. This is in accordance with the LEA view of governing bodies as a mechanism to keep in touch with the views of the community. A related LEA concern is the need to ensure that governing bodies are aware of LEA policies and knowledgeable about expectations of other parts of the local education system. It is likely that these types of authority are characterized by an open style of policy-making which admits pressure-group activity.

The part the governing body can play in the total education policy-making process is framed by the way that the LEA decides to proceed with consultation. For the LEA, consultation can exist on several levels. First, it may be designed to illuminate a problem and enable them to receive different viewpoints prior to a decision being made by the education committee. For example, one authority in the research undertook a planning exercise for the reorganization of the schools in an area in which options were formulated at different stages in the whole process with governing bodies consulted at each stage. The entire process was structured, and governing bodies were one of a number of groups engaged in participation.

Secondly, governing bodies may be informed by the LEA once a decision has been made with the intention of keeping them informed of policies and building up support before implementation.

The consultation process designed by the LEA may be classified according to a number of factors. Participation of groups including governing bodies may take various forms. Arnstein's ladder of citizen participation contains eight levels, ranging from manipulation and therapy, through informing, consultation and placation to partnership, delegated power and finally citizen control.[10] The main dimensions of such a ladder are the degree of autonomy given up by the decision-making body and the assumption that the possession of power is necessary for groups to progress up that ladder. Similarly, participation will depend upon the stage of the policy-making process at which the views of groups are sought. This is important because at a later stage of the process the options given to groups to consider may become more restricted. Finally, the extent of participation depends upon information for effective contribution and this will vary in its content and style of presentation by the LEA.

In practice, the LEA's views about consultation and its control of that process were matched by what governors saw as the legitimate scope of concern of the governing body. These views may rule out involvement in issues of wider education policy-making as being beyond the authority of the individual governing body. A feature of a number of governing bodies in the research was their attachment to the affairs of the individual school rather than to the local education system. Which view is taken by the governing body will depend upon the type of governors and composition of the governing body. Governing bodies must themselves be viewed as political bodies composed of various groups with different values. For example, in a governing body with a majority of party political nominees their role may be to formulate and implement party policy. Another relevant factor is the existence of 'community' governors nominated by pressure groups in the local education system. These and other governors are likely to have links with other status positions in the local political environment to form what Dunleavy terms the 'burgher community'.[11] These linkages make up informal networks of influence which present selected demands to policy-makers and can frame the definition of policy issues. The implication of networks for the position of governing bodies is that they may be used by pressure-groups in certain circumstances as channels in the transmission of demands. In this way the boundaries between the different elements of the local political-administrative system become blurred. The linkages will affect the operation of the governing body in terms of its internal style and presentation of demands.

Yet it is also true that governing bodies may be in an isolated position in the political-administrative system because the main political transactions take place around them, rather than through them. Equally true is that party-nominated governors may not be active members of their ward parties, and do not take part in the formulation of party education policy-making so that governing bodies are insulated from the pressures of the local political system. Our research clearly showed that, in general, pressure groups seek to exert pressure on the LEA which they view as being the main locus of power rather than on governing bodies. However, the political-administrative system changes over time as the configuration of power changes. Governing bodies may constitute a possible pressure channel, which may be used by groups when particular types of issue emerge. An issue such as the possible closure of a number of schools increases the likelihood that governors will display a concern with LEA policy-making and act as a pressure group upon the LEA. In one authority where there were plans for the reorganization of its schools, governing bodies were used by the schools to exert pressure upon the authority to protect their interests.

In general, the ability of governing bodies to formulate or change policies is limited. Both councillors and officers stated in the research that the views of governing bodies could be forecast, and therefore only served to confirm the direction of policy. Only if there was a concerted and unified opposition from governors (which was viewed to be unlikely) would policy change dramatically. On major issues of majority party education policy opposition would be less effective, and in some cases policies were introduced without governing bodies being consulted. In one authority in the research the abolition of corporal punishment had become LEA policy despite widespread opposition from governing bodies in the authority; this was because this issue had been a major element on the party manifesto. In another case a governing body facing the closure of the school was debarred by the clerk from discussing the decision in formal governing body meetings because it was interpreted that the governing body could not criticize LEA policy. These cases illustrate what Ham has identified as the importance of power in participation.[12]

School governing bodies may thus constitute one element in the education policy-making process. In general, they are reactive rather than proactive, or providing a continuous contribution. They coexist amongst other elements such as teachers' unions, political parties, pressure groups and head teachers. Although these groups may be represented on the governing body, they see it as just one amongst a number of channels of communication rather than being a prime element.

School governing bodies and administration

The second main activity of governing bodies as shown by the research is to act as a mechanism of positive support for the school in providing contact with the LEA. This is viewed by governors to be an important function. It is different from participation in policy-making because it involves a more spontaneous and fluid relationship with the LEA and allows the governing body in some cases to be proactive in its demands.

The LEA's view of this function varies. In documents such as the notes of guidance for governors it is generally identified as a crucial activity for governing bodies which helps the LEA to keep in touch with the affairs of individual schools. Yet in this concern an important factor is the amount of autonomy in administrative functions possessed by the governing body.

Governors in general see the governing body as an important source of pressure upon the LEA: this is in accordance with what governors see as their responsibility in providing support. It is also recognized that the governing body possesses the authority to assess the needs of the school and to mediate between school and LEA. Although this view was generally found amongst all governors interviewed, it was particularly marked amongst teacher and parent governors. Likewise, head teachers view the governing body as a potential pressure group which can exert pressure to reinforce other requests to the authority.

The form of contact with the LEA takes place at different levels. The LEA clerk—where he exists—is most often used as the first formal contact with the authority. In some cases, the clerk has an influence over the exact wording of resolutions making specific demands to the authority, and is able to influence the governors' stance on certain issues. Governors rely upon the clerk because it is judged that he possesses the necessary knowledge of where to send resolutions and the contacts to follow up progress.

When the LEA does not clerk the governing body the chairman or correspondent becomes the main intermediary with the authority. The position of the chairman depends upon the category of governors and their individual statuses. Where the chairman is a majority party councillor this is viewed by the rest of the governing body as a useful asset. The chairman then has contacts with key councillors and senior officers and some status in the eyes of the LEA. But even where the chairman is a key councillor it does not automatically benefit the governing body. In the one case in the research where the chairman of the governing body was also chairman of the education committee, he stated that he owed a loyalty both to the governing body and the LEA, which meant that on certain issues he would defend LEA policy and distance himself from the governors' demands.

Other LEA-nominated governors can be used by governing bodies to influence the LEA. Local education authorities in the research often saw this type of governor as one who would be conversant with its policies and, if necessary, would defend them. However, most governors in this category do not necessarily possess the relevant information about policies or procedures, and do not regard themselves as defenders of the LEA. This was particularly true of minority party governors. In some cases they are able to use party political networks to raise issues with councillors.

In these cases the governing body is acting as a pressure group. Although in most cases bargaining takes place through using 'key notables'—leading political figures—in some cases governors themselves engage in direct lobbying of the education or schools sub-committee. The style of bargaining and the relative success of various strategies depend upon a number of interrelated factors. As we have seen, the nature of administrative contact between LEA and governing bodies influences the pattern of activity. If there is a formalized system of clerking and processing of governing body requests governing bodies are more likely to have a ready route of access and be used as a mechanism for the LEA to receive issues of concern. But although this channel may benefit the governing body, it can also reduce its scope of action as it becomes incorporated into the administrative process.

Secondly, the type of issue and the way it is viewed by the LEA is also a key

School Governing Bodies and the Political-Administrative System 211

factor. Local education authorities in the research had definite views on what was 'reasonable action' and a 'legitimate' demand which influenced how they processed such requests.[13] For example, officers in the research stated that a demand by governors for extra resources had less chance of success in a period of financial stringency. From our research, governors were well aware that their powers of exerting pressure in these circumstances were limited.

A third factor is that governing body activity depends upon the style of administrative relationship between the LEA and its schools. The governing body might not be used as an intermediary with the LEA if the head has his or her own well-established contacts. Also on issues such as building it was customary for some authorities to have a detailed administrative process for identifying requests for repairs. In these cases, the governing body might only be used if the system broke down, or in the case of delay when extra pressure was viewed to be desirable by the head teacher.

Lastly, governing body activity depends upon the composition of the governing body; the governors' own view of the purpose of the governing body; and also on the governors' own contacts elsewhere in the political-administrative system which affects strategies adopted. For example, teacher governors in some cases saw the governing body primarily as a forum of support for the school and raised issues of resource deficiencies in meetings in order that their fellow governors should act upon these and request additional resources from the LEA.

SCHOOL GOVERNING BODIES AND THE POLITICAL-ADMINISTRATIVE SYSTEM: AN ASSESSMENT

The previous analysis of the role of governing bodies in the local political-administrative system shows how they are conditioned by exogenous factors, particularly the stance taken by the LEA. It shows that their role is multi-modal depending upon the type of issue they face. Yet this analysis should not be viewed as static for it is clear that changes in the local political-administrative system, for example a change from an élitist to a pluralist distribution of power, have repercussions on the possible roles of the governing body. Similarly, the presence of new governors with links with the political system may lead to changes in the roles adopted. Yet an important conclusion from our research is that, in general, governing bodies do not have systematic relationships with community groups, and that such groups are more likely to seek to exert pressure upon the LEA. School governing bodies are not used by community groups as a major channel of contact to exert pressure upon the school and the local education authority. In part this is because they lack visibility in the local education system and also because community groups commonly perceive governing bodies as lacking any real power or purpose. It is the LEA which is seen by these groups to be the major power-holder and so direct contact is the most favoured strategy.

In assessing what part the operation of school governing bodies plays in this system, our research confirms the earlier findings of Baron and Howell that governing bodies operate on the periphery of the network because they do not have links with any structure except the LEA.[14] Yet this should not lead automatically to the view that they completely lack power. This contrasts with the views of other writers. For example, Bacon, in his analysis of school boards in Sheffield, presents an élitist account of education policy-making with the local educational establishment composed of key officers and councillors forming an 'administrative-political élite'.[15] According to this analysis, school boards developed in Sheffield in the context of problems facing the educational establishment in the 1970s—the need to maintain authority and executive control and to ensure public support for the introduction of new policies. In this context school boards aided the introduction of new and contentious policies and provided an alternative way for the local educational establishment to gain information and elicit public opinion. This was achieved through the process of the co-option of possible challenging interests. Therefore school boards did not make any challenge to the existing structure of power.

From our research it is difficult to reach conclusions of such a generalized nature which would be applicable to all cases. Our account presents a more complex view of governing bodies engaging in multiple forms of contact. By using such a framework several important factors become evident. First, different institutions in the local education system are engaged in different linkages with each other. Governing bodies as one such element occupy a unique role because they may constitute the various interests present in the system and such overlapping membership assumes importance. Secondly, because of the different values held by individual governors, governing bodies lack clear organizational identity. Their functions therefore have to be negotiated because they are used by different constituent groups for their own purposes. Of particular importance is the power of the LEA to determine the composition of the governing body, its functions and mode of relationships. These control patterns obviously exist at different levels and allow governing bodies different degrees of autonomous action. The twin notions of compliance and discretion determine the operation of governing bodies. What Bacon and others view as complete control by the administrative—political élite does not completely determine their operation. Our analysis echoes Howell's view that within limits governing bodies can exploit their access to sources of power and can remain a potential source of conflict with the LEA or school.[16] In our research there were a limited number of examples of governing bodies exerting pressure upon the LEA and refusing to acquiesce in legitimating policies. Yet in the end result they were not always successful. Although occupying a weak position, governing bodies are not completely debarred from action of a particular kind, although this is likely to be individual rather than involving groups of governing bodies.

NOTES AND REFERENCES

1. For example, see Benson, J. K., The inter-organisational network as a political economy, *Administrative Science Quarterly*, vol. 20, no. 2, 1975; and Archer, M.S., Educational politics: a model for their analysis, in Broadfoot, P. (ed.), *Politics and Educational Change*, Croom Helm, 1981.
2. Kogan, M., The central-local government relationship—a comparison between the education and health services, *Local Government Studies*, January/February 1983.
3. For example, Jennings, R.E., *Education and Politics: policy-making in LEAs*, Batsford, 1977; and Alexander, A., *Local Government in Britain Since Re-organisation*, Allen & Unwin, 1982.
4. Jennings, op. cit., p. 182.
5. For example, Collins, C.A. et al., The officer and the councillor in local government, *Public Administration Bulletin*, December 1978.
6. Alford, R., *Health Care Politics: ideological and interest group barriers to reform*, University of Chicago Press, 1975.
7. For a number of current problems affecting these relationships, see Dennison, W.F., *Education in Jeopardy: problems and possibilities of contraction*, Basil Blackwell, 1981.
8. See Howell, D.A., Corporate management in English local government and the education service—an interim report, *The Journal of Educational Administration*, vol. 17, no. 2, October 1981.
9. Education (School Governing Bodies) Regulations, 1981.
10. Arnstein, S., A ladder of citizen participation, *Journal of the American Institute of Planners*, vol. 35, 1969.
11. Dunleavy, P., *Urban Political Analysis*, Macmillan, 1980.
12. See Ham, C., Community health council participation in the NHS planning system, *Social Policy and Administration*, vol. 14, no. 3, Autumn 1980; and Richardson, A., Thinking about participation, *Policy and Politics*, vol. 7, no. 3, 1979.
13. See Dearlove, J., *The Politics of Policy in Local Government*, Cambridge University Press, 1973.
14. Baron, G. and Howell, D.A., *The Government and Management of Schools*, Athlone Press, 1974.
15. Bacon, A.W., *Public Accountability and the Schooling System*, Harper & Row, 1978.
16. Howell, D.A., Problems of school government, in *Education in the Eighties: the central issues*, Simon, B. and Taylor, W. (eds), Batsford, 1981.

SECTION 4

Teacher Unions and Teacher Numbers

12

Pushing for Equality
the influence of the teachers' unions — the NUT*

PAUL LODGE and TESSA BLACKSTONE

It is difficult to trace the NUT's influence on educational policy. Ronald Manzer has described[1] the existence of an 'educational sub-government' in which the various parties, the DES, local authority associations and teachers' unions consult, bargain and negotiate until an educational consensus emerges. Much of this discussion takes place privately between officials. In certain circumstances, however, Manzer suggests:

> bargaining inside the education sub-government may break down and the participants have to appeal to the political system at large for a settlement. For educational pressure groups in England and Wales such an appeal is usually made with a 'public campaign'. The public campaign is an exceptional event in the politics of the education sub-government, however; and, in general, access to political as opposed to administrative arenas is definitely of secondary importance for all the groups in the sub-government.[2]

The methods that the NUT employs to influence policy are various. They include direct dealing with departmental officials, deputations to ministers, planted parliamentary questions and membership of official working parties. At any one time it is likely to be represented on nearly a hundred bodies, including various unofficial groups as well as the more formal official ones. By this means it may exercise considerable influence on policy questions, sometimes obtrusively but, more often than not, in an unobtrusive way. It works through an extensive network of contacts, bringing pressure to bear on those with power or influence to get its views on a wide range of matters accepted. For example, there are a number of ex-teachers in the House of Commons, especially in the Labour Party. Moreover, the NUT actually

---

* This is an edited extract from Lodge, P. and Blackstone, T. (1982) *Educational Policy and Educational Inequality*, Oxford, Martin Robertson, published in *New Directions in Educational Leadership*, Harling, P. (ed.), Falmer Press, 1984.

sponsors several MPs. One instance of rare direct and visible NUT influence on educational developments is cited by Manzer. The publication in the early 1960s of a pamphlet entitled *Fair Play for Our Primary Schools* sparked off a parliamentary debate on the neglect of primary schools and probably contributed to the setting up of the Plowden Committee. For the most part, the process is less visible and, as a consequence, open to a variety of possible interpretations.

The degree to which the political arena is used may have grown somewhat in recent years, however. In the climate of rapid growth in educational expenditure which existed throughout the 1960s and the early 1970s there was less pressure on the teachers' unions to move out of the charmed circle of negotiations between the DES, the local authorities and themselves.

Since the mid-1970s, however, the almost automatic assumption of high growth that existed before has been challenged by the circumstances. The harsh combination of public expenditure constraints, a declining birth rate and some disenchantment with the importance of educational expansion to achieve economic growth or redistribution has meant that cosy discussions about how best to spend a growing budget are over. There are already signs that to defend what they have already, all the teachers' unions are resorting to a more public and political role. Moreover, a concentration on fighting to retain the *status quo* may well detract from attempts to redistribute. It may also be the case that the DES has somewhat changed its style. The department now consults more widely through the publication of Green Papers and consultative documents of one kind or another. This widens the debate beyond the 'education industry', makes it more public and may also serve to push the unions into a more overtly political arena.

Another aspect of the NUT's political position is its relationships with the major political parties. Manzer argues:

> on the whole the relationship between the union and the parties is deeply inhibited, reflecting the low temperature of educational politics, the disinclination of the union to become involved in party politics and the irrelevance of party educational policy to the overwhelming amount of national educational policy.[3]

In taking this point of view, he ignores the much closer connection the union has with the Labour Party than with the Conservative Party and overstates the 'irrelevance' of party policy to national educational policy. Although it is true that there is some caution about identifying too closely with one or other political party (many of the union's ordinary members are Conservative voters), there is little doubt that most of the union's senior officials have an affinity with the Labour Party. Their contacts with Labour Members of Parliament, with members of the Labour Party's National Executive Committee's sub-committee on education and with Labour ministers are likely to be closer and more extensive than those with their Tory equivalents. The union's executive clearly draws its members from a range of political opinion. Two of its more prominent members over the last two decades have been members of the Communist Party, and there have been Conservative as well as Labour presidents. However, in general it is fair to say that the union's political position has been to the left of centre rather than to the right, in terms of both its leadership and the policies it espouses.

This has implications for the stance that it is likely to take upon most questions of educational equality. The union is likely to attach some importance to achieving greater equality in general and, more specifically, greater equality through education. The Labour Party is committed to change in order to bring this about, while the Conservative Party on the whole is not, and Labour policies on education have been more in line with NUT policies than have Conservative educational policies. The union has tried to influence the policies of both parties in government in order to create more equality. Its advocacy of certain policies may, however, have less to do with its commitment to such an ideal and more to do with self-interest. Cynics might argue that any espousal of greater equality has as much to do with trying to expand the system to create more jobs and more opportunities for promotion for teachers as with trying to improve the opportunities of certain groups of children. The real test comes, perhaps, when self-interest and moves designed to create greater equality conflict with each other. There are special tensions which are peculiar to 'professional' unions. On the one hand, they wish to represent the interests of their members with respect to pay, job opportunities and working conditions; on the other, they wish to be a responsible and influential force in the pursuit of wider aims concerning professional standards which they perceive to be in the national interest.

The rest of this article will examine the view that the NUT has taken of some of the relevant policy areas, namely, nursery education, positive discrimination, the abolition of selective schools and the raising of the school-leaving age. In so doing, it will from time to time touch on the professional/union conflict.

NURSERY EDUCATION

The union has long espoused the case for education for children under 5. Since the early 1960s it has produced several documents on the need to expand nursery schools and classes. The first of these involved a survey of maintained nursery education, carried out in 1962. It found that all the nursery schools in the sample, and most of the nursery classes, had long waiting lists. More than half of the schools had more names on their waiting lists than pupils in their schools. In the period leading up to the creation of the Plowden Committee, the union was the first organization to emphasize the large gap between demand for, and supply of, nursery places and to stress the need to close the gap. In its own evidence to Plowden it recommended that nursery education should be available at the age of 3 and that 'there should be a statutory obligation on the local authority to provide facilities on the scale necessary to meet the full demand for such education in its area'. It explained the need for nursery education partly in terms of 'waste of ability' and 'differences of opportunity between one area and another', commenting particularly on the importance of the child's linguistic environment: 'Of all the cultural inequalities that widen the differences between child and child, it is the richness or poverty of its early linguistic development which demands most attention.' It went on to say that 'an adequate nursery school system and the provision of infant school education from the age of 5 are both indicated if there is to be equal educational opportunity for all our children'.[4]

The evidence also referred to the need to help parents of deprived children because of the strong link between early nurture and later ability to benefit from schooling. Interestingly, however, the document did not advocate bringing parents into the nursery schools but suggests instead the expansion of services available to mothers through child welfare clinics and education for parenthood in the secondary school curriculum. This may simply have reflected the view that intervention should take place only before the child starts school, or indeed before the child is even thought about. It may also have reflected the union's wariness of proposing that parents should be brought into the schools on a large scale. It did, however, suggest that informal contacts between parents and teachers were important elsewhere in the report. It backed parent-teacher associations but sounded a note of caution about their development replacing these informal contacts.

The document concluded by stating: 'we have emphasized but not, we think, over-emphasized the social role of the primary school as the great provider of equal opportunity for all our children'. To achieve this, it argued that it was essential that children should enjoy 'the benefits that highly skilled and therefore highly trained teachers can confer'. It went on to warn against any possible departure from this desideratum for purely economic considerations.

To some extent, the Plowden Committee made just such a departure. It recommended a major expansion of nursery education along the lines proposed in the NUT's evidence, so that eventually it would be available for all children whose parents wanted it. However, the expansion was to be staffed in part by nursery assistants rather than entirely by fully qualified teachers. There would be a minimum of one teacher per two nursery classes, and the nursery assistants would work under her supervision and guidance. In its public response to Plowden, in a document in which it commented on the major issues of the report, the union said nothing about this recommendation. Indeed, its comments on the nursery education proposals were confined to three sentences. However, in its private negotiations with the Labour government at the time the latter was considering the Plowden Report's recommendations, it strongly opposed the proposal to staff the expansion partly with nursery assistants. In a series of lectures on aspects of government, Shirley Williams castigated the NUT for doing so.[5] She had been a minister of state at the DES at the time and argued that the union's opposition prevented the government from expanding nursery education at a time when there were still serious problems with teacher supply in primary schools, as well as constraints on public expenditure, making the cheaper nursery assistants doubly attractive. She put this forward as an example of the undesirability of excessive secrecy in British government. Had the union's opposition been made public, there would, she implied, have been a public outcry, which would have greatly strengthened the government's hand in innovating in a way which the union opposed. Alternatively, the union might have been more constrained to avoid the embarrassment of public criticism. How far this was true is, of course, a matter for speculation. It is, however, hard to escape the conclusion that in this case the union's legitimate concern with the interest of the teaching profession was in some conflict with its desire to expand nursery education in order to equalize opportunity for all children. The case that no expansion was better than some expansion partly staffed by nursery assistants was and is hard to sustain. However, it can perhaps be understood in terms of a dilution of the quality of the professionals working with young children at the time when emphasis was being placed on imposing higher standards through, for example, longer and more demanding training.

The union persisted in its opposition to the employment of nursery assistants in the 1970s. It also continued to advocate nursery education expansion in order to alleviate inequality throughout the decade. It issued four different pamphlets. The first was a survey of nursery education in Wales.[6] The Welsh report stressed the importance of giving priority to areas of social need. Consistent with the Welsh tradition of an early start to primary education, it recommended provision from the age of 2. This was followed by another pamphlet on pre-school provision in England and Wales.[7] The pamphlet was marked by its attack on playgroups. By this time the playgroup movement had become an established form of provision rather than just a stop-gap, which was how it had been perceived in the 1960s. Moreover, it had a number of powerful advocates. Bridget Plowden had retracted from the commitment of her report to nursery classes on the grounds that the participation of parents was crucial and that this could be more easily achieved in playgroups. A. H. Halsey, whose action research studies in educational priority areas had examined the work of playgroups,[8] was also giving them his support partly because of teacher opposition to parental help in schools. The NUT appears to have been willing to accept them as long as they were seen as a temporary expedient. As soon as they became more than this, it took a different view.

As far as the NUT was concerned, playgroups were second-best, stop-gap measures. This was partly because of a genuine belief that standards are higher where professionally trained staff are employed and partly, no doubt, to protect the role and status of nursery teachers.

Not only did the NUT oppose the expansion of nursery education using nursery assistants rather than teachers, but it also criticized the 1971 White Paper's proposals to expand provision by attaching nursery classes to primary schools.[9] It also criticized the White Paper for failing to allocate sufficient financial resources to nursery education, claiming that it would cost more than anticipated. Whether the union was correct about this or not, in general such criticism may well be counter-productive when governments are under severe public expenditure constraints, since it may serve to discourage them from expanding at all rather than encourage them to provide further funds. The union then argued: 'we strongly disagree with the almost total exclusion of nursery schools from the proposed provision'. It admitted the advantage of nursery classes, particularly that of greater continuity, then went on to claim that nursery schools had many advantages too. However, the only one it cited was that nursery classes were likely to be accommodated in mobile classrooms or in inadequately converted infant classes. Any objective observer would regard this as a somewhat weak claim for nursery schools. In fact, the real reason for the NUT preference for nursery schools was its belief that they provided better promotion prospects for nursery teachers. Although it did not reveal this in the 1974 document, it made the point quite clearly in *The Needs of the Under-Fives*:

> The union believes that authorities should seek to ensure that nursery teachers have an opportunity to obtain promotion without necessarily having to apply outside of the nursery sector. This requires a restoration in the balance in the programme so that the number of places in nursery schools and nursery classes is nearly equal.[10]

Since nursery schools are considerably more expensive than nursery classes, their development might well have slowed up the expansion of the number of available places. This is another example of a conflict in the union between its goal to promote opportunities for its members and its genuine desire to obtain more nursery provision, especially for the disadvantaged child.

One further example of this concerns its views on parental participation, which have already been touched on. In the 1974 document it argued:

> Teachers welcome parental support and are prepared to put their training and experience at the disposal of parents. Nevertheless, we see dangers in that it may be assumed that such community of interest confers an unqualified right upon parents to intervene in the educational function of the school as and when they see fit ... teachers are responsible for the welfare of all children and have to hold a balance between the needs of the individual and the community, in a way parents do not normally have to bear in mind. The union therefore believes that the Department of Education and Science and the local education authorities should give proper emphasis to this responsibility, and that they should institute further consultation on this matter with the teachers through their professional associations.[11]

POSITIVE DISCRIMINATION

Under section 11 of the 1966 Local Government Act, local authorities are able to claim 75 per cent of the cost of the staff who are employed to make special provision for 'immigrants from the Commonwealth whose language or customs differ from those of the indigenous community'. Any local authority is eligible to make this claim if 2 per cent or more of its school population are the children of Commonwealth immigrants. In July 1978 the NUT issued a report which was critical of the operation of this legislation.[12] Its criticisms were based on a survey of local authorities, which revealed that the amount of grant claimed varied enormously between authorities and that it bore little relationship to the number of immigrants within their boundaries. It also showed that staff employed under section 11 were frequently not being used to carry out specific tasks to help minority group children. Indeed, some head teachers did not even know that they had section 11 staff.

The union put forward a number of positive proposals to improve both the Act and its implementation. These included abolishing certain limitations (such as those that restricted the application of the Act to people from the Commonwealth and those resident in the country for less than ten years) to take in all minority groups and some constructive suggestions on how such extra staff might be used. Among them were recommendations to use liaison officers between the community and the schools, to create education visitors to visit homes and to provide more resources for the teaching of English. It could be argued that in backing amendments to section 11 and more effective use of the legislation, the union was in the enviable position of being able to support change which would benefit disadvantaged children and would also provide staff in schools 'extra to establishment' and thus benefit the teaching profession. In this case there was no conflict of interests. However, some of the NUT's proposals for use of section 11 staff were unlikely to have a direct impact on reducing the burdens of the classroom teacher. It would therefore be unduly cynical, and rather unfair, to argue that this was the union's main goal with respect to section 11.

A further report was produced the following year[13] in response to a Home Office Consultative Document on replacing section 11 of the 1966 Local Government Act. This welcomed some of the Home Office's new proposals and reasserted the NUT's view that ethnic minorities must be given high priority in educational programmes within a wider strategy to deal with racial disadvantage. The second report confirms the view that the NUT has played a positive role in trying to improve educational opportunities for ethnic minorities.

These is further confirmation of its consistently concerned record in this area in two other publications. *All our Children*, published in 1978, summarized the way in which the union believes schools can contribute to a tolerant multi-racial society. In its conclusion it recommended that all teachers should 'champion the cause of social justice for all students in their classes, schools and communities'. It also suggested that the schools could and should be seen as agents of racial harmony. In this context it backed a curriculum that recognized cultural diversity in schools. One practical outcome of this was a Schools Council project on need and innovation in multi-racial education, which the NUT proposed along with the National Foundation for Educational Research and the National Association for Multi-Racial Education. There was, however, a touch of complacency about the document's definition of the role of the school when the NUT quoted from its own evidence to the 1973 Select Committee on Race Relations: 'our educational system [is] non-discriminatory in intention and in fact'. The union went on to explain the fact that children separate into different minority groups as they get older and become more ethnically aware, or indeed intolerant, in reaction to pressures in the wider society. Such pressures are undeniable but do not mean that the educational system has nothing to answer for with respect to discrimination against minority groups. There was, in fact, no reference in this document to the need for positive discrimination towards minority group children. The DES argued at the time that general policies towards the disadvantaged would benefit black and brown children. The department tended to down-play the extra dimension to the social and economic disadvantages from which these groups often suffer. Possibly to avoid stigmatization, it argued that policies should be geared not specifically towards minorities but towards the disadvantaged generally.[14] While the NUT did not actually say this, its omission of any reference to positive discrimination for ethnic minorities could mean that it accepted the DES line. However, it is perhaps dangerous to interpret lack of explicit comment as acquiescence. All the indications, including its strong stance on section 11, are that the NUT has favoured positive discrimination for ethnic minorities.

One way in which the DES decided to tackle disadvantage was to found the Centre for Information and Advice on Educational Disadvantage. This was set up in 1975 as an independent body to promote good practice. The union gave the new centre strong backing in *All our Children*. However, it did not say anything in this pamphlet about its potential role with the disadvantaged among ethnic minorities. When the new Conservative government took office in 1979 it embarked on an attempt to reduce greatly the number of QUANGOs. Although it was not especially successful and the great majority of QUANGOs remained intact, the Centre for Educational Disadvantage was one of the victims. The NUT roundly condemned the government for its decision to close the centre. Max Morris, an ex-president of the union and vice-chairman of the centre, claimed that its valuable work on ethnic minorities and the 20 per cent of the school population who get no qualifications would be wiped out.[15]

The second document which demonstrates the NUT's commitment to minority groups is *Race, Education and Intelligence: a teacher's guide to the facts and the issues*, also published in 1978. This pamphlet was commissioned by the NUT from biologists and psychologists at the Open University, including Steven Rose, a well-known critic of Jensen's and Eysenck's theories about racial differences and levels of intelligence. The pamphlet set out clearly for practising teachers the arguments against assuming any biological basis for differences that may occur. How much influence a document of this kind has is, of course, impossible to assess.

THE ABOLITION OF SELECTION

The third area of policy in which we wish to examine the NUT's position over the last fifteen years or so is the abolition of selective schools. It is a policy that the NUT has forcefully advocated since the mid-1960s. Prior to this there is not much evidence of extensive NUT initiative to promote this cause. The reason for this is unclear. It perhaps reflects a tendency by the union to support certain changes when they become part of the political agenda rather than to fight for their inclusion on the agenda in the first place.

It was not until the election of a Labour government in 1964 that the union apparently considered it worth devoting much time to the advocacy of comprehensive schools. In that year it published *The Reorganisation of Secondary Education*. This seems to have been designed as much to demand that certain conditions, such as adequate accommodation, should be fulfilled in the reorganization schemes as to make the case for reorganization. It was no doubt issued in an attempt to influence a new Labour government not to proceed too fast *if* that meant that schemes would not be backed by extra resources and teachers would not be extensively consulted about the planned changes. The same year the NUT submitted its evidence to Plowden.

A careful reading of the NUT's evidence to Plowden leaves little doubt that the union was in favour of the abolition of selection at the time. However, its view was often expressed in an oddly muted way. Whether this reduced the impact of what it said is hard to say. One example of its reticence and caution is as follows. The Plowden Committee had asked in its list of questions for those giving evidence whether selective education was desirable. In its reply the NUT said, 'In some ways we regret that we are called upon to answer the question at this particular time.' Because some authorities had already begun reorganizing 'in a very hasty and ill-considered way', decisions about this question were in some ways too late, it argued. At the same time, in some ways they were too early, it claimed. It was hoped that effects of Plowden's recommendations, including demonstration of the potential of all children, would help in the battle to persuade parents and teachers of the effect of environment upon the educational development of children (a surprising admission). This needed more time. In the light of all the evidence on this subject already available at that time, this is a strange statement.

However, perhaps the findings of research had not yet percolated through to many teachers.

Although there is no doubt about where the union stood on this issue—it was in favour of comprehensive schools—its advocacy of the abolition of selection was certainly cautious and pragmatic rather than uncompromising and idealistic, perhaps because it was anxious to ensure that the reform would work. Its advocacy of change was hedged about with preconditions, notably those concerning buildings. Much emphasis was placed on the need for purpose-built accommodation. Constraints on new building were accepted as a reason why the tripartite system should continue in some areas. There are two possible interpretations of why the NUT placed so much emphasis on school buildings. The first is that it was anxious that comprehensive schools should succeed and therefore insisted that, for example, schemes which put together two schools on different sites should be avoided. There was not, however, much evidence to support the importance that it attached to buildings. The second interpretation was that it was primarily concerned with the job opportunities and working conditions of teachers and was anxious to protect these even at the risk of slowing down the development of comprehensive schooling. There were certainly fears that the senior posts in comprehensive schools would all go to ex-grammar school teachers and that ex-secondary modern teachers would suffer accordingly. After the publication of Circular 10/65, which invited local authorities to submit plans for the reorganization of secondary education, the NUT's house journal, the *Teacher*, came out in support of the circular.[16] However, the editorial also criticized the government for failing to provide extra money, which it claimed could delay the exercise by up to thirty years. It also indicated concern that reorganization would be at the expense of primary education, stating, 'the inequalities that the present tripartite system tends to encourage find their first beginnings in the primary school'. As many of the union's members were primary school teachers it was presumably politic to say this. However, if the government had acted upon the criticism, there would have been even fewer resources for comprehensive schools and therefore, on the NUT's own argument, an even greater delay in establishing the new system.

By the end of the 1960s the NUT had adopted a tone of greater urgency about the implementation of secondary reorganization. Possibly fearing the return of a Conservative government, which might have stopped further progress towards comprehensive schools, it began to demand legislation to enforce reorganization on local authorities. At the 1969 Conference it passed a resolution calling on the government to provide the necessary money and to legislate in order to bring about comprehensive education. From then on practically every annual conference of the NUT has passed a resolution on comprehensive schools. During the 1970s there were only three years when such a resolution was not passed, and the topic was the subject of resolutions more often than any other. This perhaps indicates better than anything else the degree to which, by then, the NUT attached importance to the issue in spite of a somewhat cautious position earlier. Moreover, many of the conference resolutions were phrased in terms of a belief that the comprehensive principle is the only basis for providing equal opportunity for all children. And by 1977 the demand was for 'an immediate end to all forms of selection'. Two years later conference instructed the executive to encourage the membership to refuse co-operation in selection procedures. By the end of the 1970s, then, the union was taking a fairly militant position about selection.

Several possible reasons can be postulated to explain this change. First, the political climate was marked by a sharpening of the debate. With each change of government there was an immediate attempt to change the policies of the previous government. The NUT was drawn into this debate and could not easily sit on the fence. Second, there was probably a change in the general attitudes of the NUT's membership: teachers trained in the 1960s were exposed to educational research which demonstrated that social as well as academic selection was taking place. Third, dissatisfaction over the fairness and reliability of selection methods had probably grown.

Beside conference resolutions, there are three documents, published between 1969 and 1979, which reveal a certain amount about the NUT's position on reorganization. One of the ambitions of Edward Short, who was Secretary of State for Education during the latter part of the 1966–70 Labour government, was to produce a new Education Act to replace the 1944 Act. His hopes were not fulfilled. However, he did prompt others to think about what a new Act should contain. Among them was the NUT, which produced a document entitled *Into the Seventies*, in which it put forward its ideas. In the introduction it made clear its views about the essentially regressive nature of educational expenditure. The more privileged the pupil, the more money is spent on him. Second, it identified wastage.

> The outstanding characteristic of the system is its profligate waste of ability. There is waste of ability before the child enters school, waste at 11+, waste at school leaving age ... The present distribution of educational resources still very often means that the 'haves' receive positive discrimination in their favour, while the 'have nots' lose even the little that might be theirs.[17]

It went on to propose that the new Act should legislate for comprehensive education over the whole of the compulsory age range.

The second of the documents mentioned above addressed itself specifically to attacking the Conservative government's slowing down of the process of going comprehensive in the early 1970s. In a pamphlet provocatively entitled *What is Mrs Thatcher up to?* it launched a personalized attack on the Secretary of State for Education. It was more 'political' than any previous statement on this subject published by the union.

What is Mrs Thatcher up to? is an example of political pamphleteering at its best. It is cleverly conceived, punchy and persuasive. If Mrs Thatcher were the kind of politician who could be embarrassed by attacks of this kind, it might have succeeded in making her feel uncomfortable. The third of the 1970s NUT pamphlets, entitled *Education in Schools*, which touched on secondary reorganization, is in a quite different style, perhaps because it was published in a different political context. It listed and briefly commented on the main recommendations in the government's Green Paper, *Education in Schools* (1977). This Green Paper followed the 'Great Debate' which was stimulated by the speech of the Prime Minister, James Callaghan, at Ruskin College, and it covered a wide range of issues. One of its many recommendations concerned secondary reorganization. It stated that comprehensive reorganization must be completed, though it was self-congratulatory about the substantial progress so far and went on to argue that what was needed in the wake of reorganization was a period of stability during which standards might be improved. The pamphlet questioned the government's claims about the extent of the achievement so far. It suggested that although 75 per cent of pupils were nominally in comprehensive schools, this figure exaggerated the true proportion. It included pupils in schools where only those in the lower forms were in 'comprehensive' classes because of the recent nature of reorganization. It also included pupils in comprehensive schools which were coexisting with selective schools. The NUT went on to urge the implementation of the 1976 Education Act requiring all authorities to submit plans for reorganization. Only then, when recalcitrant authorities had been brought into line, would the period of stability be justified.

ROSLA

Thus by the end of the period we are considering the union was strongly committed to the abolition of selective schools, in strong contrast to its slightly tentative position a decade or so earlier. Its position on the raising of the school-leaving age to 16 seems to have been strong and consistent advocacy of it from the early 1960s. Some might argue that adding an extra compulsory year to secondary education greatly increased pupil numbers and therefore the demand for teachers, so that the union could hardly have advocated anything else. However, some teachers' organizations, notably the NAS, strongly opposed raising the leaving age significantly, to the detriment of existing pupils and their teachers. The NUT did not accept the arguments of the other associations. In a short paper stating its view of the issue the union explicitly attacked the argument that resources should be directed towards those who want to learn rather than those who are unwilling. It pointed out:

> views not so very dissimilar were being expressed a hundred years ago, when the principle of compulsion was being applied for the first time at a much earlier age. But more important, the fact that teachers were aware of the hostility of some of the present leavers against the school and its ethos, should be taken as a criticism of our present attitudes and methods, rather than as a reason to welcome the departure from school of such youngsters at the earliest possible opportunity.[18]

It is difficult to detect exactly what position the NUT took on the question after the Crowther Report was published in 1959 recommending that the school-leaving age should be raised. However, once the government had announced in 1964 that it would implement the recommendation, the union was active in encouraging preparation for it and in demanding extra resources for buildings, staff, in-service courses and curriculum development. However, its commitment to raising the school-leaving age was not sufficiently influential to prevent the government from deciding in 1968 to postpone the measure by two years, from 1970–1 to 1972–3, as part of a package of public spending cuts. The NUT's Annual Conference in 1968 adopted a resolution deploring the decision to delay implementation. Among the reasons cited were that it would 'deny opportunities to underprivileged children' and would 'delay the satisfactory reorganization of secondary education', as well as restricting 'the output of better trained and skilled manpower'. Thus it emphasized both redistribution and manpower requirements. Voluntary staying on, which had increased, was thought to be insufficient; moreover, those who left early were most likely to be those who had already suffered other social disadvantages.

After this the union concentrated on the problem of how to implement the change, dismissing as irrelevant any further discussion of whether it should be introduced. It carried out a survey of all LEAs to find out what was being done to prepare for the raising of the leaving age and published its findings in a pamphlet entitled *16: Raising the School-Leaving Age*. The pamphlet claimed that many authorities complained of being hampered by inadequate resources, and as a consequence the union pleaded for greater generosity on the part of central government. However, it went on to say that there were substantial differences between LEAs in the quality of preparation, which had little to do with resources. One of the less obvious issues it touched on was the influence of examinations on the secondary school curriculum. The retention of all pupils until they were 16 would require that more thought be given to the examination system, though few authorities had apparently considered this. Finally, the pamphlet foresaw that the raising of the school-leaving age would strengthen the case for abolishing two separate systems of school-leaving examination. This is a policy which the union advocated as early as 1970 and has strongly espoused since then.[19] One of the reasons it put forward in favour of a common system was that it would remove 'the divisive element implicit in the present dual system'.[20] In backing five years of compulsory secondary education for all children, the union did not explicitly anticipate the need for completely different forms of assessment, such as pupil profiles, which would be required if a substantial minority of pupils were not to be left without any form of paper qualifications whatsoever on leaving school.

The union's position on the raising of the school-leaving age can be summed up as the conventional liberal progressive one, which backed the measure strongly as a means of extending opportunities to less privileged children. Disparities in staying-on rates between different social groups and different parts of the country could be wiped out by this means. It did not question whether the extension of compulsion was desirable in principle. It did not consider whether the most obvious alternative method of extending opportunities in this age group—the expansion of part-time education for 15–18-year-olds, possibly on a compulsory basis—might be a more desirable use of the resources. It was, however, hardly in the NUT's interests to do so. The union represented schoolteachers, and the alternative policy would have meant expanding the further education sector rather than the secondary schools.

CONCLUSION

In this article so far we have examined the position that the NUT adopted on the key issues of policy designed to create greater equality. What conclusions can we draw about the NUT's influence? As we said in the introduction to this article, it is not possible to prove influence. We can only speculate on the basis of the fairly limited evidence we have available.

What we have said has been based largely on an analysis of NUT publications and conference resolutions. What is difficult to ascertain is the impact of such publications. Who reads NUT pamphlets? How many people read them? How seriously are they taken by policy-makers in central and local government? How far do they influence ordinary NUT members? Are the members' attitudes and practices modified as a result of reading these pamphlets? If so, presumably this will have some indirect effect on policy formulation at the local level, and possibly at national levels, insofar as the teaching profession as a whole, rather than just its representatives, is seen to be strongly opposed or strongly in favour of particular changes.

Another important question is how closely the public position taken by the union in the pamphlets it produces accords with the position it takes up in the private negotiations it enters into with central government in particular. When attempting to put pressure on the government through deputations to education ministers or through private discussions with senior officials, it may adopt a stance slightly different to the one it adopts publicly. It may feel able to take a more self-interested position than it would if its views were exposed to public scrutiny. In some circumstances the reverse may be true. It may feel more able to advocate policies in the interests of children, parents or the nation, rather than simply in the interest of teachers, when it is not exposed to its own members' scrutiny. Whichever is correct, it must be emphasized that the extent to which the union can privately depart from the public position it takes must be constrained. If it did so frequently and extensively, it would rapidly lose credibility with the 'insiders' in the decision-making process and would probably eventually lose some of its influence.

Where the union does adopt a somewhat different position in different contexts, this may not necessarily be the result of a cynical disregard for the principles of consistency and integrity. It may be because there are genuine differences of opinion between different sections of the union. So far we have assumed homogeneity. In fact, as in all large organizations concerned with political and policy issues, there are differences of opinion which are sometimes of a serious kind. Most of the work that goes into NUT publications is done by full-time officials, mainly in the Education Department. This work is scrutinized by members of the executive and its committees before being published. Hence it often represents a consensus and may mask differences of opinion that emerge elsewhere. However, in spite of all these provisos, it seems reasonable to assume that the publications are a fairly accurate reflection of the union's general position and that they are read by those responsible for making policy, who have to take into account the likely response of the teaching profession as a whole and of the NUT in particular.

Apart from the example of the pamphlet on primary schools mentioned at the beginning of the article and the 1970 proposals for a common examination at 16, there is no other evidence of the NUT's actually initiating new policies in the areas we are considering. Its mode is, in general, responsive rather than initiatory. Its opposition to particular proposals, such as the partial staffing of nursery classes with nursery assistants, may serve as an informal veto. Its opposition to extensive parental involvement is another example. Its views on this are in part a function of strongly-held professional values about freedom and autonomy in the classroom. Professionalism of this kind has undoubtedly produced tensions when certain kinds of change have been advocated. As the *Schoolmaster* stated with respect to the Beloe Report, 'it has always been a source of pride to the profession, and a very proper one, that in this country the teacher has the unalienable right to decide what to teach and how to teach it, and insofar as he is the best judge of the child's readiness to learn, when to teach'.[21] On the other hand, its continual backing of certain policies may help to speed up their implementation. Its espousal, if a little belated, of the abolition of selection at the age of 11 over a number of years may have helped somewhat to reinforce the introduction of comprehensive schools.

We suggested earlier that the union's position has been on the radical side of the political spectrum rather than the conservative. (One result of this is that its public stance may vary a little according to which party is in power.) However, Manzer has argued that 'in promoting the education of working-class children the NUT was part of a general movement in British society to improve the condition of the working class'.[22] He suggests there was a social idealism that was shared by administrators and teachers alike during the post-war years. He does not give the union any special credit for espousing the cause of equality. On the contrary, he claims that the NUT must now be regarded as a powerful conservative influence in the politics of English education. This conservatism is explained by the union's traditional professional concern for the education of the individual, its refusal to sacrifice long-standing educational ideals, the distractions created by divisions inside the teaching profession, and the threat to the collective role of teachers in the policy-making process posed by a more national orientation and centralization of educational policy.[23]

Does this judgement stand up in the light of our analysis of the NUT's position on our four policy issues? What has emerged shows the NUT as both idealistic and self-interested, both conservative and radical. In certain respects it has dragged its feet, as a consequence possibly reducing the educational opportunities of working-class children. In other respects it has fought hard to expand educational opportunities for the less privileged members of the community. Its record is by no means unblemished, as we have indicated. Nevertheless, Manzer's assessment seems a little too sweeping and harsh.

NOTES

1. Manzer, Ronald A. (1970) *Teachers & Politics*, Manchester University Press.
2. Ibid., p. 3.
3. Ibid., p. 19.
4. *First Things First*, memorandum submitted to CACE, under the chairmanship of Lady Plowden, London, NUT, 1964.
5. Williams, Shirley (1980) The decision makers, in *Policy and Practice: the experience of government*, London, Royal Institute of Public Administration.
6. *Nursery Education in Wales*, London, Welsh Committee of the NUT, 1972.
7. *The Provision of Pre-School Education in England and Wales*, London, NUT, 1974.
8. Halsey, A.H. (1972) *Educational Priority: EPA problems and policies*, London, HMSO.
9. *The Provision of Pre-School Education in England and Wales*, p. 15.
10. *The Needs of the Under Fives*, London, NUT, 1977, p. 29.
11. *The Provision of Pre-School Education in England and Wales*, p. 12.
12. *Section 11*, London, NUT, 1978.
13. *Replacing Section 11*, London, NUT, 1979.
14. *Educational Disadvantage and the Needs of Immigrants:* observations on the Report of the Select Committee on Race Relations and Immigration, DES, London, HMSO, 1974.
15. Morris, Max (1979) quoted by Castle, Mary, Second thoughts urged on 'arbitrary' closure of disadvantage centre, *Teacher*, 23 November.
16. See issue of 12 July 1965.
17. *Into the Seventies*, London, NUT, 1969, p. 4.
18. *The Union View of ROSLA*, London, NUT, 1971.
19. See *A Certificate of General Secondary Education*, London, NUT, March 1970.
20. *Examining at 16-Plus: the case for a common system*, London, NUT, 1978, p. 5.
21. See issue of 30 September 1960.
22. Manzer, op. cit., p. 38.
23. Ibid., p. 158.

13

The National Union of Teachers

KEN JONES

To read the educational output of the National Union of Teachers is to experience the power of the past over the present. Looking back, the union emphasizes its overriding aim of securing expansion of opportunity; it stresses the reasonableness of its cause and the supporters the cause has attracted, across the political spectrum. Governments may sometimes have obstructed expansion, short-sighted councils may have sought immediate economies at the expense of long-term interests, but the lesson of history is that allies will be found to press the struggle on. The future of the nation's children is the future of the nation itself, and enough will realize this axiom to make the union's efforts eventually worthwhile. This outlook is plainly that of a body which claims not simply trade union status but co-responsibility for the education service. It colours the rhetoric and strategy of the union's present campaigns, which enumerate once-consensual themes:

> All children should have equal opportunity to develop their abilities and talents to the full.
>
> Access to a public education service of the highest quality is a fundamental right for all children....
>
> The united support of all who care for the nation's future is vital if these principles are to be upheld and our children offered the opportunities they deserve.[1]

These propositions are offered as restatements of well-known truths, which scarcely need argument. The full range of the present educational crisis—which comprises more than cuts and crass anti-egalitarianism—is not discussed.

That 'equal opportunity', as it has previously been defined, has foundered on inequalities of class, sex, race and power; that 'quality' has become a term of an immensely problematic sort; that 'united support' cannot easily be invoked when the community of 'those who care' is divided about the value

---

Source: From Lawn, M.A. (ed.), *The Politics of Teacher Unionism: International Perspectives*, Croom Helm, London, 1985.

and purpose of education—these problems, which are all aspects of a breakdown of consensus, are not registered. Yet these difficulties are at the heart of the union's current situation which arises from the combination of economic recession with a very marked shift in the relationship of major social forces to state education. The union's traditional pathways of advance are blocked. The assumption that educational expansion is synonymous with economic benefit is not widely shared. Governments no longer think that the teaching force can be relied upon to adjust itself to official perceptions of educational need; on the contrary, it is argued that new routes of policy-making have to be constructed that by-pass the union's channels of influence. The teaching force must not only contract. Just as important, it must be subject to increased control both of its educational work and its conditions of service.

The NUT thus faces a Conservative government committed not only to financial restraint, but to radical revision of the 1944 educational settlement. This settlement, and its renewal in the 1960s, provided the conditions for the extension of the union's influence, as well as the matrix in which the attitudes of its leaders and members were formed. The union has been accustomed to rising membership, educational expansion and increasing curricular influence. The accelerating revision of the settlement has shaken the NUT. Its membership falling, its influence lessened, the conditions of service of its members worsening, the union is attempting to develop a new strategy that in its basics revives and consolidates its traditional outlook, and yet also faces problems that require responses more associated with trade union than professional forms of struggle. This article examines the tensions that arise in this difficult process.

No single great governmental battle plan has forced the union onto the defensive. But the cumulative effect of a number of distinct processes has been to face the union with problems on every front.

SALARIES

The average salary of a teacher has fallen—by comparison with average earnings in the work force as a whole—by about 30 per cent since 1975.[2] The early 70s were a time of teacher shortage and successful pay campaigns. By contrast, 1984 finds management in a strong position. Teacher numbers are falling—by 10 per cent between 1979 and 1983. Teacher unemployment is rising to an official level of about 15,000,[3] 3-4 per cent of the teaching force.

In addition to their low pay increases, many teachers find that their automatic progression by yearly increments has come to a halt: they have reached the top of their particular pay scale, and no further movement is possible without promotion. Promotion is difficult because, with a fall in student numbers, schools are less able to make appointments above the lowest scale of the five scale salary structure.

The teaching unions have turned their attention to renegotiating the salary structure. The employers (representatives of local authorities with whom teachers negotiate on the Burnham national salary committee) have used the occasion to link issues of pay to those of the management and control of the teaching force. Their proposals for restructuring would make salary progression dependent upon assessment of the teacher. There would be a three-year 'entry grade' for new teachers, with the elimination at the end of this period of teachers who were declared professionally incompetent, or who failed to display something called 'long-term career potential'. There would be an annual assessment of teachers on the 'Main Professional Grade' with accelerated progression through the pay scales for teachers certified as good, and the withholding of increments from those who did not satisfy. A condition of being paid at all would be a willingness to accept as contractual activities which are now voluntary: lunch-time supervision, staff meetings, 'in service training', parents' evenings. These proposals will, of course, be modified in negotiation. Even so, it is clear that the employers envisage a teaching force more flexible in its interpretation of 'professional duties' and subject to assessment as a condition of advance. And, since criteria for assessment will be influenced by new educational policy goals, employers will also be able to develop a surer means of translating curriculum policy into school practice.

JOB SECURITY

The years since 1979/80 have been marked by a reduction in educational provision which has in many cases increased workloads and lowered morale. 'Morale' in this context should be understood in a strong sense. It is not simply a question of increased stress arising from a decline in resources. It entails, also, a sense of the breakdown of an educational project: that of attempting to develop a pedagogy based on principles of equal opportunity. The attitudes created by the expectation of unemployment, the perception of a lowered public status, the pressures from inside and outside the school to emphasize differentiation of curricula, and the new vocationalism, all combine to create a general crisis of teaching purpose.

The particulars of job security should be set against this background.

Compulsory redundancy is very rare—though hundreds have been prevailed upon to accept premature retirement with compensation, and thousands have left teaching voluntarily, under similar agreements. But redundancy is not the only threat to job security. The number of teachers employed on fixed-term (temporary) contracts is slowly increasing; an NUT survey put the proportion in 1983 at 4.6 per cent of the teaching force. About half have been placed on such contracts in order that their employers can more easily eliminate jobs in time of cutback.

Compulsory redeployment is also on the increase. The White Paper of March 1983 on *Teaching Quality* recommends its use, not just as a means of dealing with a teacher 'surplus' at a particular school, but as a permanently available tool of managerial policy.

This policy, though directly affecting only a small number, can only weaken the sense that all teachers have of belonging to a particular staff at a particular school. It 'decollectivizes' the teacher's conception of his/her status, and thus helps to increase the influence of centralized authority both within the school, and within a local authority area.

EDUCATIONAL INFLUENCE

In the union's best years, government influence on the curriculum was indirect. Teachers, though subject to advice, resisted stipulation. The main advisory body on the curriculum was not a government department but the autonomous Schools Council, on which the union was strongly represented. The Council is now dissolved and has been replaced by committees on the curriculum and examinations appointed by the Secretary of State. At the same time there is an abundance of state and independent initiatives, all of which have the effect of reclaiming from teachers much of the curricular ground they occupied in their heyday. The proposed common examination at 16+ will lessen the influence teachers have exercised through the CSE exam boards. Encouraged by the DES, the two main (private) vocational examining bodies are to promote a new 'practical' curriculum leading to a system of pre-vocational and technical awards.[4] Likewise, the government's 'Technical and Vocational Education Initiative', funded not by the DES but through the Manpower Services Commission, represents a direct national influence upon a curriculum traditionally open to school-based decision. Other government initiatives, outside the control, even, of the DES, are setting a context for the school curriculum that installs at the heart of the educational system a goal different from that of equal opportunity, in that by stressing the relationship between education and occupational destiny it emphasizes that the school must provide appropriately vocational forms of education for students destined for relative failure in the labour market. The Youth Training Scheme has an educational basis which is rudimentary in the extreme.[5] Yet its educational criteria are influencing school curricular developments and the union can do little to modify them.

As the union's national influence on the curriculum diminishes, its members experience in their schools the emergence of different criteria and new demands. Stimulated by DES circulars, local authorities are requiring of their schools an account of their curricular objectives. As the schools redefine their work, the initiative passes from the subject departments to the administrative centre; and the recommendations of heads and deputies, curriculum co-ordinators and working parties are increasingly inflected by the new vocationalism.

ACCOUNTABILITY

The corollary of teacher control of the curriculum has always been an objection to 'outside interference', whether governmental, industrial or parental. In practice this has entailed not only a justifiable suspicion of government's centralizing tendencies but also a resistance to dialogue with popular organizations about educational objectives. At a time of consensus, the weakness of this latter position was not crucial: teacher activity could at least parallel the public mood even if there was little explicit interaction. However, when with the publication of the *Black Papers* in the late sixties the right wing began to depart from the consensus, teachers had to face something more than the usual lobbying and infighting against particular government policies. They now had also to cope with a populist critique of the comprehensive principle which, utilizing the slogan of accountability, appealed over the heads of the usual protagonists of debate to win some support among parents and public opinion. The NUT has found it difficult to respond to a challenge of this kind. Too much associated with the character of postwar reform to respond critically to the shortcomings of 'equal opportunity', it has never investigated the sources of discontent with the school system and is thus vulnerable to criticisms which play upon concern about the discipline and knowledge presently transmitted by the school in order to advocate a return to a form of schooling in which order and a sense of purpose would allegedly be secured by the unambiguous matching of types of education to types of future occupation.

Mainstream Conservative policy borrowed from the *Black Papers* the slogan of accountability and deployed it as a tactic in educational debate. The accuracy of the charges that linked a supposed decline in 'standards' to the secretive and unresponsive nature of the system was questionable; but this was less important than their political effect. Conservative policy was able to exploit a gap—caused partly by failures of communication and partly by real differences in educational conception—between the activity of teachers and the expectations of parental opinion.

A diluted form of 'parental choice' is now embodied in the 1980 Education Act, which gives parents the right to indicate a preference for a particular secondary school. It is a device which assures some schools of substantial demand and certain survival, while alongside them unpopular schools face falling rolls and the possibility of closure. Given that parental choice is exercised in a manner influenced by the new themes of educational policy, schools are under pressure to provide an education in line with the redefined priorities. It thus serves as another pressure towards conformity and as a further, if distant, instrument of control over the teaching force.

This survey should be enough to indicate that the problems the NUT faces are not simply the classic ones of trade unionism in a period of recession. Though they encompass the defence of jobs and conditions, they also go beyond it. Teacher autonomy in determining the curriculum, relative freedom from management control, and organizational influence upon national policy-making have been among the union's major objectives, and have formed the practical content of its claim to professionalism. Each aspect of this policy is now under threat. Much of the anger that fuelled the union's 1984 salary action—which involved refusal to take on 'voluntary' activities, or to cover for absent teachers, as well as widespread strike action—arose as a response to this combination of factors, and not from the pay issue alone.

Before examining the responses of union policy to these issues, it is necessary to look at the varied composition and attitudes of the union and of the teaching force. These must be appreciated before any account of the development of union policy can become comprehensible. It is useful to begin with a description of some of the major points of division among teachers.

SALARY AND MANAGERIAL FUNCTIONS

Salary differentials are large enough to sustain differences in outlook between groups of teachers, especially when combined with the interests arising from the managerial functions carried out by a surprisingly large percentage of the work force.[6] In September 1981 there were nearly 60,000 head teachers and deputies in employment: 13 per cent of all teachers. Of the rest 9.5 per cent were on Scale 4 or senior teacher scale.[7] Though it is impossible in any exact way to read off from teachers' position in the school hierarchy their attitude towards trade union issues, there is a rough but evident correlation between status and 'political' practice. The tendency for heads to leave the NUT or NAS/UWT over the last decade in order to join less militant head teacher organizations is one indicator of this.

PRIMARY AND SECONDARY TEACHERS

Secondary teachers are on average better paid, have greater opportunity for promotion, and more time in school to prepare lessons. Working in larger units, they are better able to resist or escape close supervision of their work. Protected by their numbers, more remote from parental pressure, and less vulnerable to the argument that militancy causes children to suffer, they are—though in many senses better off than their primary colleagues—more likely to take 'industrial' action. Yet, in the NUT, primary teachers are the majority: the implications of a situation in which the part of the union with the lesser implantation within its own sector plays the more militant role needs further consideration.

GENDER

Sexual discrimination permeates teaching. Women are 59 per cent of the teaching force. They occupy the lower salary scales, hold 96 per cent of part-time contracts (which are usually temporary), and 81 per cent of full-time temporary contracts.[8] They are less likely to be graduates and more likely to be 'non-specialized' teachers or to work in the less prestigious areas of the curriculum.

The effects of discrimination are as pervasive in the major teaching unions as they are in the schools. The NUT (which has a much better record on 'equal opportunities' than its rivals) has only 8 women on an elected executive of 42—yet nearly 60 per cent of its membership is female, and in every region of the union there are more women than men members. Over two-thirds of women primary teachers are in the union, but less than half of male primary teachers. In secondary schools, too, women members outnumber men: nearly one in two women secondary teachers are in the union; less than one in three men. Yet these proportions are not reflected in the composition of school and area leaderships.

UNION MEMBERSHIP AND POLITICAL ALIGNMENT

Only about half the teachers in England and Wales belong to the NUT—about 220,000. Of the rest, the National Association of Schoolmasters/Union of Women Teachers claims 120,000 and the Assistant Masters and Mistresses Association 80,000.[9] Both organize mainly in secondary schools. The Professional Association of Teachers (23,000) and the head teacher associations claim the rest.

Only the NUT and NAS/UWT are affiliated to the TUC. PAT never strikes; AMMA hardly ever. The NAS/UWT built its reputation as a militant union of male teachers—'the men's movement' it called itself.[10] It gained many members in the 1960s, as a result of its salary campaigns. It maintains a militant rhetoric on questions of pay and conditions, and has a highly competitive attitude towards recruitment. It is much more distant than the NUT from the reforming tradition in education. It is less concerned with the establishment of alliances with extra-educational bodies, and less likely to co-operate at local level with non-educational unions. It is inclined, in its educational pronouncements, to authoritarianism, as befits a union which for many years championed the cause of 'men teachers for boys'.

Although it established itself as a union in the course of campaigns against equal pay (which would, it said, reduce the male teacher's salary, and prevent him earning a 'family wage') it has in recent years been forced to moderate this stand, first by the Sex Discrimination Act, and recently by the need to maintain membership levels—a concern which is leading to attempts at recruitment in primary schools.

It will be plain from this account that union membership and political orientation to some extent overlap. It would be improbable that a Labour voter would join PAT, and unlikely that any organized socialist tendency of teachers would arise outside the NUT. No union, though, can claim that its membership is firmly aligned on the left. An opinion poll[11] taken before the 1983 general election indicated that 44 per cent of teachers, the majority in primary schools, would vote Conservative. The rest were fairly evenly divided between SDP/Liberal and Labour Party. These differences are probably not reproduced in exactly the same form in the NUT, where Conservatives are less assured of support. Nonetheless, the general picture of political heterogeneity does also hold true for the union.

But differences in overall political allegiance are not directly translated into particular alignments in NUT debate. They are, instead, refracted through conceptions that the nature of the union requires a special form of politics. Executive members who have long been in the Labour Party will argue against activity that might be considered as over-sympathetic to Labour. Thus, also, campaigns—such as that to defend existing abortion rights—which achieve reflex (if not always vigorous) support in the trade union movement as a whole are shunned by NUT leaders. The basis of this dissociation between private belief and public action is discussed later. One of its results has been that it falls to those groups—particularly the Socialist Teachers' Alliance—which were originally connected with organizations to the left of the Labour Party, to defend positions which in other, non-teaching, unions would be common ground.

It is important that, of this catalogue of divisions, none is seen as politically immutable. The teaching force has always been divided—particularly along lines of sexual discrimination and status. The degree of sharpness of the political splits that arise from such differences has depended upon the effectiveness of the strategy advanced by the major organizations: the rise in NAS membership in the 1960s after a salaries debacle attributed to the NUT is one case in point.[12] The secession of the now defunct NUWT from the NUT on the issue of equal pay is another.[13]

Having considered some of the main features of the NUT's ideology, of the policy changes it has to face, and of its constituency, it is now possible to look more closely at the effectiveness of its strategy, as a means of maintaining the strength and influence of the union in the context of a sharp and sometimes frantic fight to defend educational provision.

The NUT has always presented itself as the transcender of differences; with justice, it points to its non-sectional nature. Unlike AMMA it has no history of representing the interests of grammar school teachers in an exclusive way; unlike the NAS/UWT it has no record of explicit support for the almost literally patriarchal demands of male teachers. Its aim has been to unify a profession. The two terms of this brief phrase have to be read together. The unity that it seeks is of a specifically professional kind. The union has for many years supported the setting up of a General Teaching Council, which would have the power to control both entry to the profession, and discipline within it. If such a body were to be established, it would increase the consultative weight of teachers and raise their status.

It is doubtful whether this aspiration is realistic. If teaching is a profession, it is largely a self-recognized one. Neither in pay nor security, institutional authority nor curricular influence do teachers share the position of doctors or lawyers. The trend is rather the other way. Yet although the hope of professional self-government is ill-founded, it has real effects. The NUT, having set out its aspirations for the future, cannot in the present behave in a manner which departs too sharply from them. Professionalism, while not incompatible with episodes of 'industrial action', certainly inhibits the systematic development of a trade union orientation.

A too-consistent pattern of militancy, political alignment and educational controversy seems from the perspective of professional unity to jeopardize the union's highest ambitions, since the conferral of self-government upon an unruly teaching force would be impossible.

In this way professionalist traditions lock into and reinforce the union's reliance upon the achieving of educational progress, not through combativity or political partisanship, but through alliance with the broadest possible forces on a narrow front of issues.

The phrase 'unity of the profession' can be glossed in another way too: that it is only as a profession that unity can be achieved. This is the rational basis of professionalism at the present time. For even when the hope of a self-governing profession is shown to be false, it can still be argued that among such a heterogeneous teaching body, political alignment is ruinously divisive, and that it is only a teaching force which demonstrates a deep concern, quite beyond politics, for the fate of education, which can secure public support and its own cohesion. This argument overlooks the deepening ideological divisions among teachers. Nevertheless it is employed within the NUT to justify the union's abstention on an important range of issues. It is the basis of a double, self-denying exclusion. It discountenances, first of all, the formation of a school-based politics of the curriculum. It is not for NUT members to develop collective policies on what should be taught in their school; that is the responsibility of the heads, in consultation with their staffs. This is a responsibility which can be devolved to individual teachers, but which cannot be mediated via the school union group. This conception rests in turn upon a belief that the nurture of children is a task which is politically and ideologically unproblematic and must therefore be kept free from political controversy and 'interference'.

Yet state educational policy, though doing lip-service to education's non-political status, has in reality taken a series of political initiatives that have shifted the ground of educational common sense rightwards, and are changing the ideological character of an important part of the school curriculum—14–19. The union's belief in the neutrality of the educational process does not assist it in coping with these developments.

The second forbidden zone is that of extra-educational politics. The union's constitution codifies the relationship it should have with political parties and the trade union movement: a distant one, that is made still more remote by the way that the present executive interprets the union's 'aims and objects'. For an issue to be supported, it must have an explicit educational content; for an organization to be worked with it must have educational objectives.

The problem with this approach is that it is not at all symmetrical with government policy. For the government, education occupies just a few degrees of a wider arc of vision. Thus measures to privatize aspects of education (meals, cleaning, some YTS courses) are not unique to the sector, but part of a broader policy. Likewise, the fall in education spending is not independent of the rise in spending on defence. When the union decides that only a single aspect, selected from the general movement, is relevant to its concerns, then it renders impossible co-operation with other unions across the broad front. Here arises the union's dilemma. The nature of the problems that it faces impel it towards consideration of issues that arise outside the educational sector. But traditional politics and the pressing fears that a politicized union, in attempting to alter a century-old configuration of teacher attitudes, will lose members and influence, pull it back towards conservatism. In the arguments of the majority of the union's executive this difficulty is the reason for a high rate of abstention on 'political' issues, exemplified in the union's votes at the TUC, and in its attitudes to central issues of trade union politics.

But while professionalist ideas are still powerful in the NUT, they are increasingly modified by the pressing necessities of trade union action.

It is not as if the changes described at the beginning of the article have occurred outside the teachers' organizations, and are only now provoking a debate on the strategies needed to deal with them. In an uneven, spasmodic and overlapping way, changes in teachers' status, educational spending and curricular policy have been in motion since the mid seventies. Combined with changes in the composition of the teaching force, they have already had an effect on the relationship of teachers' organizations to each other, and on their internal life.

As early as the end of the sixties, in the late afternoon of consensus, long, premonitory shadows were being cast. The pay strikes of 1969/70 brought about the growth of 'trade union' methods of struggle and organization, and, in reaction, the development of 'non-political' and non-militant organization. This was the period when the NAS and NUT affiliated to the TUC, as well as that of the founding of the PAT.

Throughout the seventies these shadows took on more substance. Legislation of the Labour Government of 1974–79 strengthened the process of trade unionization by encouraging the development of training courses for local union officers. At school level, the function of the NUT 'correspondent' was evolving into that of 'representative'. At the same time, the generation of activists who had come into the union at the end of World War II reached retiring age. These men were gradually replaced, in the local union structures, by members of the generation which arrived in teaching in annual batches of 40,000 in the early seventies. The processes of trade unionization and generational change were speeded up as the union came into collision with the cuts. A more hectic pace of activity and the demands of a higher level of mobilization have led in many areas to a recomposition in union leadership.

Developments in union organization have been accompanied by a drift of union policy to the left. This movement centres on local action against cuts. In addition, where the TUC is united behind an action, the union, seeing in unanimity a legitimization of action, has sometimes offered support: on the TUC 'Day of Action' against government policy in 1980, and, in support of the health workers, in 1982. These are the modest frontiers of expansion into areas which, because they encompass broader-than-educational objectives, are new territory for the union. They find their cautious parallels in union policy in the endorsement by union conference of the need for 'an alternative economic policy' to that of the government. (The indefinite article establishes a distance between the union's policy and that of the TUC and Labour Party.)

Neither educational action, nor that of the wider sort, should be seen simply as developments of *policy*. The process of organizing action alters (even temporarily) the composition, structures and outlook of the union's local associations. Always, there are a few members who resign; others become involved in the union for the first time; in circles which extend beyond the usual activists, NUT policies are debated and questioned. In this process, the previous certainties of union life are put in doubt—without, necessarily, approval being given to a coherent new strategy.

These were all features of the highest recent point of teacher union militancy—the NUT's seven-week strike in the London Borough of Barking and Dagenham in 1982. The strike is worth examining for what it reveals of the potential of teacher militancy, of the relationship between the NUT and non-teaching unions, and of the way that parents responded to teacher trade unionism. Implied in the strike were fragments of a strategy that, developed in a coherent way, could with some optimism address the present educational crisis.

The Labour council of Barking and Dagenham announced in September 1981 that it intended to cut 160 teaching jobs—about 10 per cent of the total number—starting the following April. About 30 of these jobs would be lost through compulsory redundancy. This package provoked a strike—the union's longest since the 1920s—which was in many ways squarely in the NUT tradition: ultimate control, and conduct of negotiations, rested at Hamilton House; strikers were fully sustained by the union; the issue which triggered it related to the defence of existing levels of jobs and provision. But the way it was organized has a significance of its own, in what it showed of the way that, in order to oppose severe attacks on their jobs and on education, teachers adopt new tactics and new relationships with parents and with other trade unions.

Apart from the more rapid tempo of union life—mass meetings at least weekly, strike committees every other day—the action was remarkable for its combination of union militancy with popular support: the two were not at all incompatible. A measure of the extent of 'trade unionization' in the NUT was the readiness of teachers to carry out the controversial public activity of picketing. Official picket lines appeared outside primary and secondary schools—intended, though, to turn away supplies rather than teachers in other unions. Unionized oil-tanker drivers refused to cross the pickets; the council therefore employed scab drivers. Teachers lay down in front of their lorries, tracked them to their depots and spread word of the council's tactics in the local Labour movement. Next, a council driver was suspended for respecting the picket lines. The resulting strike of the council's drivers was almost fully sustained by donations from NUT members.

Just as important, the local union was able, first to mobilize and then to work alongside newly-created organizations of parents. Widespread leafleting and the assiduous collection of names at lobbies led to a volatile inaugural meeting of a 'Parents' Action Committee' which in turn set up groups in about half the schools. These parents organized meetings in the schools, occupations of the town hall, and demonstrations in Barking and in Central London. Although many parents did not support the strike, efforts to organize a 'go back to work' campaign failed, since the 'Parents' Action Committees' clearly had the initiative.

The union was able to build such support because it linked the issue of jobs to that of educational provision. A fight against redundancies alone would have had nothing like the same impact. In the context of cuts of this size, in an area which was predominantly working class, the slogan of equal opportunity became the basis of a militant, if limited, campaign and inspired an attitude among parents which was strong enough to sustain the burden of making arrangements for child-care during a long strike.

In the policy of the union nationally, however, the relationship between militancy and parental support is not explored. Propaganda aimed at parents is written for those who are thought to inhabit the middle ground of politics—'young executives in tree-lined suburbs' as one union leader put it—who must be won away from Thatcherism to a belief that 'investment in education is the basis for national prosperity'. Unsurprisingly, the committees, demonstrations and occupations of the Barking strike are not a reference point. Nor is its insistence on equal opportunity as a working-class right. Instead, the union executive appeals to another tradition, that descends from Disraeli to Edward Heath, and that sees educational expansion as entirely compatible with conservative social philosophies. An early parliamentary justification for universal schooling is quoted with approval:

> Upon the speedy provision of elementary education depends our industrial prosperity .... Upon this speedy provision depends also ... the good safe working of our constitutional system.[14]

So the occasional necessities of strike action are bound within an overall framework that endorses the most conventional values of education policy.

The strike was fairly successful—nearly two-thirds of the threatened jobs were retained, and there were no redundancies. But, like every action, it had its cost and aftermath. 'TEACHERS TRIUMPHANT' wrote the local paper, hyperbolically, and as if the strike was a sporting contest in which the winners would be secure in their victory for all time. In reality, the strike represented an enormous collective investment of energy, of a kind which could not easily be repeated.

The action over, members returned to their schools: some frustrated that the action had not achieved all it seemed to promise, others to schools where censorious heads and non-strikers (the other teaching unions at no point joined in) exerted the pressures of conformity. Nevertheless, the strike not only brought lasting benefits, in terms of the number of jobs protected, but also demonstrated the way in which militant trade union action can develop in ways which alter the usual relationship of the NUT to other sections of society.

It is not only the union's response to 'economic' questions which has changed. The women's movement has also had an effect on union policy. In danger of being outflanked from the left, and responsive to changes in the ideological climate, the executive has taken up issues related to 'equal opportunities', and in 1976 produced a memorandum on the issue. This document concentrated on aspects of sexism in the curriculum, women's conditions of service, and questions of promotion. Since then, there has been a gradual movement towards consideration of the role of women in the union.

The 1984 Conference of the union voted to set up national union structures which would have the effect of encouraging the organization of women: an 'equal opportunities' department; an advisory committee on 'equal opportunities'; the possibility of an annual conference on 'equal opportunities'. Small steps, but important in that they establish a framework for future activity. A lot has still to be done. At the moment, the union has six national officers, all men; six senior officials, one of them a woman; twelve regional officials, all men. Local associations are, in the main, led by men. The union is beginning to become aware that these proportions comprise a problem, but its most usual way of explaining the difficulty is to refer to the (learned) passivity and non-assertiveness of women: the problem lies in the consciousness of women, rather than the activity of men. This diagnosis, itself symptomatic, explains the untroubled persistence of a range of behaviour, from the generic use of the masculine pronoun to the platforms weighted down with male speakers and the prioritization of the major areas of the union's activity. It is a factor which helps explain the union's relative neglect of primary as against secondary education, as well as the absence from its main campaigns of discussion of the way in which the issues involved—from salaries to nursery education—particularly affect women.

It is important to see changes in the NUT as only one side of the response of teacher organizations to the changes in educational politics. If the activity of 1969/70 prefigured some welcome changes in NUT policy, it also foreshadowed some less heartening developments. It was in the aftermath of the pay strikes of those years that the PAT was founded—an organization whose policies are less important than its embodiment of a single principle: that teachers, being professionals, should not take any form of industrial action, let alone strike. Thus the PAT abstracted, from the strategy of professional unity and educational reform developed by the NUT, just one element, and then exaggerated it.

Though the present Conservative government has been eager to recognize PAT, its influence is not great. But its existence as, in effect, the newest teachers' union provokes important questions: why is it that the unification of the education system which has occurred with the ending of the 11+, and the many problems that teachers have faced over the last decade have not created either a general unification of teachers' organizations, or else established more firmly the hegemony of the NUT, as the union most willing to take defensive action? Why is it, rather, that the trends of consciousness most acutely dramatized in the founding of the PAT actually seem to have increased their strength in the teaching force, so that it is necessary to speak not simply of a 'drift to the left', but of a more complex process of polarization?

To ask these questions is to draw attention to a number of developments: the fact that AMMA, far from collapsing with the decline of the grammar schools, seems to have established a stable position; that the NAS/UWT, which has done far less than the NUT to oppose cuts in education, claims not to have lost members during the recent fall in teacher numbers; and that the NUT is struggling to prevent, not just a decline in its numbers, but also a fall in its share of the teaching force.

These 'membership' issues are an index of the attitudes of teachers to the problems of recession and sharp educational change. Whereas, undoubtedly, the number of those willing to campaign against education cuts has grown, so has a reluctance, on the part of others, to involve themselves in activity of a sort which is strenuous, controversial and contrary to the policy of the government they may well have voted for. The attitudes of parents, heads and colleagues combine with the belief that the 'children come first' to produce quiescence. In addition, the overall political crisis of the Labour Party and trade union movement provides no attractive or plausible alternative to the difficulties of the present, and makes it less likely that teachers will see anything purposeful in union activity. It is not that, in this situation, the NUT's competitors have any effective strategy to put forward—but their continued numerical strength is the indicator of a considerable political problem.

Are, then, the kinds of radical policy implied in the previous sections really a feasible basis on which to maintain the NUT's strength? Will they not simply sharpen the divisions within teaching and ensure the collapse of the union's remaining positions? Against these self-made and anticipatory accusations of ultra-leftism, the first point to make is that, while the union's traditional strategy is capable of some defensive victories, it is, overall, demonstrably losing ground. It is the failure of the old approach—rather than the wholesale adoption of something new—which gives rise to the union's crisis of strategy, and the membership problems associated with it. (Though the fact that the conflict between the two approaches is unresolved and ubiquitous adds to the union's problems, a dimension which is absent from the policy development of other, less ambitious, teacher organizations.)

To offer a detailed 'solution' to the complex of political and ideological problems that face the union would be both grandiose and implausible. Nor do I want to suggest that there is only one possible solution to the union's crisis, and that the adoption of a left-wing programme will simultaneously raise the level of militancy, win over wavering members and establish widespread popular support. On the contrary: even if the dangers outlined earlier in this article were all to be realized, the union would still have a role, albeit diminished, in educational politics, as well as a large membership.

So rather than asserting in inevitablist fashion that *either* the union must move to the left *or* collapse, I would argue from the perspective that teachers have the potential to play a useful part—trade union and, more important, educational—in the development of a popular left-wing current in Britain. At the same time, for the union to adopt such a position would allow it to make a more effective critique of state educational policy, to construct alliances to replace those that, developed in an earlier period, are now ineffectual, and to produce a less sectoralist answer to the conservative populism which has influenced parental opinion. This, in turn, would strengthen its position among teaching unions.

A precondition of a successful change in overall strategy is a militant 'trade union' response to issues of jobs, conditions and pay. But this hardly represents in itself an adequate alternative to the rightward drift of educational policy. That alternative would have to incorporate, not just defensive responses, but a fully-rounded educational politics.

The first area where, from this perspective, change is needed is that relating to policy on the *content* of education. Much of the effectiveness of populist assertions that 'education isn't working' has stemmed from two propositions: first, that education has become irrelevant to the 'world of work'; second, that the standards of the state school—largely as a result of the shortcomings of teachers—are too low.

No progress is possible unless these propositions are questioned.

Vocationalism presents the functioning of the economy as something quite beyond social determination, and consequently offers no understanding of the world of work for which it claims to prepare students. It is an approach that has been challenged surprisingly little. Yet it is possible to discover, even in the unspectacular history of British 'civic' education, alternatives to it, which present economic decisions as subject to popular control. This, for instance, is from the teachers' manual of the largest pre-MSC effort at mass education on economic questions, the Army Education Council's wartime *British Way and Purpose*:

> Few people are likely to confuse masses without work, half-derelict mining communities, the slums of Glasgow, the under-sized bodies of under-nourished children, or the shocking scars on the loveliness of the English countryside with any heavenly thing.... The war has been among other things an excellent teacher of economics. It has shown conclusively that unemployment is not inevitable.... Given a clear expression of the democratic will of the people ... there is no reason why we should not make the fullest use of all our resources to create a much finer civilization than anything we have ever known.[15]

Such eloquent arguments can be utilized against the politically-willed depoliticization that is embodied in the educational content of the YTS. At present, the union has little to say about the content of the Youth Training Schemes, or their school-based derivatives. It concentrates on questions of administration, selection, resources. In questioning the educational content of the schemes, the union would be beginning the work of formulating different objectives for state education, and of influencing public debate on those objectives.

Likewise on the issue of standards. The present Secretary of State has been able to win a strategic advantage by seizing as his own the issue of 'intellectual standards'. This is the high ground of educational debate, which any opposition aspiring to popular success must take.

In reality, the claim to intellectual seriousness is not soundly based. It is not just that the segregation implicit in vocationalism excludes the majority of students from the high levels of education to which Sir Keith Joseph, the Secretary of State for Education, claims to aspire. It is also that the curriculum he defends in the name of high intellectual standards is archaic and seriously incomplete. It should be quite possible for the NUT to come forward as an advocate of a curriculum which aims to deliver a knowledge of the world well in advance of what the Secretary of State can offer: instead of vocationalism, a general and critical education around the world of work, including its planning and decision-making aspects; a greater commitment to the study of science in a social context; the incorporation of ecological, north-south and feminist themes into many areas of the curriculum; the development of media and communications studies. Because such a synthesis could justifiably claim to create a much higher level of understanding among a larger number of students than present policy will allow, it would have the advantage of combining intellectual force with its radical momentum, and could achieve a real popular resonance.

There are two further areas in which change is required. That aspect of professionalism which is suspicious of parental and student demand lessens the chances of winning broad support for change. It is through encountering and debating criticism from the 'consumers' of education that the union will be best able to take an authoritative position in a movement for reform.

Secondly, an alliance on educational issues should be complemented by an alliance with the Labour movement on broader questions of social and economic policy than the NUT at present allows. It is difficult to see how otherwise a strong section of teacher opinion can be won to support of a movement of the left. Continued abstention on major issues insulates the NUT, not only from controversy, but also from exploration of alternative economic and social policies to those of the government, and thus impoverishes all aspects of its work, educational as well as trade union.

It is possible, then, for the union to establish itself as a force capable of leading a response to those new issues of educational debate which are at present a virtual monopoly of the right. Winning hegemony on issues of curriculum content, vocational education, and the relationship between education and economic and social policy would allow a membership campaign based on the union's ability to present a popularly-accepted case for educational change: the union would be offering its members more than a grimly attritional defence of equal opportunity and diminishing provision. (Though this defence would remain essential.) It would not end the division of teacher opinion—but it would greatly strengthen its progressive wing. At the same time, a greater alertness to feminist issues, and a manifest willingness to ensure that the local and national leaderships of the union—as well as its base—are predominantly female, would do a lot to increase the involvement of primary and women members, as well as opening up new areas of educational policy.

The support for campaigns on cuts and pay shows that there are considerable reserves of militancy within the union. The difficult thing is to extend these attitudes into areas which the union has not previously entered. The development of educational battles in Britain depends to a considerable extent on whether this enterprise is accomplished.

NOTES

1. *Our Children, Our Future*, NUT pamphlet, London, 1983.
2. Memorandum on Salaries, presented by the NUT Executive to the 1984 Conference.
3. Statistics presented by the DES to the Pay Data Working Party of the Burnham Committee, 1983. The NUT considers this figure to be an underestimate.
4. *Times Educational Supplement*, 6 January 1984.
5. See Green, A., Education and training: under new masters, in Donald and Wolpe (eds.), *Is There Anyone Here From Education?'*, London, 1983.
6. Management Panel of the Burnham Committee—Submission to Arbitral Body on Teachers' Pay, 1982.
7. Ibid.
8. NUT Survey of Fixed Term Contracts, 1983.
9. *Times Educational Supplement*, 24 September 1982.
10. *Action 1919-69: a record of the growth of the NAS*, NAS pamphlet, 1969.
11. *Times Educational Supplement*, 27 May 1983.
12. Kogan, M., in *Educational Policy-making: a study of interest groups and Parliament*, London, 1975, gives the following figures for NAS membership increase: 1960—22,651; 1973—60,230.
13. Pierotti, A.N., *The Story of the National Union of Women Teachers*, Kew, 1963.
14. Quoted in the NUT Executive Memorandum to the 1983 Conference: *Education for National Survival*.
15. *The British Way and Purpose*, Directorate of Army Education, 1944.

14

Teacher Numbers
the framework of government policy

KIERON WALSH, ROLAND DUNNE, BRYAN STOTEN
and JOHN D. STEWART

THE LOCUS OF RESPONSIBILITY

The management of the teaching force in a period of declining rolls is first and foremost an issue for the local education authority in determining the extent to which the teaching force should be reduced as rolls fall and the manner in which that reduction is carried out.

The local education authority makes its decision on this issue as on other issues within a national framework. That national framework consists of four main elements:

the nationally negotiated framework of salaries and conditions of service;
the statutory framework of power and duties;
the financial framework set by central government;
the policies of central government expressed in advice and guidance.

This article is concerned with central government's policies for the size of the teaching force. These policies do not have any binding force upon local authorities which are free to make their own decisions on the size of the teaching force, although they may be influenced by the views of central government.

Those views are, however, not directly expressed to local authorities. There are no current circulars or letters in which the Department sets out its policy on the size of the teaching force or directly on the reduction required as a result of declining rolls. General guidance about teacher numbers and

---

Reproduced by permission of the publishers NFER-Nelson Publishing Co. Ltd., Danville House, 2 Oxford Road East, Windsor, SL4 1DF, from *Falling School Rolls and the Management of the Teaching Profession*, © 1984 Walsh, Dunne, Stoten, Stewart.

staffing standards has been included in the past in the Joint Circulars on local authority expenditure, which normally used to be issued in connection with the Rate Support Grant settlement. DES Circular 14/76 relating to the Rate Support Grant settlement for 1977/78, the last circular containing such guidance, was before the main decline in pupil numbers. It is not that the Department regards the subject of declining rolls as outside its concern. It has given guidance on the elimination of surplus accommodation, reflecting its greater involvement in issues relating to the building stock.

The Department regards surplus places as a heavy drain on resources. It is also concerned that schools whose rolls fall below a reasonable minimum, which can vary with type and age range, are likely to be educationally inefficient. There are, of course, resource and educational issues involved in the question of the size of the teaching force. An outside observer might reflect that the apparent greater direct involvement with the issue of surplus places than with teacher numbers is a result of past involvement in the loan sanction procedures and continuing block approvals for capital expenditure.

The Department has, of course, highlighted the general issue of declining rolls in such documents as *Reports on Education*. But the only clear public expression of its policy on the reduction of the teaching force is through the Government's financial plans for public expenditure generally and for local government expenditure in particular and in ministerial statements about educational expenditure related to those plans (e.g. the Secretary of State's statement to Parliament on 8 November 1982).

PUBLIC EXPENDITURE PLANNING

The Government each year issues a White Paper on its Expenditure Plans for the coming year and for two or three further years beyond. This White Paper is the culmination of the Government's process of planning public expenditure. It expresses the Government's views on the level of public expenditure and on its priorities between different programmes and between activities in those programmes.

In that process of planning public expenditure, local government expenditure is treated as an integral part of public expenditure and in the White Paper local government expenditure is not distinguished from central government expenditure in the breakdown of each main programme.

The presentation in the White Paper on the programme covering Education and Science, Arts and Libraries (cf Table 2.10 in the Government's Expenditure Plans 1982–83 to 1984–85, Cmnd 8494) includes, therefore, expenditure on schools, divided between capital and current expenditure and between under-fives, primary, secondary, special and other. Those expenditure figures which in the latest White Paper were expressed in cash terms, take account of pupil projections and are based on government policy on the number of teachers. A table is included in the White Paper setting out the pupil projections including the allowance made for under-fives and for pupils over the school-leaving age and setting out planned teacher numbers and the implications for overall pupil-teacher ratios.

The expenditure planning process underlying this table is carried out by the Department but also draws upon the work of the Expenditure Steering Group for Education Services (ESGE) set up under the Consultative Council on Local Government Finance. The Group consists of senior civil servants from the Department of Education and Science, officials of the local authority associations and education officers and treasurers also representing the associations. ESGE reviews the plans for educational expenditure in the period preceding the Government's decisions on its plans both for educational expenditure and for local government expenditure. It reviews those plans in accordance with the remit given by the Consultative Council on Local Government Finance, normally as proposed by the Government. Thus, in 1982, ESGE along with the other expenditure groups was asked to consider:

(a) the likely outturn of expenditure for 1981–82;
(b) the likely outturn of expenditure for 1982–83;
(c) the prospects for the level and pattern of expenditure in 1983–84 and the later years;
(d) the measures which would be required to contain expenditure within the cash plans for each of the years as set out in Cmnd 8494 (i.e. the previous year's White Paper on the Government's Expenditure Plans);
(e) the implications of the plans for services.

This remit represented the Government's proposals, which were challenged by the Associations at the Consultative Council, but which the Government defended as merely the first stage in the process of discussion.

ESGE work feeds into decisions on the Government's expenditure plans for education, which are then expressed in the next White Paper on the Government's Expenditure Plans. Those decisions also provide the basis for the Rate Support Grant settlements.

The Rate Support Grant Report specifies the level of relevant expenditure accepted by the Government for grant purposes. It sets out the breakdown of that expenditure into main programme areas, including Education and School Meals and Milk as separate categories. The report also specifies the percentage of that expenditure on which the Government will pay grant, the way the block grant mechanisms will be applied and the way grant will be distributed between local authorities.

Broadly then the Government decides the number of teachers that local authorities could afford to employ within its cash plans based on the work of ESGE, work carried out in the Department and any representations it receives. That decision is published in the White Paper on the Expenditure

Plans and is a component of the level of expenditure accepted for Rate Support Grant in the Rate Support Grant settlement for the coming year.

THE IMPACT ON LOCAL AUTHORITIES

These decisions by central government on the number of teachers it considers should be employed by local government have no necessary connection with the actual decisions made by local authorities. The only connection between the two levels of decision is through the financial arrangements. The decision by central government influences the total amount of Rate Support Grant available for local authorities, but is only one component of that amount. The grant depends first on the Government's decision on the aggregate level of expenditure it will accept for grant purposes, in which expenditure on education is but one component—although a major one—and the amount for teachers' salaries is a major part of that component. The total grant, however, also depends upon the decision made by the Government on the percentage of local government expenditure on which grant will be paid. The actual grant received by a local authority depends, of course, on the grant distribution arrangements. Each authority has a figure set for its grant-related expenditure, i.e. its share of the total expenditure planned by central government. The grant received by the local authority depends on its grant-related expenditure assessment, which represents the Government's assessment of its needs for expenditure, and upon its resources as measured by its rateable value.

The grant-related expenditure assessment is built up by a number of factors deemed to represent the need for expenditure. The factors related to education do not include any direct measures of the number of teachers required. They include factors such as the number of school pupils of primary school age, of secondary school pupils aged under 16 and of school pupils aged 16 and over. The need for expenditure represented by these factors can reflect the Government's views on the number of teachers. The relationship is however not clear and direct and in any event other factors in the grant-related expenditure assessments also reflect expenditure on teachers, e.g. factors covering sparsity of school population and social and environmental problems.

A local authority could not deduce from its amount of grant or from the figure for grant-related expenditure the amount of expenditure that was implied for teachers' salaries nor indeed the number of teachers. The Rate Support Grant is a non-hypothecated grant which is added to the amount which the local authority raises from other sources of income and together these may represent more or less than the figure for grant-related expenditure. The local authority is free to spend grant and other sources of income as it sees fit to meet its statutory obligations. Even if the amount of expenditure allocated for teachers in GREA were clear the local authority would be under no obligation to spend that amount. It could spend more or less and employ more or less at its own discretion.

Government policy on teacher numbers is part of the general background to the Government's policies on local government finance. It is a factor in determining the Government's policy on the level of local government expenditure to be aimed at. It underlies therefore the Government's assessment of whether local government is over-spending. It is a factor in determining the level of grant. But that policy still has no necessary or direct effect on the decision made by LEAs on teacher numbers.

It remains important to understand the Government's policy but not as a direct control, rather as an influence both on the educational policy and on the financial policy of local authorities in managing the teaching force in a period of declining rolls.

THE 1982 WHITE PAPER POLICY

The policy set out in the Government's Expenditure Plans 1982/83–1983/84, Cmnd 8494, is set out in Table 1.

Table 1 *Government plans for teacher numbers: 1982 White Paper*

	Total school population '000s	Teacher numbers (full-time equivalents) '000s	Pupil-teacher ratio
1980/81	8184	429	18.6
1981/82	7973	418	18.6
1982/83	7725	405	18.6
1983/84	7504	390	18.7
1984/85	7330	380	18.7

N.B. The last column cannot be derived directly from the first two columns because under-fives are included in the first column as the actual numbers and not as full-time equivalents, which are used in the calculation of the pupil-teacher ratios.

The White Paper states that:

> The plans envisage that in the period up to 1984–85 the number of teachers will be reduced from the higher number in 1981/82 broadly in line with the reduction in the projected total numbers of pupils, but with some tightening of staffing standards especially as the balance of pupil population continues to shift to older age groups. The Government look to local authorities in cooperation with their teachers so to manage the contraction of the teacher force as to minimize its impact on curricular opportunities (p. 40).

As the phrase 'some tightening of staffing standards' makes clear, the Government was seeking an increase in pupil–teacher ratios. This was reflected in the figures for pupil–teacher ratios, but over and above the visible increase in these figures, there was an implied increase. In the mid-1980s the proportion of secondary school children (especially of those over the school-leaving age) will increase.

Table 2 Pupil numbers assumed in 1982 White Paper: 1980/81 and 1984/85

	1980/81 '000s		1984/85 '000s	
Under-fives	428	5.3%	398	5.5%
Other primary	3797	47.1%	3286	45.5%
Secondary under school leaving age	3530	43.7%	3209	44.5%
Secondary over school leaving age	310	3.8%	325	4.5%
	8065		7218	

From Table 2.10.1, Cmnd 8494.

Such a change would mean a marginal reduction in overall PTR, if constant PTRs were maintained for primary, secondary and post-16 pupils.

The White Paper made no provision for what has been described as the operating margin. This has two separate components. The first component allows for structural diseconomies as a result of the changing composition of the schools, allowing for the need for smaller schools to have lower PTRs than larger schools.

The second component allows for the diseconomies of change, due to the short-term difficulties of adjusting teacher numbers in line with pupil numbers.

Maintenance of staffing standards would have required a reduction in overall PTRs both because of provision of an operating margin and the changing age composition of the school population. In fact the plans marginally increased the PTR.

THE 1983 WHITE PAPER

The policy set out in the Government's Expenditure Plans 1983/4 to 1985/6 (Cmnd 8789) is set out in Table 3.

The White Paper involves a change in the degree of precision with which the planned level of future teacher numbers is specified. Maximum numbers or ranges are substituted for the specific numbers given in previous White Papers.

The White Paper does not state the underlying policy as to staffing standards beyond saying in para. 2.10.7 that they represent some improvement in pupil–teacher ratios compared with the January 1982 level. In fact the PTR for 1983/4 at 18.2 represents a significant change from the PTR at 18.7 set out for that year in the previous White Paper (Cmnd 8494). It would appear that broadly policy has now become the maintenance of staffing,

Teacher Numbers

Table 3 Government plans for teacher numbers: 1983 White Paper

	Total school population '000s	Teacher numbers (full-time equivalents) '000s	Pupil-teacher ratio
1981–2	7854	420	18.5
1982–3	7606	411	18.3
1983–4	7391	up to 400	18.2
1984–5	7223	390–395	18.0–18.3
1985–6	7099	380–385	18.2–18.4

which after allowing for changing age composition and the operating margin does imply a slight decrease in the pupil–teacher ratios.

CHANGES IN POLICY

Cmnd 8494 represented a change of policy for 1982/3 and beyond. The number of teachers for 1982/3 was larger than in the previous White Paper (Cmnd 8175). This was due to two factors. The first was changes in pupil projections due to the 'numbers of 16-year-olds staying on in full-time education' (p. 40). The other factor was that the reduction in teacher numbers in 1981/82 by local authorities was not expected to be as great as planned by the Government. 'The Government have also had regard to the estimated 7000 extra teachers in post in 1981/82 compared with the planned number' (p. 40). In effect the Government accepted as a *fait accompli* some of the additional teachers employed by local authorities. Cmnd 8789 again revised planned teacher numbers upwards partly in the light of actual employment, although it was argued, given cash planning, 'the number of teachers within these cash plans will depend crucially on the level of pay settlements for teachers' (pp. 46–47).

Table 4 shows the changes in the Government's policy over a longer time span.

The figures marked with an asterisk are actuals; they are immediately followed by estimated figures for the current year, in which the plan is being drawn up. The figures for the following years constitute the Government's planned numbers. The figures for 1979–80 and for 1980–81 include figures for Scotland and Wales. They illustrate however the change in policy from the Labour Government of 1974–79, to the succeeding Conservative Government.

Whereas the Labour Government were proposing that the decline in school rolls should be used, in part, to improve pupil–teacher ratios, the Conservative Government in accordance with their policy of reducing public expenditure proposed to use the decline in school rolls mainly to serve their

Table 4 Plans for teacher numbers as outlined in White Papers 1979/80 to 1983/84

	1979–1980 Cmnd 7439	1980–1981 Cmnd 7841	Teachers '000s 1981–1982 Cmnd 8175	1982–1983 Cmnd 8494	1983–1984 Cmnd 8789	1979–1980 Cmnd 7439	1980–1981 Cmnd 7841	PTRs 1981–1982 Cmnd 8175	1982–1983 Cmnd 8494	1983–1984 Cmnd 8789
1977–78	520					19.3*				
1978–79	521	527				19.0	18.8*			
1979–80	520	519				18.7	18.7	18.7*		
1980–81	517	505	438*			18.3	18.7	18.8	18.6*	
1981–82	512	491	424	429*		18.0	18.6	18.8	18.6	18.5*
1982–83	502	479	411	418	420*	17.8	18.4	18.8	18.6	18.3
1983–84		460	398	405	411		18.6	18.8	18.7	18.2
1984–85			386	390	up to 400					18.0–18.3
1985–86				380	390–395					18.2–18.4
					380–385					

Figures from Cmnd 7439 and Cmnd 7841 are for Great Britain. Figures from subsequent White Papers are for England only.

policy of reducing public expenditure, proposing in some White Papers a marginal reduction in PTRs and in some White Papers a marginal increase.

THE WORK OF ESGE

The reports of ESGE provide additional information on the Government's plans and the basis on which they were derived. Since we took as the starting point for our analysis the White Paper on the Government's Expenditure Plans, 1982–83 to 1984–85, we shall take the ESGE Report presented in July 1981 which provided the basis for the decisions recorded in that White Paper.

ESGE carried out their remit of considering the implications for the

Table 5 ESGE analysis of the implications of 1981/82 White Paper for Teacher Numbers

	\multicolumn{5}{c}{FTE '000s Academic Years Provisional Plans}
	1980–1981	1981–1982	1982–1983	1983–1984	1984–1985
(1) Teacher numbers provided for in Cmnd 8175	424 429 (actual)	411	398	386	378
(2) Teacher numbers required to maintain 1979–80 levels of provision per pupil	431	422	411	401	391
(3) Year on year rundown implied by Cmnd 8175 teacher numbers (i.e. (1) above)		−18	−13	−12	−8
(4) Estimated number of posts at (3) above which might be vacated by natural turnover and premature retirement at currently forecast level		−8.5	−7	−6.5	−5
(5) Estimated number of posts at (3) above which would need to be shed by increased premature retirement, redeployment and compulsory redundancies [(3)−(4)]		−9.5	−6	−5.5	−3
(6) LAA side's view of prospective teacher rundown on LEAs' present policies		415	402	391	383
(7) Year on year rundown implied by (6)		−14	−13	−11	−8

education service of 'containing expenditure within the Government's planned totals for each year included in the previous year's White Paper' (Cmnd 8175). The key analysis is set out in Table 5.

In examining the plans for 1982/3 and beyond, ESGE confronted the problem that actual teacher numbers in 1980/81 were 5000 more than had been assumed in the plans set out in Cmnd 8175. They had therefore to accept a significantly greater reduction if the Cmnd 8175 plans were to be achieved. ESGE calculated the scale of reduction from January 1981 to January 1984 now required as 43,000, representing the addition of the 5000 posts to the 38,000 reduction originally required. That represented a reduction of 10 per cent in the teaching force and at just over 14,000 per annum, a rate of reduction above that previously achieved.

The Group estimated that just over 20,000 of the 43,000 posts would on present policies be left vacant by local authorities as a result of natural wastage and premature retirement. The issue remained as to how the further reduction of over 20,000 posts might be achieved.

The Group considered that the maximum that could be achieved through increased premature retirement and increased redeployment was an additional 10,000 posts, leaving a reduction of over 10,000 posts to be achieved in other ways.

The Group examined the critical issue of how many of the posts in which vacancies occur actually lead to a loss of a post, either directly or by using redeployment. Although natural wastage was expected to be higher than the planned rate of reductions ESGE concluded that the required reduction could not be achieved without compulsory redundancy—except by leaving some essential vacant posts unfilled, at a severe cost to the quality of education in the schools involved.

ESGE calculated that the policies necessary would impose costs approaching £20 million per annum, the cost of additional premature retirement being estimated at about £3 million per annum and the cost of the compulsory redundancies at about £15 million per annum, if only the statutory minimum terms applied, although that level of compulsory redundancy was more likely to be implemented by authorities if more generous terms were available.

ESGE highlighted the problems of compulsory redundancies. There was a general tendency in LEAs to protect levels of teacher employment at the expense of non-teaching expenditure. In particular there had been practically no compulsory redundancies and many LEAs had committed themselves to no redundancy policies. The implementation of compulsory redundancy would present practical problems for LEAs, both in the time taken and in the criteria to be applied.

The Local Authority Associations' representatives recorded their view that the maximum reduction that could be achieved even if LEAs accepted reduced staffing standards and loss to the curriculum was below that required by Cmnd 8175. As Table 5 shows, the main difference between the Local

Authority Associations' views and the Government was in the period 1980-81 to 1981-82 when the Cmnd 8175 targets implied a reduction of 18,000 or 4000 more than the Local Authority Associations thought possible. As already noted the 1980-81 actual was 5000 higher than in Cmnd 8175 and to maintain the previous end of year target for 1981-82 required a further reduction of that 5000. In effect the Associations were arguing that 5000 additional teachers at the start of 1981-82 had to be accepted as a *fait accompli* and that the rate of reduction should be not increased.

In practice the Government decided in November 1981 that an additional £300 million should be allocated to aggregate educational expenditure in 1982-83. The Department of Education and Science used part of these additional resources to modify its targets for the teaching force. It now recognized that in 1981-82 the teaching force was likely to be 7000 more than planned in Cmnd 8175, and to maintain the Cmnd 8175 targets for 1982-83 now meant a reduction of 18,000 which was unrealistic. The Department also recognized that the number of pupils staying on after 16 had increased, creating a need for additional teachers. The changed targets were:

Table 6 Targets for reduction in teacher numbers: 1981/82 and 1982/83 White Papers

	Cmnd 8175 Teachers '000s	Cmnd 8175 Reduction required '000s	Cmnd 8494 Teachers '000s	Cmnd 8494 Reduction required '000s
1980-81	424 (429)		429	
1981-82	411	−18	418	−11
1982-83	398	−13	405	−13
1983-84	386	−12	390	−15
1984-85			380	−10

Note: 424 was the projected figure included in Cmnd 8175 for 1980/81; 429 was the outturn.

The Department had not altered its policy, only its phasing. Although requiring the same rate of reduction in 1982/83, it required a higher rate of reduction in 1983/84 than that in Cmnd 8175. As a result by 1984/85 its planned number of teachers at 380,000 was close to that outlined to ESGE before the change, but allowed for an extra 2000 because of additional pupils over the school leaving age.

There remained a problem. Reductions of 13,000 and 15,000 were significantly higher than had previously been achieved. Between 1979-80 and 1980-81 and between 1980-81 and 1981-82 the rate of reduction had in each case been 9000. The local authority representatives on ESGE argued that this rate of rundown could be achieved in future years and possibly slightly higher rates, but that the rate of rundown required by central government was too high.

The dilemma confronted by ESGE in its 1982 report, however, was not merely that the reductions considered achievable by local authorities were well below those envisaged in the Government's plans as set out in Cmnd 8494, but that the introduction of cash planning in government public expenditure planning meant that, following the 6 per cent pay award in April 1982 rather than the 4 per cent assumed in Cmnd 8494, a 29,000 reduction was now required in 1982–83 and not the 13,000 set out in Cmnd 8494.

The scale of the reduction required was 16,000 or almost 4 per cent more than in the original plan. The reason why a pay settlement 2 per cent more than allowed for in the cash plan led to a requirement for a 4 per cent greater reduction in manpower was that those reductions were assumed to start from the beginning of the academic year in September, which would itself be nearly halfway through the financial year. In the second year, the full salary effect comes through leading to a see-saw pattern illustrated in Table 9.

The Government's decisions as recorded in the next White Paper (Cmnd 8789), however, follow the previous pattern in giving recognition to the current position, both as to the actual number of teachers which was higher than planned and to existing cash levels. The decisions went further, however, in broadly accepting the views of ESGE. As we have seen Cmnd 8789 implies a lowering of the pupil–teacher ratio, in order to maintain standards and a significantly higher number of teachers than Cmnd 8494 or any of its immediate predecessors.

The various positions taken on the size of the teaching force are summarized in Table 7.

Table 7 Government and Local Authority views on teacher numbers

Teacher numbers '000s	Cmnd 8175	Cmnd 8494	Implications of Cmnd 8494 after 6% increase	ESGE 1981	Local Authority Associations' views ESGE 1982 A	ESGE 1982 B
1980–81	424†	429*	429*	429*	429*	429*
1981–82	411	418†	420*	415	420*	420*
1982–83	398	405	391	402	411	411
1983–84	386	390	388	391	402	400
1984–85		380	358	383	393	390
1985–86			389		384	380

* Actual. † Estimated.
N.B. The Local Authority Associations' representatives in 1982 put forward two possibilities. Alternative B implies greater financial pressure than A.

CONCLUSIONS BASED ON THE ANALYSIS

1. In practice the annual rundown in teacher numbers has so far never been more than 9000. Up to 1978–79 the number of teachers was still increasing. Since then teacher numbers have moved as shown in Table 8:

Table 8 Actual movements in teacher numbers: 1978/79 to 1982/83

	Teacher numbers	Annual reduction
1978–79	441,000	
1979–80	438,000	−3,000
1980–81	429,000	−9,000
1981–82	420,000	−9,000
1982–83	414,600	−5,400

These reductions have been achieved without any significant use of compulsory redundancy. The Government's plans have required and continue to require larger reductions. It is clear that those plans are unlikely to be implemented without new policies being introduced.

2. The introduction of cash planning resulted in an implied planned reduction in the number of teachers, of 29,000 in 1982–83, which was above any level accepted as possible by the Associations and above any level previously proposed by the Government.

A relatively small overspend in cash terms can have very significant effects on the plans for manpower reduction. In this instance a two per cent excess in the salary award led to an increase in the rundown required from the 13,000, which as we have seen was put forward by the Department in the interests of realism, to 29,000. Cash planning if strictly applied can lead to policies for manpower rundown far above the maximum levels previously accepted. Changes of this order in short periods of time can clearly not be achieved without radical change in present policy, the use of compulsory redundancy on a very significant scale, and resulting effects on the curriculum.

It will, however, be noted that the figures showing the effects of cash planning on the rundown show considerable fluctuations from year to year and that by 1985–86 planned total numbers have climbed back to over 380,000. This, however, shows the difficulty of combining cash planning with the systematic planning of manpower reduction. These problems may, however, lessen if lower rates of inflation are maintained, since that is likely to mean there are fewer differences between actual price levels and assumed price levels.

3. The overall process of drawing up plans for reductions in teacher numbers by local authorities which are only partially achieved in practice reduces the credibility of those plans. In practice the tendency has been to revise those plans to recognize 'realism'. That is what happened with the plans included in Cmnd 8175 which were revised upward in Cmnd 8494. Cmnd 8789 again revised plans upward.

The process of yearly revision upwards of the planned manpower levels may destroy the credibility of the procedure. Yet such revision is inevitable if the plans are not to destroy their own credibility. There is a gap between plans and practice that can only be bridged, either by revising plans or changing practice. It is normally easier to change the plan than to change practice.

4. The gap between plans and practice may seem large when measured as the gap between a planned change and the actual change. The gap seems relatively small when measured as the gap between the planned level and the actual level. Both perspectives are required. On the one hand it has to be recognized that the total level of the number of teachers has never been more than two per cent above that planned by the Department and has normally been changing in the direction required by the Government. Such a degree of conformity between plans and practice could be claimed as more than reasonable. It could equally be said to indicate that annual change takes place in small increments and it is hardly surprising that there should be such conformity. In this perspective it is the degree of difference between planned change and actual change that is significant and that difference can be well over 40 per cent.

5. The work carried out by ESGE depends upon a methodology designed to show the consequences of existing policy or of change in policy. That requires procedures for estimating the impact of possible changes.

Procedures have been developed:

(a) For estimating the extent of the rundown in teacher manpower on the basis of present policies. These procedures probably amount to little more than an interpretation of past experience.
(b) For estimating the level required to maintain existing standards, with which proposals can be compared. These procedures have to take account of the changing age composition of the school population. This is achieved by applying different weightings to pupil numbers in different age groups to arrive at loaded pupil numbers to which overall PTRs can be applied. These procedures also have to allow for 'the operating margin' both in respect of the diseconomies of scale and the effects of change. The former is allowed for by allocating a fixed number of teachers per school of each type, irrespective of size. The latter is allowed for as a margin for a one year lag effect.

The procedures are not fixed and can be varied from year to year. Work is currently being carried out on a curriculum based model.
(c) For estimating how rundown might be achieved and the extent to which vacancies accruing by natural wastage can be turned into vacant posts either directly or on various assumptions about redeployment policies, the extent of premature retirement and of compulsory redundancy. These procedures require assumptions to be made on the extent of turnover on which recent statistics are not available. These procedures also require assumptions to be made about the extent of interchangeable posts in schools.

The key characteristic of these procedures is that they are operated at

the macro level and depend upon assumptions made at that level. The assumptions made are unlikely to correspond to practice in particular local authorities.
(d) For estimating the costs of the various plans. There have to be procedures to calculate:
teachers' salaries, allowing for salary drift; costs of redeployment, premature retirement and compulsory redundancies.
These costs are probably capable of a fairly high degree of accuracy, since they can be checked against recent experience.

The output from these procedures represents the figures for expenditure that are used in the White Paper on the Government's expenditure plans and in the Rate Support Grant Settlement.

6. The procedures carried out by ESGE, although using material supplied by local authorities, appear strangely remote from individual LEAs. There is no direct connection between the plans being prepared by local authorities to deal with the management of the teaching force in a situation of declining rolls and the work of ESGE. There is no systematic feed-in of those local authority plans, nor is there any communication to LEAs of the results of ESGE's work. Indeed, ESGE reports are circulated to members in confidence. As already stressed the main output of the process is set out in the White Paper on the Government's Expenditure Plans, which cannot be regarded as a main means of communication between the Department and local authorities. The ESGE process is undertaken not because of the requirements of educational planning in the Department of Education and Science, but because of the public expenditure planning process of central government.

THE WORK OF ACSET

The discussion has been conducted so far in respect of the Department's policies for teacher numbers as they develop within public expenditure planning and as influenced by the work of ESGE. The Department also needs to consider teacher numbers as part of its policies on the supply and education of teachers on which it is advised by ACSET (Advisory Committee on the Supply and Education of Teachers).

ACSET's work, which is fully discussed in Blackstone and Crispin (1982), is inevitably concerned with a longer time-span than we have been concerned with in the analyses so far. ACSET has to consider the intake into the teacher training system and must therefore be concerned with the longer term in which students about to enter training will be employed. The policy of the Department on the training of teachers is an influence on the supply side of the local authorities' approaches to the management of the teaching force, but it is an influence that operates over the longer term. It is not a direct influence on present staffing levels.

ACSET does, however, set out projections for teacher numbers for a period of up to 15 years ahead. The report of the Committee (DES, 1982) projected the teacher numbers as at April each year (see Table 9).

These projections can be an important influence on local authorities' concern that their policies for the rundown of teacher manpower will enable them to have a balanced teacher force that takes account of future changes. The importance of the projections lies in the extent of the proposed decline and the anticipated point at which numbers will need to increase given alternative assumptions about the birth rate and hence pupil numbers.

Table 9 Teacher numbers as projected by ACSET

	(Full time teachers only in thousands)			
	Low*	Lower*	Upper*	High*
1981	—	—	433.0	—
1982	—	—	422.5	—
1983	—	—	409.5	—
1984	—	—	394.5	—
1985	—	—	384.0	—
1986	—	—	377.0	—
1987	—	—	370.0	—
1988	360.5	363.0	363.0	364.0
1989	352.5	358.0	358.5	361.5
1990	346.5	355.0	357.0	362.0
1991	343.5	354.5	358.5	365.5
1992	342.5	356.5	363.0	371.5
1993	344.5	360.5	370.0	380.5
1994	347.0	366.5	379.5	391.5

From Table 3 of the 1982 Report.
* Based on constant PTRs but different pupil numbers, reflecting variant projections of future births.

The breakdown into primary and secondary teachers is of particular importance, since the projected numbers of primary teachers increases from 1986 as Table 10 shows for the upper projection.

The number of secondary school teachers will continue to decline according to Table 10 up to 1991, but the number of primary school teachers will increase from 1986, and by 1990 will be more than in 1983. The figures set out here show the national context within which local authorities have to develop their policy.

The projections prepared by ACSET are very closely related to the public expenditure planning process described above. This is not immediately apparent because they are presented in a different way from those set out earlier in this article.

1. The White Paper figures are for England only (although Welsh numbers are given separately). The ACSET figures are for England and Wales.

Table 10 Primary and secondary teacher numbers as projected by ACSET

	Primary	Secondary
1981	189.0	244.0
1982	180.0	242.5
1983	171.5	238.0
1984	163.5	231.5
1985	160.5	223.5
1986	161.5	215.5
1987	162.5	207.5
1988	165.0	198.0
1989	169.5	189.0
1990	175.5	181.5
1991	180.5	178.0
1992	185.0	178.0
1993	190.5	179.5
1994	196.5	183.5

2. The White Paper figures are for January. The ACSET figures are for April.
3. The White Paper figures include unqualified teachers (mainly instructors). The ACSET figures exclude them.
4. The White Paper figures are for full-time equivalents. The ACSET figures are for full-time teachers.

These are, however, only differences in present figures. As the 1982 report makes clear, 'in the period up to and including financial year 1984/85 these projections have been constrained to be consistent with the planning figures for total teacher numbers in England and Wales published in the Government's Expenditure Plans' (Annex A, para. 5). Beyond 1984/85, ACSET worked on an extrapolation of the primary and secondary PTRs implicit in the teacher numbers planned by government for January 1985. These PTRs are applied to the projections of pupil numbers.

The work of ACSET can therefore be seen as closely related to the policies derived from public expenditure planning.

THE ISSUES EXPLORED

The two key issues identified in the discussion above are:

1. The relationship between the process of planning teacher numbers at national level and the public expenditure planning process, and in particular the problems created by the introduction of cash planning.
2. The relationship between the process of planning teacher numbers at national level and the actual policies adopted in local authorities.

1. Manpower planning and public expenditure planning

The first issue that has to be faced is whether the Department of Education and Science is concerned with policies for the reduction in the number of teachers in their own right, as well as part of the process of public expenditure planning. If it is so interested, then there is a case for a much more developed process within the Department, working where appropriate with the Associations. It would involve the systematic collection of information on manpower plans from local government.

Particular problems arise because of the introduction of cash planning. The requirements of cash planning are simple. If expenditure is planned in cash terms, then any salary award or other increase in costs over and above that assumed in expenditure planning must result in a cutback in inputs. As the White Paper on Teaching Quality (Cmnd 8836) states, 'the number of teachers that can be employed within the cash plans will depend on the level of pay settlements for teachers' (para. 19). Thus a salary award for teachers over and above that allowed for should result in a reduction in the number of teachers over and above that originally planned for, unless a reduction can be made elsewhere in local authority spending.

The dilemma is obvious. On the one hand there is the planning of the reduction in teacher numbers, based on the preservation of curriculum opportunities and minimum compulsory redundancies. Sudden increases in manpower rundown because of the impact of cash planning and salary awards throw into disarray the results of that process and could, if they were to be implemented, require of local authorities sudden alterations of policy. Such changes would have harmful effects on schools and are consequently unlikely to be implemented.

Without entering into its merits it is clear that a simple insistence on cash planning can throw manpower planning processes into total disarray. If the principles of cash planning are to be maintained, then procedures have to be introduced that will phase additional manpower reductions required as a result of implementation over longer periods of time.

2. The relationship between national and local policy processes

There is a gap between the actual policies at local level and the national policies for manpower reductions embedded in both the ESGE and PESC procedures and resulting expenditure levels set by central government. Blackstone and Crispin (1982) have described the position in slightly different terms:

> The main reason for this incomplete planning system is the tension between central control and local autonomy. This results in a dangerous division of responsibility between national planning (DES) and local employment (local authorities) which fails to maximize the effective use of skilled manpower, in this case teachers (p. 70).

On one level this gap can merely be accepted, recognizing that it can mean that the policies underlying the national expenditure decisions may not be applied locally. This can either result in local authorities spending more on education than has been allowed in national expenditure, or spending more on teachers' salaries, but cutting back more on other educational expenditure. In practice, both tendencies are present. This position can be accepted by the Government recognizing as present reality the consequences of local authority decision-making. Alternatively they can increase the financial pressure under which local authorities make their decisions, either by reducing grants generally or by the use of penalties directed at authorities whose expenditure is above that specified by the Government—that decision is, however, likely to be taken after consideration of the whole pattern of local authority expenditure and not merely expenditure on education generally or on teachers' salaries in particular.

In practice the Government has pursued both the policy of increasing financial pressure and of taking account to a degree at least of the consequences of past decisions on teacher numbers.

If, however, the Government wishes to achieve a closer relationship between its policies for manpower reduction and the policies of local authorities, there is a wide range of options that are in theory at least open to it.

It would be possible for the Government to take powers to ensure its policies were in fact carried out. It could for example take direct statutory powers to compel the required teacher reductions or, as would be more likely, to introduce an educational planning process requiring local authorities to submit policy plans for approval—covering their policies for teaching manpower, probably as part of wider educational policies.

This approach would represent a fundamental change in the relationship between the Department and local education authorities. Indeed, it would represent a direct control over local government unparalleled in other services. True the Department previously applied a teacher quota system to local authorities, but that was a means of ensuring the fair distribution of a scarce resource.

The Government could change the financial relationship between central government and local authority from a general financial relationship to a special financial relationship for education, which would give central government a much greater influence on educational expenditure. The proposal for an educational block grant was designed for this purpose. The arguments about educational block grant extend well beyond the management of the teaching force. In this context we merely note that if that block grant had been related to grant-related expenditure assessments based on factors similar to those currently in use, then although increasing DES influence on educational expenditure in general, it would not have increased that influence on the allocation of expenditure to teachers' salaries or teacher numbers, since GREAs contain no factor directly measuring the requirement. Influence over local education authorities through an education block grant would not have extended to the allocation of expenditure between teacher salary costs and other budget heads. The possibility exists that the block grant system could be further modified to give the Department direct influence over teacher numbers and the resulting salary expenditure. The possibility that an educational block grant could be a first step leading on to further financial control has been one of the issues raised in discussion on the proposals.

The measures set out above involve significant increases in the direct control exercised by the Government over local authorities in the exercise of their education function. It is, however, possible to envisage measures which while giving the Government no more control over local authorities and in no way altering the balance of central–local relations, improve the network of influence and communication.

The relationship between central government and local authorities in the government of education has only to a limited extent depended on the exercise of direct controls, although of course, both local authorities and central government have operated within a clear statutory framework. It has depended more upon a complex network of influence often backed by views at both local and national level.

There are arguments for extending the channels of communication between central and local government on the policies for reducing teacher numbers in relation to declining rolls. At present the processes centring on ESGE and the related processes in the Department appear isolated from the actual policy processes in the local authorities.

There could be a more systematic feed-in to those processes of the policies being adopted by local authorities, who could be invited to prepare policy plans covering a number of years on their policies for teacher numbers, including premature retirement, redeployment and related issues, although this might be resisted as a preliminary to the use of such policy plans for direct control.

There could be publicity given to the work of ESGE and direct statements by the Government about their own conclusions communicated by the Department to local education authorities. If the Government wishes local authorities to reduce education manpower by amounts that involve greater premature retirement, more redeployment and even compulsory redundancy, then that should be clearly stated and appropriate advice sent out. The Department would set out its views clearly on these issues and not merely let them be implied in the White Paper on Public Expenditure. The White Paper on Teaching Quality issued in March 1983 (House of Commons, 1983), as this research was being written up, does contain a statement of the Government's views on some of these issues.

Each of the alternatives for change put forward here implies further involvement by central government, even if only at the level of consultation and advice. The alternative favoured by those concerned to clarify the relationship between central government and local authorities on the basis of greater local accountability would be to question the need for an involvement by central government in teacher numbers. As we have seen, that involvement has arisen, not from any direct concern by the Department, but because of the requirements of public expenditure planning. So long as the White Paper on Public Expenditure and the processes underlying it treat local government expenditure in the same detail and on the same basis as central government expenditure, the Department must be involved in detailed calculations of teacher numbers, since teachers' salaries are such a major component of local government expenditure. But there is no necessity for the Government's procedures for planning public expenditure to include local government expenditure in this way. Such a change would obviously have implications beyond the issue of teacher numbers, but is included to show that there are alternative approaches.

We have set out as alternatives:

maintenance of present procedures;
direct controls over teacher numbers;
increased financial influence over teacher numbers;
new processes of information consultation and advice;
a lessening of central government's concern.

The alternative followed will depend on an assessment of the viability of the present position and of likely future trends and on the extent of the disparity between central government and local education authorities' policies and on changing views on central-local relations.

A degree of divergence between central government's and local education authorities' policies is implicit in the very existence of elected local government. It may be concluded that the divergences are not sufficiently great on this issue to justify changes over and above what is required to open up better channels of communication and advice.

REFERENCES

Blackstone, T. and Crispin, A. (1982) *How Many Teachers? Issues of Policy, Planning and Demography*, Institute of Education, University of London.
Great Britain. Department of Education and Science. Advisory Committee on the Supply and Education of Teachers (1982) *The Initial Teacher Training System*, London, DES.
Great Britain. Parliament (1981) *The Government's Expenditure Plans 1981-82 to 1983-84*, London, HMSO (Cmnd 8175).
Great Britain. Parliament (1982) *The Government's Expenditure Plans 1982-83 to 1984-85*, London, HMSO (Cmnd 8494).
Great Britain. Parliament (1983) *The Government's Expenditure Plans 1983-84 to 1985-86*, London, HMSO (Cmnd 8789).
Great Britain. Parliament. House of Commons (1983) *Teaching Quality*, London, HMSO (Cmnd 8836).

# SECTION 5

A Policy Re-examined: equality of opportunity

15

Education and Social Policy

JOHN LAWSON and HAROLD SILVER

The Elementary Education Act of 1870 was the most workable piece of compromise legislation in English nineteenth-century history. It did not introduce free or compulsory education, but it made both possible. It did not supersede the voluntary schools, it supplemented them. It brought the state into action in education as never before. It created, in the school boards, the most democratic organs of local administration of the century....

The public elementary schools, to be provided by the boards, were intended to and did rest on the same central assumption as the voluntary schools which they were called on to supplement—they were for the children of the poor, providing an independent system for the lower class. Although lower-middle-class children came to some extent to benefit from their existence, the elementary schools were viewed as catering for the class of children ranging from the 'street Arabs' to those of the 'respectable' working class. They were self-contained and not preparatory to a grammar school or any other education. Although the voluntary and public elementary schools were rival systems in one respect, they formed a socially coherent system in another respect: the identification of this system with the working class did not alter in the remainder of the nineteenth century and was only slowly eroded in the twentieth century. A pamphlet on the public elementary schools published by the National Union of Teachers early in the twentieth century begins with the typical statement: 'Six million children are in the Public Elementary Schools of England and Wales. They are the children of the workers, to be themselves England's workers a few years hence.'[1]

LADDERS

The 1870 Act itself made access to higher-than-elementary education inevitably a more prominent issue. Apart from evening and adult education,

Source: Lawson, J. and Silver, H., 1973, *A Social History of England*, Methuen, London.

such access became available mainly in two ways—the evolution of a higher stage within the elementary system, and the scholarship ladder from the elementary to the grammar school.

Under some school boards elementary schools kept children in extra-grade classes or 'higher tops'. Others provided central facilities for children in the upper grades to be grouped in schools which were seen initially as elementary and later, especially by the Bryce Commission, as secondary. Some church opinion protested that such higher education supported out of public funds, even in voluntary schools, was 'an education the curriculum of which cannot possibly be defined as "elementary"'.[2] In London, church and other opposition in the school board prevented the creation of higher-grade schools until the 1890s.[3] A feeling that the higher-grade schools competed unfairly with the grammar schools was widely expressed, especially where grammar schools with entrance scholarships for boys from elementary schools found the supply of good candidates diminishing when a good higher-grade school was established locally.

The higher-grade schools acted in some cases as stepping-stones to the grammar school and university but were seen generally as routes to skilled and clerical occupations. The chairman of the Manchester school board expressed the view in 1887 that neither the higher-grade schools nor the scholarship ladder to the Manchester grammar school was really catering for the children of the poor, but for a slightly higher class which was now benefiting from the elementary system, including the children of the 'labour aristocracy', the better-paid 'upper strata' of the working class whose social position was very often identical with that of the lower middle class.[4] The grammar-school scholarships were going to children of clerks, warehousemen and shopkeepers. Asked whether the thirty or so scholarships to the grammar school were going to 'what you call the poor', he replied: 'No; I am afraid that Manchester is an example of what the ladder is not.' The higher-grade schools, also, charged a 9d. fee, 'which is prohibitory so far as the labouring classes are concerned. The higher grade schools are not open to the labouring classes as they ought to be.'[5] The higher-grade schools remained socially identified, however, with the working-class elementary system.

The concept of a ladder to higher education was associated in these decades partly with the greater emphasis being placed on social justice, and partly with the indignation among men like T. H. Huxley at the social waste of failing to recruit all available talent. The ladder itself evolved as a direct result of three main developments—the establishment of entrance scholarships as part of the reform of the endowed schools after 1869, an awareness of the increasing number of able working-class children being revealed in the board schools, and developments in technical education, notably at the end of the 1880s.

Attempts to organize a systematic scholarship ladder began in the 1870s. Provision for the admission of poor scholars to the endowed schools had, as we have seen, been severely curtailed, and the social composition of the classical grammar schools narrowed in the nineteenth century. The reforms of the Charity Commissioners and those under the 1869 Act began to increase the number of scholarships available. A variety of local schemes began to emerge, though the number of poor children who attained grammar-school education remained very small....

At the end of the century, therefore, there was keen awareness of the deficiencies in the scholarship system. There were also, in other circles, worries and hesitations about the social effects of extending it....

TOWARDS A UNIFIED SYSTEM, 1900–1938

There was at the beginning of the twentieth century no less an awareness than before of the existence of 'two nations', of the barriers of social class. Elementary education continued to be seen as something specifically provided for the working class. Increased school and university provision had not altered the definitions that surrounded the different strata of education. Socialists in the 1920s were to describe the distinction between 'elementary' and 'secondary' education as 'educationally unsound and socially obnoxious', and to campaign for the abandonment of the nineteenth-century concept of elementary education as 'the discipline of a class'....

THE 1902 EDUCATION ACT

At the end of the nineteenth century important factors were altering attitudes towards the pattern of education as it had evolved since 1870. The elementary system had produced what seemed to some people anomalous pseudo-secondary features in its higher-grade schools and evening classes. The still insecure financial basis of very many grammar schools was in many cases being further eroded by these developments. The voluntary schools were being outpaced by the school boards; many of them, in a period of general decline in church attendance, were in serious financial difficulties, bearing what A. J. Balfour (shortly, as prime minister, to carry through the 1902 Act) called an 'intolerable strain'. The voluntary agencies, though divided as to the desirability of further state aid and intervention, were increasingly pressing for greater assistance, as 'a due recognition of the magnificent work they have done, not for a quarter of a century, but for many centuries, in training up the people in godliness and honesty'.[6] State intervention was in society generally being more actively advocated and tolerated. The Bryce Commission had recommended in 1895 the creation of a central authority for education, although, it hastened to add, 'not in order to control, but rather to supervise the Secondary Education of the country, not to override or supersede local action, but to endeavour to bring about among the various agencies which provide that education a harmony and co-operation which are now wanting'.[7] A Board of Education was created in 1899. Local councils had also entered the education field (mainly under the Technical Instruction Acts) as competitors of the school boards....

There were, of course, legitimate criticisms of the boards. Many of the smaller ones were inefficient. The separate administration of board schools, grammar schools, Science and Art Department grants, technical instruction committees (and the independent management of voluntary elementary schools) was chaotic. The new council education authorities, what is more, would have advantages....

The Act itself designated as local education authorities the Councils of Counties and County Boroughs.... Instead of dealing with 2500 school boards and the managers of over 14,000 voluntary schools, the Board of Education would now deal with 318 local education authorities. The Act converted, said one supporter, 'our long-endured educational chaos into something approaching a regulated system'.[8]

The most far-reaching effect of the 1902 Act was its influence on the structure of elementary and secondary education. The Act, says Professor Eaglesham, 'helped to contain, to repel, and in some respects to destroy the upward striving of the elementary schools'. Morant has been defended against the charge of hostility to the scientific and technical work that was central to the experience of the higher-grade schools,[9] but it is clear that his view of the nature of secondary education was in the public-school mould. On the question of advanced work under the school boards, he wrote in a memorandum '...it cannot be doubted that this policy of letting School Boards supply a sort of Pretence-Secondary School has headed off the natural local pressure in the big towns for the development of true Secondary Schools'.[10] His view of elementary education was based on a strong sense of social hierarchy. He and Balfour had 'similar middle-class educational values, similar doubts about the abilities of the masses'.[11] By defining the board schools as strictly elementary, and then bringing them into a relationship with the newly strengthened grammar schools, Morant (and with him Gorst, Balfour and Webb) defined also a strictly class relationship to be tempered only by the introduction of a formal system of transition from one system to the other.

SECONDARY EDUCATION TO 1918

The Act gave the grammar schools a new financial security and a clear structure within which to work. The role of the schools provided or aided by the local authorities was defined more explicitly in the *Regulations for*

Secondary Schools issued in 1904, in which Morant echoed some of the doubts about the higher-grade type of curriculum. The regulations, according to a well-known description, 'failed to take note of the comparatively rich experience of secondary curricula of a practical and quasi-vocational type which had been evolved in the Higher Grade Schools'.[12] ...

Secondary schools run by voluntary bodies were able, following the 1902 Act, to receive grant from both the local authority and the Board of Education. After 1919 these schools had to choose between receiving grant from the LEA or direct from the Board; those in special relationship with the Board (there were nearly 250 by the Second World War) acquired 'direct grant' status. In terms of social composition they were or tended to become closer to the independent public schools than to the provided or aided grammar schools.

The new local authorities immediately began to survey the secondary education needs of their areas. The story of secondary education from 1903 to the First World War is a combination of two main themes—the building up of the system of schools and, as we shall see, the introduction of the free-place system. The number of grant-aided secondary schools increased from nearly 500 in 1904-5 to over 1000 in 1913-14 (and the number of pupils from nearly 64,000 to nearly 188,000). The number of schools continued to increase into the 1920s, but the main feature of wartime and post-war expansion was the size of schools, as the demand for grammar-school places grew. The average number of pupils in grant-aided secondary schools was 182 in 1913 and 290 in 1921. In the first decade of the century London was educating some 5 per cent of its children aged ten to fifteen in public secondary schools.[13] In 1904 Morant created a secondary branch of the inspectorate. The free-place system was introduced in 1907; it made recognition for a grant dependent on the school taking upwards of a quarter of its children from elementary schools. The new system both brought relief to the grammar schools and introduced a greater element of social-class diversification into their structure. ...

The need to provide more secondary-school places for intending elementary teachers was an important factor in attempts to improve the ladder from the elementary schools. In 1906 approximately half of the scholarships in secondary schools were held by pupils pledged to teaching. As a result of the 1902 Act there was to be, in one description, 'a ladder, not a stairway—to the universities for the poor boy and girl of parts; there was to be a reservoir from which would come the ten thousand teachers required each year by the state elementary schools'.[14] In 1907 the free-place system was introduced, by which grants to secondary schools were made dependent on their keeping at least a quarter of their places, without fee, for pupils from elementary schools. Entrance was conditional on passing an 'attainment test' at approximately the age of eleven, which had grown in popularity as the best age of transfer since the end of the nineteenth century. ...

Demands were to increase in the years that followed for the ladder to be made into a stairway, and for fees to be reduced or abolished....

The war ended with an ambitious Education Act, a report on the insufficiency of science teaching, and the creation of the Burnham Committee, in which teachers and the local authorities were to negotiate teachers' salaries. All three reflected trends in social organization and social and educational philosophies apparent since the late nineteenth century. The 1918 Act was intended to provide a new national momentum in implementing established ideas; like many other hopes for the post-war implementation of radical social policies it ended in a struggle to cope even with existing provisions, given the demands for economy in public spending from the beginning of the 1920s.

THE 1920s AND 1930s

The 1920s and 1930s saw the growth of a movement to end the parallel systems of elementary and secondary education, and to replace them by an end-on system of primary and secondary education. 'Secondary education for all' was the slogan; the Hadow Report of 1926 was its most representative document. By the beginning of the 1920s the NUT and the labour movement were pressing for a remodelling of the system. In 1922 a major policy document of the Labour Party entitled *Secondary Education for All*, edited by R. H. Tawney, considered that the only proper definition of 'secondary' education was in fact 'the education of the adolescent'—the phrase that came to be used for the title of the Hadow Report; R. H. Tawney was also a member of the committee which produced the latter. Although there were calls for experiments with 'multiple-bias' schools, the general aim of the movement was to establish a two-stage educational process, with the grammar schools as one type of secondary school, and with maximum opportunity for entry.

This movement to revise the relationship between elementary (the word was not officially interred until 1944, two decades after the Hadow Committee proposed that it should be) and secondary schools had its roots not only in the increased demand for secondary education, but also in the economic and political conditions of the inter-war years, including juvenile unemployment....

When the Labour Party issued its policy statement *Secondary Education for All* in 1922 it used data obtained in Bradford to show that secondary education had become 'the aspiration of families who, twenty years ago, would have withdrawn... [children] from school at the earliest age which the law allowed'; throughout the country, however, large numbers of children were still debarred by their parents' poverty or the shortage of free places. The existing scholarships and places were described in the document (varying the 'ladder' image) as 'bridges' or 'slender hand-rails' between the elementary and secondary systems. For more than 90 per cent of the children concerned 'the primary school is like the rope which the Indian juggler throws into the air to end in vacancy'. Its proposal was 'the creation of a system of universal secondary education extending from the age of eleven to that of sixteen'.[15] The Hadow Committee's main conclusion was that education should be conceived as two stages, primary and secondary, with a break at about eleven. In addition to existing grammar schools, schools on the pattern of selective and non-selective central schools—to be known as 'modern schools'—should be made available for all children. Existing elementary schools could at least be divided into junior and senior departments. The movement for secondary education for all accepted the Hadow Report 'as ground on which we think the battle for improvement can hopefully be fought.... It aims at secondary education, not for a selected few, but for all children. To this principle we admit no exception.'[16]

Secondary Education for All and the Hadow Report marked the climax of movements of opinion which aimed to raise the elementary education of older children to 'secondary' status. [...]

The Hadow Report won swift and widespread support. The Board of Education in 1928 published a pamphlet applauding its recommendations and urging local authorities to adopt the principles laid down in it, and to prepare public opinion for the changes.[17]

Many authorities tried to implement the scheme in full; others began to open new senior schools and to create senior departments.... Such expansion or reorganization did not go without opposition. Fisher's Act (1918), and especially its proposal for continued education beyond the school leaving age, provoked the wrath of the Federation of British Industries, whose education committee declared that industry would be unable to bear the burden of releasing its juvenile labour over the age of fourteen for eight hours a week, and that only a small minority of children were 'mentally capable of benefiting by secondary education'.

For the individual grammar school the free and special places meant a broadening of its social basis. For the nation as a whole at the outbreak of the Second World War education was still, in Tawney's words, based on a combination of 'a not unkindly attitude to individuals with a strong sentiment of class and a deep reverence for wealth'.[18] The benefits of the ladder were unevenly distributed geographically and among the different social strata eligible to benefit from it....

In this highly selective system a preoccupation with the age and methods of selection naturally increased. Even the Cross Commission had been told in 1886 by a chief inspector of schools of the difficulty of securing 'encouragement for those who are slow at learning at first, but who are not necessarily slow afterwards'. Transfer at 11 plus came to be justified in the twenties and thirties in terms of physical and psychological growth. The Hadow

Committee described 'a tide which begins to rise in the veins of youth at the age of eleven or twelve'. The Spens Committee declared that 'general intelligence' was best measured up to the age of 11, 'when certain qualitative changes in the child's personality... become noticeable'.[19] The early free-place examinations consisted of papers in English and arithmetic, sometimes a general paper, and, increasingly from the 1920s, intelligence tests. The claims for such tests were at first tentative. In 1928, for example, the Board of Education reported that twenty-one out of seventy-five local authorities investigated were using intelligence tests (four or five using 'standardized' or 'recognized' tests, and about half of the others using tests constructed by expert examiners). The board indicated that opinion was 'deeply divided upon the question of the value and suitability of the tests themselves, and upon the relevance of the usual arguments for and against them'. Its conclusion was that 'a general use of these tests in making awards would be premature'. In the 1930s claims for the tests became more insistent; the Board of Education followed the research cautiously, but by 1936 could say: 'Evidence has accumulated which suggests that the value of what are known as intelligence tests is higher than had been supposed provided that such tests are constructed, and their results used, under expert guidance. It is therefore recommended that such a test be included in every examination for the award of special places.'[20] The Spens Committee, two years later, was impressed by evidence that 'with few exceptions, it is possible at a very early age to predict with some degree of accuracy the ultimate level of a child's intellectual powers'. This confidence in the possibility of identifying different levels of ability seemed also to justify the emerging pattern of secondary education, with grammar, modern and technical schools. 'Different children from the age of 11,' said the Spens Report, 'if justice is to be done to their varying capacities, require types of education varying in certain important respects.' Although the committee saw the need for experiments with 'multilateral' schools, it 'could not advocate the adoption of multilateralism as a general policy'.[21]

The committee also recommended the eventual raising of the school-leaving age to 16. An Education Act had determined that the leaving age would be raised to 15 in September 1939, but war intervened.

EDUCATION AND SOCIAL IDEALS 1939–1972

The most important provision of the 1944 Act was that which proclaimed that 'public education shall be organized in three progressive stages to be known as primary education, secondary education, and further education'. Local authorities were now required to provide secondary education, and schools would 'not be deemed to be sufficient unless they are sufficient in number, character, and equipment to afford for all pupils opportunities for education offering such variety of instruction and training as may be desirable in view of their different ages, abilities and aptitudes'. The school-leaving age was to be raised to 15 from 1945 (subsequently postponed for two years), and to 16 at a later date. The scheme for county colleges was revived, providing for compulsory part-time education up to 18 (in the event this was again not implemented). The Board of Education was turned into a ministry, and part III authorities were abolished.

When the 1944 Act was implemented the system of direct grant schools was retained, with modifications. Of the 231 existing schools, 160 retained direct grant status, 36 were rejected and 35 became independent. Four LEA grammar schools were accepted onto the list (another 27 applied and were rejected). Direct grant schools had to reserve at least a quarter of their places for non-fee-paying children from local authority primary schools. Some took more: Bristol grammar school, for example, in addition to its 25 per cent of free places had another 25 per cent of 'reserved places' if the local LEAs wished to take advantage of them; at King Edward's school, Birmingham, the LEA paid the fees of half of the boys.[22] In 1950 nearly 83,000 children (more than half of them girls) were attending direct grant schools, the social composition of which had since their creation come increasingly to resemble that of the public schools.

The educational reforms which were to take effect from 1945 were intended to remove some of the stigmas attached to lower-class education, provide a new pattern of opportunity, and set education in a framework of improved welfare and social justice.

SECONDARY EDUCATION AND SOCIOLOGISTS

Like the pre-war Spens Report, the Norwood Committee reported in 1943 in favour of different types of secondary schools for different children. It even used the language of the 'progressive' educationist to make its main recommendation—that, 'in accordance with the principle of child-centred education the definition of "secondary education" should be enlarged so as to embrace three broad types of education'. It asserted that English education had 'in practice recognized the pupil who is interested in learning for its own sake ... the pupil whose interests and abilities lie markedly in the field of applied science or applied art', and thirdly the pupil who 'deals more easily with concrete things than with ideas'.[23] The Spens Committee, in 1938, may have had to rely on overconfident psychological evidence; the Norwood Report of 1943 was concerned not with evidence but with assertion. It had less of a basis in discriminating analysis and concern for data than any other modern report on education; it was produced by a narrow committee and, it has been said, the circumstances in which it was published were 'a perfect example of that departmental procedure which to the uninitiated seems like official chicanery'. The report contained 'obscurities and inconsistencies, perhaps not quite unintentional'.[24]

In spite of the report's poor reception Labour ministers of education after 1945 accepted the tripartite argument and interpreted the 1944 Act in the light of it. A pamphlet on *The Nation's Schools* issued by the Ministry of Education in 1945 was withdrawn after protests about its tripartite assumptions. *The New Secondary Education,* issued by the ministry in 1947, followed the same lines, however. 'Different types of secondary education will be needed', it affirmed, 'to meet the differences that exist between children' and it reproduced the description of three different kinds of children who could be identified for three different types of schools. A ministry pamphlet on school-building asserted, in 1957 under a Conservative minister, that 'we now hold that there should be different kinds of schools to provide for variety in the ages, aptitudes and abilities of children themselves and to suit local circumstances'. Labour leaders continued, throughout the 1950s, to defend the retention of the grammar school.

At the end of the war the organization of secondary schooling on comprehensive lines had only sporadic support. The 'multilateral' or 'bilateral' concepts of separate types of education within the same building (or in separate schools on the same campus, as favoured by the Liberal Party) competed with the concept of comprehensive schools which took children of all abilities in the area....

There was a widely held view that the grammar schools could and should have an enhanced contribution to make, and were too profoundly rooted in history and experience to be sacrificed to a new and partisan idea. There was also a view that the secondary modern schools which had replaced the senior classes of the elementary system could make, with essentially non-academic children, a new sort of contribution to the pattern of secondary-school life. These assumptions were challenged in the 1950s in three ways: the experience of the existing comprehensive schools was being collated (notably by Robin Pedley), doubt was growing about the part of intelligence tests in educational selection, and sociologists began to play an influential part in educational thinking.

The main criticism of intelligence testing was based on its claim, firmly accepted in the 1930s and 1940s, to be able to measure intelligence divorced from social determinants. Uncertainty about the relationship between intelligence and environmental factors was being voiced in the late 1940s, and in 1953 Brian Simon in *Intelligence Testing and the Comprehensive School* built on some of the early doubts of psychologists and others about the accuracy and validity of the instrument they had evolved. By the following year sociologists and social psychologists investigating social mobility were publishing results which accepted that 'there is suggestive evidence that working-class children do relatively less well on the tests of attainment which comprise 66 per cent of the selection examination'.[25] By 1957 the argument about the validity of tests and the arguments about the desirability of selection had become difficult to disentangle. The margins of error in the 11-plus were wide enough to allow of the wrong allocation of considerable numbers of children. Innate or general intelligence was admitted to be less easy to define or measure than had previously been thought. Intelligence quotients were demonstrated to be affected by coaching, and were not unrelated to previous social and educational experience. Professor P. E. Vernon, an important figure in the history of intelligence testing, himself helped to throw doubt on their use as a mechanism of selection. By the early 1960s it was possible for the Robbins Committee to pass a historical verdict:

> Years ago, performance in 'general intelligence tests' was thought to be relatively independent of earlier experience. It is now known that in fact it is dependent upon previous experience to a degree sufficiently large to be of great relevance. And once one passes beyond tests of this kind and examines for specific knowledge or aptitudes, the influence of education and environment becomes more and more important.[26]

It was from the 1950s that sociologists began seriously to investigate the relationship between 'previous experience' and the distribution of educational opportunity. When the Central Advisory Council reported in 1954 on *Early Leaving* it found that in its grammar-school sample there would have been 927 children from unskilled workers' homes if the proportion had been the same as in the population as a whole; there were in fact 436. Of these, two-thirds left without as many as three passes at ordinary-level GCE (which had begun to operate three years earlier); only one in twenty entered for two or more advanced-level subjects, representing 1.4 per cent of the total number taking advanced-level courses. In seeking explanations the council felt itself to be 'in territory that had so far been little explored; and it is probable that many economic, social and perhaps biological factors have escaped us'.[27] Sociologists were, in fact, already exploring this territory. Jean Floud, A. H. Halsey and others began to publish research data on the differential access of children from the two main social classes to grammar schools. In 1956 Floud, Halsey and Martin published *Social Class and Educational Opportunity*, demonstrating how class affected chances of a grammar-school education. What the research of the 1950s showed was that post-war educational expansion

> benefited the children of all social classes—not just those of the less prosperous groups.... The widening of educational provisions does not by itself reduce social inequalities in educational opportunity ... no less than nine in every ten of the lowest social group were still deprived of a grammar school education in the 1950's; the proportion so deprived was barely a tenth smaller than thirty or forty years before.[28]

If *Early Leaving* was the first report of an official committee on education to ask mainly sociological questions, the Central Advisory Council's 1959 report on education, *15 to 18* (the Crowther Report), was the first to look for systematic sociological answers. It set out to explore the implications of economic and social change for the education, full-time and part-time, of young people in this age range. Problems of population and family, and changes in teenage employment and interests, for example, were of central importance to it. It was concerned with the school's role in preparation for family life and adulthood. It looked at the earlier age of marriage among girls, and suggested that this required a new approach to the education of girls of 17 and 18 still in full-time education. It considered aspects of increased economic prosperity ('the community is about one-third richer in material wealth than it was in 1938') and believed that the effects of prosperity had been beneficial to education, though educational expenditure had in the previous twenty years 'been doing little more than keep up with the general expansion of the national income'....

THE 1960s: INEQUALITIES AND OPPORTUNITIES

An important feature of education in the 1960s was the increased role of the central government in developments of many kinds. The debate about educational principles and practice dominated the reports of the national committees. Outstanding reports of the sixties covered the universities, less able children, primary and public schools, the youth service and the recruitment of scientists. The reports reflected in general the growing concern about evidence of underprivilege and the problems of manpower. The Crowther Committee's concern with sociological analysis and the definition of educational objectives was repeated in the reports of the 1960s. They also showed a concern, implicit or explicit, with national economic needs, with the rights and requirements of the individual, the distribution of resources and acceptable philosophies for educational processes. Out of such reports came developments which strengthened the role of the state in education: the Ministry of Education was reconstituted, a national Schools Council was created, a government scheme for a system of higher education to run parallel with the universities was implemented, educational priority areas were designated, and ministers played a more intimate part in decisions on comprehensive-school schemes and the pay of university and school teachers.

Two reports which were to be of profound importance for educational development appeared in 1963—the Newsom Report, *Half our Future*, on children of average and less than average ability, and the Robbins Report on *Higher Education*. Both accepted and reinforced the premise that social factors had deprived poor children of adequate educational opportunities....

THE 1960s: SECONDARY EDUCATION

Questions of educational opportunity had their most strident public discussion in the 1960s in terms of secondary education, and specifically of comprehensive schools. Of the 3 million or so pupils in maintained secondary schools in the early 1960s some quarter of a million were in non-selective schools. In 1962 there were 106 comprehensive schools, maintained by 23 local education authorities (more than 100 authorities had none)....

The Labour Party nationally was won over to the idea of comprehensive schools in the mid-1960s. In 1965 the Labour government announced plans 'to end selection at eleven plus and to eliminate separatism in secondary education'; local education authorities which had not done so were to submit plans 'for reorganizing secondary education in their areas on comprehensive lines'. Circular 10/65 in which the Department of Education and Science issued their instructions described six main forms of comprehensive organization and left it to local authorities to select their preferred pattern (the six included schools for 11- to 18-year-olds, two-tier schemes, and schemes which used 'middle schools' or sixth-form colleges). During the lifetime of the Labour government the majority of local authorities adopted reorganization schemes of one kind or another, in some areas against a background of pronounced controversy, disputes between parents and local councils, and marches and protests. Support for the comprehensive idea was also increasing in the Conservative Party; the Conservative government elected in 1970 withdrew circular 10/65, but the movement towards reorganization was not halted. By 1970 115 authorities had had reorganization plans approved for all or most of their areas (those of thirteen authorities had been rejected, and ten authorities had so far refused to respond to the requirements under 10/65). By 1970 even authorities which had embarked reluctantly on reorganization found it inexpedient to turn back.

Support for an opposition to complete comprehensive reorganization had continued along established lines. Its opponents argued that by removing the choice of schools comprehensive education undermined freedom, and by eliminating the grammar school it did away with a known tradition of academic excellence; that it substituted schools which tended to be too large, and in which brighter children were penalized; and that secondary modern schools had not yet been given a fair chance. Quintin Hogg said in Parliament, for example, that:

> If Labour Members would go and study what was being done in good secondary modern schools they would not find a lot of pupils biting their nails in frustration because they had failed the 11-plus. The pleasant noise of the banging of metal and the sawing of wood would greet their ears. The smell of a cooking meal, produced with expensive equipment, would come out of the front door to greet them. They would find that boys and girls were getting an education tailor-made for their bents and requirements.[29]

The supporters of comprehensive education argued in general that it undermined privilege and inequality, and that comprehensive schools could provide broader and more flexible courses and opportunities, including for the more able pupils. The record of the comprehensive schools in GCE examinations and university entrance began to come under close scrutiny....

In 1971 there were some 1300 comprehensive schools in England and Wales taking about 35 per cent of the secondary age group: the greatest increase in numbers had come some two to four years after circular 10/65. The percentage of new comprehensive schools of an all-through type (from 11 or 12 to 18) fell from the early 1960s, although these still formed the main block of comprehensive schools—in 1968 well over half were of this kind.[30] The pattern of comprehensive organization was changing markedly from that of the large, pioneer all-through schools—of London, for example. More than half of the comprehensive schools were at this point in time, however, coexisting and competing with grammar schools for their intake. 'Genuine comprehensive schools', it was being pointed out, 'are hard to organize where coexistence or creaming takes place.' The problem was most acute in urban areas which retained grammar schools, a policy which 'inevitably forces certain comprehensive schools into a second-class rôle'.[31] ...

Educational opportunity in the 1960s was being seen in terms of the quality and suitability of education as well as the structure of the system. It was being assessed in relation to the likelihood of a child's staying on at school beyond the age of 15, and the differences in academic performance and access to higher education that were attributable to social class and regional differences. Like the Robbins Report, sociologists continued in the sixties to point to the absence 'of sufficient informed and persistent action to compensate for built-in inequalities of conditions, attitudes and behaviour'. They emphasized the likelihood that children living in poor housing conditions would attend schools with a poor record of, for example, 11-plus successes, and would find themselves 'allocated to the lower streams at school and their school performance will tend to conform accordingly. In general they are less likely to receive encouragement from their parents. Between the ages of 8 and 11 years, the working class and middle class children will thus tend to grow further apart in operational ability.' The survey on the basis of which these comments were made went on to look at the same children when they reached secondary schools. It came to the conclusion (in 1968) that 'the social class differences in educational opportunity which were considerable at the primary school stage have increased at the secondary and extend now to pupils of high ability. Thus nearly half the lower manual working class pupils of high ability have left school before they are sixteen and a half years'.[32] ...

EDUCATIONAL PRIORITIES

Change has always to be kept in perspective. In very many schools the developments of the 1950s and 1960s made little or no impression. Newly trained teachers had to trim enthusiasms to established situations. There were still primary schools without indoor lavatories, teachers without equipment, and schools of all kinds in old and unsuitable buildings. Attitudes do not change uniformly or overnight. A book which in 1968 traced the background of 'children in distress' described those schools where children 'seem to shed their distress the moment they cross the threshold', but others 'where it is still possible for a visitor to be told in a voice audible to the whole class, "These are our 11+ failures"', and which take the view that 'a child's social background is not their concern'.[33]

Social priorities are established in the framework of economic possibility and the state of political and public opinion. The uncertainties of the British economy in the 1960s were accompanied by heightened public controversy about educational and social policy. Political and social ideals were being re-examined under new pressures. The political radicalisms and protest movements of the late 1950s and 1960s were based not only on grievances connected with foreign policy, but also on concerns about social priorities, child poverty, neglect of the aged, antiquated hospitals, and the continued underprivilege of low-income and immigrant groups in the affluent society. The evidence of underprivilege went alongside the evidence of its distribution. Regional differences in education had been shown up persistently in the statistics but attracted little attention. They were most forcefully analysed in 1969 by Taylor and Ayres in a discussion of divergent standards of living and educational opportunity between regions. The 'two nations' of the nineteenth century, it was suggested, still existed in terms of educational opportunities in the second half of the twentieth century.

NOTES AND REFERENCES

1. Steer, N.B., *Our Public Elementary Schools, and How They Are Staffed*, London, undated.
2. Moore, Thomas, *The Education Brief on behalf of the Voluntary Schools*, London, 1980, pp. 18-19.
3. Rubinstein, David, *School Attendance in London 1870-1904*, Hull, 1969.
4. See Hobsbawn, E.J., The Labour aristocracy in nineteenth century Britain, in *Labouring Men*, London, 1964.
5. Royal Commission to Inquire into the Working of the Elementary Education Acts (1886), (Cross Commission) *First Report*, Vol. 1, p. 796.
6. Reynolds, Bernard, Church schools and religious education, in Magnus, P. (ed.), *National Education*, pp. 50-51.
7. Commission on Secondary Education (1895) (Bryce Commission) *Report*, Vol. 1, p. 257.
8. Magnus, P., *Educational Aims and Efforts 1880-1910*, London, 1910, p. 217.
9. See Banks, O., *Parity and Prestige in English Secondary Education*, 1955.
10. Eaglesham, Eric, *From School Board to Local Authority*, London, 1956.
11. Eaglesham, E.J.R., *The Foundations of Twentieth Century Education in England*, London, 1967.
12. Board of Education, *Secondary Education* (Spens Report), London, 1938.
13. Campbell, F., *Eleven Plus and All That: the grammar school in a changing society.* (1956) pp. 9-10.
14. Petch, James A., *Fifty Years of Examining*, London, 1953.
15. Tawney, R.H. (ed.), *Secondary Education for All* (1922), pp. 25-6, 37, 62, 77.
16. Bradford Independent Labour Party, Report IV, p. 3.
17. See Board of Education, *The New Prospect in Education*, London, 1928.
18. Tawney, R.H., Introduction to Leybourne, G. and White, K., *Education and the Birth-rate*, London, 1946, p. 12.

19. Board of Education, *Secondary Education* (Spens Report), London, 1938.
20. Board of Education, *Memorandum on Examinations for Scholarships and the Free Places in Secondary Schools*, London, 1928.
21. Board of Education, *Secondary Education* (1938), pp. 124–5.
22. Hill, *Bristol Grammar Schools*, pp. 216–17.
23. Board of Education, *Curriculum and Examinations in Secondary Schools*, London, 1943, pp. 2–3.
24. Petch, J.A., op. cit., pp. 165–8.
25. Himmelneit, H.T., Social status and secondary education since the 1944 Act: some data for London, in Glass, D.V. (ed.), *Social Mobility in Britain*, London, 1954.
26. *Committee on Higher Education* (Robbins Committee), Report, London, 1963, p. 49.
27. Central Advisory Council for Education, *Early Leaving*, HMSO, London, 1954.
28. Little, A. and Westergaard, J., The trend of class differentials in educational opportunity in England and Wales, *British Journal of Sociology*, Vol. XV (1964).
29. Reported in *The Times Educational Supplement*, 29 January 1965.
30. Benn, C. and Simon, B., *Half-way There*, Penguin, London, 1970.
31. Ibid., pp. 307–8.
32. Douglas, J.W.B., Ross, J.M. and Simpson, H.R., *All Our Future*, Peter Davies, London, 1968.
33. Clegg, A. and Megson, B., *Children in Distress*, Penguin, London, 1968.

16
Poverty and Educational Priority

KEITH BANTING

The first major extension of the poverty debate came in 1967 when the Central Advisory Council on Education (CACE) issued a dramatic call for a national programme of compensatory education.[1] Education, the Council argued, should be employed in a concerted effort to break down the social barriers that trap young children in poverty. The most deprived urban areas should be designated Educational Priority Areas (EPAs) and receive exceptional educational resources, the best and most generous educational facilities in the land.

The existing educational system was universal, seeking to provide equal services to all. But as the CACE report put it, 'Equality is not enough.'[2] The EPA idea of 'positive discrimination' invoked another conception of educational equality. The aim was not simply to provide equal services but to achieve more nearly equal outcomes; and the narrowing of inequalities in educational attainment seems to dictate unequal services. In effect, the proposal implied a large change in the purposes of the educational system and the principles on which it was based. Potentially, EPAs represented what one observer described as the only really new educational policy since 1944.[3]

The politics of EPAs reveal the intellectual and institutional processes of policy innovation moving in patterns remarkably similar to those in the field of family poverty. The proposal was essentially social-science theory translated into public policy; the original inspiration for EPAs came from ideas developing in the academic community in the early 1960s. But the Plowden Council's recommendation ran into sharp conflict with the institutional structure of education, and in the end the proposal was fundamentally remoulded to fit the existing contours of administrative and political life. The resulting policy turned out to be but a pale reflection of the

Source: From Banting, K., *Poverty, Politics and Policy*, Macmillan, London and Basingstoke, 1979.

original idea. EPAs provide a fascinating view of the emergence of a new idea, its diffusion in the political world, and its transformation in the policy process.

I. EPAs: THE EMERGENCE OF AN IDEA

The Central Advisory Council was a unique institution in the field of social policy. Under the terms of the 1944 Education Act, the Minister of Education was required to appoint councils of outside experts to advise him or her on educational theory and practice, and throughout the post-war years the councils produced major reports on different educational problems. Since their memberships were drawn from professional educators and academics, the various CACEs functioned as direct links between the concerns of professionals and those of administrators. Their reports absorbed, extended and legitimated ideas and theories emanating from educational experts.[4] Unlike in other social policy areas, the interchange between the intellectual and institutional worlds had been institutionalized.

In June 1963 Edward Boyle, the Conservative Minister of Education, announced the appointment of a Central Advisory Council to examine primary education. There had been no comprehensive review of primary education since 1931, and it had emerged as an obvious subject for study. The Council was chaired by Lady Plowden and its membership included the usual large number of headmasters, inspectors and educational committee chairmen. But there was also a larger than usual contingent of academics, reflecting the concern of Boyle and the Ministry to draw on new developments in the social and biological sciences. Two of the academics appointed were David Donnison and Michael Young. These men had backgrounds in sociology and social administration, and the fact that they were both on the left of political centre helped balance the political composition of the council.[5] Young was also included as a representative of a new breed of educational activist. He was the author of the brilliant educational satire, *The Rise of the Meritocracy*,[6] and the founder of the Advisory Centre for Education, a group which campaigned for greater parental participation in the schooling of their children. Together Donnison and Young were critical for the emergence of the EPA idea.

By the time the Plowden Council began its deliberations, it could draw on two major streams of social criticism. The first was the rediscovery of poverty; while the Plowden group was at work, Abel-Smith and Townsend published their full findings and launched the Child Poverty Action Group (CPAG) campaign. The second was the growing realization in professional circles that education was not having much impact on either poverty or inequality. In 1944 the new Education Act had established for the first time a comprehensive state education system, including secondary education for all. Since then, further and university education had expanded rapidly. British society was devoting more and more of its resources to educating the young; educational spending was rising dramatically not only in real terms but also as a percentage of the gross national product. Great expectations had surrounded this expansion. According to Churchill, the 1944 Act would ensure equal opportunity for all, and for his Labour partners in the wartime Government the Act represented the results of a generation's educational ambition and effort.[7]

But the social promise of 1944 was not being fulfilled. Although general educational levels were rising, marked class differentials in attainment remained, and the children of the poor were making the least progress of all. The lead in gathering the relevant evidence was taken by academics, since once again the information in the hands of the central government was inadequate. Special surveys were required, and, as in the other cases, influence was exerted by those capable of carrying them out. Sociologists, in particular, became increasingly interested in education, one of the first important studies being conducted by Floud, Halsey and Martin, and others following over the next decade.[8] These private efforts were extended by government commissions, such as the CACEs and the Robbins Committee on Higher Education, which commissioned major research projects and nationwide surveys.[9] The statistical appendices to their reports soon numbered hundreds of pages and in themselves became important contributions to educational sociology.

The cumulative message of these various studies was clear. At each stage of education, working-class children did less well than middle-class children; and the poorest children—the sons and daughters of unskilled workers—did worst of all. The number of such children in grammar schools was disproportionately low. Indeed poor children tended to leave school as soon as they legally could; 92 per cent of the sons of unskilled workers stopped their education at age 15.[10] Children of fathers in professional and managerial occupations were twenty times more likely to enter university as those of fathers in semi-skilled or unskilled jobs.[11] More revealingly, these differentials had been remarkably stable over the post-war period. As one academic survey concluded: 'Middle-class pupils have retained almost intact their historic advantage over the manual working class.'[12] The major expansion of education at the higher levels, in which so much faith had been placed, in fact represented an unintended shift of educational spending towards the upper income groups.

Members of the Plowden Council were aware of this pattern. As left-wing intellectuals, Donnison and Young were particularly concerned; and when the Council broke down into smaller groups to prepare the various sections of the report, they became the core of Working Party No. 2, which examined social influences on educational attainment. They were joined by two others also interested in the social sciences: Timothy Raison, a Conservative journalist who later became founder editor of *New Society*, and Maurice Kogan, the Council Secretary, a young civil servant who later became Professor of Government and Social Administration at Brunel University. The working party commissioned elaborate surveys and research projects, invited extensive evidence from outside experts, and travelled to other countries to look at experiments there. Throughout, its members were looking for educational policies that would have some impact on poverty and inequality.

Definition of the problem

What could be done? Were class differences in educational attainment simply given facts about which the schools could do nothing? Or could the educational system be employed as a mechanism for reducing poverty? The EPA proposal emerged from attempts to grapple with this problem. Virtually all educationalists accept that educational achievement is the product of a complex interaction between inherited ability and environment; but sharp disagreements centre on the weight that should be given to each....

The genetic perspective implies that, short of genetic engineering, class differentials are relatively immutable and are not worth trying to eradicate. The environmental perspective, on the other hand, implies that social changes, including possibly a different pattern of educational provision, might significantly increase the educational success rate of the poor. Clearly a marked shift between these perspectives could have important consequences.

EPAs were a product of such a shift. The 1960s saw the high-water mark of the environmental perspective and of faith in the capacity of education to change society. The shift in professional opinion can be seen in the major educational reports. During the interwar years, those active in education paid the greatest attention to genetic inheritance and its measurement. The 1931 Hadow Report and the 1938 Spens Report, for instance, accepted the advice of psychologists such as Cyril Burt that the important factor in educational attainment was inborn cognitive ability.[13] But after the war this perspective was increasingly challenged. Sociologists entered the lists. Their academic orientation inclined them to social explanations of achievement, and they began the laborious task of tracing the educational progress of different classes. The major CACE reports of the 1950s faithfully reflected this evolution in the intellectual debate, and by the 1960s there was a wealth of evidence to support the conclusions of the Robbins Committee that working-class children were much less successful on average than middle-class children of similar ability, as measured by IQ tests.[14] Even these analyses were thought to understate the differences, as a child's score on an IQ test was itself environmentally influenced. Indeed experts increasingly argued that there was no means of measuring pure inherited ability. One could only guess at the relative influence of genetic and environmental factors, and throughout the 1960s the prevailing assumption in professional debate was that social influences were very powerful indeed. One survey of British educational research reported that some 'writings in education and sociology suggest that the genetic element in intelligence is either so small as to be educationally insignificant or it is non-existent'.[15] While not everyone went that far, the pendulum had clearly swung a long way from the assumptions of the 1930s....

The Plowden Report called for a national policy of 'positive discrimination': deprived urban areas should be designated 'educational priority areas' and should receive the most generous and innovative educational provision.

EPAs reflected professional faith rather than knowledge. Crucial assumptions were untested. The Council had not attempted to measure 'innate ability' and could not really demonstrate how important environmental influences such as parental encouragement actually were.[16] There was little hard evidence that extra educational resources would in fact produce better results.[17] Nor had the Council examined the geographic distribution of poverty to see if designating specific urban areas would actually cover most poor children. In fact, within two years some of the assumptions underlying compensatory education were being seriously challenged. A string of negative evaluations of Head Start reopened a furious debate about the relative importance of genetic and environmental factors and the extent to which education can compensate for social deprivation; and other studies questioned whether poverty was sufficiently concentrated geographically in Britain for an EPA strategy to work.[18] But the proponents of EPAs were fortunate. There is a time lag between professional and political debate, and their recommendations were to outlast the swell of professional confidence that produced them.

Thus the process of social monitoring and analysis was once again dominated by professionals and social scientists, in this case operating both independently and through government research bodies. They documented the problem, defined its causes, and prescribed innovative policy. Now the critical question became whether their ideas would find sufficient support to be translated into public policy.

II. EPA POLITICS: AN IDEA IN SEARCH OF A CONSTITUENCY

As the invention of a small group of intellectuals, EPAs needed strong political backing to avoid being put on the proverbial dusty shelf. The poor parents whose children were to benefit could not provide a political constituency; they remained unorganized and unassertive throughout. Support would have to come from somewhere else. The Plowden Council did its best to create its own constituency. It attached 'absolute priority' to the

EPA proposal over all other recommendations in the report,[19] and after the report's publication members of the Council campaigned strenuously for their ideas. Unlike previous CACE chairmen, Lady Plowden was unwilling to fade away. She exhorted Ministers and senior officials in private; she spoke publicly to educational interest groups and teacher conferences; she wrote articles for the press and visited countless schools; she was co-opted onto the Inner London Education Authority's schools sub-committee and pressed for action at that level. In addition, she and her colleagues turned themselves into public auditors, reconvening on each anniversary of the report's publication to assess progress and resume the call to action.

A second and more private campaign was waged by Donnison and Young, together with a few other left-wing intellectuals such as A. H. 'Chelly' Halsey, the Oxford sociologist. These men were old friends of the Secretary of State for Education in the Labour Government, Anthony Crosland. They had worked with him on educational questions when he was in Opposition and now they used their private contacts with him to press the EPA case. During his period as minister, Crosland regularly sought the advice of such educationalists sympathetic to Labour. A series of evening seminars on specific issues was held at his London home and at least one session was devoted to 'what to do about Plowden'.[20] At about the same time, Halsey entered the Department of Education and Science (DES) as a part-time adviser to Crosland and pushed for action from inside. Although the EPA campaign involved the same type of social scientists and policy experts as did CPAG, it was a very different effort. There was no organization: Lady Plowden and the academics conducted their respective efforts with minimal co-ordination; there was no staff, headquarters or journal; there was little consistent cultivation of the media. In fact, the EPA idea depended largely on the un-coordinated enthusiasm of a few individuals searching for a constituency.

EPAs, pressure groups and the public

The EPA proposal found few other champions outside the institutions of government. Its biggest impact was undoubtedly within the educational community; the Plowden Report became an instant best seller, the subject of debate in the educational press and a standard component in teacher training curricula. But while interest in the EPA idea was widespread, none of the major educational groups mounted a sustained drive to secure its implementation; indeed their main concern was often to ensure that EPAs were not implemented in a way that would jeopardize their own primary goals. Although some Local Education Authorities (LEAs) were enthusiastic, their national representative, the Association of Education Committees (AEC), was cautious. The association was potentially divided by the proposal; many rural areas also had poor schools and were worried that an EPA policy would delay their own programmes.[21] As a result, the AEC welcomed the principle of EPAs but did not consider it a high priority.[22] The reaction of the teachers' unions was similar. The National Union of Teachers (NUT) formally endorsed the principle and the National Association of Head Teachers (NAHT) gave Lady Plowden a standing ovation.[23] But the teachers never regarded EPAs as the most important part of the Plowden Report, and the proposal was scarcely mentioned during the debate on it at the NUT conference.[24] More importantly, while the NUT accepted EPAs in principle, it was opposed to several of the key details of the proposal as advanced by the Plowden Council, as will be seen.

The educational organizations apart, no other organizations took much interest. The TUC formally welcomed the Plowden Report but did little else.[25] The press gave the report generous coverage when it was first published, and the EPA recommendation received general editorial approval,[26] but this initial interest never turned into the sustained attention that family poverty enjoyed. Within six months the proposal had virtually disappeared as a regular editorial feature and news coverage shrank to a trickle. Nor did EPAs ever become a major issue for the public....

Politicians would undoubtedly have been very nervous if the Plowden Council had called for a major programme of positive discrimination. As the Association of Municipal Corporations (AMC) put it mildly, 'discrimination ... within an authority's areas is not always easy'.[27] Certainly a dramatic and visible shift of educational resources to schools in poor neighbourhoods would have been controversial. But the Government was not being asked for radical redistribution. From the beginning, the Plowden Council had explicitly rejected such a strategy as politically self-defeating,[28] and Lady Plowden later warned of the 'danger of being unfair to middle-class children through pushing the priority area policy to extremes.'[29] The Council's milder proposal would only delay educational improvements in more affluent areas for a few years. The political dangers were thus less acute; as one official put it, the idea of disquiet among the affluent 'never bothered us much'. On the other hand, EPAs did have modest political attractions. These were not seen primarily in terms of extra votes in poor areas; in the early years, the Government even refused to publicize which areas were receiving benefits in case local residents disliked being labelled educationally deprived.[30] But at the national level programmes such as EPAs do have some publicity value, as hard-pressed ministers can make attractive announcements about helping the poor, often at modest cost to the Treasury.

Still, EPAs had not really found their constituency outside government. Approval in principle was widespread among educational groups and the press, but, as one minister summed it up, 'Except for a few researchers, the degree of outside pressure was minuscule.' The fate of EPAs thus depended heavily on the response within government.

EPAs and policy-makers

Policy elites reacted ambivalently to EPAs. On the plus side, there was virtually no opposition in principle to the proposal. During the 1960s political debate on education was pervaded by a vague environmentalism; while the details of academic research had little impact, the main thrust of the environmentalist outlook did find echoes among politicians and civil servants....

Departmental interest was declining, however, by the time Plowden reported. In 1964 a new Permanent Secretary, Sir Herbert Andrew, arrived from the Board of Trade. He had little experience in educational administration and was strongly sceptical of sociological research, much of which he regarded as thinly veiled ideology. He also believed in the tradition of the detached administrator and was worried that the DES had become too emotionally committed to educational expansion and reform. Andrew sought to change the department's general orientation. Existing personnel were shuffled and new officials brought in from other departments to fill important positions. By the time the Council's report was published in 1967, the senior positions in charge of schools policy were filled with officials considered much more detached. As the shuffle progressed, both officials and academics sensed a lessening of interest in the new ideas and research being produced by the educational intelligentsia.

One sign of this was a hardening of the Department's attitude towards the CACE. By the mid-1960s it was clear that 'the Department didn't like it', as Crosland put it.[31] The Council generated extra work for officials who had to prepare papers for it and develop responses to its recommendations. In addition, those recommendations often conflicted with the priorities of the Minister, the department or outside groups. As one senior official complained:

> They kept coming up with monumental reports recommending spending millions of pounds we didn't have. So all it did was put the Minister in awkward positions. Ministers never got any credit out of it and they never got any advice they couldn't have had by inviting three or four people to lunch. It was rather a bugbear.

The new Permanent Secretary publicly opposed the statutory requirement that there be such major research-advisory bodies[32] and, after Plowden, no further CACEs were appointed. Even before the Plowden Report was finished, the Council began to detect a certain departmental coolness.

Individual recommendations such as EPAs received greater sympathy. 'Everyone in the department thought it was quite a good idea', recalled one official. 'No one was hostile', echoed another....

The dominant view was that EPAs were a good idea but not a desperately important one. The Department was willing to advance the policy in places, and its support was important. But only those parts of the proposal that did not conflict with existing priorities or relationships were actively pursued.

Political judgements were equally qualified. The response of the major parties depended primarily on the extent to which the EPA idea corresponded with existing party policies. The authors of the proposal were most disappointed by the Labour Government's reaction. Historically Labour had not regarded education as a major instrument of social reform, but interest had grown after the war. The right wing of the party, in particular, argued that educational and social policy were more important to achieving equality than economic changes like nationalization.[33] ...

There was a lag, however, between the professionals and the politicians. During the 1950s academic work had focused on secondary education, and the Labour Party had absorbed that emphasis. Their policies on comprehensive reorganization and the school-leaving age were repeated in countless speeches and codified in successive manifestos. By comparison, the structure of primary education was not seen as a pressing area of reform.

The EPA advocates were fortunate that Crosland was Secretary of State for Education when the report was published. Crosland was an intellectual. He had been an Oxford don before entering political life and, more importantly, he was attuned to educational sociology. He had long argued that educational reform was crucial to equality and his views on the subject, as expounded in his major book, *The Future of Socialism,* owed much to conversations with Michael Young and the research of people such as Halsey.[34] Primary schools were not one of his priorities as minister, and he was cool to the Plowden Report as a whole. But he pronounced the EPA idea 'utterly convincing'.[35] Crosland was a critical sympathizer, however. From the social scientists' point of view, their old friend failed to grasp positive discrimination as a basic approach to education; he was sceptical of the mechanics of their proposal; and he did not attach nearly the same importance to it. But Crosland did at least initiate action on parts of the proposal in his last months at the DES.

After Crosland left the Department in August 1967, no other minister of education took such a personal interest in EPAs....

The Conservatives' reaction to Plowden was considerably warmer because in general it reinforced their educational views. Conservatives were divided over the comprehensive school issue; but at the very least they all could agree that comprehensive reorganization should not take precedence over other educational needs. In particular, the party demanded higher priority for primary education, and the shifting of the CACE spotlight onto the inadequacies at the primary level provided them with extra ammunition. The EPA part of the report also received Conservative support. Only a few of the party's educational spokesmen, such as Edward Boyle, were particularly knowledgeable about the newer social-science theories of educational success,[36] but 'positive discrimination' fitted well with the developing emphasis on selectivity in the party's policies. Even before the report was published, the 1966 Conservative manifesto had promised 'special help to areas where there is most need', and the EPA proposal gave an added boost to this approach.[37] Yet, again, support was qualified; except for Boyle and a few others, EPAs excited little real enthusiasm in Conservative ranks.[38]

In short, Educational Priority Areas had not found a major political constituency. Sympathy was widespread, but no real champion emerged. Obituaries soon appeared: the various educational journals announced that Plowden was being 'pushed aside', dying 'of neglect', and heading 'for peaceful oblivion', with the remains to be left 'on a shelf to gather dust'.[39] In the case of the EPA recommendation, the obituaries were not so much premature as overstated. There was sufficient sympathy among policy elites to ensure that some action would be taken. But without more powerful backing the proposal was highly vulnerable to being 'improved' to death by administrators and interest groups. The transformation of the idea was about to begin.

III. EPA POLICY: AN IDEA TRANSFORMED

... The Council did not envisage separate programmes that totally bypassed the existing educational structure; rather, they sought to redistribute resources within the school system. Their idea was deceptively simple. The central government should carefully select the most deprived urban areas for special treatment; schools in those areas should receive more teachers, expanded nursery education, improved buildings and the most modern equipment. In addition, the schools should make determined efforts to increase parents' interest in their children's education.

The task of responding to this package fell to the DES. But doing so was administratively complicated. In the first place, the Department itself was not well designed to handle such a proposal. EPAs represent an area approach to policy; but the DES is structured along functional lines, and no single section of the department was ever responsible for all aspects of EPA policy. The building and nursery education parts of the Plowden proposal fell to the Schools Branch; ideas about staffing poor schools fell to Teachers Branches I and II, and the special machinery established for negotiations with the teachers' unions; actual classroom practice and parent participation involved the Inspectorate (HMI); research fell to the Planning Branch; and the expenditure implications naturally involved the Finance Branch. The department's response was thus developed by officials in the various branches. Senior people in the Schools Branch collated advice in the early months, but the lack of centralized responsibility for the proposal within the DES undoubtedly complicated the policy response in the longer term....

The DES also faced a major constraint in the larger structure of educational administration....

Changes in a social service such as education require the manipulation of a complex structure over which the central government has only partial control. Education is provided by the Local Educational Authorities. The DES influences what LEAs do, through a number of specific legal powers and financial provisions as well as through more informal means of persuasion. But within the framework of national controls significant areas of local discretion remain, and in such areas the Minister cannot issue commands and expect automatic compliance.[40] Educational changes also involve the teaching profession. Teachers' unions influence not only salaries and working conditions but also larger aspects of educational policy.[41] The more a policy directly affects the teacher and his or her behaviour in the classroom, the more it requires the compliance and even the co-operation of teachers. Where the EPA proposal conflicted with the goals of the teaching profession, the chances of its being implemented were sharply reduced.

The department was also under powerful resource constraints. Educational spending was growing dramatically, both in real terms and as a proportion of total public expenditure. But the main determinant of this increase was sheer growth in pupil numbers.... Demand for longer schooling added to the pressure: more pupils were staying on after the legal school-leaving age, and the numbers in further and university education more than doubled in the 1960s. Although expenditure was growing, there was, as the DES put it, 'little respite from the sheer job of simply coping with numbers'.[42]

With little flexibility in the education budget, new programmes such as EPAs had to compete with the spending proposals of other departments.... The Plowden Report was published in the middle of Callaghan's drive to restrain public expenditure, and after the November 1967 devaluation there were actual cuts in educational programmes and commitments. The financial prospects were bleak. And the manpower situation was not much more encouraging. Qualified teachers were in short supply, and expansion in EPA areas could only come by diverting staff from other sectors. Growth at the secondary level was already threatening the staff position at the primary level, and improvements in the primary and pre-school sectors were going to be difficult to bring about....

Thus, in formulating its response to the EPA proposal, the DES had to contend with limited resources and a dispersed structure of control over education. Together, these forces modified the Plowden recommendation in fundamental ways. The resulting transformation can be best seen by looking at the fate of each of the major elements of the original package.

A national programme

The Plowden Council had called for a national programme of compensatory education, involving co-ordinated changes in virtually all aspects of education in carefully selected urban areas. Such a co-ordinated programme, the Council argued, had to be directed by the central government. They recommended strong central direction through two mechanisms: the official designation of EPA schools by the DES, and a special formula to channel funds to those schools. LEAs would be required to rank their schools according to specific criteria of social need. The DES would then merge these lists into a single national ranking and designate the 10 per cent most deprived as 'priority schools'. These would qualify for favourable treatment, financed through additional Exchequer grants. Regular reports would be sent back to the DES so that progress could be monitored.[43]

The national programme died an instant death. The proposal would have required a shift in the power relationships in education, with a considerable expansion of the role of the DES. Important parts of the EPA package involved areas of local discretion; under existing legislation the DES had no legal right to change an LEA's current expenditure decisions or to alter the distribution of teachers, aides, equipment and so on between schools within its jurisdiction. The DES could draw up any national lists it wanted to, but it could not force LEAs to favour schools so designated. 'We simply had no power to intervene', insisted a senior official. This discretion was preserved by convention and by the power of established educational groups. The central government could have taken additional powers to intervene, but members of the Department regarded such intervention as inappropriate, at least in the EPA case:

> You can either run schools through local authorities or through the Government, but not both. You can't have the Department telling the local authority which of its schools deserve more funds.
>
> Central designation was just contrary to the whole way that thinking about government relationships has developed, at least since the introduction of the general grant in 1958.
>
> People kept suggesting that you could change a relationship in one special area and not in general. But if you are going to tell the local authorities which schools are the worst, you will soon be drawn into everything, including the choice of blotting paper.

These conventions were strongly reinforced by the major educational groups whose power would be affected by central designation. In a rare show of unanimity, the idea was denounced by all of the AEC, the ILEA and the NUT.[44]

Even without such opposition, designation of EPA schools would have been politically difficult. Officials could envisage conflicts with the local authorities over the weight to be attached to diverse criteria of social need, and formal designation might also generate greater protests from rural areas. 'The burden of departmental advice', recalled one official, 'was that setting up a national list of EPA schools would be a difficult, slow and contentious process.' In addition, formal designation would also give an official *imprimatur* to the social needs of a large number of schools. Since adequate funds to assist all of them might not be forthcoming, central designation would only provide a public yardstick of governmental failure. Politically, it was safer to recognize only as much need as it was intended to deal with.

There was nothing immutable about all this. The central government could have expanded its role, improved the resources of the DES for making such judgements, and simply shouldered the complexities involved. Legislation conferring additional powers or establishing a specific grant could have been sought, as was done for the Urban Programme. Or the Government could have adopted a stronger promotional attitude by designating schools and exhorting compliance through less formal methods, as was being done in the case of secondary reorganization. But only a government firmly committed to a national programme of compensatory education could be expected to change the established system against the opposition of the major interest groups affected. That commitment was lacking. In 1967 the formal designation of EPA schools was dismissed 'more or less out of hand', explained one official. 'Fortunately—speaking as an administrator—that question was disposed of quickly', echoed another. Crosland 'took no persuading to reject it', recalled a third. In the Commons, no one spoke in favour of central designation. Crosland simply rehearsed the objections and concluded that 'every local authority knows which are its own EPA schools and we can therefore achieve the results within the present administrative framework'.[45] This position was maintained subsequently, the department even rejecting a demand that they give 'strong and detailed guidance' to local authorities about positive discrimination in their expenditures.[46]

With the rejection of a national programme of co-ordinated action, responsibility for the various aspects of the original proposal was fractured among different jurisdictions, with no common criteria as to which schools should benefit. Each jurisdiction had to decide whether to respond at all and to set its own terms. As a result, the concept of 'EPA' itself began to undergo an important change. Originally it had meant a national programme of compensatory education. But when no national programme was launched, it came to represent a general attitude towards education, a vague idea that ongoing programmes should be biased a little in favour of poor areas, wherever possible. This conception was far more compatible with the existing administrative structure and on this basis some progress was made. The idea began to have a modest effect on existing programmes, and an EPA element was built into several new programmes which were being propelled forward by stronger political forces than EPAs could ever muster on their own.

Buildings

While the administrative framework militated against some elements in the EPA package, it had the effect of expanding the significance of others. The clearest case was the building element. The Plowden Council had ample evidence of the survival in slum areas of grim nineteenth-century school buildings, with their 'narrow passages; dark rooms; unheated and cramped cloakrooms; unroofed outside lavatories;... and the ingrained grime of generations'.[47] The Council did not stress buildings in their proposal. Rather than advocating wholesale replacement of slum buildings, they recommended a 'minor works' allocation for small improvements in each EPA school; indoor sanitation, classroom renovation or simple redecoration, they argued, would make schools pleasanter places. But the proposal was deliberately modest; the average grant suggested was only £5000, one-quarter of the normal limit for such projects.[48] Change in actual school buildings was definitely not the essence of compensatory education.

Administrative convenience, however, transformed buildings into the central government's main response to the proposal. School building is one activity over which the DES does have significant direct control: although the LEA makes the initial judgement about needs and actually constructs the building, the Department must approve each individual project. The DES already had developed the administrative capacity to regulate building programmes, and a special building programme, unlike a national list, would not disrupt relations with the LEAs and the teachers. Indeed, after the publication of the report in 1967, the AEC urged such a response on the Department.[49] If the DES was to respond to the EPA proposal at all, a building approach would involve the least disruption to the existing administrative framework.

Education policy-makers were used to thinking about the problems of slum areas in terms of poor buildings. A survey conducted by the DES in 1962 had revealed that over 50 per cent of primary schools dated from the nineteenth century and that 75 per cent were seriously deficient by modern standards; the NUT had published a similar survey in the same year; and in 1963 a CACE report re-emphasized the sorry state of secondary schools in slum areas.[50] Policy-makers were embarrassed....

A special EPA building programme was therefore doubly attractive to the DES. It would be administratively simple and would remedy an embarrassment in existing policies. The Department did not pretend that a building programme really constituted a strategy of compensatory education. Indeed the departmental brief recommending an EPA building programme to Crosland conceded that it could not be expected 'to counter the complex effects of social deprivation'; only after a meeting with ministers was a concluding flourish about education 'compensating for the effects of social deprivation and...overcoming family poverty' tacked onto the circular that announced the programme.[51] But the more important elements of the Plowden proposal involved greater administrative complications. When the DES was looking for a simple response to Plowden, buildings proved irresistible. 'In the educational world, the timing was right', recalled an official; 'no one challenged it.' Crosland concurred. In a generally cautious Commons speech on Plowden, he was most encouraging about the building possibilities.[52]

A special building programme still had to circumvent the restraints on public expenditure. The prospects for significant new money were virtually non-existent and Crosland agreed to cut another programme, school meals. Demands for an increase in school meal charges and a reduction in the subsidy involved had been growing in Parliament,[53] and the Chancellor of the Exchequer had tried to get cabinet approval for such an increase in November 1966. But the social security ministers had managed to delay the issue, insisting that it be considered in connection with family allowances and other social reforms.[54] They were hoping to sacrifice school meals in favour of extra social spending elsewhere. In early 1967 the press contained a good deal of speculation that the price to be paid for EPAs was an increase in school meal charges, and in February Crosland publicly promised to consider the increase.[55] At the same time Crosland was having to contend with social security ministers who argued that any savings on school meals should be applied to the proposed family allowance increase that was being discussed at the same time.[56] In the final public announcement in July, the annual saving of £25 million from the school meal decision was presented as an offset of the cost of the more controversial family allowance increase. But Crosland's acceptance of the increased charges was crucial. As one of the officials involved put it,

> The Chancellor wanted to keep the whole thing as balanced as possible. Crosland said that he was willing to accept a significant increase in the charges for school meals provided that he got money for school buildings. Without that he would not have got the money.

The strategy worked: £16 million were authorized over two years for a special building programme in EPAs.[57] ...

Although this was the first major acceptance of the EPA principle, it received little public attention. The allocation was announced in the same Commons statement as the increase in family allowances, and in the controversy over the family allowance decision the EPA policy sank from view. None the less, the EPA idea continued to affect the building programme. Crosland's special programme was simply a first step. Despite the hurried introduction of the programme, the proposals submitted by the LEAs to the DES totalled £43 million. But only £16 million was available, and the special programme was not extended beyond the initial two years. In the 1970s, however, the pressure of pupil numbers began to ease at the primary level, leaving greater flexibility in educational spending. Simultaneously the Conservatives came to power determined to give primary education a higher priority, particularly by mounting a drive on old school buildings. In 1971–72 an additional £18 million was made available for replacements in socially deprived areas; in 1972–73 a major four-year programme was launched to replace pre-1903 buildings and in the first year a substantial part of the programme was devoted to deprived areas.[58]

Staffing

In the original Plowden proposal, the single most important element was improved staffing in EPA schools. Schools in deprived urban areas suffered from a depressing cycle of rapid teacher turnover, unfilled vacancies and temporary substitutes. The report urged that the quota for teachers allocated to various areas should be raised for authorities with EPA schools. But since deprived schools often could not fill even their existing allotment of positions, some 'additional incentive' was required. To attract and hold more experienced and successful teachers, the Council recommended a salary supplement of £120 per year for teachers in EPA schools. They also recommended more generous provision of teacher aides than in the rest of the country, with one aide for every two classrooms.[59]

The DES was sympathetic, but once again its powers were limited. It did make marginal adjustments in the quota,[60] but the more important salary proposal had to be thrown into the machinery established for the negotiation of teachers' salaries. Bargaining was conducted through the Burnham Committee, composed of a Teachers' Panel representing the various unions and a Management Panel representing the local authorities and the DES. From the outset the salary supplement was controversial; even before negotiations began, the representatives of both the teachers and the local authorities indicated coolness towards it. The AEC disliked a flat-rate supplement for all teachers in EPAs but left open the possibility of a higher number of 'responsibility posts', which carry a higher salary, in such schools.[61] The NUT, however, was the major stumbling-block. During the 1960s the union's primary goal was a much higher basic salary scale and it was not happy about the endless variety of special supplements that were regularly proposed. They felt that such differentials created troublesome distinctions between teachers and drained away resources from a higher basic scale. In the same week that the Plowden Report was published, the NUT executive rejected a remarkably similar supplement for teachers in immigrant areas.[62]

The minister and the DES decided to recommend some form of supplement, although, in the words of one official, 'We told Crosland that we weren't likely to get much.' They were right. The bargaining situation was tense in 1967. The Management Panel's salary offer was restricted by the Government's incomes policy and was far below union demands; the teachers, on the other hand, were showing greater militancy and were committed to selective sanctions if negotiations failed. With the novel prospect of a partial strike on the horizon, the Government was not in a position to insist on something like EPA supplements in the face of continued union opposition. They could only hope to win over the Teachers' Panel to some limited supplement.

The Government was partially successful, and an exploratory compromise was announced. But it was limited and difficult to administer fairly. The Committee set an arbitrary limit of £400,000 for such supplements, and the unions insisted on a flat-rate payment to all teachers in each EPA school.[63] In combination, these two decisions greatly restricted the number of schools in which supplements could be paid. Even though Plowden's figure of £120 was reduced to £75 per teacher, only 2½ per cent of all schools—rather than Plowden's 10 per cent—could be covered before the money ran out. When LEAs submitted their lists of schools that they felt should qualify, the DES decided that it could not choose from among the large number involved without creating serious anomalies. The Department tried to get the Burnham Committee to reconsider its approach, but the Committee refused; so in November 1968 the Department went ahead, anomalies and all.[64] ...

The second of the Plowden staffing recommendations—a more extensive use of teachers' aides, especially in EPAs—ran into even more determined opposition. The use of such assistants was already a controversial issue. The DES and the LEAs had been recommending greater use of 'auxiliaries' as a solution to teacher shortages; but the teachers' unions strongly opposed the use of unqualified personnel in teaching duties, and feared that semi-qualified auxiliaries would fatally blur the distinction between qualified and unqualified teachers. After lengthy negotiations an uneasy compromise had been reached.[65] The Plowden Report's more emphatic advocacy of aides arrived just after this fragile accord had been accepted, and its approach to the issue pleased no one. The NUT was outraged: 'These are monstrous proposals', declared its President.[66] The DES and LEAs did not want to jeopardize the earlier accord by pushing harder. It was therefore left to local decisions, made in keeping with the accord, to determine the use of teachers' aides, 'including of course the special needs of educational priority areas'.[67]

Thus the demands of established educational groups ensured that the staffing elements of the original EPA proposals emerged only in a truncated and, as will be seen, largely ineffective form.

Parental participation

The fate of the other elements of the original proposal that the Plowden Council considered essential, such as increased parental participation, also depended on the willingness to co-operate of those actually running the schools. The Report laid great stress on parental involvement, community schools and home-school liaison, especially in EPAs, where parental encouragement of the children's education was thought to be particularly lacking. But once again institutional obstacles blocked rapid change. Such matters fell to the LEAs and individual headteachers: more importantly, any progress required overcoming the teachers' traditional desire for professional autonomy and their intense suspicion of Parent-Teacher Associations on the American model. While the NUT was willing to consider the general principle, it insisted that the idea should not be imposed on teachers.[68] At no time was central direction even suggested. 'You can't force a teacher to be nice to a mother by government decree', argued one Plowden member; 'it must be a voluntary movement', echoed Shirley Williams.[69] The Government easily fell into a passive role and limited itself to publishing a pamphlet on good home and school relations. There was never any co-ordinated effort to stimulate parental involvement in EPA areas.

Nursery education

Nursery education was another central element in the original Plowden conception. Newer research was emphasizing how early environmental influences took their toll, and there was a strong belief that compensatory education should start as early as possible. The Plowden Report had advocated nursery education for all, but children in EPAs were to receive priority treatment. Nursery schools should start immediately in these areas and only spread out to more affluent areas as resources became available. Even then, EPAs were to have a permanently higher level of provision, with 50 per cent of poor children attending full-time rather than part-time as envisaged for the rest of the country.[70]

In 1967, however, the Plowden appeal was blocked by other educational programmes that had more political backing. An expansion of nursery education would have required transferring money and teachers away from other sectors of education. But for decades both Conservative and Labour Governments had committed themselves to lowering the size of primary and secondary classes first, and they were reluctant to drain away teachers, particularly from the hard-pressed early years of primary schooling that were the most likely source of nursery teachers. The Plowden Council had sought to circumvent these obstacles. Priority to deprived areas was, in effect, a socially defensible means of phasing in nursery education slowly; a full nation-wide service was not expected until the 1980s. To overcome the manpower problems, they recommended that 'nursery assistants' carry out the main work, with qualified teachers only in a supervisory capacity. Those qualified teachers were to be diverted from the infant schools by a slight raising of the age of entry to school for some children. But the manpower proposals were controversial in the educational world and Crosland deferred them for 'a great deal of study'. The nursery element of the EPA proposal went with it; Crosland was only willing to promise 'to give priority to EPA areas when we are in a position to make some further relaxation on the establishment of new nursery classes'.[71] On its own, the EPA proposal did not possess sufficient political force to break the log-jam.

Yet these obstacles were easily blown away by a much greater political force: race. The popular response to Enoch Powell's speeches on race in April 1968 created a major controversy, and the Government responded immediately with a new Urban Programme designed to assist poor urban areas with heavy levels of immigration. Given the haste with which the programme was rushed into operation, it could do little but gather up and extend existing policies and ideas, and the nursery element of the EPA proposal was swept up into it. Nursery classes did well because, as one official put it, they were 'administratively ready-made'; the school building machinery already existed and classes could be put in place rapidly. The entire DES share of the Urban Programme was spent on nursery education in socially deprived areas. By 1972, some 18,000 new nursery places had been provided, representing a real beginning on the report's call for 50,000 new places in EPAs for four-year-olds plus additional provision at a later date for 3-year-olds.[72]

A general expansion of nursery education did not occur until well into the 1970s, when the pressure of 'basic needs' began to ease. By that time, a major public campaign for nursery education had developed. The drive was well organized by a group called the Campaign for Nursery Education; it enjoyed strong public support, especially among middle-class families; it received consistent backing from the press, the NUT and most LEAs; and it found aggressive parliamentary champions in all parties. 'Politically it was a pushover', recalled one DES official. In 1972 the Conservative Government accepted the principle of universal nursery education and launched a ten-year programme to phase it in. The legislative authority for such an expansion had long existed; all that was required was a DES circular, and during that summer the drafting of the circular began in earnest. But whether the Conservative Government would deny its middle-class supporters and bias the new provision towards poor areas was unclear.

The EPA advocates remained few in number. Lady Plowden was still active, but among the academics the lead increasingly fell to Chelly Halsey. In 1967, when the prospects for major action seemed bleak, Halsey and Michael Young had launched another research effort designed to keep the EPA idea alive. Using their contacts with Crosland and Young's position as chairman of the Social Science Research Council, they obtained joint DES-SSRC funding for four small EPA demonstration-research projects. The programme was directed by Halsey, and by the summer of 1972 he and the project staff were writing up and publicizing their findings. The demonstration projects gave the EPA campaign new research ammunition and an organizational base for the first time. The small staff of men and women involved believed in EPAs and championed the idea publicly; indeed, after the research was completed, the Liverpool project turned itself into a continuing organization called Priority and published a variety of pamphlets and books on the subject.[73]

The influence of these EPA advocates on the nursery education circular, however, was highly dependent on the sympathy of the relevant officials in the Schools and Planning Branches of the DES. These officials drew Halsey into the Department's deliberations. They arranged meetings with the Secretary of State; they offered him advice on the most effective way to formulate his recommendations; they arranged for the research findings to be published by HMSO before the final policy decisions were announced; they sent drafts of the circular to him for comment. In part the Department was co-opting a potential source of public criticism. But in addition many officials were sympathetic to the EPA idea. Its underlying assumptions were increasingly absorbed into departmental thinking; during the same period, for instance, officials were arguing before a Commons committee that 'underprivileged children have an exceptional need for the additional stimulus which can most effectively be provided before the age of five'.[74] Indeed one official argued that Halsey simply 'gave emphasis to the view already current in the Department. The Department was able to pray Halsey in aid of a policy it had decided to pursue anyway.'

Halsey argued strongly that nursery education could be a powerful instrument of compensatory education, but only if it were organized properly. He pressed in two directions.[75] First, he reiterated the original Plowden appeal for strong DES direction. There was a fear that local authorities might not favour their deprived sections because the most forceful demands for nursery education came from middle-class parents. Halsey therefore argued for a new branch of the DES to take responsibility for EPA policy, stricter reliance on objective criteria to identify needy areas, and a financial formula modelled on the Urban Programme to channel money directly to such areas within each local authority. Secondly, he sought a new structure of nursery education to involve parents more. He advocated 'nursery centres', a hybrid structure combining elements of professional nursery schools and amateur parent-run play groups.

Much of the spirit and language of Halsey's arguments were incorporated into the final circular. But at the level of hard administrative directives, his influence was muted. There was to be a modest EPA element in the nursery-school programme: in the initial stages allocations were to be weighted in favour of authorities with the greatest social need. But once again central direction was rejected. The DES could only hope that local authorities with such deprived areas would actually give priority to them.[76] More importantly, although nursery education was initiated in deprived areas first, there was no requirement to fulfil the central EPA idea of permanently higher level of provision there.

Halsey's arguments for a new structure of nursery education had even less impact. The Conservative Secretary of State for Education, Margaret Thatcher, was sympathetic to the idea of greater parental participation, but once again the structure of educational government posed difficulties. Educational administrators were sceptical about whether 'Halsey's Hybrids' would be successful, especially in deprived areas. They believed it administratively easier and cheaper to use the existing machinery and provide nursery education through existing primary schools with standard staffing arrangements.[77] Halsey's ideas also excited the NUT's determined opposition. The idea of parental involvement was still suspect and the union disliked the parent-run playgroup movement, on which Halsey's proposal was partly based. The NUT insisted that nursery education be provided in the professionally run educational system, and they attacked Lady Plowden for arguing that social-science evidence demonstrated that pre-school education would have little lasting effect if parents were not centrally involved.[78] Confronted by administrative convenience and interest-group opposition, the proposals of a solitary social scientist like Halsey withered. The circular made clear that nursery education would be provided through existing primary schools. An early draft of the circular had urged LEAs to 'take all possible steps to encourage parents to play a more active role' and included a paragraph of detailed suggestions from Halsey's report. But after objections from the teachers' unions, these recommendations were progressively watered down until the final circular simply asked LEAs to 'extend opportunities for collaboration' and dropped the detailed suggestions completely.[79]

The evolving pattern

The original EPA *proposal* was clearly a failure. No national programme of compensatory education was ever implemented....

Nevertheless, important improvements in educational provision came to poor areas earlier than they otherwise would have. The greatest casualty was the idea of an integrated programme. Some local authorities were more enthusiastic than others, and a variety of local responses developed. Where DES approval was required, the department could often only hope that LEAs would adopt a common approach in preparing their submissions.[80] Diverse criteria even characterized those aspects of EPA policy that did flow from the central government. The criteria set by the DES for the special building programme were different from those for the salary supplement settled on by the Burnham machinery, which in turn were different from those set under the Urban Programme for the early nursery school elements.[81] In addition, with no formal designation of EPA schools there was no commitment to assist all similarly deprived schools. In the DES programmes an arbitrarily determined amount of money was allotted and LEAs were asked to bid for it. Consequently some schools received one type of assistance but not others. While 570 schools qualified for salary supplements, only 158 benefited from Crosland's special building programme. Anomalies were inevitable.

IV. EPILOGUE

EPA policy reveals the intellectual and institutional processes of policy innovation in conflict.... The problem of educational deprivation was not put on the political agenda by the dynamics of political conflict. Rather, it flowed from a change in the way in which policy-makers interpreted their environment. Social-science information made them aware of the problem; social-science theory defined its nature for them; and social scientists charted the new course of action presented to them. These intellectual initiatives succeeded in shifting the terms of educational debate in Britain.... Concepts, once diffused throughout the policy world, persist long after the initial campaigns have subsided.

However, the salience of the issue and the final policy response were determined by more immediate institutional forces. EPAs never found a major constituency in the world of educational politics. The idea was sustained by the enthusiasm of a small number of intellectuals and professionals, coupled with the sympathy of an equally small number of administrators and politicians. But the educational system is a complex organization, governed by a firmly established framework of administrative-group relations, and sustained political pressure is required to change it. EPAs lacked that kind of support and, as the proposal entered the final phases of the policy process, it was remoulded to fit the contours of the educational world....

NOTES AND REFERENCES

1. Central Advisory Council for Education (England), *Children and their Primary Schools*, London, HMSO, 1967. Hereafter cited as Plowden Report.
2. Ibid., para. 149.
3. Corbett, Anne, *Much To Do About Education*, 3rd edn., London, Council for Educational Advance, 1973, p. 6.
4. See Kogan, Maurice, The Plowden Committee on Primary Education, in Chapman, R.A. (ed.), *The Role of Commissions in Policy-Making*, London, Allen & Unwin, 1973; also Kogan, Maurice and Packwood, Tim, *Advisory Councils and Committees in Education*, London, Routledge & Kegan Paul, 1974.
5. Young had served as Secretary of the Labour Party Research Department throughout Attlee's premiership. On the appointment of the academics to the Plowden Council, see Kogan, Maurice, *The Politics of Education*, Harmondsworth, Middx., Penguin, 1971, pp. 133–4.
6. *The Rise of the Meritocracy, 1870–2033*, Harmondsworth, Middx., Penguin, 1970.
7. Bryce, Maurice, *The Coming of the Welfare State*, 4th edn, London, Batsford, 1968, p. 319; Parkinson, Michael, *The Labour Party and the Organisation of Secondary Education*, London, Routledge & Kegan Paul, 1970, p. 80.
8. Floud, Jean, Halsey, A.H. and Martin, F.M., *Social Class and Educational Opportunity*, London, Heinemann, 1956; Fraser, Elizabeth, *Home Environment and School*, London, University of London Press, 1959; Douglas, J.W.B., *The Home and the School*, London, MacGibbon & Kee, 1964; Douglas, J.W.B., Ross, J.M. and Simpson, H.R., *All Our Future*, London, Peter Davies, 1968.
9. Central Advisory Council for Education, *Early Leaving*, London, HMSO, 1954; *Fifteen to Eighteen*, London, HMSO, 1959; *Half Our Future*, London, HMSO, 1963. Also Committee on Higher Education, *Report*, London, HMSO (Cmnd 2154), 1963, hereafter cited as Robbins Report.
10. *Fifteen to Eighteen*, Vol. 1, p. 8; also *Early Leaving*, pp. 17–23 and appendices.
11. Robbins Report, Appendix One, Part III, pp. 38 and 53; also the main report, pp. 49–52.
12. Douglas et al., *All Our Future*, p. xii.
13. *Report of the Consultative Committee on the Primary School*, London, HMSO, 1931, including the advisory memorandum by Cyril Burt. Also *Report of the Consultative Committee on Secondary Education with Special Reference to Grammar Schools and Technical High Schools*, London, HMSO, 1938.
14. Robbins Report, pp. 49–54; also Appendix One, pp. 38–46.
15. Butcher, H.J. (ed.), *Educational Research in Britain, 1968*, London, University of London Press, 1968, p. 263.

16. Reported in Young, Michael and McGeeney, P., *Learning Begins At Home*, London, Routledge & Kegan Paul, 1968.
17. Plowden Report, ch. 3.
18. Jensen, A.R., How much can we boost I.Q. and scholastic achievement?, *Harvard Educational Review*, 39, 1–123, 1969. Jencks, Christopher, *et al.*, *Inequality: a reassessment of the effect of family and schooling in America*, New York, Basic Books, 1972. On the geographical distribution of poverty in Britain, see Ackland, H., What is a bad school?, *New Society*, 9 September 1971, pp. 450–3.
19. Plowden Report, para. 1185.
20. Kogan, *The Politics of Education*, p. 185.
21. Plowden priority areas seen as a threat, *Daily Telegraph*, 16 May 1967.
22. AEC Executive Committee Minutes, Appendix One, 'Memorandum on the Plowden Report', 30 March 1967; also Sir William Armstrong in *Education*, 20 January 1967. For the similar position of the general local authority organisations, see Association of Municipal Corporations, Observations on the Report of the CACE, *Municipal Review*, September 1967; and County Councils Association, Observations on the Plowden Report.
23. NUT, Plowden: the union's comments on some of the major issues, 1967; for the NAHT response, see *Guardian*, 31 May 1967.
24. NUT, *Annual Report: 1967*, pp. 44–47; also NAHT, Commentary on the Plowden Report, 1967.
25. *Guardian*, 9 September 1967.
26. See leading articles in *The Times, Guardian, Financial Times, Daily Mail* and *Sun*, all 10 January 1967; *Observer* and *Sunday Times*, 15 January 1967. The *Daily Telegraph*, which disliked the proposal, was in a distinct minority (10 January 1967).
27. AMC, Observations.... On the pressure for equal treatment at the local level, see Kogan, Maurice and van der Eyken, W., *County Hall: The Role of the Chief Education Officer*, Harmondsworth, Middx., Penguin, 1973, p. 165.
28. Plowden Report, para. 173.
29. *Guardian*, 23 August 1967.
30. House of Commons Debates, 776, cols 182–3 (written answers).
31. Quoted in Kogan, *The Politics of Education*, pp. 173–4. On early departmental uneasiness about the Councils, see Kogan and Packwood, *Advisory Councils and Committees in Education*, ch. 2.
32. Testimony to the Select Committee on Education and Science, Session 1969–70, *Teacher Training*, Minutes of Evidence, pp. 417–24.
33. See Crosland, C.A.R., *The Future of Socialism*, London, Jonathan Cape, 1956.
34. See, for instance, Crosland's testament to his discussions with Young in *The Future of Socialism*, p. 235.
35. HCD 743, col. 755.
36. For Boyle's testimony on the impact of educational sociologists on his own thinking, see Kogan, *Politics of Education*, pp. 91–2.
37. Conservative Party, *Action Not Words* (1966); for the Conservatives' welcome of Plowden, see Boyle, HCD 743, col. 738; also Corbett, Anne, The Tory educators, *New Society*, 22 May 1969.
38. Boyle was the only person to refer to EPAs at Conservative party conferences (*Conservative Party Annual Conference Report*, 1967, p. 61, and 1968, p. 46).
39. *TES*, 2 June 1967; *Education*, 7 April 1967; *Guardian*, 15 September 1967; *TES*, 1 March 1968.
40. See Griffith, J.A.C., *Central Departments and Local Authorities*, London, Allen & Unwin, 1966.
41. See Manzer, R.A., *Teachers and Politics in England and Wales*, Manchester, Manchester University Press, 1970, and Coates, R.D., *Teachers' Unions and Interest Group Politics*, Cambridge, Cambridge University Press, 1972.
42. *Education: A Framework for Expansion* (London: HMSO, Cmnd 5174, 1972), para. 4.
43. Plowden Report, paras. 153–4, 169–70.
44. NUT, Union's comments..., p. 3; AEC Memorandum...; for ILEA opposition, see *Education*, 7 July 1967, p. 1. On general LEA opposition to centralization see Kogan, Maurice, *Educational Policy-making*, London, Allen & Unwin, 1975, ch. 6.
45. HCD 743, col. 756. For a satire on the government's refusal to initiate a co-ordinated programme, see *Education*, 17 November 1967.

46. HCD 755, cols 1651–2. For similar refusals to seek to influence LEAs on specific parts of the proposal, see also HCD 760, cols 1602–3; and 806, col. 453.
47. Plowden Report, para. 133; also paras 1080–5.
48. Ibid., para. 170(iv).
49. AEC, Memorandum...
50. DES, *The School Building Survey, 1968*, London, HMSO, 1965; NUT, *The State of Our Schools* (1962); CACE, *Half Our Future*.
51. DES Circular 11/67. I am indebted to the Department for checking the files on the origins of this clause.
52. HCD 743, col. 756.
53. See, for instance, Estimates Committee, Session 1966–67, *Fifth Report*.
54. Crossman Diary, 17 November 1966.
55. *Guardian*, 3 February 1967.
56. Crossman notes a lengthy argument in cabinet on this (Diary, 19 July 1967).
57. HCD 751, cols. 56–8.
58. DES, *Reports on Education*, No. 71.
59. Plowden Report, paras. 158–62, 170.
60. DES Circular 1/67 and DES Letter to Chief Education Officers (RS 26/9), 13 June 1968.
61. AEC Memorandum....
62. For the rejection of the supplement in immigrant areas, see *The Teacher*, 20 January 1967; NUT coolness to the EPA version is seen in ibid., 13 January 1967. On the NUT's general salary goals, see Manzer, *Teachers and Politics*, ch. 5.
63. For an account of the bargaining, see *The Teacher*, 1 March 1968.
64. HCD 769, col. 167; and 773, cols 890–1.
65. *Education*, 20 January 1967. On the background to the dispute, see Manzer, *Teachers and Politics*, pp. 103–7.
66. NUT, *Annual Report 1967*, pp. 46–7. The union was particularly upset at the idea that teachers agreeing to work with aides would receive higher pay. See also AEC, Memorandum...
67. HCD 806, col. 453 (written answers); also 743, col. 761.
68. NUT, The Union's comments... On teachers' attitudes towards such participation, see Kogan, *Educational Policy-making*, pp. 57–61; and Young and McGeeney, *Learning Begins at Home*.
69. HCD 753, col. 588.
70. Plowden Report, para. 165.
71. HCD 743, cols 756–9. On the factors blocking expansion of nursery education see Blackstone, T., *A Fair Start*, London, Allen Lane, Penguin, 1971.
72. DES Evidence to the Expenditure Committee (Public Expenditure Sub-Committee) Session 1971–72, p. 47. For the Plowden Report's estimate of the needed places, see Table 36, col. 11.
73. Midwinter, Eric, *Projections*, London, Ward Lock Education, 1972; *Priority Education*, Harmondsworth, Middx., Penguin, 1972; and *Education and the Community*, London, Allen & Unwin, 1975.
74. DES, Memorandum on Nursery Education, Expenditure Committee (Public Expenditure Sub-Committee), Session 1971–72; also the testimony of J. R. Jameson and J. D. Brierly.
75. Halsey, A. H., Memorandum on pre-school provision in EPAs (no date); Notes on meeting with Mrs. Thatcher (26 July 1972); Notes on draft circular on nursery education (7 September 1972). The Projects' findings were published in Halsey, A.H. (ed.), *Educational Priority*, London, HMSO, 1972.
76. *Education: A Framework for Expansion*, para. 28.
77. Their reservations were detailed in a letter from J. R. Jameson (Assistant Secretary, Schools Branch) to Halsey, 25 May 1972; and DES Minute from Jameson to Rodwell, 4 July 1972.
78. *Observer*, 17 June 1973. The NUT's position is outlined in its pamphlet, *Provision of Pre-school Education* (no date).
79. Draft Circular on Nursery Education, 22 August 1972; DES Circular 2/73.
80. HCD 758, cols 203–4 (written answers).
81. See, for example, *Education*, 24 March 1967.

17

Class Inequality in Education
two justifications, one evaluation but no hard evidence

JAMES MURPHY

Though no necessary relationship exists between class disparity in education and class inequality in education, educational commentators have conventionally taken the existence of one to indicate the existence of the other, and have sought by exposition to justify this convention by two rather different strategies. The first strategy, which might be called 'the structural exclusion account', is an argument much favoured by the more radical academic of a Marxist persuasion, whilst the second, which might be termed 'the cultural dispossession account', is an argument adopted for the most part by less radical commentators of a Fabianist persuasion. Though both accounts offer somewhat contrasting, sometimes antithetical, justifications for this convention, in that the first explains class difference in educational representation in terms of 'structural bias', the second in terms of 'cultural handicap', neither account, however, actually sustains this equation in a manner which is, in a social scientific sense, respectable. The reason in each case is the same, for neither account takes seriously class difference in educational aspiration.

TWO ACCOUNTS: TWO JUSTIFICATIONS

At source, the structural account takes class disparity in education to be the consequence of the unequal distribution of power and privilege in capitalist society. Variously interpreted, such inequality in power and privilege is taken at the highest level of abstraction to be responsible for class differentials in

Source: From Murphy, J., Class inequality in education, *British Journal of Sociology*, Vol. 32, No. 2, 1981, pp. 182–200.

access to knowledge,[1] and at a more comfortable level of reflection to be responsible for class differentials in access to selective education.[2] One step removed, such inequalities in power and privilege have been seen as responsible for the class differential provision of educational resources[3] and for the class differential consumption of such resources.[4] Less directly, the unequal distribution of power and privilege has been taken as instrumental in structuring ability[5] and in shaping attitudes to education.[6] Rarely taken to be conspiratorial, never taken to be accidental, the exclusion of the working class from selective and higher education has at a lower level of abstraction been attributed to the culturally loaded 'ethos' professed by the school,[7] to the culturally loaded curriculum presented by the school[8] and to the culturally loaded tests adopted by the school.[9] Covert rather than overt class bias has been further identified in the expectation of teachers[10] which results in the working class being differentially tracked into educationally terminal schools,[11] streams[12] and colleges.[13] More recently, the working class have been seen as excluded by the zoning strategies of the school, which through residential segregation[14] or white flight[15] cut the working-class child off from that emerging condition for educational equality—access to affluent classmates.[16]

By this account the working class stand structurally excluded. The cultural account, on the other hand, whilst rarely denying the determinate influence of inequality in power and privilege, preferred for its part to focus in general on the cultural consequences of such structural influences and in particular on those emotional, psychological attributes which through extended habituation with poverty effectively deprived the working class of an equal chance. Acknowledged by the main architects of this account to be structurally generated,[17] the immediate source of prevailing educational inequality was, however, identified as residing primarily in these cultural, emotional and psychological conditions. Though now in something of a decline, it was an account which was at the time uncompromisingly deployed as by Plowden, who echoing Moynihan declared that 'the educational disadvantage of being born the child of an unskilled worker is both financial and psychological'.[18] Uncompromisingly advanced, it was a view which was uncompromisingly sustained by research, which identified in the cultural milieu of the working class a matrix of factors and forces which through extended socialization left the economically disadvantaged, educationally disadvantaged. Like the range of 'bias' identified by the structural account as in need of eradication, the range of handicaps identified by the cultural account as in need of amelioration was likewise comprehensive. Perhaps not surprisingly, given its centrality in Lewis's classic description of 'the culture of poverty', the one handicap most recurrently cited as hindering the realization of educational equality was the existence within the working class of 'a strong present-time orientation, with little ability to defer gratification and plan for the future'.[19] Sometimes regarded as a cultural imperative, sometimes as a personality attribute, such impulsiveness on the part of the working class has long been canvassed by 'cultural' theorists and indeed by structural theorists of catholic taste, as effectively depriving, dispossessing and disinheriting the working class of an equal chance.[20] Taken as responsible for the low achievement and early leaving of the working class, this reluctance to make sacrifices, as Bourdieu puts it,[21] has long been complemented by the often noted low cultural saliency of education in the culture of poverty.

To these more obvious handicaps, subsequent research added more, which, if rather more subtle in their operation, were no less debilitating in their effects. Deriving again from a focus on the distinctive socialization experienced by the working class, an experience typically characterized by inadequate maternal instruction and paternal interest,[22] the working class emerged handicapped further, limited on the one hand conceptually,[23] and restricted on the other linguistically.[24] By this account, then, the working class stand 'culturally dispossessed' of a fair start.

Structurally excluded or culturally dispossessed, the persistence of working-class under-representation stands in both accounts as an enduring testament to the persistence of unequal educational opportunity. The inevitable consequence of structural bias in the first account and the predictable outcome of cultural handicap in the second, class disparity not surprisingly emerges in both as class inequality.

TWO JUSTIFICATIONS: ONE LIMITATION

Paradoxically, however, this equation of educational disparity with educational inequality has yet to be sustained in either account, for whilst it is, of course, true that both accounts, rooted as they are in the empirical tradition, advance much in the way of observation, it is however equally true, if less apparently so, that both accounts offer little, which when viewed even with charity could be construed as constituting evidence of educational inequality. The reason in each case is the same. In each account all that has been documented is the obvious: namely, that there are class differences in education. As evidence of class differences in education, such observations are, to be fair, difficult to fault, for it is indeed the case that it takes longer to count middle-class heads in selective education than it does to count those of the working class. More specifically it is probably also the case that there exist differences in facilities and funding—though in America less striking than was previously thought[25]—that there are differences in teacher quality and in teacher turnover, and that for sake of clarity that what counts for knowledge in the school is more in accord with middle-class expectations than working-class expectations. In addition, one would not want to deny the observations that teachers tend to regard the working class as less able, that the working class are alienated by the school, that they participate less in extracurricular activities and that they leave earlier.

Likewise, with the cultural dispossession account one does not wish to deny that there are cognitive, linguistic, emotional and motivational differences between the classes or indeed that the working class have a lower measured IQ, though in this instance, one might question whether some of the imputed qualities such as lack of impulse control, linguistic deprivation and cognitive impairment are as class specific as they are made out. Reservations aside, such observation provides on the whole convincing and varied evidence of class differences in education. As evidence of class inequality in education, however, such observations are without exception difficult to accept, for at no point do such observations warrant, at least in sociological terms, the critical interpretation placed upon them—the interpretation that such difference, be it real or imagined, constitutes, as in the structural account, evidence of exclusion or, as in the cultural account, evidence of dispossession. It is unwarranted, for by a curious oversight neither the structural nor cultural account have controlled for the eminent possibility, suggested by such observations—that such difference is simply difference. This point can be put more fully if rather more formally, and it is this, that since it makes little sense in a pluralistic society to speak of exclusion or dispossession, unless there is evidence in the first instance that those 'excluded' or 'dispossessed' actually wanted what they are supposedly excluded from or dispossessed of, it appears by the same token a critical if minimal condition for converting class disparity in education into class inequality in education that, other things being equal, universal demand for such education be first documented, or if demand for education is less than total, that such differential demand be itself shown to be the product of structural or cultural inequality. When and only when one or other of these holding conditions has been met have the sociological as opposed to ideological grounds for claiming class inequality in education been established, for then and only then has that ever present possibility that such difference is simply difference been sociologically and scientifically contained.

Contrary to appearances, however, such holding conditions are nowhere fulfilled; for it is significant on further inspection that the empirical requirement for such a conversion has been met in both accounts by an experiential rather than evidential response, by an experiential response, moreover, which, taking education to be a natural aspiration of man, quietly circumvents the need to document either the universality of educational demand or the inequity of differential demand. Though this experiential response is typically implicit, the consequent suspension of enquiry that attends such a belief is recurrently betrayed by arguments which, in presuming education to be a natural desire, transform these holding conditions from being matters of empirical dispute into matters of indisputable fact. Based on collective conviction rather than on reflexive inspection, on a conviction more exactly that suspends inspection, these holding conditions remain, in the arguments of the Egalitarian, strikingly unmet.

THE DIFFERENT MANIFESTATIONS OF THIS LIMITATION

An attribute of both structural and cultural accounts in general, this failure to meet the documentary demand for converting class difference in educational representation into class inequality in education provides a common, if less than ideal, bond between otherwise diverse perspectives and conflicting sentiments. By a perverse irony, moreover, it is a failure which is at its most apparent when it is at its most critical, notably in the commentaries of those who most influence the direction and most determine the structure of this debate.

Notable in this regard is the pioneering work of Glass, who from an observation that '...of undergraduates...only a quarter were the sons and daughters of manual workers', proceeds to claim the need for further reconstruction '...if we are to combine diversity of educational provision with equality of educational opportunity'.[26] Whilst the rationale for such a conversion is not without merit, for Glass cites evidence for explaining such differential representation as the consequence of differential demand, it is a rationale, however, that is empirically less than adequate. It is less than adequate for at no point does Glass actually show such class differences in attitudes to be contingent on structural bias. Simply put, there is no evidence, cited or otherwise, for taking class differences in demand to be the product of structural or cultural inequalities. There is by the same token no reason, at least empirically speaking, for converting class disparity in educational representation into class inequality of educational opportunity.

Likewise, in that other authoritative statement on post-war reform, Douglas makes a similar if uncharacteristic jump from observed difference to proclaimed inequality. As with Glass, Douglas starts with the observation, that

> ...in the upper middle class there are 14 pupils in grammar schools for every one in a technical school whereas in the lower manual working class, there are only two pupils in grammar schools for every one in a technical school[27]

and proceeds despite recurrent emphasis on class differences in parental aspiration[28] and in pupil attitudes[29] to declare that

> this is a distribution of selective secondary school places that can hardly be justified in terms of social equity or, for that matter, of national interest.[30]

As with Glass, the incompatibility of such a distribution with social equity is passed over as self-evident, and above sociological debate.

In an equally striking fashion this same failure to empirically resolve this question is evident in that most recent example of demographic analysis, the Oxford Mobility Study. A longitudinal comparative study of social mobility in Britain, it considers amongst other issues, '... the chances of proceeding from given class origins to a university degree for those educated before and after the 1944 Act'.[31] The finding, in line with previous demographic research, is not unpredictable, for whilst '... all origin categories have increased their output of graduates, the proportion of graduates remains correlated with origin and the differences between them have increased'.[32] The interpretation, again in line with previous demographic research, is, if unwarranted, not unpredictable, for such a statistic at least in the view of its leading author is taken to 'show no clear trend towards the elimination of class inequalities in educational attainment'.[33] In one sense, a superficial sense, Halsey is indeed correct, for as the statistic is about social class differences in education, and not about social class inequalities in education, it does not, indeed cannot, indicate anything about class inequalities in educational attainment. In another sense, a rather more substantial sense, however, Halsey is, if not incorrect, at least premature in his judgement about the prevailing class inequalities in education, for it is a judgement that follows neither from a documentation of universal educational demand nor from a documentation as inequitous, of differential demand for education. Unhampered by such evidential considerations, it is a judgement that remains in the last analysis tentative rather than definitive. Such empirical indifference at this point of critical significance undermines also Halsey's more recent deliberations on the inequity of British education, for once again, though this time with Heath and Ridge, Halsey reaches the same verdict from the same unsubstantiated equation of class disparity in education with class inequality in education. This time, however, such an experiential leap from educational disparity to educational inequality has resulted not only in the empirical but also in the conceptual bankruptcy of the claim, for it is a claim which is made despite recurrent acknowledgements of class disparity in educational aspirations, despite what is described in the penultimate line of the text as '... the stubborn resistance of class and class related culture'.[34] Their analysis of 'post-secondary education' is a case in point, where acknowledging from the start that by this rung of the educational ladder '... half have chosen to have done with formal learning'[35] they proceed nonetheless to promptly ignore this remark by presenting as evidence of '... class inequalities at different stages of the educational system',[36] statistics which simply describe class disparities at different stages of the educational system. Taken as confirming that '... class inequalities are crucial at each successive stage of the educational career',[37] such evidenced disparity is presented by Halsey, Heath and Ridge as a testament to '... class bias in selection'.[38] Like the first claim, this claim of class bias is, however, not sustained empirically, for though the authors freely take the rapidly reducing numbers in post-compulsory education to be in a large measure the consequence of 'new found freedoms'[39] in general and of 'the enormous drop-out of working-class boys' in particular[40] they singularly fail to contain the spectre of self-selection suggested by the former, and the spectre of class disparity in self-selection suggested by the latter. Studiously ignoring rather than strenuously exorcizing this spectre of class different tastes for education, Halsey, Heath and Ridge end up with an indictment of British education which is not only empirically premature, in that it fails to control for class different taste before claiming class inequality, but is in addition conceptually confused, in that it derives from a computation of 'unequal chance' which simply entails 'different choices'. It is a confusion neatly embedded in their summarizing remarks, where, evaluated as the consequence of unequal chances, class disparity in education is then explained as the consequence of different choices. As they put it:

> ... The boy from a privileged school or from a privileged social background had a much higher chance than his unprivileged contemporary of gaining a place at university. These inequalities however were very largely a consequence of earlier decisions in the educational process.[41]

Wanting it both ways, Halsey, Heath and Ridge end up with an explanation and evaluation of class disparity in education, which is sociologically less than enlightening, for whilst it is not inconceivable that different choices might on occasion be the consequence of unequal chances, the point here, however, is that, in so taking different choice and unequal chance to be one and the same, Halsey, Heath and Ridge not only confuse the matter altogether, but fail in the process to document what is here crucial, namely that class disparity in educational aspiration is, in some sense or other, the product of inegalitarian forces.

A characteristic of empirical research, this failure to document the inequity of differential aspiration, also flaws more theoretical treatments of class inequality in education. Notable in this regard is the influential thesis of Bourdieu and Passeron, a thesis which not unlike that of Halsey, Heath and Ridge evaluates class difference in educational representation as inegalitarian[42] yet explains such inequality as the consequence of class differences in educational aspiration—'pupils of working-class origin', as they put it, 'are more likely to eliminate themselves from secondary education by declining to enter'.[43] Unlike Halsey, Heath and Ridge, however, Bourdieu and Passeron are somewhat perturbed by this mis-match between an evaluation which proclaims inequality and an explanation which invokes differential aspiration, and accordingly they try to re-align the evaluation with the explanation by taking differential aspiration to be itself a consequence of inequality. It is an adjustment, which if not particularly novel, is nonetheless strikingly radical, for it turns on the intervening claim that 'subjective expectations' are the deterministic consequence of 'objective conditions'.[44] It is an adjustment, however, which has little to commend it empirically, for far from carefully documenting the existence of this posited relationship between 'subjective expectations' and 'objective conditions', Bourdieu and Passeron merely protest its existence. In one sense, however, this is all that is required, for this dramatic reversal of the traditional view of reality and individuality turns on a more fundamental claim, on what Bourdieu and Passeron take to be the indispensable principle of sociology, namely that '... every power to exert symbolic violence... adds its own specifically symbolic force to those power relations'.[45] Lacking the clarity of Descartes' 'cogito ergo sum', this first principle of Bourdieu and Passeron lacks also its compulsion, for even if one were persuaded that '... every power which manages to impose meanings and to impose them as legitimate... adds its own specifically symbolic force to those power relations',[46] it is a moot point in a society with half its population 'declining to enter secondary education'[47] whether education is in fact covered by a principle which is concerned only with those powers which 'manage to impose meanings'. Without some additional and in this instance rather ethnocentric assumption to the effect that individuals of all classes are naturally predisposed to education, Bourdieu and Passeron's first principle does not clearly, still less logically, embrace education.

Other theorists, however, are rather more direct and get around the complication raised by class difference in educational aspiration by spontaneously declaring such a difference to be itself an example of educational inequality. Thus Evetts, for example, when faced with what she describes as 'apathetic and directly hostile parents',[48] side-steps the need for further evidence by declaring that such a difference is also inegalitarian. As she disarmingly puts it, such factors as 'motivation, parental interest, norms of aspiration, teacher quality etc. are known to be unequally distributed between social groups'.[49] Others, if no less direct, are, however, rather more abrupt, as, for example, Husen, who manages to get around the need for further evidence by blindly affirming on the one hand Orwell's famous dictum that 'some are more equal than others' and by blandly citing, on the other, as an example of such inequality, class differences in educational orientations. As he puts it:

> Since, from the outset 'some are more equal than others', for instance have better educated parents, we find in both socialist and capitalist countries striking class differences in participation in advanced education.[50]

Evidently for Husen, as for Evetts, such disparity is self-evidently inequality, which is fortuitous for in neither case is any evidence advanced for so taking differential aspiration to be inequality.

Other theorists for their part get around the problem posed by class difference in educational aspiration by simply ignoring it altogether.[51]

Such failure to take seriously the holding conditions for converting class disparity in education into class inequality in education is as much an oversight in American research analysis as it is in European research. One typical example of such empirical indifference is to be found in that uncompromising indictment of Bowles and Gintis of 'the total functioning of U.S. education', 'a system' which they claim 'provides eloquent testimony to the ability of the well-to-do to perpetuate, in the name of equality of opportunity, an arrangement which consistently yields to themselves disproportional advantages'.[52] It is a claim that rests in part on the observation that 'children from less well off families are ... less likely to have graduated from high school', and in part on the further observation that such a difference is not 'simply a reflection of unequal intellectual ability or ... of different levels of scholastic achievement in high school'.[53] It is a claim, however, that is as it stands unwarranted, for even if these alternatives had been adequately controlled, the further alternative that such differential attainment is the consequence of differential aspiration is left running wild. True the authors try to 'head off' this possibility by asserting that such difference in years of schooling '... thwarts the aspirations and need of working people',[54] but it is an attempt that is less than convincing, for not only is this asserted universality of demand empirically unsupported by hard evidence, it is logically undermined by a later claim '... that the educational aspirations of unorganized common people ... are almost impossible to discover'.[55] Rarely, however, is such a failure to document the inequity of differential aspirations quite so explicit, for typically such a failure is masked in both the cultural and structural account by an evaluation of differential aspiration which presumes in each case that such difference is in some sense pathological. Though such an assumption, once sustained, would of course relieve both the cultural and structural theorist of the obligation to document the inequity of differential aspiration, the point here, however, is that rarely if ever has such an assumption actually been justified.

Until its current demise, the classic example of such a practice was to be found in the cultural account, where without a shred of empirical support one commentator after another observed class difference in aspiration, called it deficit, and demanded its remediation, in the name of equality.

Bronfenbrenner's review of the literature on cultural difference is in this regard typical, for like the theorists surveyed, Bronfenbrenner simply takes cultural disparity, whatever its form, to be the main source of educational inequality. Indeed on this Bronfenbrenner is uncompromising, as is well illustrated by his opening remarks 'whatever their origin, the immediate overwhelming and stubborn obstacles to achieving quality and equality in education now lie in the character and way of life of the American negro, as in the indifference and hostility of the white community'.[56] However, empirically speaking he is not convincing, for when he comes to sustain this assertion the main evidence advanced is not evidence of the inegalitarian determination of such cultural difference in motivation but is, more simply, evidence of cultural difference in motivation between the negro and white child. Described as a 'lack of motivation' on the part of the negro child, this difference in motivation between negro and white children is then taken not as a good reason for questioning the prevailing view on the inequity of negro attainment but paradoxically as a good reason for rejecting the prevailing view of educational equality. 'Objective equality of opportunity is', he declares, 'not enough. The negro child must also be able to profit from the educational situation in which he finds himself. This he cannot do, if he lacks the background and motivation necessary for learning.'[57] Unfortunately for Bronfenbrenner, however, this last observation weakens rather than strengthens his case, for whilst it would of course be a mockery, by any view of equality, if the school disabled the negro child, what is here rather more pertinent however is whether in fact, given cultural differences in motivation, such a situation actually prevails. On this Bronfenbrenner is unhelpful, for apart from calling it a deficit, Bronfenbrenner does not at any point specify in what sense such motivational disparity is inegalitarian. True, Bronfenbrenner does try to render this indictment of the American negro and the American educational system more plausible, by suggesting such motivational difference is rooted in deeper cultural factors such as paternal absence, latent femininity, exaggerated masculinity, impoverished environments and inadequate socialization; however, such a strategy serves only to confound rather than clarify his claim for not only is the egalitarian status of such cultural difference left empirically unexamined, but the relationship of such cultural factors with educational motivation is likewise left unspecified. Pushing further back into his analysis the empirical requirement for converting educational disparity into educational inequality, Bronfenbrenner ends up burying rather than meeting this requirement, for what now needs to be documented as inegalitarian is not the determinants of representational disparity but the determinants of aspirational disparity. Failing to document either, Bronfenbrenner ends up with an indictment of American education which is empirically empty.

However, if the cultural account provides the classic example of how to side-step the empirical requirement for converting educational disparity into educational inequality, the structural account provides the most systematic in the work of Boudon, whose thesis on educational inequality never once meets, or indeed tries to meet, the documentary requirement for converting educational disparity into educational inequality. A somewhat surprising failure in a theory of educational inequality, such a failure is, in this context, however, not in the least unexpected. It is not unexpected for by the opening paragraph of his Preface Boudon has already admitted that when he is talking about class inequality in education he is in fact talking about class disparity in education. As he puts it clearly and unequivocally,

> By inequality of educational opportunity (IEO), I mean the differences in level of educational attainment according to social background.[58]

A frank admission; it is, however, not quite a full confession, for in addition to taking educational inequality to mean educational disparity, Boudon in the next breath takes them to mean one and the same, by taking as given that a measure of educational disparity is a measure of educational inequality. As he puts it, again unequivocally,

> Thus a society is characterized by a certain amount of IEO if, for instance, the probability of going to college is smaller for a worker's son than for a lawyer's son.[59]

For Boudon, then, educational inequality means educational disparity only in the sense that they both mean the same. Whilst semantically there may be little to choose between these two assumptions, as both play fast and loose with the traditional distinction between disparity and inequality, the latter is sociologically speaking rather more critical than the former. It is more critical, for whilst the former gives good reason to suspect that what Boudon is about to present as a theory of educational inequality is yet another theory of educational disparity, the latter gives little reason to expect either, for with educational disparity and educational inequality so tightly linked such that educational disparity is, regardless of its determination, a measure of educational inequality, Boudon is left with a model of the world which simply cannot handle difference, indifference or dissent as a legitimate educational response. Hardly the assumption that theories of educational disparity, not to say educational inequality, are made of; such, however, is Boudon's central assumption. Underwriting both the descriptive and explanatory elements of his theory, it is an assumption which leaves Boudon with a theory of educational inequality which is at once empirically unwarranted and conceptually unconvincing.

At an empirical level, the assumption that a measure of educational disparity is a measure also of educational inequality is nothing, if not convenient, for by this assumption, all that is evidentially required to demonstrate the existence of class inequality in education is to indicate the existence of class disparity in education. An undemanding requirement in a society characterized on all fronts by class difference in educational representation, it is for Boudon, however, a particularly felicitous requirement, for in setting aside the normal requirement of demonstrating class discrimination before claiming class inequality, it allows Boudon to side-step what is, by the normal requirement, the most striking deficiency of his data—notably its singular lack of evidence, cited or otherwise, of class discrimination in education. Too seductive to resist, when the only data in the bank is data on class disparity, it is an assumption that leaves Boudon with a theory of educational inequality, whose statistical precision is somewhat out of phase with its sociological compulsion. Nowhere is such a mis-match clearer than when Boudon sets out to build up an international profile on educational inequality, where after a complicated statistical preamble on how to convert raw data on class differences in educational representation into a form which admits of cross-cultural comparison, Boudon proceeds, without further ado, to take such statistics as parsimonious measures of class inequality in education. Thus, having derived what he calls a 'disparity index'—a disparity index is 'a crude estimation of the number of times a youngster with a high social class background has more chance of attending college than youngsters with a low social background'—he concludes that 'IEO is high in all countries when college level is considered'.[60] However, as the disparity index for these countries is not uniform, his general conclusion on the high rate of inequality is accordingly modified to fit the fluctuations in his 'disparity index'. Thus, since the disparity index for Portugal is unusually high and since the disparity index for Belgium is relatively low, Boudon infers the same is true of educational inequality—as he puts it,

> IEO rates are similar in most continental countries of Western Europe except for Portugal, where they appear as higher, and Belgium where they appear as lower.[61]

Similarly, because of their low rating on the disparity index, Norway, Sweden and the United States are seen 'to have relatively low IEO rates',[62] and since East European countries return a similarly low rating when '... the same kind of disparity index'[63] is applied to their rate of college attendance, Boudon concludes with similar ease that '... the IEO rates of Eastern Europe are probably closer to those of the U.S.'.[64]

Capable of generating rather more fine grained observations on educational inequality, this disparity index when applied, as, for example, to changes over time in the class composition of education, enables Boudon to arrive at the conclusion that IEO likewise changes. Thus finding that over time '... the probability of, say, a worker's son attending high school increases much more considerably than the probability of, say, a professional's son',[65] Boudon is moved to claim that '... Western societies are characterized by a steady and slow decline of IEO'.[66]

A convenient if less than convincing equation at an empirical level, this equation of educational disparity with educational inequality proves at a conceptual level to be neither, for it leaves Boudon with a 'contradiction' of some consequence and a 'paradox' of some intractability.

The contradiction is perhaps best illustrated by taking as seriously, as does Boudon, his measure of class inequality in education, for if it is indeed the case that class disparity in education is a measure of class inequality in education, then whatever the origin of such 'disparity', it cannot at least in logic be 'difference'. For Boudon, however, it is, for Boudon not only parsimoniously measures class inequality in education by class disparity in education, but equally parsimoniously explains such disparity in educational representation by difference in educational aspirations. Indeed, as Boudon is at pains to stress on a number of occasions, this is the distinctive feature of his theory of IEO. As he puts it:

> ... it introduces the assumption that people will make different choices according to their position in the stratification system.[67]

Or as he subsequently elucidates:

> ...in other words, it is assumed...that...they behave within decisional fields whose parameters are a function of their position in the stratification system.[68]

More simply described as 'differences in aspiration as a function of social background',[69] these secondary effects of stratification, as he calls them, are taken by Boudon as explaining class differences in education. As he puts it,

> ...the secondary effects of stratification on IEO are, other things being equal, probably much more important than their primary effects. In other words, the attendance at college of a disproportionate number of students from the higher class is probably much more attributable to the different systems of expectations generated by different social backgrounds than to the different cultural backgrounds.[70]

Class differences in educational aspirations, then, explain class differences in educational representation. Whilst this is not a particularly surprising claim in educational research, it is in this context somewhat confusing. It is confusing, for what Boudon is now left with is an index of class inequality, in the form of class differences in educational representation, whose origin is not in inequality but in difference. Of course, such a contradiction is not, in any sense, irredeemable or insuperable, for were such differences in aspiration shown to be inegalitarian, such a contradiction would indeed be quickly resolved: in this context, however, this contradiction is not quite so clearly dispatched, for Boudon never once actually shows such difference to be inegalitarian. Whilst strictly speaking such a failure casts a dark shadow over the internal coherence of Boudon's thesis, and thus over his conclusion that '...stratification is the principal factor responsible for inequality of educational opportunity',[71] a more charitable interpretation might possibly grant that Boudon technically resolves the contradiction, for he does at least on two occasions suggest that such aspirational diversity is the consequence of economic inequality.[72] On innumerable occasions Boudon does, it is true, assert that such aspirational diversity is the consequence of stratification,[73] but as stratification even in his terms describes only difference—'we assume stratification generates and actually describes a number of differences between people'[74]—such assertions naturally do not count in this matter. However, even if Boudon is given the benefit of the doubt and even if his assertion about the causative influence of economic inequality is accepted as successfully averting the contradiction, such a resolution leaves in its wake a rather more ticklish problem, for in assuming differential aspiration to be inegalitarian, Boudon merely 'trades in' one logical contradiction for a sociological paradox of rather greater intransigence.

The paradox, like the contradiction, can be simply described, for as a direct consequence of such a resolution Boudon is now left with a theory of IEO, which, if logically consistent, is no longer sociologically competent. It is no longer competent, for with aspirational as well as representational disparity now assumed to be inegalitarian, Boudon is left with a theory of educational inequality which ends, as it starts, by begging the very question in contention by assuming educational disparity to be educational inequality. Making the one assumption that he cannot make if he is to demonstrate the inequity of class disparity in education, Boudon not only reduces sociology to the status of a metaphysical underlabourer, whose task is to justify rather than verify conventional beliefs, but so neuters reality of its complexity and diversity that what now stands as sociologically problematic about the inequity of class disparity in education is that it was ever seen to be sociologically problematic.

At its most influential, however, this failure to document the inequity of class disparity in education flaws the otherwise critical and empirical work of Jencks and his associates. It is a commentary, in addition, which illustrates in a particularly graphic form the confusion which attends such a failure.

Having at their disposal a mass of statistical evidence on the quantitative and qualitative differences that exist between the classes, Jencks and his associates break with tradition by treating seriously, at least at the outset, class differences in educational aspirations. A recurrent concern, such sensitivity furnishes 'Inequality' with its most iconoclastic prescription. It is a sensitivity more particularly that underwrites at a prescriptive level that uncompromising demand for the provision of alternative benefits for those who get relatively few benefits from education, a prescription that turns in the first instance, and last analysis, on taking as 'basic' class differences in aspiration. As they put it more trenchantly, 'If people do not want to attend school or college, an egalitarian society ought to accept this as a legitimate decision and give these people subsidized job training, subsidized housing, or perhaps simply a lower tax rate.'[75] It is a sensitivity in addition that undermines at a descriptive level the explanatory certitude of the traditional debate, for it leads the authors to freely admit the ambivalence that such aspirational diversity creates for the explanation of class differences in educational representation. It is an ambivalence that is constantly indicated, as when the authors deliberate on the clear-cut differences in representation that obtain at every level of American education. Thus, in explaining class differences at the pre-school level, the authors, mindful of differences in expectations, concede 'we cannot say how much of the inequality we observe is due to variations in taste and how much is due to vagaries in public provision of such services'.[76] Likewise at the secondary level sympathetic to the differential educational attitudes the authors conclude that the differential attrition rates of the classes '... does not necessarily prove that poor or black students have less opportunity to use high schools than other students'.[77] Similarly, when accounting for the even more striking class differences in higher education, Jencks and his associates go no further than is warranted by the evidence, cautioning that '... it is hard to say to what extent the selectivity of higher education represents a denial of equal opportunity and to what extent it results from variations in people's appetite for education'.[78] Cautious almost to a fault, and sensitive to the limitations of their statistical data, Jencks and his associates break with tradition by advancing at a descriptive level explanations of differential representation that are strikingly if not surprisingly indeterminate.

Such a break with tradition, so striking in the prescriptive and descriptive elements of 'Inequality', is however at an evaluative level less than complete, for whilst such an admission of aspirational diversity undermines, as the authors rightly observe, many widely held educational beliefs, it paradoxically has no such implication for that most widely held of educational beliefs that class disparities in educational representation reflect class inequalities in educational opportunity. For Jencks and his associates class difference in educational representation is evaluated as it always has been, as class inequality in educational opportunity: an evaluation that, notwithstanding the acknowledged indeterminacy of the presented evidence in this regard, is paradoxically taken as warranted by such evidence. As the authors put it '... the evidence reviewed ... suggests that educational opportunities are far from equal'.[79] True, additional argument and supplementary statistics are advanced to warrant this critical step from explanatory ambivalence to evaluative confidence, but it remains for all that a shift warranted by no evidence at all, or by evidence of something else. Thus when discussing the difference, or as Jencks significantly puts it '... the inequality that obtains at the pre-school level',[80] the unresolved question as to whether such difference is contingent on 'variations in taste' or on 'vagaries of provision' is quickly if not empirically resolved by the 'throw-away' line, 'both are apparently involved to some degree'.[81] It is an observation, to be pedantic, that if true is less than illuminating because apart from prejudging the nature of differential representation, by precluding without evidence the possibility that it could be the sole consequence of one or the other, such an observation leaves empirically unspecified not only the precise contribution of each factor, but more importantly the egalitarian significance of each factor. Given that class differences in educational aspirations are, for Jencks and his associates, 'basic', the critical empirical requirements for converting class disparities in educational representation into class inequalities in educational opportunity turns critically on first resolving this dilemma of taste or provision.

Likewise at the secondary level, the explanatory dilemma as to whether such differential attrition rates are the upshot of class different expectations or class different opportunities for education, is taken as resolved by the further observation that '... public funds are being used to subsidize a service used by the middle-classes more than by other groups'.[82] Although attractive, such a resolution is seductive, for the precise egalitarian significance of such additional evidence depends once again upon first resolving whether class differences in education reflect class differences in educational opportunity or class difference in educational expectations. Of itself, such evidence of differential subsidy whilst no doubt correct, is not particularly helpful, for as the economic correlate of differential representation it says little about the determinants of such representational rates and, as such, about the equity of such rates. It is quite simply irrelevant, for what is here in contention is not the economic consequences of differential representation, interesting though they be in another context,[83] but whether such evidenced class differences in educational consumption are the product of something else other than what Jencks heretically professes but here religiously ignores, namely class differences in taste.

CONCLUSION

Though this concern with the failure of educational research to document the inequity of class disparity in education is no doubt pedantic, it is not, at least in a pluralistic society, unnecessarily pedantic. It is not unnecessarily so, for once class difference in educational aspiration is taken seriously, the equity or otherwise of class difference in educational representation becomes a sociological problem rather than an ideological given. Of course should class disparity in education transpire, after investigation, to be class inequality in education, then the beliefs of the reform establishment would stand vindicated: however, should such disparity transpire after inspection to be only that, or even partly that, conventional certitudes on the inequity of class disparity in education would be well dented.

NOTES

I would like to thank Professor Michalina Vaughan (Department of Sociology) and Mr Charles Desforges (Department of Educational Research) for their critical comments on previous drafts of this paper.
1. Althusser, L. Ideology and ideological state apparatuses, in Cosin, *Education Structure and Society*. Middlesex, Penguin, 1972. Bernstein, B. Classification and framing, in Young, *Knowledge and Control*, London, Collier-Macmillan, 1971. Bourdieu, P. and Passeron, J.C., *Reproduction*, London, Sage, 1977.
2. Westergaard, J. and Little, A. The trend of class differentials in educational opportunity, *Brit. J. Sociol.*, vol. 15, 1964, pp. 301-16. Douglas, J.W.B. et al., *All Our Future*, London, Panther, 1971. Boudon, R. *Education, Opportunity and Social Inequality*, New York, Wiley, 1974. Hurn, C. *The Limits and Possibilities of Schooling*, Boston, Allyn & Bacon, 1979. Sarason, S. An unsuccessful war on poverty, *American Psychologist*, vol. 33, 1978, no. 9, pp. 831-46. Halsey, A.H., Heath, A.F. and Ridge, J.M. *Origins and Destinations*, Oxford, Clarendon Press, 1980.
3. Glass, D.V. *Social Mobility in Britain*, London, Routledge & Kegan Paul, 1954. Williamson, W. Patterns of educational inequality in West Germany, *Comparative Education*, vol. 13, 1977, no. 1, pp. 29-44. Byrne, E. *Planning and Educational Inequality*, London, N.F.E.R., 1974.
4. Jencks, C. et al., *Inequality*, London, Allen Lane, 1973. Bowles, S. Unequal education and the reproduction of the social division of labour, in Halsey and Karabel, *Power and Ideology in Education*, Oxford, Oxford University Press, 1977. Glennerster, H. Education and Inequality, in Rubinstein, *Education and Equality*, Middlesex, Penguin, 1980.

5. Floud, J. Social class factors in educational achievement' in Halsey, A.H. (ed.), *Ability and Educational Opportunity*, Paris, O.E.C.D., 1961.
6. Liebow, E. *Tally's Corner*, Boston, Little-Brown, 1967. Evetts, J. *The Sociology of Educational Ideas*, London, Routledge & Kegan Paul, 1973. Husen, T. *Social Influences on Educational Attainment*, Paris, O.E.C.D., 1975. Emmerij, L. *Can the School Build a New Social Order?* Amsterdam, Elsevier, 1974. Hummel, C. *Education Today for the World of Tomorrow*, Paris, UNESCO, 1977. Husen, T. *The School in Question*, Oxford, Oxford University Press, 1979. Bisseret, N. *Education, Class Language and Ideology*, London, Routledge & Kegan Paul, 1979.
7. Whyte, W.F. *Street Corner Society*, Chicago, Chicago University Press, 1955. Jackson, B. and Marsden D. *Education and the Working Class*, Middlesex, Penguin, 1968. Wax, M. and Wax, R. Great tradition, little tradition and formal education, in Wax, Diamond and Gearing, *Anthropological Perspectives on Education*, New York, Basic Books, 1971. Willis, P. *Learning to Labour*, Hants, Teakfield, 1977.
8. Bernstein, B. Education cannot compensate for society, in Rubenstein and Stoneman, *Education for Democracy*, Middlesex, Penguin, 1975. Cardinet, J. School evaluation and equality of opportunity, in Carelli and Morris, *Equality of Opportunity Reconsidered*, Lisse, Swets & Zeitlinger, 1979.
9. Ginsburg, H. *The Myth of the Deprived Child*, New Jersey, Prentice-Hall, 1972. Ogbu, J. *Minority Education and Caste*, New York, Academic Press, 1978. Coles, G. The learning-test battery: empirical and social issues, *Harvard Educational Review*, vol. 48, no. 3, 1978, pp. 313-40.
10. Rist, R. Student social class and teacher expectations, *Harvard Educational Review*, vol. 40, 1970, pp. 411-50. Baratz, S. and Baratz, J. Early childhood intervention, *Harvard Educational Review*, vol. 40, 1970, pp. 29-50. Hobbs, N. *The Future of Children*, San Francisco, Jossey Bass, 1975.
11. Himmelweit, H. The school and society, in Anderson, *Education for the Seventies*, London, Heinemann, 1970.
12. Ford, J. *Social Class and the Comprehensive School*, London, Routledge & Kegan Paul, 1969.
13. Karabel, J. Community colleges and social stratification, in Halsey and Karabel, *Power and Ideology in Education*, Oxford, Oxford University Press, 1977.
14. Rist, R. *The Invisible Children*, Mass., Harvard University Press, 1978.
15. Coleman, J. Recent trends in school integration, unpublished—see Pettigrew, T. and Green, R.L. School desegregation in large cities: a critique of the Coleman 'White Flight' thesis, *Harvard Educational Review*, vol. 46, 1975, pp. 1-53.
16. Jencks, C. 1973, op. cit.
17. Lewis, O. *The Children of Sanchez*, New York, Random House, 1961. Moynihan, D.P. *The Negro Family: A Case for National Action*, Washington, U.S. Department of Labour, 1965. Hess, R. The transmission of cognitive strategies in poor families, in Allen, *Psychological Factors in Poverty*, Chicago, Markham, 1970. Bronfenbrenner, U. The psychological costs of quality and equality in education, in Allen, *Psychological Factors in Poverty*, Chicago, Markham, 1970, pp. 210-25. Bruner, J. Poverty and childhood, *Oxford Review of Education*, vol. 1, no. 1, 1975, pp. 31-58.
18. Plowden Report, *Children and Their Primary Schools*, Central Advisory Council for Education, London, H.M.S.O., 1967, p. 31.
19. Lewis, O. 1961, op. cit., p. xxvi.
20. Bronfenbrenner, U. 1970, op. cit. Bruner, J. 1970, op. cit., Berthoud, R. *The Disadvantages of Inequality*, London, Macdonald & Janes, 1976.
21. Bourdieu, P. The school as a conservative force, in Eggleston, *Contemporary Research in Sociology of Education*, London, Methuen, 1974, p. 34.
22. Hess, R. and Shipman, V. Maternal influences on early learning, in Hess and Bear, *Early Education, Current Theory, Research and Action*, Chicago, Aldine, 1968.
23. Hess, R. 1970, op. cit., Rohwer, W. Prime time for learning, *Harvard Educational Review*, vol. 41, 1971, pp. 316-41.
24. Bereiter C. and Engleman, S. *Teaching Disadvantaged Children*, New Jersey, Prentice-Hall, 1966.
25. Coleman, J. et al., *Equality of Educational Opportunity*, Washington, U.S. Government Printing Office, 1966. Jencks, C. 1973, op. cit.
26. Glass, D.V. 1965, op. cit., pp. 404-6.

27. Douglas, J.W.B. 1964, op. cit., p. 154.
28. Ibid., pp. 81–89.
29. Ibid., pp. 89–97.
30. Ibid., p. 154.
31. Halsey, A.H. Towards meritocracy, in Halsey and Karabel, *Power and Ideology in Education*, Oxford, Oxford University Press, 1977, p. 177.
32. Ibid., p. 177.
33. Ibid., p. 177.
34. Halsey, A.H., Heath, A.F. and Ridge, J.M. 1980, op. cit., p. 219.
35. Ibid., p. 176.
36. Ibid., p. 184.
37. Ibid., p. 185.
38. Ibid., p. 185.
39. Ibid., p. 179.
40. Ibid., p. 185.
41. Ibid., p. 193.
42. Bourdieu, P. and Passeron, J.C. 1977, op. cit., pp. 71, 72, 92, 156, 162, 224.
43. Ibid., p. 153.
44. Ibid., Part 3.
45. Ibid., p. 4.
46. Ibid., p. 4.
47. Ibid., p. 153.
48. Evetts, J. 1973, op. cit., p. 70.
49. Ibid., p. 62.
50. Husen, T. 1979, op. cit., p. 178.
51. Ford, J. 1969, op. cit., Baratz, S. and Baratz, J. 1970, op. cit., Bruner, J. 1970, op. cit., Westergaard, J. and Resler, J. *Class in a Capitalist Society*, London, Heinemann, 1976. Hauser, R. and Featherman, D., Equality of schooling, *Sociology of Education*, vol. 49, 1976, no. 2, pp. 99–119.
52. Bowles, S. and Gintis, H. *Schooling in Capitalist America*, London, Routledge & Kegan Paul, 1976, p. 30.
53. Ibid., p. 30.
54. Ibid., p. 30.
55. Ibid., p. 229.
56. Bronfenbrenner, U. 1970, op. cit., p. 211.
57. Ibid., p. 211.
58. Boudon, R. 1974, op. cit., p. xi.
59. Ibid., p. xi.
60. Ibid., p. 44.
61. Ibid., p. 44.
62. Ibid., p. 44.
63. Ibid., p. 47.
64. Ibid., p. 47.
65. Ibid., p. 53.
66. Ibid., p. 53.
67. Ibid., p. 36.
68. Ibid., p. 36.
69. Ibid., p. 86.
70. Ibid., pp. 84–5.
71. Ibid., p. 193.
72. Ibid., pp. 162, 193.
73. Ibid., pp. 30, 36, 77, 84, 86, 112.
74. Ibid., p. 29.
75. Jencks, C. 1973, op. cit., p. 23.
76. Ibid., p. 18.
77. Ibid., p. 19.
78. Ibid., p. 19.
79. Ibid., p. 37.

80. Ibid., p. 18.
81. Ibid., p. 18.
82. Ibid., p. 19.
83. Jencks, C. *et al.*, *Who Gets Ahead*, New York, Basic Books, 1980.

Index

A Basis for Choice (FEU, 1979) 162
Ability levels 282
Academic standards 182
Academic freedom 15
Academic quality 176, 180
Academic salaries 185
Accountability 200, 237, 271
Administration, science of 86
Administrative convenience 65, 69, 304
Administrative culture 203
Administrative-political élite 212
Administrative rationalization and implementation of innovations 95
Adult education 275
Advisory Centre for Education 292
Advisory Committee on the Supply and Education of Teachers 265
Advisory staff, schools 203
Age composition of school population 264
Apprenticeship 170
Architects and Building Branch 145, 150
Articles of government 198, 204
Aspiration, class disparity 321, 323, 327
Assessment of Performance Unit 17, 28, 110
Assistant Masters and Mistresses Association 239, 241, 246
Association of Education Committees 115, 296
Association of Municipal Corporations 297
Attainment, social influences 293
Auld Report 17
Autonomy 40, 46
  governing bodies 204, 209
  school 197
  teacher 238
  university 178, 184
Auxiliaries 307
Avon 17

Barlow Committee 174, 180
Binary line 180
Binary system 14
Birth rates 27, 218
Blackie, J. 153

Black Papers 16, 28, 237
Block grant 111, 175, 253, 269
Boudon, R. 324
Bourdieu, P. 321
Bowles, S. 323
Boyle, E. 12, 14, 148, 151, 176, 292, 299
Bronfenbrenner, U. 323
Brooke, H. 176
Budgets, LEA 134-138
Building programmes 12
  universities 178, 184, 185
Buildings, school 226, 284, 303
Building standards 150
Burgher community 208
Burnham Committee 235, 280, 306
Business and Technical Education Council 161

Callaghan, J. 17, 161
Campaign for the Advancement of State Education 115
Campaign for Nursery Education 309
Capitalism 66, 93
Case study methodology 1
Cash limits 33
Cash planning 257, 262, 263, 267, 268
Central Advisory Council on Education 154, 155, 285, 291-293, 298
Central government 1960s 286
Centralization of powers of government 182
Centralized systems 48, 55
Centre for Information and Advice on Educational Disadvantage 224
Centre and locality in education 103, 268-270
Certificate in Pre-vocational Education 162
Certificate of Secondary Education 18, 150
  examination boards 236
Child-centred education 283
Child Poverty Action Group 292
Circular 10/65 108, 152, 287
City and Guilds 161, 169
Class bias in selection 320

335

Class differences in educational attainment 293, 294
Class disparity in educational aspiration 321
Class inequality in education 315
Clegg, A. 68, 70, 72, 75–77
Client needs 197
Climate of opinion 105
Closure of courses 188
Colleges of education 181
Community governors 207, 208
Community groups 211
Community Relations Council 197
Community-school liaison 223
Community schools 307
Compensatory education 301, 308
  nursery education 310
Comprehensive education 20, 21, 75
Comprehensive schools 225
Comprehensivization 16, 68, 109, 150, 227, 287, 299
  centre-local relationships 108
Comptroller and Auditor General 185
Compulsory education 89
Compulsory redundancy 235, 244, 260, 263, 264, 270
Consensus 2
Conservative government 1950s and 60s 71
Conservative government 1979 15
Consultative Council on Local Government Finance 132
Continuing education 181, 281
Continuity in education 19
Contracts 235
Corporal punishment 209
Corporate management 17, 109, 141, 203
Corporation 29
Council for National Academic Awards 14
Councils 134
Crosland, A. 14, 21, 148, 151, 155, 296, 299, 303, 304, 308
Crowther Report 148, 154, 179, 229, 285, 286
Curricular objectives 236
Cultural account 316
Cultural differences in motivation 323
Cultural handicap 315
Curricular objectives 236
Curriculum
  centre-local relationships 110
  control of 18
  cultural diversity 224
  further education colleges
  school-based politics 241
  school governing bodies 204
Curriculum based model 264
Cuts, university funding 187

Day release 170
Decentralized systems 48, 56, 62
Declining rolls 251, 271
Demographic contraction 103
Demographic research 320
Department of Education and Science 1, 21, 29, 30, 126, 145, 268, 296
  EPAs 300
  power of 105
  UGC 179, 182
Department of Education and Science ministers 148
Department of Employment 161
Department of the Environment 141
Department of Health and Social Security 181, 188
Determination 69
Direct grant schools 279, 283
Dirigisme 191
Disadvantaged children 223
Discretionary powers 129
Diseconomies of change 256
Diseconomies of scale 264
Disjointed incrementalism 2
Disparity index 326

Early retirement 190
Earmarked grants 175
Eccles, D. 12, 13
Economic contraction 103
Economic values 21
Economy and education 25
Education Act 1870 275
Education Act 1902 277
Education Act 1918 280
Education Act 1944 11, 68, 104, 106, 150, 175, 282, 292
Education Act 1964 67, 72
Education Act 1976 228
Education Act 1980 237
Education Act 1981 17
Education cuts 247
Education and the economy 25
Education officers 199, 202
Education policy and values 11
Education and social policy 275
Education White Paper 1972 26
Educational expansion 12, 14, 25, 176, 234
Educational objectives 286
Educational opportunity 285, 286, 288, 316, 319, 325
Educational Planning Paper No. 2 146
Educational politics, model for analysis 39
Educational Priority Areas 286, 291, 294–296, 299
  building programme 304
  nursery education 308

Index

parental involvement 307
  staffing in schools 305
Educational sub-government 217
Egalitarianism 20
Elementary schools 275, 280
11 plus 13, 281, 287
Employer based schemes 162
Employers 166
Employment needs 167
Environment and achievement 294, 295
Environment and educational development 225
Environment and intelligence 284
Equality 14, 20
  NUT influence 219
  positive discrimination 291
Equality norm 19
Equal opportunity 227, 233, 237, 244
Ethnic minorities 223, 224
Evening classes 277
Evetts, J. 322
Examinations, secondary school curriculum 229
Exchange theory 44
Expansionism 12, 14, 25, 234
Expansion, universities 176
Expenditure planning 26, 252
Expenditure Steering Group for Education Services 253, 259, 264, 268
Expertise 44, 49
External interest groups 46
External transaction 42, 45, 57

Family allowance 305
Family life, school's role 286
Fees 186
  overseas students 189, 192
Financial pressure 269
Finniston Report 180
Floud, J. 285, 293
Free-place system 279
Full-time students 160
Further education 282
Further education colleges 160
Further Education Unit 165

GDP 25, 26, 31
Gender 239
General Certificate of Education
  comprehensive schools 287
  ordinary level 285
General systems theory 44
General Teaching Council 241
General factors and achievement 294
Gintis, H. 323
Glass, D. V. 319

GNP 55
Grammar schools 246, 276, 278
  differential access 285
  social composition 277
Grant-aided secondary schools 279
Grant funding 107
Grant related expenditure 111, 128, 129, 131, 254
Grant related expenditure assessments 254, 269
Grant Related Poundage 130
Grants, universities 174, 188
Grants Working Group 131
Great Debate 3, 28, 161, 228
Green Paper, *Education in Schools* (1977) 110, 161, 228
Growth rate guidelines 139

Hadow Report 280, 281
Halsey, A. H. 221, 285, 293, 296, 309, 310, 320
Head teacher organization 238
Head teachers 203, 210, 238
Her Majesty's Inspectorate 13, 150, 152, 168, 300
Higher education 13
  class differentials 316, 328
  from expansion to contraction 14, 25
Higher Education in the 1990's 179, 181
Higher-grade schools 276
Horsborough, F. 12
House of Commons 217

Immigrants 308
  section 11 223
Incrementalism 138
Industrial action, teachers 240
Inflation 183, 185, 263
Inherited ability 294
Innate ability 295
Innovation in social policy 95
Inservice training 17
Institutional values 21
Intelligence quotients 285, 294
  working class 318
Intelligence tests 282, 284
Interest groups 42, 43, 45, 49, 52, 54, 56, 57, 202, 296
Internal initiation 42, 44, 59
Interventionism 28, 126

Jencks, C. 328
Job losses 27
  universities 188

Job security, teachers   235
Junior high school   68, 75
Joseph, K.   248

Key notables   210
Kogan, D.   191
Kogan, M.   148, 191, 294

Labourers, non-wage to wage   88
Labour Government 1945   11
Labour Government 1964   14
Labour market   88–91
Labour power   88, 89
Ladder of citizen participation   207
Latin   76
Layfield Report   126
Learning disabilities   32
Leicestershire Plan   75, 76
Lindsay, Lord   176
Local Authority Associations   260
Local autonomy   268
Local community   200, 202
Local Education Authorities   1, 28, 74, 108, 111, 125, 197
  budget documents   134–137
  Education Act 1902   278
  EPAs   300
  power of   104
  relationship with school governing bodies   198
  teacher numbers   251
Local Education Authority nominated governors   206
Local Government Act 1966, section 11   223
Local Government Planning and Land Act   128, 133, 141, 151
Local government reorganizaton 1974   201
Local Income Tax   126
Local state   77
Locality and centre in education   103

Manpower-oriented higher education policy   191
Manpower planning   268
Manpower Services Commission   3, 5, 6, 18, 26, 160, 166, 236
Manpower Services Commission/Department of Education and Science, competitive or co-operative   167
Manzer, R.   217
Marxism   65, 66, 74, 80, 94
Medical manpower needs   181
Medical schools   188
Middle schools   67, 72

Militancy   243, 249, 306
Ministers, DES   148
Ministry of Education   106
Minority groups   223
Morant   278
Motivation, cultural differences   323
Multi-cultural education   204
Multilateral schools   282

NAFE   128
National Advisory Body for Local Authority Higher Education   15, 192
National Association of Governors and Managers   115
National Association of Head Teachers   297
National Association for Multi-Racial Education   224
National Association of Schoolmasters   228
National Association of Schoolmasters/Union of Women Teachers   239, 241, 246
National Foundation for Educational Research   224
National state   77
Natural wastage   260
Needs of society   176, 181
NEDO   164
Negotiation
  external transaction   42, 45, 57
  interactions   60
  interest groups   50
  internal initiation   42, 44, 59
  political manipulation   42, 45, 53
  process of   52
Negro, motivation   323
Newsom Report   14, 286
New Training Initiative   162, 167
Non-Advanced Further Education Colleges   30
Non-teaching staff   203
Norwood Report   79, 283
Nursery assistants   221
Nursery centres   310
Nursery education   26, 219, 300, 308
Nursery teachers   222
NUT   115, 217, 280
  ideology   233
  Plowden Report   297
  salary supplements   306

Open University   14, 181
ONC   160
Organization for Economic Co-operation and Development   105, 149, 153, 159
Overseas student fees   189

Overseas student numbers 186
Oxbridge 76
Oxford Mobility Study 320

Parental aspiration 319
Parental choice 237
Parental interest 322
Parental participation 115, 222, 292, 300, 307
Parental pressure 238
Parents 17
  playgroups 221, 310
Parents' Association Committee 244
Parents' associations 197
Parent-teacher associations 220, 307
Parent/Teacher Ratio 140
Parkes, D. 191
Partnership 3, 5, 125, 174
  UGC and universities 181
Part-time education 230, 283
Party political organization 206
Party political policy 201, 218
Passeron, J. C. 321
Pay settlements for teachers 257
Picketing 244
Pile, W. 145, 155
Play groups 221, 310
Plowden Report 14, 17, 32, 110, 115, 154, 155, 218, 219, 220, 225, 291, 292, 295–297, 301, 307
Pluralism 1, 4, 65
Policy and Resources Committee 139, 140
Political and administrative system of education 195
Political alignment of teachers unions 239
Political manipulation 42, 45, 53
Politics of administrative convenience, middle schools 65
Politics of education 39
Polytechnics 14, 26, 179, 180
Positive discrimination 14, 224, 227, 291, 295, 299
Post-secondary education 320
Poverty and educational priority 291, 316
Pratley, B. 163
Premature retirement 235, 260, 264
Pre-school provision 221
Pressure groups 32, 197, 202, 207, 208, 210
Primary education 226, 292, 299
Primary schools 17, 218, 281, 288, 304
Primary school teachers 238, 266
Prime institution 197
Priority 309
Professional Association of Teachers 239, 246
Professional group 57, 59
Professionalism 241, 246, 249

Programme Analysis and Review 147
Progressive primary education 16
Projectionism 146
Proletarianization, passive and active 88, 89
Promotion 219, 234
  women teachers 245
Proposals for a Certificate of Extended Education 162
Public accountability 203
Public Accounts Committee 178, 184, 185, 187
Public expenditure 252
  cuts 183
Public expenditure and education 31
Public expenditure planning 268
Public Expenditure Survey Committee 33, 131, 147, 183, 268
Public participation 202
Public sector growth 32
Public sector of higher education 180, 183, 184
Public schools 16
Pupil attitudes, class differences 319
Pupil numbers 138
Pupil profiles 229
Pupil-teacher ratios 253, 255, 256, 262, 267

QUANGO
  Centre for Educational Disadvantage 224
  University Grants Committee 190
Quinquennial planning, UGC 178, 184

Race 308
Race Relations, role of the school 224
Raising the School-Leaving Age 229
Ranson, S. 166
Rates 126, 127
Rates Support Grant 107, 127, 128, 139, 151, 253, 254
Recurrent grants, universities 177, 184, 186
Redeployment of teachers 199, 236, 260
Redundancy, teachers 235, 244, 245, 260, 263, 264, 270
Research Councils 190
Resources 2, 31, 113
Resource allocation, UGC 173, 180, 183
Resource availability in society 47
Resource dependency theory 113, 116
Resource distribution 125
Resource holders, relations among 47
Resource utilization 34
Responsibility posts 306
Retrenchment 191, 192
Robbins principle of social demand 15
Robbins Report 13, 32, 146, 176, 177, 180, 285, 286, 293, 294

ROSLA 228
Royal Commission on Local
    Government 126
Russell, R. 165
Russian studies 179

Salaries 185, 234, 238, 254, 269, 271, 280, 306
Salary supplement, EPA schools 306
Scholarship ladder 276, 279
School boards 275, 278
School buildings 226, 284, 303
School closure 208
School governing bodies 195, 198, 199, 207, 211
School-leaving age 12, 20, 228, 282, 283
School management 198
School meals 305
School rolls 251, 257, 271
Schools Council 150, 224, 236, 286
SCOTEC 160
Secondary education 106
    reorganization 68, 77, 226
    sociologists 283
Secondary modern schools 284
Secondary schools 278, 280
Secondary school selection 13
Secondary school teachers 266
    salary 238
Secretary of State 110
Section 11 staff 223
Selection at 11 plus 13, 287
    NUT and abolition of 225
Selection, intelligence tests 285
Selective education 14
    class differentials in access 316
Self-evaluation of schools 204
Sex Discrimination Act 240
Sexism in the curriculum 245
Sexual discrimination in teaching 239
Short, E. 227
Signposts 163
Sixth-form colleges 68
Slum buildings 303
Social demand 15
Social influences on educational attainment 293
Social mobility 284, 320
Social policy and education 275
Social policy innovations 95
Social policy and the theory of the state 85
Social values 20
Sociologists and secondary education 284
'Soft' concept of equality 12, 15
Special education 32
Spens Report 79, 282, 283
Staffing in EPA schools 305

Staffing standards 255
Staff: student ratios 185
State 55, 78
    economy-polity-social system relationships 116
    social policy and the theory of 85
State apparatus 95, 98, 153
State educational system 41, 42
    Marxism 66
Staying-on rates 230
Strike action 243
Structural limitation 69–71, 75
Student fees 186
Student maintenance awards 185, 186
Student numbers 138
    forecasts 184
    universities 177, 180
Student places, universities 183
Student unit cost 183
Subject-based sub-committees, UGC 188

Tapering multipliers 131
Tawney, R. H. 280
Tax bases 130
Taylor Report 17, 109
Teacher autonomy 2, 238
Teacher control of the curriculum 237
Teacher education 17
Teacher governors 211
Teacher militancy 243, 249, 306
Teacher numbers 246, 251
Teacher quota system 269
Teacher supply 25, 221
Teacher training system 265
Teacher turnover 306, 317
Teacher unemployment 234
Teachers 19, 111
    job opportunities and working conditions 226
    salaries 185, 234, 238, 254, 269, 271, 280, 306
Teachers' aides 307
Teachers Supply Branch 145
Teachers' unions 19, 109, 217
Teaching staff appointments 199
Teaching quality 268, 270
Technical education 12, 276
Technical Instruction Acts 278
Technical stream 166
Technical and Vocational Education Initiative 18, 29, 162, 167, 236
Technician Education Councils 169
Tertiary reorganization 204
Thatcher, M. 16, 152, 227, 310
Theory of the State 85
Thresholds 131
Todd Commission 180, 181

Index

Trade unions 217, 233
Training for Jobs 162, 167, 168
Transfer at 11 plus 281
Triangle of tension 2, 104
Tripartite system 226
TUC 239, 242, 243, 297

Unemployment 29, 31, 32
   teacher 234
Union membership 239
Universal comprehensive education 16
Universal nursery education 309
Universal secondary education 281
Universities 55, 152
   role of 181
   scholarship ladder 279
   student numbers 177
University autonomy 178, 184
University College of North
   Staffordshire 175
University funding 14
University Grants Committee 14, 15, 173
   status 182, 187
Unqualified teachers 267
Urban Programme 303, 308, 310

Values 11–21
Vernon, P. E. 285
Vice-Chancellors' Committee 174

Vocational education 159
Vocationalism 167, 235, 237, 248

Wage-labour 88–90
Wealth creation 21
Weaver, T. 148
West Riding of Yorkshire 68, 71, 72
White Paper, *Teaching Quality* 236
White Paper, *Training for Jobs* 162, 167, 168
Wilkinson, E. 79
Williams. S. 221, 307
William Tyndale Junior School 17
Wolfenden, J. 177
Women teachers 239, 245
Woodhall, M. 146
Work experience 162
Working class 276
   aspirations 321, 323, 327
   educational attainment 293
   educational opportunity 316
World of work 248

Yellow Book, 1976 110
Young, M. 292, 299, 309
Youth labour protection laws 97
Youth Opportunity Programme 160
Youth Task Group Report 162
Youth Training Scheme 29, 162, 166, 167, 169, 236, 248
Youth unemployment 29